TORTURE AND THE TWILIGHT OF EMPIRE

HUMAN RIGHTS AND CRIMES AGAINST HUMANITY
Eric D. Weitz, Series Editor

Echoes of Violence: Letters from a War Reporter by Carolin Emcke

Cannibal Island: Death in a Siberian Gulag by Nicolas Werth.
Translated by Steven Rendall with a foreword by Jan T. Gross

TORTURE AND THE
TWILIGHT OF EMPIRE

FROM ALGIERS TO BAGHDAD

Marnia Lazreg

PRINCETON UNIVERSITY PRESS

PRINCETON AND OXFORD

PUBLISHED BY PRINCETON UNIVERSITY PRESS, 41 WILLIAM STREET,
PRINCETON, NEW JERSEY 08540
IN THE UNITED KINGDOM: PRINCETON UNIVERSITY PRESS,
3 MARKET PLACE, WOODSTOCK, OXFORDSHIRE OX20 1SY

LIBRARY OF CONGRESS CATALOGING-IN-PUBLICATION DATA

LAZREG, MARNIA.
TORTURE AND THE TWIGLIGHT OF EMPIRE : FROM ALGIERS
TO BAGHDAD / MARNIA LAZREG
PRINCETON UNIVERSITY PRESS.
P. CM.
INCLUDES BIBLIOGRAPHICAL REFERENCES AND INDEX.
ISBN 978-0-691-13135-1 (HARDCOVER : ALK. PAPER) 1. TORTURE—
ALGERIA— HISTORY—20TH CENTURY. 2. ALGERIA—HISTORY—
REVOLUTION, 1954–1962—ATROCITIES. 3. ABU GHRAIB PRISON.
4. IRAQ WAR, 2003—ATROCITIES. 5. TORTURE. I. TITLE.

HV8599.A4L39   2007   956.7044′3—DC22   2007014846

BRITISH LIBRARY CATALOGING-IN-PUBLICATION DATA IS AVAILABLE

THIS BOOK HAS BEEN COMPOSED IN SABON

PRINTED ON ACID-FREE PAPER. ⊚
PRESS.PRINCETON.EDU

PRINTED IN THE UNITED STATES OF AMERICA

1 3 5 7 9 10 8 6 4 2

For Ramsi and Reda

CONTENTS

Chapter 11

ACKNOWLEDGMENTS

B ECAUSE OF ITS subject matter, writing this book required fortitude. In moments of discouragement, Ramsi and Reda were always
there with the right words and a reminder that writing about the
struggle for freedom from torture is part of the larger struggle for the hu-
manization of life in which I am engaged.

I am grateful to a number of scholars for helping me in one way or another to think through a particularly complex subject matter at different
stages of its elaboration. When the book was still a tentative idea, Wolf V.
Heydebrand and Melvin Richter provided incisive comments and invaluable suggestions. Virginia Held helped me to understand debates in moral
philosophy. As the manuscript began to take shape, I was fortunate to
meet Peter Paret at the Institute for Advanced Study. He generously gave
of his time to share with me his vast knowledge of military history and to
alert me to invaluable bibliographical sources in addition to reading a part
of the manuscript. I feel especially indebted to him. At the Institute, over
enjoyable luncheons, I also learned from Morton White's philosophical
insights into conscience and politics.

Eric D. Weitz, the editor of the series, made a difference in the completion of this book. His sharp critical insights, rigor, and commitment
helped me to better understand my thoughts, and remain focused. Working with him was a particularly gratifying experience. My deep appreciation goes to Brigitta van Rheinberg for her unwavering interest in the
manuscript and for encouraging me to bring it to fruition in a shorter for-
mat. It is understood that I alone am responsible for all the arguments and
interpretations developed herein.

In 2003 and 2005 I was the recipient of two travel grants from the
CUNY Research Foundation that helped to defray the cost of collecting
data. The Gender Equity Project at Hunter College gave me course release
time in 2003–2005. As an Associate of the GEP, there is much that I am
grateful for. In 2004–2005 the Institute for Advanced Study, Princeton,
with the support of Acting Dean Judy Friedlander, Hunter College, provided me with the freedom to focus solely on reading and writing in a
most enchanting environment.

ABBREVIATIONS

ACA	Assemblée des Cardinaux et Archevêques (Assembly of Cardinals and Bishops)
ALN	Armée de Libération Nationale
ASSRA	Adjointes Sociales Sanitaires Rurales Auxiliaires
CAOM	Centre des Archives d'Outre Mer in Aix-en-Provence
CDR	Centre de Reéducation
CEPH	Centré d'Etudes des Problèmes Humains
CICR	Comité International de la Croix Rouge (International Red Cross Committee)
CIMADE	(Comité Inter-Mouvements Auprès des Evacués)
CMI	Camp Militaire d'Internés
CRA	Centre de Renseignement et d'Action
CRS	Compagnies Républicaines de Sécurité (Riot Police)
CRUA	Comité Révolutionnaire d'Unité et d'Action
CTT	Centre de Tri et de Transit
DOP	Détachement Opérationnel de Protection
DP	Division Parachutiste
DST	Direction de Surveillance du Territoire
EMSI	Equipes Médico-Sociales Itinérantes
FIS	Front Islamique du Salut
FLN	Front National de Libération
GPRA	Gouvernement Provisoire de la République Algérienne
GPW	Geneva Convention III on the Treatment of Prisoners of War
HLL	Hors-La-Loi
HUMINT	Field Manual on Human Intelligence Operations
IGAME	Inspecteur Général de l'Administration en Mission Extraordinaire
MIA	Mouvement Islamique Armé
MNA	Mouvement National Algérien
MSF	Mouvement de Solidarité Féminine
MTLD	Mouvement pour le Triomphe des Libertés Démocratiques
OAS	Organisation de l'Armée Secrète
OPA	Organisation Politique et Administrative
OR	Officier de Renseignments
ORU	Organisation Rurale-Urbaine
OS	Organisation Spéciale

PJ	Police Judiciaire
PAM	Prisonnier pris les Armes à la Main
PCA	Parti Communiste Algérien (Algerian Communist Party)
RAP	Renseignement, Action et Protection
REP	Régiment Etranger Parachutiste
RPIMa	Régiment de Parachutistes d'Infanterie de Marine
SAS	Section Administrative Spécialisée
SAU	Section Administrative Urbaine
SHAT	Service Historique de l' Armée de Terre
SNP	Sans Nom Patronymique
ZEA	Zone Est Algérois

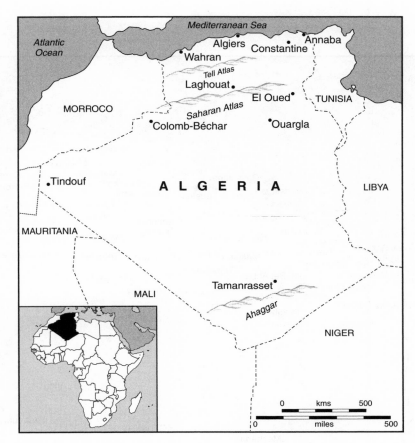

Map 1.
Adapted from University of Texas Perry-Castañeda Library Map Collection.

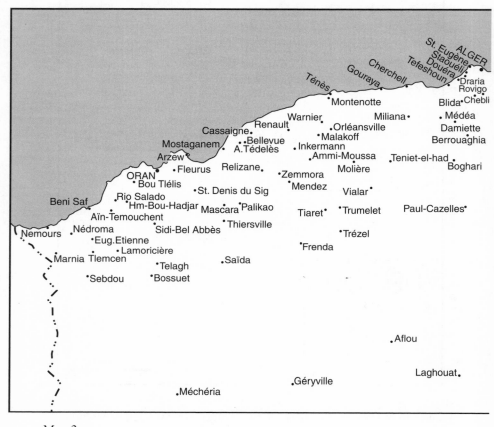

Map 2.
Adapted from "Algérie Nord. Limites Administratives. Ministère de l'Algérie, 1957."

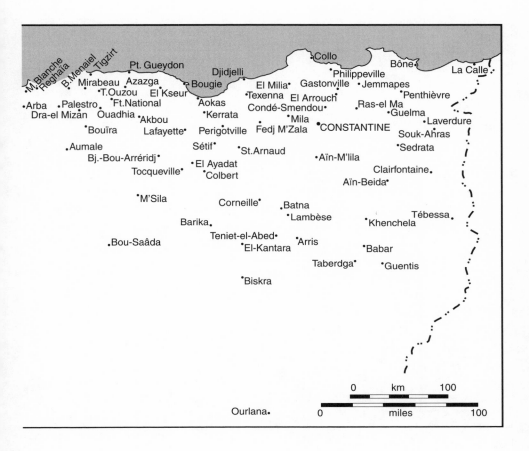

M.Blanche
Reghaïa
B.Menaiel
Tigzirt
Pt. Gueydon
Collo
Bône
La Calle
Mirabeau
Azazga
Djidjelli
Philippeville
Arba
T.Ouzou
El Kseur
Bougie
El Milia
Gastonville
Jemmapes
Penthièvre
Palestro
Ft.National
Aokas
Texenna
El Arrouch
Ras-el Ma
Dra-el Mizan
Ouadhia
Akbou
Kerrata
Condé-Smendou
Guelma
Bouïra
Lafayette
Perigotville
Mila
Laverdure
Fedj M'Zala
CONSTANTINE
Souk-Ahras
Aumale
Sétif
St.Arnaud
Sedrata
Bj.-Bou-Arréridj
Aïn-M'lila
Tocqueville
El Ayadat
Clairfontaine
Colbert
Aïn-Beida
M'Sila
Corneille
Batna
Tébessa
Lambèse
Barika
Khenchela
Bou-Saâda
Teniet-el-Abed
Arris
Babar
El-Kantara
Taberdga
Guentis
Biskra

0   km   100

Ourlana
0   miles   100

INTRODUCTION

IN THE COURSE OF A discussion about the Algerian war, a disenchanted man in his twenties who worked in the mailroom of a government institution where I had been employed in the early years of independence when I was still a student said to me: "The French army broke my testicles! And here I am recording mail day in, day out." A shy young woman at the time, I had not quite grasped the enormity of the pain and suffering that this man had experienced, nor had I understood his trauma, although I glimpsed the depth of the anger that gleamed in his eyes. It was my first encounter with a person who had been tortured during the war. I often remember that look. Years later, it helped me to understand the sexual core of torture and, by implication, the silence in which it had been wrapped in Algeria: that men, just like women, had been systematically raped.

In the summer of 2001, while I was in Algiers carrying out interviews for another research project, two publications appeared. The first one was by an Algerian woman, Louisette Ighilahriz, a former revolutionary, who broke silence about the torture and rape she had endured during her interrogation by Colonel Graziani and his men in 1957.[1] This was the first time since the independence of Algeria that a woman wrote about her sexual abuse at the hands of paratroopers. The other book was by a retired French general, Paul Aussaresses,[2] who not only admitted to having tortured numerous Algerians, but also described the methods he used in a detached manner, expressing no regrets and making no apology. A number of war memoirs had already been published by retired Algerian generals, to which were added young deserters' accounts of torture committed by the Algerian military against Islamist suspects, and confessions to assassinations by former Islamists. I grew intrigued by these tales of torture and war from both sides of the Mediterranean and was unsure of their significance.

In France, Aussaresses' confession created a stir, sparking a flurry of legal actions against him, and renewed interest in a chapter of French history that government and public opinion had wished to bury in silence. It occurred to me that the Evian Accords that put an end to the Algerian War in 1962 had not mentioned torture, but had declared a moratorium on legal actions for all acts of violence committed during the war. There was to be no equivalent of the Nuremberg trials. I thought again of the man in the mailroom.

Oddly, writers dealing with French veterans of the Algerian War often think that Algerian combatants had an easier time of it.[3] They claim that Algerian combatants did not suffer, as French soldiers allegedly did, from having to keep their involvement in a problematic war silent. Unlike their French counterparts, the story goes, Algerian combatants returned home victorious and were celebrated for their success. They were able to put the war behind them and move on with their lives, while French soldiers returned to a life in the shadows, resented by their society for having defamed it, and abandoned by a government that had failed to treat them in the manner that it did veterans of previous wars. Perhaps this is a case of the grass looking greener on the other side, or a circuitous way of bemoaning defeat.

The memory of torture and other atrocities has fed a steady stream of French narratives that unburden the self as they shed light on the core of a dishonorable war. Memory retrieval has been aided by professional studies made possible by the opening of the military archives in 1993.[4] The cumulative effect of this speaking and writing about the war has resulted in a trivialization of the significance of torture as glossy pictures turn war into an orgiastic intellectual entertainment.[5] Speaking authoritatively about both sides of the war, a new generation of French historians felt entitled to change its name and the identity of its initiators: It was a "war of independence" they asserted, not a "revolution" as Algerians who won it have claimed; and nationalists are turned into "independentistas."[6] Thus a long-standing monopoly over meaning enables the empire to reproduce itself by deconstructing itself with one hand, and recomposing itself with the other.

In this climate of recovery of the colonial past, French legislators passed a law on February 23, 2005, that attempted to rehabilitate colonialism by proposing (in Article 4) that school curricula present it as a positive system of rule, especially in North Africa.[7] They also rehabilitated formerly convicted and deported citizens (an oblique reference to members of the clandestine Organisation de l'Armée Secrète) opposed to the independence of Algeria who became eligible for monetary compensation.[8] The management of what French historians have of late called "la mémoire," has become a political affair.[9] Torture and related atrocities cast serious doubt on the plausibility of the ongoing revisionist history of "empire," French as well as British, which seeks to extol the benefits of colonial domination for the colonized and downplay its cost as collateral damage.[10] This relegitimation and rehabilitation of the French "civilizing mission" elides a discussion of whether the colonial empire was inevitable. It eschews the fundamental core of colonial ventures: the extension or preservation of the interests of the colonists not the natives. Had colonial systems been motivated by an alleged gift of "civilization," a cultural charity, it is incomprehensible that the gift failed to reach the majority of natives.

In this book, I take a different approach. I examine torture as an analytical category and practice (that is, a conscious and rule-bound activity) through which to understand how, between 1954 and 1962, the militarized colonial state normalized terror to forestall the collapse of the empire in an age of decolonization. In tracing the etiology and methods of state terrorism, I explore the justifications that allowed for the routinization of torture in a "total" war of decolonization-recolonization. From this perspective, the book seeks to uncover torture's layered meanings for practitioners and victims; the role it played in techniques of population screening[11] and social engineering; and its use as a catalyst for imperial identity formation and crystallization. Torture was not, as was often claimed by military officers, an epiphenomenon of the war. It was central to the army's defense of a colonial empire in its waning years. The systematic use of torture was the logical outcome of revolutionary-war theory (*guerre révolutionnaire*) and doctrine developed in the 1950s by a group of veterans of colonial wars, especially in Indochina. Many had also fought in World War II. They were men who had suffered a loss of honor and relevance in fast-changing postwar France. The Algerian War offered them a last opportunity at recouping both. In this context, systematic torture was not just an instance of violence committed by uncontrolled soldiers; it was part and parcel of an ideology of subjugation that went beyond Algeria's borders.[12] Algeria became a testing ground for fighting "revolutionary" wars in Africa and Latin America.[13]

Torture was intimately linked to colonial history and to the nature of the colonial state. It had been used in the aftermath of the invasion of Algeria in 1830 when rape, beatings with a *matraque*, exposure of naked bodies, and starvation were frequent.[14] Thereafter, it was not uncommon at the hands of colonial policemen and gendarmes who used the methods of electricity and water on communists and nationalists. But it had not risen to the level of a system as it did after 1954.[15] Rather, it was part of a general pattern of police brutality exercised on a native population that lacked the legal protection enjoyed by French colonists.

Algeria was invaded in 1830, but French control was not established securely until the 1870s. Resistance was first organized by Emir Abd-El-Kader, who set up the first native government since the incorporation of Algeria into the Ottoman Empire in the sixteenth century. After his defeat in 1844, a series of tribal-based uprisings took place episodically until 1871, when the last one of significance was crushed in the Grande Kabylie. After each uprising, land was confiscated by the colonial state, and heavy fines exacted from the insurgents. The military administered the countryside through the Arab Bureaus until their demise in the 1870s. Throughout this period, tensions arose between the settlers who had been given land confiscated from the native population, and the military. Settlers perceived the military—which had wrought untold violence against the Algerian population—as protecting the interests of rural Algerians. From 1884 until 1946, Algerians were governed by a special legal system—the Code de l'Indigénat—that severely restricted basic civil liberties and criminalized attitudes as anodyne as "insolence." Algerians were neither free men in the Roman sense, nor slaves. They were neither full-fledged citizens as Frenchmen were, nor subjects. Theirs was a qualified "citizenship" best captured by the expression "protected subjects."[16] They did not become full-fledged citizens until 1958. Their legal status was that of "French-Muslims," which meant that they could not be accorded citizenship rights on account of their religion. The war of decolonization (1954–62) was the culmination of a long process of economic immiseration, political disenfranchisement, and colonial intolerance of Algerians' attempts to agitate for change within the system. There is ample evidence to demonstrate, as the Front de Libération Nationale (FLN) has claimed, that all nonviolent options to change the inequities of colonial rule had been exhausted. For example, a liberal law passed on September 20, 1947, gave Algerians, including women, citizenship rights —even as it instituted a double electoral-college system, one for Algerians, the other for colonists.[17] However, opposition from the settlers' lobby thwarted its implementation. The war was as ferocious as the occupation in the nineteenth century. It saw the rise of a generation of young nationalists[18] initially organized into two rival parties, the FLN and the Mouvement National Algérien (MNA). In a relatively short period of time, the FLN established itself as the sole party waging a war of decolonization against a determined army supported by settlers with powerful influence on the government in Paris, and a stratified colonial population of over one million, comprised primarily of descendants of immigrants from southern Europe.

In a repetition of nineteenth-century colonial history, the state relied on the military for not only waging the war, but also administering the rural population. The Fourth Republic was the casualty of the ensuing military encroachment on politics. May 13, 1958, was a turning point in the war: Charles de Gaulle was brought back to politics by a group of generals, staunch advocates of a French Algeria, among whom were Raoul Salan and Jacques Massu (an unabashed advocate of torture), who hoped he would decisively end the war in favor of France. However, after continuing to wage the war for four more years while proposing various political settlement formulas, including a measure of autonomy for Algeria, de

Gaulle opted for recognition of independence. Before making his final historic decision, he extended to Algerians unconditional citizenship in 1958. A highlight of the war prior to May 13, 1958, was the "Battle of Algiers" in January 1957: the Casbah was surrounded by paratroopers seeking to break an FLN-ordered eight-day strike and dismantle the underground Autonomous Zone responsible for urban guerilla warfare using the "bomb strategy."

On the ground, the colonial population had been waging its own counterrevolutionary war through the establishment of a clandestine terrorist movement, the OAS (Organisation de l' Armée Secrète) targeting Algerians and French advocates of Algeria's independence. However, as de Gaulle appeared less reliable than the hard-line generals expected, they staged a short-lived putsch in April 1961. Subsequently, the state tried to regain its control of the military. The declaration of Algeria's independence on July 3, 1962, after the signing of the Evian Accords, put an end to the war, and helped the French government restructure the military and return it to its domain.

The state in Algeria was the bifurcated colonial modality of the state in France. For all practical purposes, the French state that considered Algeria an extension of France, comprised of three (extra) departments, empowered its agents differently whether they were located on one or the other side of the Mediterranean. State terror became established in Algeria, at the behest of the French government in France. It did not affect the majority of the French population in France, although it curtailed its civil liberties to some degree. Jails throughout France were filled with Algerian political prisoners (many of whom were transferred from Algeria) and their French supporters; torture was inflicted on suspects in Parisian police stations;[19] and over two hundred Algerians were killed and thrown into the Seine on October 17, 1961, by orders of the police prefect of Paris, Maurice Papon.[20] Nevertheless, torture was not routinized in France as it was in Algeria.

If the historical context of colonialism facilitated the emergence of torture as a method of control, the war itself crystallized the stakes and clarified for the military the importance of the use of unbridled force and terror. War, as a situation in which normative restraints on life and death are suspended, has close affinities with torture. As Elaine Scarry has shown, war's relation to torture is mediated by the labor of "civilization," a concept dear to colonial officers in Algeria. Torture partakes in the work of the civilization in whose name it is practiced,[21] and in which it finds its justification against the alleged barbarity of the enemy. War and torture feed into each other in the same way that torture and terror do.

Justifications of torture play a crucial role in its routinization; they require for their efficacy a suspension of disbelief: They harness an array of reasons of unequal value and importance that must be accepted as a whole. If looked at separately, each loses its weight, weakening the whole. The dictionary points to the root of justification as making "just," whereas explanation "makes flat." I take the position that intentional assault against the body physical or the body social is not justifiable, albeit explainable. In wars, "just" or "unjust," belligerents are bound by rules of engagement, which are meant to avoid or minimize the occurrence of atrocities.[22] In Algeria, justifications of torture found fertile ground in the myths spun on natives' flawed nature and a narcissistic view of French cultural supremacy.

In this book, I do not review or engage in discussions of what degree of physical punishment rises to the level of torture as these generally constitute preliminaries to defending torture as a legitimate form of interrogation. I simply propose that torture is the deliberate and willful infliction of various degrees of pain using a number of methods and devices, psychological as well as physical, on a *defenseless*, and *powerless* person for the purpose of obtaining information that a victim does not wish to reveal or does not have. It is the powerlessness of the victim, the inability to defend herself and her absolute vulnerability to the torturer that captures the specific character of torture. Slapping a victim may seem a mild form of punishment, and not torture. But, when the slap is inflicted repeatedly by a large soldier, or a group of soldiers going at it together, in a manner such that the victim loses her balance and her hearing, it becomes a method of torture. Torture is methodical: It has a beginning, an evolution, and an end. It unfolds holistically,[23] according to a design, and with various tools, of which the slapping hand is one. It is multilocal and multimodal. It cannot be conceived piecemeal. It is the totality of the torture *situation* that needs to be grasped in order to understand that torture is not definable in terms of bodily harm or psychological torment alone. It is not only what goes on during the electrical or knife-carving sessions that defines torture. It is also the preliminaries—what French torturers called "softening" the victims—as well as what happens between torture sessions that could last one to three days, and at times several weeks on and off.

The torture situation is not summed up by a torturer and his victim thrown together in a room with a few instruments. It is a structured environment with a texture of its own, a configuration of meanings, a logic and rationale without which physical, let alone, psychic, pain is incomprehensible and ineffective. In the social situation of torture, memory, identity, and culture weave a network of ideas and perceptions, experiences and ideals that define a genuine battle between two embodied realities: in this case, colonial France with its unbounded power and mythologies, and colonized Algeria, with its claim to a full share of humanity.

Conversely, the fact of doing torture allows the torturer to voice (albeit freely) *his* identity claims. General Aussaresses could not help evoking the Battle of Valmy of 1793 while torturing an Algerian in 1957. Torture thus appears as a political practice that unfolds in a social *situation* from which it is inseparable. In this respect, the stated end of torture, intelligence, does not and cannot define torture: Torture in Algeria was not primarily about information, although some useful information was collected.[24] Information can be had without the use of torture as a French intelligence officer found out.[25]

As with its colonial counterpart, the democratic state in crisis is especially attracted to torture because it is pure power, and affords absolute control. Although politically onerous, engaging in torture for liberal democracies also provides an expedient and instantaneous response to a crisis defined as one of "security." Tapping into torture-power is, for the state, a manner of re-sourcing itself, rejuvenating itself by re-creating itself, refashioning its existence as the power of instrumental reason.[26]

Torture converts abstract power into concrete power (the potential for coercion into actual coercion). But, unlike police power that randomizes physical abuse, torture, when *ordered* for reasons of state in spite of the legal prohibition against it, targets its victims in a systematic manner. As a source of pure power, torture allows no immediate counterpower that physically harms the torturer. Torture is no less than absolute power over body and mind targeted at their molecular constitutive elements. It scars the body and sears the mind. The power conveyed by torture is unique insofar as it is transformative. No one who undergoes torture can forget it or find it justifiable.[27]

Torture-power makes possible, and feeds into terror. In this book, I will often use terror and torture interchangeably, although they are analytically distinct. Without torture, terror would lose its capacity to sustain fear and silence in its victims. Torture may take place without terror, but terror needs torture to magnify its impact. The colonial state in Algeria engaged in five related acts of terror: torture, rape, disappearances, summary executions, and reprisals. The last three seldom occurred without torture, and torture seldom occurred without rape. Terror and torture worked together like Jekyll and Hyde, feeding on each other, supporting each other, filling in for each other.

The establishment of a climate of terror from 1954 to 1962 in Algeria was a reenactment of a historical precedent. The generals in Algeria carried out a counterrevolutionary war not so different from the revolutionary war waged in the late 1700s. Although the French Revolution had abolished judicial torture, physical and psychological torment by other means did not end, and massacres of internal enemies were common during the Great and *petite* terrors.[28] The wheeling onto the public square of the dreaded guillotine, set up to behead those labeled counterrevolution-ary, was the functional equivalent of the tortures by portable electric gen-erators (*gégène*) in Algeria. Itinerant torture was a sort of *guillotine sèche*.[29] In either case, the individual had no recourse, couldn't protect herself. Terror claims its victims in a manner similar to torture "in the dark of the night, far from the living, anonymous, without echo, without witness, and without a last will."[30] The ends of terror are sometimes in-voked to justify its use. Hannah Arendt distinguishes terror undertaken by revolutionary leaders eager to unmask hypocrisy and preserve politi-cal virtue from ideological terror: Robespierre is counterposed to Stalin.[31] Yet, state terror is no more justifiable than state-sponsored torture. The burden of torture on the French colonial state is all the heavier in that for intellectuals such as Merleau-Ponty France is a "country favored by his-tory."[32]

National (qua "insurgent") movements of liberation also use torture. Theirs is a discrediting recourse to torture as punishment—which consti-tutes one aspect of torture as analyzed in this book—that does not attain the sophistication of the means and functions of torture employed by the militarized state. The pain endured by victims is no less real. Although their use of torture cannot be justified, such movements cannot be equated with the colonial states against which they fight. The entanglement of states with torture is frequently justified by reference to the violence per-petrated by these oppositional movements. But states have obligations to preserve the law, not to violate it. More importantly, because they have the monopoly on the use of force, states are morally as well as politically obligated to use it judiciously in a manner that preserves the physical and moral integrity of all their citizens.

The book is divided into four parts. Part I focuses on the imperial pol-itics of torture as it analyzes the theoretical-doctrinal foundations of the systematic use of torture. It examines revolutionary war as well as the an-tisubversive doctrine that it spawned. It traces the ensuing militarization of the colonial state and delineates the role played by torture and terror in psychological action as exemplified by three selected models of "paci-fication."

Part II constructs an "ethnography of torture" detailing the language in which torture is spoken, its sexual core, its functions in identity crys-tallization. It also examines the military use of women in expanding its psychological action strategy.

Part III addresses the interface between conscience and imperial iden-tity that sustains tolerance or rejection of torture and terror. It examines the management of conscience by torturers and observers of torture, and the moral justifications proffered by the Church, individual chaplains, and right-wing Catholics. It also analyzes perspectives on torture's meanings expressed by three influential intellectuals, Jean-Paul Sartre, Frantz Fanon, and Albert Camus differently positioned vis-à-vis Algeria, and representing different aspects of political consciousness and identity.

Part IV focuses on the philosophical and moral issues raised by torture through an examination of moral philosophers' justifications of the exceptional use of torture. It also discusses the reemergence of torture as a tool of state terror in postindependence Algeria and the United States in Iraq and Guantanamo Bay.

The data for this book was gathered over a period of five years. I have used the Archives Nationales in Algiers, the archives of the Service Historique de l'Armée de Terre (SHAT) now the Service Historique de la Défense in Vincennes, the Centre des Archives d'Outre Mer in Aix-en-Provence (CAOM), as well as the Bibliothèque Nationale François Mitterrand in Paris. I have also used interviews with two regional leaders of the Islamist movement in Algeria, one former urban Islamist guerrilla, and one surrendered member of the rank-and-file, to elicit their views on the uses of terrorism and torture. These interviews were part of a larger book project that is resulting in two books, of which this is the first. Although these interviews are not crucial to the present book, they have helped me understand how terror is justified. I have also used confessions of French torturers, and eye-witness accounts by both Frenchmen and Algerians, war diaries kept by protagonists from both sides of the war, as well as monographs. Diaries have been an invaluable source of information about the war and torture. They prove remarkably accurate when checked against declassified military documents. However, even though they record torture situations, and episodes of reprisals with detailed realism, some diaries were kept for purposes of absolving guilt, rather than for genuine personal records of feelings about the daily minutiae of the war. Caution had to be exercised in drawing conclusions from such accounts. The memory of the war, like all memory, fades after a while, which makes the plethora of recent accounts of the war obtained through interviews of former soldiers carried out by French social scientists somewhat unreliable. In addition, occasional reluctant discussions I have had with Algerians who have survived torture convince me that existing confessions of former torturers or witnesses to torture have left a whole range of sexual practices (such as incest) enforced during torture séances unspoken. But, no matter their accuracy, these narratives constitute good documentary evidence of states of mind, and feelings in the post–Algerian War era.

I found it stimulating, albeit risky, to combine archival research with the sociological need to look for patterns, structure, and agency. More importantly my need as a historical sociologist to find the theoretical implications of constellations of events was at times counteracted by history's absolute disdain and unconcern for neatness and orderly thought. Reading the historical record filled me with a mixture of awe and trepidation. Awe because it is enormous, uneven, with the trivial and the significant assembled together. In folder after folder, lay, stamped with the word "secret," the directives and instructions that led to the untold pain, suffering, and death of women, men, and children. Trepidation because I feel encouraged to take a subject matter that belongs to a very complex and layered history in a different direction with the help and insights afforded by interdisciplinary tools of analysis.

I hope this book will contribute to the study of injustice and powerlessness of which torture was the most telling expression under colonial domination. My purpose is to provoke concerned scholars into a reflection on the link between the state-sponsored human degradation that took place in Algeria in the mid-1950s under the guise of "pacification," and the wanton abuse of prisoners at, among other places, Abu Ghraib, Iraq, Guantánamo Bay, Afghanistan, and in the countries to which torture is outsourced including Egypt, Jordan, and Morocco. The similarities between the French generals' arguments in favor of terror methods ostensibly to fight terrorism, and those made by the Pentagon, White House legal counsels, and well-intentioned intellectuals are striking. The logic is the same, and in spite of the emergence of human rights as a test of a country's political maturity and commitment to democracy, the merits of torture are debated and defended by politicians and lawyers who claim realism as their cover. The similarities between the Algerian and Iraq wars are not fortuitous. There is ample evidence that the conduct of the Algerian War has been a source of information, if not inspiration, for the U.S. government. The film *The Battle of Algiers* has been used by the Pentagon as a training tool,[33] and President Bush asserted on *60 Minutes* on January 14, 2007, that he was reading a history of the Algerian War recommended to him by Henry Kissinger.[34] Prior to delving into this history, Mr. Bush read Albert Camus's novel *The Stranger*, apparently to get insight into Algerian-qua-Muslim culture from an opponent (albeit popular writer) of Algeria's independence. There are many reasons why the Algerian War would be of interest to the Pentagon's prosecution of the war against Iraq: Algeria and Iraq are predominantly Muslim societies whose cultures are deemed inferior, their political aspirations misunderstood or unrecognized; U.S. authorities, like French officers, are convinced that they *know* their enemy's culture, when in reality they approach it through an ethnocentric conceptual grid that serves geopolitical interests; resistance to the U.S. military occupation is carried out by an underground movement using urban guerilla methods similar to the FLN's; torture as a technique of interrogation is used in Iraq as it was in Algeria; the military is faced with an elusive enemy that frustrates its capacity to win a clear victory in spite of its technical superiority. Hence Algeria and Iraq appear interchangeable; and the French Empire is revisited for its value as a primer for American imperial politics.

On a final note, I will depart in this book from a tradition in French historiography, and refrain from using the term "métropole" to refer to France, the center of colonial power. I will instead use the expression "colonial state" to which I will add the qualifier "in France" or "in Algeria," wherever its area of operation might be. I will also refer to the men and women who fought in the *maquis* as "combatants," not "rebels" or "insurgents." The vocabulary used during the Algerian War continues to be employed normatively when it needs to be questioned for defining the war from the perspective of counterrevolutionary doctrine.

PART I

IMPERIAL POLITICS AND TORTURE

Chapter 1

REVOLUTIONARY-WAR THEORY

At the bottom of this deceptive logic,
the army included torture in its arsenal in order to win.
—General de Bollardière, *Bataille d'Alger, bataille de l'homme*

THE SYSTEMATIC USE of torture by the military as well as the police was not simply a response to acts of terrorism committed by the FLN as was claimed. It was the direct outcome of *guerre révolutionnaire* (revolutionary-war) theory, elaborated by a number of (colonial) military officers in the 1950s. Even though the theory did not initially advocate torture, it informed an antisubversive war doctrine that could not be implemented successfully without its use. Without the theory, torture could not have been systematized. Similarly, without torture, the antisubversive war doctrine could not have been implemented. Within this theoretical and operational context, torture became a structural imperative. To begin with, the antisubversive war doctrine rested on the twin principles of force and intelligence in an ambitious plan of total control of the population. Intelligence was to be gathered on *all* aspects of the war. At the same time, the *permanent* display of force was meant to be a deterrent of "terrorist" acts. Torture became the most elemental expression of the use of force as preventive and anticipatory punishment for "subversive" acts that may not have taken place, in addition to being a routine method of interrogation for information-gathering.

Revolutionary-war theory was as much a theory of modern war as it was a sociological statement about the relationship between state, nation, and empire. It tapped into deep-seated nationalist feelings among the French public, and articulated a critique of a political system in the throes of an identity crisis in which the military figured prominently.

Simply described, revolutionary-war theory held that war in the post–World War II world is a "new" kind of war. It is *subversive*, fought not with regular armies but with bands of guerillas or people's armies—as had been the case in China and Indochina—finding refuge and support among the population. From this perspective, the aim of revolutionary-qua-subversive movements is to seize power with the help of international commu-

nism (eager to destabilize Western democracies in their colonies by ally-
ing itself with nationalist, Pan-Arabist and/or Pan-Islamist movements)
and establish totalitarian regimes. The theory suggested that to combat
revolutionary war, conventional armies must adjust their methods and
adopt antisubversive strategies that borrow from their adversaries. Revolutionary terror must be met with counterrevolutionary military terror
in a four-pronged and integrated strategy ultimately aimed at the "pacification" of the population, the new war "terrain." The main principles of
the strategy were:

1. Search and destroy the Organisation Politique et Administrative
(OPA) of the revolutionary movement ensconced in villages (and some
city neighborhoods) in order to cut guerillas off from their social support.
Replace every destroyed OPA in rural areas with a new French OPA.[1] Re-
group and resettle villagers freed of the OPA and place them under close
military control. Maintain permanent *contact* with the population through
two mechanisms: a tight grid (*quadrillage*) of family- and neighborhood-
based structures similar to the guerilla organization, reporting to local
military posts; and the provision of sociomedical services by special civil-
military structures, the Sections Administratives Spécialisées.

2. Search and destroy military operations using light mobile units targeting guerilla "bands" and regular "rebel" units.

3. Systematically search for intelligence, with the use of torture, to intimidate the population, demoralize "rebels," and signal France's determination
to fight; torture is carried out as an "antidote" to terrorism during searches,
operations (with mobile torture equipment), and in detention centers.[2]

4. Apply new techniques of psychological warfare featuring propaganda as well as brainwashing to "conquer the minds and souls of women
and men,"[3] undermine the revolutionary movement's standing with the
population, and reindoctrinate captured combatants before enlisting
them to fight alongside the colonial army.

The clarity of revolutionary-war theory was compelling. But it was also
misleading as it reduced complex sociopolitical and economic problems
to logical propositions amenable to precise military interventions. Ironically, the doctrine sought to win the hearts and minds of the people all the
while advocating the destruction of their physical and social environment,
and the remaking of their selves through torture and psychological action
as shown in figure 1.1.

In the words of General Allard, the aim of the antisubversive war was:
"Destruction and Construction. These two terms are inseparable. To destroy without building up would mean useless labor; to build without first
destroying would be a delusion."[4] Before subjecting revolutionary-war
theory to close scrutiny, it is essential to inquire into the sociopolitical conditions that made its emergence possible.

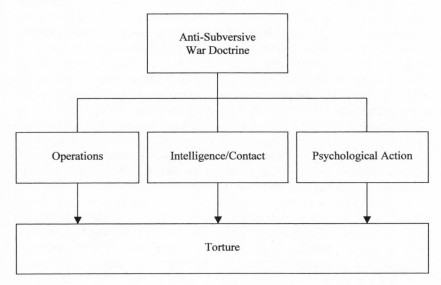

Fig. 1

Political Context of Revolutionary-War Theory

The extreme character of revolutionary-war theory and the uncompromising comprehensiveness of the antisubversive doctrine reflected a specific French nationalist tradition among the military. France's defeat by Germany in 1870–71 had been a traumatic experience for the military as well as a generation of intellectuals such as Jules Michelet, Ernest Renan, and Fustel de Coulanges, who described their views in exasperated nationalist and eschatological form.[5] Nationalism expressed a need to assert as well as recapture France's past glory in order to wash off the memory of defeat. It found an immediate outlet in a renewed interest in colonial expansion. The scramble for Africa at the end of the nineteenth century was cause for passionate debates between Jules Ferry, a proponent of colonialism, and Georges Clémenceau, its opponent. Since colonial ventures were primarily the business of military officers, debating the colonial question was a manner of shoring up the army's reputation.

Pride in a beleaguered French nation was given an intellectual and political impetus by Action Française, an ultranationalist movement spearheaded by classicist Charles Maurras. The strand of nationalism (or *nationalisme intégral*)[6] that Action Française represented found an echo among generations of French intellectuals and military officers, gripped by Maurras's unbound faith in rebuilding France's stature in the world, as well as his daring program for restoring the monarchy.[7] The Dreyfus affair compounded the perception among the military of a nation in decline, undermined from within, and divided against itself.[8] The victory over Germany in 1918 helped the nation rejoice in the recovery of Alsace-Lorraine, but the capitulation to Nazi troops in 1940 reversed the process of national psychological recovery. Not only was France occupied, but it had also actively collaborated with Nazi Germany. To make things worse, it was foreign, American and British, not French troops that liberated it.

The military was once more at the center of a national trauma. Yet, it was blamed neither for its first, nor its second defeat to Germany; and the military blamed politicians and the instability of French democratic politics. This tendency to hold the political system responsible for military defeats continued to hold sway through the Indochinese and Algerian wars. It helped the military nurture its frustrations and lull itself with the notion that the only way it could fulfill its mission of safeguarding the interest of the nation was through a change in the political system.

The Empire again held up the possibility that the military would recapture its prestige and sense of national purpose, but the Indochina and Madagascar wars were reversals. In the aftermath of World War II, French society was more invested in national reconstruction under the Marshall Plan than in actively supporting the military's battles in faraway places. The loss of Indochina in May 1954, five months before the Algerian War started, aggravated the military's feeling of isolation and compounded its wounded honor. Losing to guerillas such as the Viet Minh was far more humiliating than losing to a regular army. The year 1954 had been a particularly bad one for the French army. As Indochina was falling, negotiations had been under way to surrender sovereignty to Tunisia and Morocco.

The empire had been a source of pride and glory: it had its heroes, spanning a century and half, such as Marshall Bugeaud who had defeated the Algerian, Emir Abd-el-Kader, in 1844, and General Lyautey (a veteran of Indochina) whose "pacification" feats in Morocco were often admiringly recounted. That Algeria, a possession-department-province, would also be contested by nationalists was an unimaginable prospect, as it was threatening to the political and cultural identity of the colonial state. Stressing the Frenchness of Algeria, a political figure once exclaimed: France stretched "From Flanders to the Congo, from Dunkirk to Tamanrasset—do not forget it!—before it narrows to Perpignan."[9] Hence the military's determination to win the next and last colonial battle that Algeria presented to it. It did so in a logical-rational manner by taking stock of global political events, closely studying the methods used by its former colonial adversaries in Indochina and its ideological enemies, the communists, primarily in China where Mao had triumphed over Chiang Kai-shek.

Revolutionary-war theory was the last fully articulated expression of French imperialism. It crystallized for the civil and military establishment the memory of a vast and long unchallenged imperial venture with its entanglement in cultural and political identity; the fear of loss of relevance in a Cold War era; and a loss of self. It was at once a revaluation of the imperial/colonial idea, and its defense at a time when European colonial empires were crumbling. It also had a *redemptive* value that accounts for the military's determination to prosecute the war to the finish. In this sense, revolutionary-war theory sought to halt the historical process that inexorably led to the self-determination of subjugated peoples as acknowledged by the 1948 United Nations Human Rights Declaration to which France was a signatory.

Framers of the Theory

The conceptual groundwork for the theory was laid out by two books written in 1952–53 by Colonel Lionel-Max Chassin, a former air commander in Indochina, on the manner in which Mao Tse-tung led the revolution in China and assumed power.[10] Chassin sparked a reflection among army officers (many of whom were also veterans of the Indochina war, and former captives of the Viet Minh in the notorious Camp One) on how wars were fought in the post–World War II era, and how to prepare for them. Simultaneously, Colonel Charles Lacheroy who had just completed a tour of duty in Indochina had started lecturing and writing about the techniques of guerilla warfare he had just observed.[11] Theorists also included principally Major Hogard, Colonel Nemo, Captain Souyris, and Colonel Trinquier.[12] The theory was taught at the Ecole Supérieure de Guerre in Paris to an international student body with nearly one fourth hailing from Latin America.[13] Although it stirred excitement primarily among young officers, the theory won over all the generals who ultimately revolted against the French government in April 1961, including Raoul Salan, Maurice Challe, Henri Zeller, and Edmond Jouhaud.[14] Advocates of the theory also included high-level politicians such as Bourgès-Maunoury, minister of national defense, along with Robert Lacoste (who served as resident minister in Algeria), in addition to General Massu (the architect of the "Battle of Algiers" and a staunch advocate of torture), and General Paul Ely, chairman of the joint chiefs of staff at the Ministry of

Defense. By 1956 the theory had made inroads in political and military circles and become the prevailing frame of reference in discussing the progress or stagnation of the Algerian War. It reached beyond France and Algeria, and was taught in such places as Argentina and Brazil, where countersubversive doctrine was used in the preparation for the 1964 military coup, and in Portugal and the United States.[15]

The theory was elaborated in increments by officers who wrote individually and on occasion collectively under pseudonyms. Military journals such as *Revue Militaire d'Information*, *Revue de Défense Nationale*, and *Messages* were their professional outlets.[16] However, Catholic journals such as *Verbe*, which belonged to *Cité Catholique*, a successor movement to *Action Française*,[17] or *Itinéraires*, were also open to the military officers qua theorists. Although by 1955–56 it had been fully developed, the theory continued to be discussed and refined into the 1960s. In 1968 Colonel Roger Trinquier published a book that pulled all the strands of the theory together, described the doctrine it informed, and examined its implementation in Algeria.[18] The theory was meant to account not only for colonial wars such as those fought in Indochina and other parts of the French and British empires, but for other wars that took place in one country, such as civil wars, partisan wars, and internal insurgent conflicts aimed at toppling local governments. Yet, the theory aimed at establishing linkages between local movements of national liberation and foreign powers, and where such linkages were not evident (as the line between internal and international conflicts is never clear-cut),[19] it simply asserted their existence. Consequently, it acquired all the trappings of a conspiracy theory. At the same time, the theory provided military officers with the opportunity to critically examine their own nation's capacity to face up to this "new" war, which they perceived as a global confrontation of good against evil.

Nature of Revolutionary-War Theory

In 1956 Bourgès-Maunoury, minister of defense, wondered: "For what reasons, given our powerful units, superior command and fire-power are we failing? Why, in other words, do the weakest hold the strongest in a position of inferiority?" This question, in a nutshell, summarizes the impulse behind *guerre révolutionnaire* theory. It draws attention to the imbalance between the unquestionable technological superiority of a modern army such as the French army, and its incapacity to beat back guerilla armies as was the case in Indochina. The minister's concise answer invoked "other unrecognized or neglected factors have emerged alongside methods [ordinarily] used to help to evaluate our adversaries."[20] These factors and methods centered on a crucial concept for theorists: "subversion." Revolutionary war was described as first and foremost *subversive*, a characteristic that, according to Trinquier, "has profoundly altered the process of fighting a war."[21] As a subversive war, revolutionary war was characterized as *permanent* and *universal*, "one in space, time and methods," from Algiers to Brazzaville.[22]

These concepts, subversion and revolution, used interchangeably with one connoting the other, are crucial to understanding the manner in which military officers constructed their theory. Subversion was "the ideal weapon for manipulating populations, dominating them, seizing power, and keeping it."[23] The concept was eminently suited to the theorists' goal of formulating a grand, universal theory to justify combating all manner of opposition to established governments no matter where they were. Subversion connotes not only the overthrow or destruction of an existing political order, but also the undermining, and corrupting of a *moral* order. Subversive forces not only operate underground, but they also engage in morally reprehensible acts of terror.

The theorists seized on this dual meaning of the concept of subversion to foreground the *psychological* dimension of the war. Revolutionary war makes use of psychological techniques to manipulate people and win them to the cause of the revolution. Thus the theory raised the specter of an insidious revolutionary movement bent upon the destruction of French qua "Western" values, and implicitly shored up colonial rule as a bulwark against an immoral and shadowy adversary. From this perspective, revolutionary wars represented a clash of civilizations. Consequently, fighting "subversion" was not only a legitimate and worthy cause, but also a mission to save France as well as Europe from destruction. The goal of keeping the presumed barbarism of "subversive" movements at bay dictated the methods with which to fight revolutionary war, as will be shown later. For the conscripted or enlisted soldier, the war in Algeria was defined as a war for the preservation of French culture, a continuation of the "*mission civilisatrice*" that had justified the French colonization of Algeria to begin with.

Given the widely shared belief in France in the superiority of French culture, fighting in the colonies was perceived as fighting for the stuff that makes one a Frenchman. In this sense, the concept of subversion helped military theorists uncouple Algerian nationalism from colonialism, and shift the cause of wars of decolonization from the inequities of colonial systems to the moral character of "insurgents." In so doing, it provided troops (and the French public) with a psychological ploy for assuaging guilt when methods of psychological warfare included torture.[24] At the same time, the concept of subversion enabled the theorists to ground the rationale for holding on to colonies in the preservation of a French identity. It implied that personal identity was grounded in the nation, and national identity embedded in the empire. Anyone objecting to this identity conflation was a traitor.

In the end, not only did the concept of subversion conceal the concreteness of the causes of the war, it also neutralized the context within which it took place.[25] It helped to subsume the specific reality of the Algerian War under the rubric of a generic war. Eager to stress the newness of *guerre révolutionnaire*, theorists sought to explain away its causes in Algeria, about which they disagreed anyway.[26] Consequently, poverty or inequality under colonialism was either flatly denied as an efficient cause, or deemed an insufficient cause unless manipulated by foreign hands, especially communists, Pan-Islamists, or Pan-Arabists;[27] it was interpreted instead as a facilitating factor. Theorists warned that delving into the socioeconomic causes of the war was a political "error" that distracted from the task of countering the war. They feared the argument according to which reforms rather than military action might be a better response to *guerre révolutionnaire*. Hence Souyris asserted that reforms cause more, not less, resistance. From his perspective "rebels" reject reforms when these are announced by the colonial government.[28] Going one step further, Hogard warned that negotiations with "rebels" were similarly "a grave illusion" that needed to be dispelled.[29] Although it may seem that the generality of revolutionary-war theory required its obviating serious considerations of context, in reality it is the defense of the context (colonial rule) of such a war that required a theory with a transnational scope. In other words the theorists were eager to demonstrate that the Algerian War was not a war of decolonization[30] (as the FLN maintained), but one of (communist) recolonization.

Crucial as it is to understanding the manner in which the theory was constructed, the concept of subversion was not sufficient to give it the power of appeal to large audiences. This was supplied by the concept of "revolution" as a defining feature of the new war. Hogard, perhaps the most lucid theorist, claimed that revolutionary war is "a war of a revolution, and a revolution in the art of war."[31] Although this may appear to be a rhetorical statement, it nevertheless reflects the theorists' concern for order and stability both in France and in her empire. The communist party in France and elsewhere was deemed the "party of the revolution."[32] Theorists' fascination with the concept of revolution was both historical and situational. As military officers, they tended to be conservative, and thus took a dim view of revolutions that they equated with chaos—typically, the army in Algeria was officially referred to as "the forces of order." Additionally, they partook in a French tradition of questioning the validity of the French Revolution. In the latter they saw a prototypical model through which to understand the role of ideology, *idées force*, or "myths" such as independence, self-determination, anti-"colonialism" with which contemporary movements motivated their members to revolt.[33]

Theorists' interest in revolution also betrayed their own desire to stage a "counterrevolution" aimed not only at fighting revolutionary war, but to "dream"[34] of bringing about a new revolution of their own in France and her last colony, as will be discussed in chapter 4. Thus antisubversive war was perceived as counterrevolutionary war, a double-entendre conveying the notion that a bad revolution can be fought to bring about a good revolution. Algeria was to become the stage on which to fight a French battle with French history, a long-yearned-for opportunity to come to terms with the ghosts of the past, pitted against one another as royalists were against republicans, and radical republicans against bourgeois republicans. Although Algerians were at the center of the pitched battles, the war in Algeria was about France and her internally contested history and identity, which inescapably included the empire.

Characteristics of Revolutionary War

Theorists found in the Chinese Revolution (whose leader, Mao Tse-tung they admired) the basic features that characterize all revolutionary wars. They pointed out that, revolutionary war has no front, no definite line of combat. Rather, it deploys on a "surface" or dispersed territory. Instead of confronting the enemy frontally, revolutionary fighters ambush him on their own terms, hit, withdraw, and vanish. For the theorists, one passage from Mao's teaching about guerilla warfare encapsulated in "sixteen key words," the essence of revolutionary-war tactics: "When the enemy advances, we retreat; when the enemy withdraws, we harass; when the enemy is exhausted, we attack; when the enemy retreats, we pursue."[35] This reductive manner of presentation of revolutionary war tactics was meant to convey, by comparison, the ineffectiveness of conventional war methods despite their superior technical advantage.[36] Implicitly, theorists intended to demonstrate that the military had to develop new, more adapted methods of countering revolutionary war. From their perspective, two crucial factors accounted for the effectiveness of revolutionary war: it takes place with the support of the local *population*, which is subjected to *psychological* technique of indoctrination; and its leaders combine military and political functions.

Population

Theorists argued that without population support revolutionary war could not endure or succeed. Population supplies guerillas with food, shelter, recruits, and intelligence. In this sense guerillas are, in Mao's oft repeated expression, like "fish in water." Theorists specified that population support could stem from spontaneous patriotism, ideological commitment, or "exasperation" caused by occupying armies.[37] Grappling with this question, Souyris wrote: "Surely, there has to be a people's yearning for independence, but the wars imposed upon us are led by revolutionary movements which exploit nationalist sentiments—when they do not trigger them—in order to seize power, thereby imitating the Marxist-Leninist type of war." By dismissing the yearning for independence that they reluctantly acknowledged, theorists stressed ideological coercion as the main cause of population support for revolutionary war. They assumed that populations were amenable to manipulation regardless of the meaning they might attach to ideals such as freedom or independence. This logic enabled the theorists to design methods of fighting the war of decolonization suited for a communist subversive war as they perceived it. The Algerian War was thus rarely understood in its own terms, but always by reference to factors or events outside its ambit. And clearly, "imitating" communist methods, and *being* communist are two different things. In support of his argument, Souyris noted that concepts such as "'collegial management, personality cult, deviation, self-criticism, political commissar, thought-action, and action-thought,' did not exist in the Arabic language, and did not belong in the 'Algerian folklore.'"[38] Nevertheless, two years earlier, in 1957, he had noted that the

> presence of communist factors is not required in order to identify the characteristics of revolutionary war. . . . Although most of the nationalist parties are not beholden to Marxism-Leninism, they nevertheless are knowledgeable about the fundamentals of this [revolutionary] war, and know how to use them according to the methods and techniques which they have learned—generally in Europe—from communist parties. In spite of this knowledge, nationalist parties often display an unmistakable anti-communism. This is why they easily win the sympathy of Americans."[39]

Theorists clearly understood that their enemy in Algeria was not international communism, as was admitted by General Massu years after the war ended.[40] Yet, they proceeded to characterize the war as if it were. They strenuously established dubious linkages between communism and Islam. Making use of superficial studies, they asserted that Muslim countries such as Algeria were "*communisables.*"[41] They also adopted the prevailing notion that Islam is intrinsically political and thus impels its adherents to engage in oppositional action as a "natural reflex."[42] Finally, combining a distorted view of Islam with ethnic prejudices, military officers argued that "certain forms of Arab thought" were structurally similar to dialectical materialism.[43]

Psychological Warfare

Military theorists were impressed with the discipline displayed by revolutionary leaders and their followers, and the methods they used to gain the support of the population, both of which they attributed to ideological indoctrination. According to Hogard, revolutionary-war methods and techniques of control of the "masses" focused on the control of the body and the mind. To buttress this view, theorists ominously described the communist organization of revolutionary war (exemplified by the Viet Minh's) as one in which each individual was ensconced in an intricate network of overlapping groups in various committees and associations, at all levels of the social hierarchy from the neighborhood to the party. Every person belonged to more than one group that encompassed all facets of social life, as for example, PTAs, sports clubs, literacy groups, unions. Everyone had a function in these "parallel hierarchies," and people knew one another in the same unit. Individuals were encouraged to engage in self-criticism as part of an ongoing reflection on the adequacy of their behavior to the goals of the revolution. These horizontal hierarchies were crossed by vertical ones often referred to as "committee hierarchies" that included administrative, political, and military committees. The two types of hierarchies were theoretically independent of each other, yet formed one integrated structure. Theorists explained that parallel hierarchies rendered the individual defenseless before the power of the revolution. Since the hierarchies overlapped and the political and the military merged, the whole community participated in one way or another in the task of defending the revolution, by shielding and providing material support to the guerillas, or taking up arms against the enemy. Hence, the people were literally in arms. However, theorists often felt that the people did not arrive at this point on their own; they were acted upon, manipulated by powerful psychological methods. They concluded that a counter-"psychological action" was crucial to overturning the revolutionary tide.

Concentration of Political and Military Power

Perhaps the single most meaningful characteristic of revolutionary war that held special significance for theorists was the dual political and military power held by revolutionary leaders. Officers who had fought in Indochina resented politicians' ultimate control over military strategy and had little respect for politicians' judgment or commitment to national security. Therefore, they strongly believed that the only way to combat revolutionary war was for the military to assume political power, which would enable them to conduct the war as they saw fit. Commandant Hogard best expressed the importance for the army of sharing in political power. He maintained that (colonial) wars are no longer "national," requiring only volunteer legions to fight native leaders, and little involvement of public opinion. Gone were the times of the "noble adversaries . . . from Abd-El-Kader to Moha-ou-Hammou, or even bandits like Samory." "The soldier today cannot, as happened at the time when wars were 'national,' ignore the political factor."[44] Underlying this reference to the forms of struggle that took place at the beginning of the colonial era in the nineteenth century was nostalgia for a time when French troops were assured of victory because of their technical advantage over ill-equipped native tribes.

In seeking to emulate guerilla leaders, theorists neglected to ponder the consequences for a modern professional army, operating in a sovereign state, of combining political and military powers. Indeed, revolutionary leaders' propensity to wield military and political power was dictated by the circumstances under which they fought a war that was largely underground. However, officers were concerned with efficiency not legality. They were fascinated by those aspects of revolutionary movements that they felt accounted for their greater efficiency over a conventional army. Nevertheless, from the military theorists' perspective, unless the army was in a position of total control over the conduct of the war, as revolutionary leaders were, it could not meet the challenge of revolutionary war.

Phases of Revolutionary War

To repeat, theorists constructed a model of revolutionry war that they felt fit all local manifestations of "revolution." Although they allowed for variations to occur, they were confident that the model was not only accurate, but permitted an assessment of the level of evolution of a war at any given time, anywhere, thus helping the army to make the appropriate response. Hogard identified five stages in the evolution of revolutionary war, each corresponding to a particular strategy. In phase one, an "active kernel" of agitators begins to use the "internal contradictions"[45] of the colony, such as poverty, unemployment, political inequality.

At the next phase, an "organization" comprised of a network of intelligence, and opposition members is set up. It is in this phase that a "climate suitable for revolution develops."[46] In phase three "armed bands" are established, and start operating; acts of sabotage begin; guerillas make their appearance.

Phase four is not reached until guerillas operate for a while, and meet with sufficient success to liberate entire zones, which they will use as bases from which to launch more operations, and typically install a provisional government. At this phase, regional military units, and in due time a regular revolutionary army, are created. The dissemination of the news of the successes of the revolutionary movement rattles the adversary and deepens the gap between the population and the government.

The fifth and last phase targets the morale of the adversary's troops. The revolutionary army launches an all-out counteroffensive with the guerillas against the adversary's troops on the Chinese model.[47]

This was the profile of the ideal-typical revolutionary war. In reality, the phases analyzed overlap, and the evolution of the war may vary according to local conditions. Nevertheless, as Hogard warns, "revolutionary war is one."[48] Based on the model he constructed, he could tell the phase of any revolutionary war by identifying its strategic features. For example, he assessed the Algerian War as being at phase three.

Theorists went beyond a thorough assessment of the lessons learned from the conduct of revolutionary wars. They additionally incorporated in their theory a rebuttal of arguments made against its validity. Although presented as a list of pitfalls to avoid, these rebuttals were in reality meant to legitimize a hard-line approach to the Algerian War. In addition to the political "error" discussed earlier, there were tactical errors. These included "errors of appreciation" such as mistaking revolutionary war for "a traditional uprising."[49] Another, and very important tactical error, resided in officers' overconfidence in their fire power to quell a revolutionary war.[50] Souyris identified two resulting pitfalls: First, "contempt for the adversary," and an unrealistic sense of winning based on the use of conventional tools of assessment of military situations, such as maps and briefings. The second pitfall may seem intriguing since it questions maps and briefings, the traditional instruments for taking stock of progress on the ground. But Souyris intended to convey at least two ideas. First, military action against revolutionary war cannot be assessed accurately because the adversary is elusive. Besides, the population is often the target of military operations, making it difficult to determine whether the real "rebels" have been hit. Second, the temptation is great to win the war on paper and lose it on the ground since maps with "their color-coded pins" cannot tell what goes on in the minds of people, and the degree to which they sympathize with "rebels." Souyris concluded that: "A map does not account for the gangrene that makes its way into the minds of the people. . . . we must see the country as the revolutionary leaders see it."[51] In other words, the social fabric of the population had to be targeted. Souyris's analysis of tactical errors indirectly addressed excesses and irregularities that took place on the ground: frequent and indiscriminate use of formidable fire power; doctoring of field reports to make operations look more successful than many actually were; a disconnect between action on the ground and its political construction at official levels.

Antisubversive War Doctrine

Revolutionary-war theory helped to elaborate principles to guide strategies and tactics to fight revolutionary war. These were based on the fundamental importance of taking the war to the adversary by using the same means he did. Named alternatively counterrevolutionary, counterguerilla, and antisubversive (I will be using all three terms interchangeably), the doctrine, informed by revolutionary-war theory, should have been termed counterrevolutionary. But, the concept of counterrevolution belonged to a tradition that included Charles Maurras and Action Française, which by this time connoted the 1940 defeat. Aware of this past, Captain H. Martin found the expression "counterguerilla warfare" more acceptable, albeit inadequate, because it reflects methods of fighting that are different from those of revolution. It also connotes the opposite idea of "plagiarism," or mimicking revolutionary war, and the idea of fighting revolutionary war with the methods of classical warfare. In the end, he argued against conceiving of counterguerilla war as a "minor form of the art of warfare."[52]

The doctrine that flowed from the analysis of revolutionary war contained all the elements that made the systematic use of torture a necessary requirement of antisubversive war. Theorists qua strategists built a logical structure espousing the contours of the theory, which began with a reflection on the nature of war. They argued that Clausewitz's definition of war as "the mere continuation of politics by other means"[53] no longer applies in a world where nations at different levels of development enter into conflict with one another. Trinquier pointed out that "war is an act of violence to subjugate populations, occupy their territory and get hold of their riches." Using a version of Vilfredo Pareto's theory of the circulation of elites, he argued that "the ultimate end of revolutions has remained the same: To take the power to command from those too weak to secure obedience from others; take privileges away from a class that has become incapable of defending itself, or did not deserve it."[54] To emphasize their will to fight as a historically determined obligation, theorists defined counterrevolutionary war as "total": Military, psychological, cultural, and economic. Consequently, "pacification" was an integrated war method that should be applied thoroughly untrammeled by any negotiation with the "insurgents" until the war is won.

A key factor in waging this total war was the *population*. Counterrevolutionary war focused on "taking hold of the population by neutralizing it, rallying it, or progressively utilizing it." The concept of neutralization evokes a double process of knocking out of operation, possibly existence, as well as rendering neutral. Under conditions of war, to render a population neutral results from military as well as psychological operations. Thus counterrevolutionary war was a war *in and against* the population. A theorist put it succinctly: "We can say that for regular forces, counterguerilla war is a form of war in which the population is a part of the terrain from which it cannot be separated."[55] The population therefore becomes the target of operations. Frequently used terms such as "conquest of the population," "taking it in hand," or "reconquering it" summed up strategists' conception of counterrevolutionary war as a new colonial war. A number of strategic techniques were identified to conquer the population, each responding to the specific characteristics of revolutionary war as analyzed by theorists:[56]

1. Changing operational strategies.

These included the systematic destruction of regular enemy forces as well as small guerilla "bands." This called for a new military strategy favoring spreading military posts out on a longer front, instead of relying solely on larger posts placed at strategic locations. The change would have the added advantage of placing the army *in* the population. The army in Algeria used a mathematical troop-population ratio adjusted to mountains and plains.[57]

2. Cutting the enemy off from outside support.

This required sealing borders and displacing border populations to refugee camps. The measure would prevent the smuggling of weapons and enemy recruits trained abroad.

3. Destroying the OPA systematically.

Although this was technically an intelligence operation, it also involved military operations against villages. General Massu remarked that the destruction of the OPA was more urgent and easier than that of the military organization because the OPA was "fixed."[58]

4. Isolating the population from the enemy.

This method was comprised of three components: The establishment of no-man's-zones, the regrouping of villages and hamlets, and the organization of the population into a tightly knit hierarchical system of control with the family as a unit.[59] No-man's-zones, also referred to as "forbidden" zones were to be set up in areas where the topography lent itself to guerilla action. These were free-shooting zones aimed at dislodging and eliminating fighting "bands." The technique required the removal of the population from the zones. The regrouping or resettlement of villages was an additional measure to prevent the OPA from reconstituting itself, to cut the enemy off from its population support, and to control the population more closely. Resettled villagers would be under the permanent control of military posts and a combination of military and civil staff (the Sections Administratives Spécialisées to provide them with basic educational and health services). Whether in rural or urban areas, the population would be organized into an intricate administrative net that would record the activities and movements of every individual according to a phased plan answering the slogan: "Force! Organize! Engage!"[60] The population was divided up into four categories: "virgin" or free of FLN action; "recovered," or secured; "unorganized" or not subjected to military indoctrination in spite of its proximity to military posts; and "rotted" or won to the FLN.[61]

5. Arming villagers, especially those who had been resettled, to fight in

self-defense against the enemy. This method presupposed preparatory psychological conditioning targeting the villagers.

6. Subjecting captured combatants to "reeducation" and enrolling them in a native auxiliary force (the Harka) to fight alongside the French army. This task also necessitated psychological *action*. Furthermore, it assumed that there was an ideology that united army and local society.

The doctrine so constructed was adapted by the generals on the ground according to their own conceptions of the sequencing of its component parts, and their priorities. For example, General Massu (and his successor, General Challe) stressed the destruction of the OPA over FLN "bands" without necessarily neglecting these. He favored a strategy that combined intelligence-gathering with "tactical mobility" (also named "nomadization") characterized by "rapid and frequent movements [of small units qua 'cells' over all types of terrain] to multiply contacts with the population and track the *katibas* [FLN's troops] in their own territory."[62] Contact with the population was meant to secure "preventive intelligence" or information that led to the capture of combatants who would supply "contact intelligence," crucial to destroying "bands."[63]

In conventional war, population is not a strategic target, except under some specific circumstances as was the case with the bombing of London by Nazi forces, or Dresden by the Allies. Theorists were aware of the fallout from waging a war in and against the population. They noted that "Christian morality" and even Machiavelli would recommend that the population be kept out of armed conflict. However, "neither Sun Tzu [who had recommended the starvation of enemy cities], nor Henry V of England (who prohibited the sack of cities in Normandy), nor Machiavelli frown on the most brutal coercion within possible means." A neutralized population would supply the "forces of pacification" with "food, shelter, and intelligence."[64] In other words, French troops would live in and off the population as the Front of National Liberation was supposed to be doing. Echoing this notion that counterrevolutionary forces should mimic the "rebels," Hogard suggested that the French soldier too should become "a militant."[65]

As noted earlier, in summarizing the Algerian modality of the counterrevolutionary war doctrine, General Challe invoked two tactics: one of "destruction," the other of "construction."[66] Destroying "the rebel politico-administrative framework, the nerve center of the rebellion,"[67] must be followed by a "construction of a new order " through "pacification," which means not only "re-establishment of personal contact with the population" but also "organizing the people, separating them into hierarchies, that is to say, substituting for the political and administrative organization of the FLN new groupings beginning at the lowest echelon of the future [social and administrative] organization of Algeria."[68] Consequently, the doctrine combined military action with *psychological action*[69] in a task of *destruction/reconstruction* aimed at social engineering. "Pacification," narrowly defined, referred to the replacement of the enemy's politico-administrative organization with a new, French one. However, given the scope of the war, and the political requirement to win it as quickly as possible, it had to take place at the same time as military operations. The danger was that military operations would be synonymous with pacification. Similarly, since "pacification" could not take place without *psychological action*, the line between the two was blurred.

Psychological warfare was the hallmark of counterrevolutionary doctrine. It targeted the enemy broadly defined (as will be discussed in chapter 6), as well as those "neutral" to the war. Some strategists, such as Hogard, suggested that psychological war be waged preventively, "well before [the appearance] of signs of violence," otherwise the army must "face the following alternative: brutal repression, which it loathes, or [taking] time to know her adversary and adapt to him."[70] Since time was of the essence, the first alternative was the only one possible. Captain Martin put it bluntly: "Counter-guerilla war means how to get rid of the individual's will to fight."[71] The importance given to psychology reflected the military's interest in keeping abreast of what was then a new technique of control,[72] in addition to gaining insights into how best to deal with the challenge of "conquering" populations having their own cultures and languages. Psychological methods of "pacification" included propaganda, brainwashing, the provisioning of social services such as medical care and basic literacy classes in rural areas, and outreach programs to women in urban centers. However, the focus of *psychological warfare* was behavior modification more than winning the population's support by providing social services. The theorists' faith in psychological action was grounded in their desire to adopt this new technique of control, in conceptions of crowd behavior formulated by Gustave Le Bon,[73] and techniques of mass manipulation developed by Serge Chakotin.[74] These authors' work provided officers with concepts such as "crowds" and "masses" that proved useful in objectifying the Algerian population as an arational aggregate of people that could be reshaped at will with the proper psychological techniques, including the infliction of pain. Le Bon's and Chakotin's theories will be examined separately in chapter 3. Psychological action, just like operations, was intimately linked to intelligence. One required the other.

The large number of articles written about revolutionary war and the strategies to combat it could not be ignored by officers in the field. The theory was discussed in military messes causing some to feel "allergic" to it, and others to write in protest of it. Among critics within the army, two stand out for their questioning of the validity and legitimacy of the theory. They wrote under the pseudonyms of Simplet (i.e., Simpleton)[75] and Ximénès.[76] While Simplet, a colonel commanding a regiment, stressed the simplifications of the theory,[77] Ximénès drew attention to the economic causes of the war,[78] which theorists had dismissed. Comparing the living standards of colonial and native populations, he noted that the former consumed 2,979 calories per capita, had an income ten to twenty times greater (than Algerians) for those who lived off agriculture, and seven times larger than that of the average Frenchman in France.[79] By contrast, the Algerians had an average daily food intake of 1, 800 calories per capita, or three quarters of the standard allowance.[80] Furthermore, Ximénès found that one tenth of the Algerian active population (of 2.3 million) was permanently unemployed, and 450,000 people, primarily in rural areas, were partially unemployed. The population reduced to partial or total unemployment hovered between 25 and 30 percent. Finally, Ximénès stressed institutional discrimination against Algerians in training and access to a range of occupations.[81] Like Simplet, Ximénès boldly exploded the myths spun by revolutionary theorists to fight an essentially political war. Nevertheless, *guerre revolutionnaire* advocates were not swayed, and the war continued to be fought according to their strategy.

In conclusion, revolutionary-war theory was a powerful logical structure born out of the military's experience with fighting colonial wars, and aimed at salvaging the last bastion of the French colonial empire in Algeria. It led to a strategy that made the systematic use of torture a war weapon. It did so by constructing a transnational conception of war that wove together a number of factors aimed at rallying a diverse audience comprised of recruits, politicians, and the public at large. It conveyed a sense of a nation in danger ill-governed by weak politicians hobbled by a dysfunctional democratic system; identified the enemy as an alliance of international communism and Pan-Islamism; conflated national identity with imperial identity, which it embedded in idealized French values; portrayed wars of decolonization as subversive wars aimed at undermining not only the existing political order but also the French and European *moral* order; presented the fight for the preservation of the colonial empire as a clash of civilizations between the forces of barbarism and enlightenment, and thus a struggle for self-defense. The theory informed a doctrine that defined the war as taking place *in* the "population," therefore in the midst of civilians. Since it did not distinguish "insurgents" from "population," the doctrine merged civilians into a generic enemy, defined as fanatical, "satanic,"[82] bent upon the destruction of the Christian "West." Dehumanization of the enemy helped later to suspend moral considerations in the selection of the methods used to fight "insurgents." Revolutionary-war theory attempted to explain imperial power relationships, whereas revolutionary-war doctrine simplified the complexity of armed struggles and distorted their modalities. One aspect of this monumental effort to save a crumbling empire is striking: the need felt by the hard-line officers to pause, and theorize at a time when Europe had, barely nine years earlier, fought bitterly (along with its colonized peoples) against the excesses of formal-logical systems of thought turned against life and liberty. This theoretical moment harked back to a Cartesian imperial assertion of the power of reason to flatten out all obstacles in its path to abstract universal assertion. Whereas Mao, the inspiration behind strategists, used theory and practice as two moments of a continuous process of steering the revolution, French officers used theory as the measuring rod of their strategies, thus opening the door to various (and abusive) modalities of its application, as will be shown in chapter 4.[83]

Despite its shortcomings, the logical system was formidable in its consequences, not only in Algeria, as will be discussed in the next two chapters, but also in Latin America where it became known as the "French doctrine," in sub-Saharan Africa (Katanga), in Iran under Shah Reza Pahlevi, and in Israel among other places. To put the doctrine in action required the incursion of the military into politics and the justice system. Hence the militarization of the state was a prerequisite to a series of strategies that combined a scorched-earth policy to annihilate combatants; population-control techniques foregrounding torture and rape to aid in psychological action (brainwashing); internment camps; unbridled reprisals; and the like. The next chapter will analyze the military's gradual ascent to the political domain, and the specific structures it was subsequently able to put in place that brought terror to the population as part of the counterrevolutionary war.

Chapter 2

MILITARIZATION OF THE COLONIAL STATE

OUNTERREVOLUTIONARY war fundamental strategy was to "attack the rebel through the population and the population through the OPA."[1] To carry out the war against the OPA-population required that the military be free of political control and accountability. Intelligence-gathering, an essential component of counterrevolutionary war, could not be easily obtained without the use of torture. But, since torture was prohibited, the army needed to be free to act according to strategy, unhindered by laws protecting civil liberties. The panic generated by the November 1, 1954, coordinated attacks launched by the FLN gave the military the opportunity to fulfill a major principle of counterrevolutionary doctrine: combining political and military power. This did not happen as a result of a military coup, but with the active cooperation of the state, which became militarized as the military became politicized. This chapter analyzes the process that led to the military's ascent to power, which helped put in place the structural framework necessary to "conquer" the population. This structure rested on a secret intelligence-gathering apparatus in which torture was systematically practiced, a system of detention centers suited to the extraction of information from suspects, and military tribunals for a swift and exemplary justice that normalized torture as a method of operational investigation. In this sense, the militarization of the colonial state was a sine qua non for the emergence of torture as a war weapon in the implementation of counterrevolutionary doctrine.

Roots of the Militarization of the State

The transformation of the colonial state from an institution that protected the rights of the colonists and administered the native population, to one that was controlled by the military took place in tandem with a heightened consciousness on the part of the civil authorities of the danger of losing Algeria, and the panic-inspired notion that they were not equipped to ensure security. In reality, the panic was not grounded. Intelligence services had functioned extremely well. They had infiltrated the underground radical faction of the nationalist movement, the Comité Révolutionnaire d'Unité et d'Action (CRUA), and planted a mole, Djilali Abdelkader Belhadj (nicknamed *Kobus*), who alerted the police to the planned attacks.[2] Furthermore, intelligence services under the supervision of Jean Vaujour, director of general security in 1954, had instructed the mole to substitute a harmless chemical (potassium chlorate) for the more deadly explosives that nationalists were planning to use on November 1, 1954, instead of arresting the conspirators. Neither the mole nor the police knew the exact date of the attacks, but both were aware that the attacks were imminent. However, Vaujour worried about a generalized "rebellion" and had misgivings about the capacity of the existing security forces to bring it under control.[3] He had traveled throughout the country and come to the conclusion that the colonial security system was inadequate in size, equipment, and training. He undertook to establish a police academy, proposed the creation of an armed mounted force recruited among the native population, and called for a greater coordination between the various security services.

A number of factors facilitated the militarization of the state. First, the November 1 attacks were assessed against the background of the particularly bloody riots of May 8, 1945, in the eastern cities of Sétif, Guelma and Constantine.[4] Keeping alive the events of May 8, 1945, had been important to colonial politicians and proprietors, notably Henri Borgeaud, as a way of judging the appropriateness of approving the appointments of officials sent by Paris to the colony.[5] Conversely, memory of the fierceness of the repression in the aftermath of the riots was often invoked as prompting the group of nationalists of the Comité Révolutionnaire d'Unité et d'Action to start the war despite the opposition of the established nationalist party of the Mouvement pour le Triomphe des Libertés Démocratiques (MTLD), of which they had been members. For the French government, May 8, 1945, meant fear of a generalized "rebellion," a sort of *levée en masse,* just as it meant for the nationalists the loss of all hope for reforming the colonial system peacefully.

Second, anchoring the fear of a large-scale repetition of May 8 was the widely held notion shared by revolutionary-war theorists that foreign hands were behind the November 1, 1954, attacks. As Vaujour put it "As to whether the [nationalist] movement . . . was triggered from abroad, most specifically from Cairo, this was the opinion shared by all the police services, DST [Direction de Surveillance du Territoire] included."[6] Third, and equally important, was a perception lag[7] frequently invoked not only by Paris appointees to the colony, but also, and later in the war, by the military: The French government in Paris was believed to be unconcerned about what was happening on the ground, or unwilling to take seriously reports warning of a possible "insurrection."[8] When considered together, these factors account for the decision made in response to November 1, 1954, to launch a repressive counterattack labeled Opération Orange Amère (Operation Bitter Orange) on December 22, 1954, targeting all shades of nationalists without distinction, who were arrested, accused of having fomented the attacks, and tortured by the police in Algiers, Oran, and Constantine. This operation came on the heels of extensive military actions against people deemed *hors-la-loi* (outlaws) in the Aurès Mountains, Grande Kabylie, and the Oran region.[9] Neither the severity of Operation Bitter Orange, nor the military operations, reassured the colonial authorities that November 1 was a short-lived episode.

Etiology of Military Ascendancy

Within a relatively brief period of time, between 1955 and 1956, the military acquired power over large swaths of the country in a broad range of social, economic, and administrative functions, the scope of which they gradually widened. The first significant step toward the transformation of the state into a repressive military machine was taken with the passage of the law of April 3, 1955, decreeing a state of emergency in Algeria for a period of six months. Article 12 of the law set the stage for a transfer of power from civil to military court. It stipulated that "When the state of emergency is established in part or the entirety of a department, a decree issued at the behest of the Minister of Justice and the Minister of Defense may authorize military courts to hear crimes and related felony cases that [normally] fall under the department's appellate court."[10] Article 6 of the law gave the governor general the power of confinement over "all individuals . . . whose activity is deemed dangerous to security and public order." Nevertheless, the law specified that "Under no circumstance, shall confinement result in the creation of camps for the detained persons." In addition, the law set the stage for censorship by permitting "the control of the press and publications of any type; radio broadcasts, film projections, and stage productions."[11] Once this step was taken, it was only a matter of time before civil authorities became less accountable to the central government in Paris and relinquished power to the military over matters of security and the administration of the native population in rural and urban areas. That the declaration of a state of emergency was a watershed is attested to by Vaujour's constant reminder that he, as well as the governor, Roger Léonard, had opposed it when it was discussed in the aftermath of November 1 on grounds that it would jeopardize the primacy of civil authority over the military. Those concerns turned out to be supported by the facts, as the civil authority in Algeria started to serve the military's conception of the war, their strategies and their needs.

A second law passed on April 23, 1955, specified the previous one and enlarged the judicial powers of the military courts. Article 1, pointed out that "In application of Article 12, of the April 3, 1955 law, military jurisdictions may be invoked at any time for acts committed after October 30, 1954 in the county courts of Batna, Guelma and Tizi Ouzou; crimes designated in Article 2 of this decree; and all related felonies." The list of "crimes" lumped together petty crimes such as "blocking traffic," "poisoning," "rape and assault on public morality," and "battery," with "armed rebellion" and "all crimes against the national security of the state." More important, the law lists among crimes, "All [terrorist] attacks defined in articles 16 and 17 of the law of July 15, 1845." Furthermore, the law also refers to "crimes defined in articles 5 and 9 of the law of May 24, 1834, concerning the possession of arms or war ammunitions."[12] The appeal to laws dating back to 1834 and 1845 connotes an admittedly logical intention of continuity in legislative practice. However, the time period invoked by the laws predated the establishment and consolidation of an ostensibly *civil* state that emerged out of the "pacification" of Algeria in the first fifty years of the occupation in the nineteenth century. The resurrection of these laws implied that the colonial state was in essence militaristic, with episodic civil ascendancy.

At any rate, the establishment of the state of emergency was extended for another six months by the law of August 7, 1955. As if expressing a worry about a possible permanency of the state of emergency, the law added that "the government could reduce this period if the situation permits." Such concerns were short-lived as the law of March 16, 1956, Article 5, gave the government in Algeria, "the most extensive powers to take all exceptional measures required for reestablishing order, the protection of people and property as well as the safety of the territory." A decree passed on the following day, March 17, spelled out these extended powers, which included the suspension or control of imports of goods; requisitions necessary to the civil and military authorities; mandatory reparations paid for damage to public or private property caused by aiding and abetting the "rebels": and "the suspension, for an unlimited period of time, of all elected officials in local government who, in any way, impede the action of the state." More important, Article 11 of the decree permitted the governor general to "establish zones in which responsibility for maintaining order devolves to the military, which will assume the powers of the police normally exercised by civil authority."[13] The military thus acquired all the extended powers granted the governor general. It was effectively in power. The democratic state allowed and facilitated the militarization of politics. In the end, it took less than two years after November 1, 1954, for the colonial state to relinquish the most significant portion of its powers to the military thereby helping it to realize the condition necessary for conducting a counterrevolutionary war according to *guerre révolutionnaire* theory. This process culminated in the transfer of police power to General Massu by Prefect Serge Barret for the whole department of Algiers, on January 7, 1957. This was the prelude to the "Battle of Algiers," immortalized by the film of the same name, which would become a model of counterrevolutionary warfare to be emulated in other parts of Algeria as well as in the world.

As generals became more involved in the administration of the population through the establishment of Sections Administratives Spécialisées, the military's definition of the situation took precedence over what was left of the civil authorities' power of oversight. Once the army fulfilled policing and social-welfare functions, it could only bypass the formal political and legal bureaucracy of the state. Obedience to command for the sake of operational efficiency trumped due process; esprit de corps overshadowed fairness of prisoners' treatment. Violations of individual rights appeared as correctives of the shortcomings of a democratic system deemed incapable of defending itself. Was the army equipped to discharge civil functions? This is a question that was not posed, and probably could not be posed, because the situation was deemed an emergency. Algeria in the mid 1950s resembled Algeria in the first half of the nineteenth century, when the military was a major actor in the colony. The evolution of this historical role played by the military in politics led to the generals in the colony-province-department attempting to dictate their civil-military will to Paris in 1958 and 1961.

Was the state of emergency absolutely necessary? Could it have been avoided? Were the benefits it was expected to yield greater than its shortcomings? Officials, such as Vaujour, who attempted to justify the state of emergency in hindsight, argued that such a measure should only be resorted to when the nation was in danger and "everything appear[ed] lost." This was not the case in Algeria at the time. Vaujour knew that the state of emergency would unleash repressive measures, including torture, which would alienate the native population. He also clearly understood that a regular army is not equipped to fight guerilla warfare. However, in ultimately supporting the decision, he invoked a typical argument, favored by the military, that: "The judicial arsenal of the regime [*sic*] was not adapted to controlling the situation that arose in Algeria, outside of the most radical means, that is to say the state of emergency." However, this argument obviates a consideration of alternatives to the state of emergency, and a discussion of the degree of efficiency of military control in the long run. Barring these, the rationale behind the establishment of the state of emergency so soon after November 1, 1954, when the FLN was still ill-equipped, and virtually unknown to the Algerian population, was wanting. As Vaujour wistfully remarks, it is fear that put in motion a war machine bent upon the destruction of the enemy, and it is fear that he claims led to torture and summary executions, among other atrocities.[14] But fear was also grounded in the ever present sense of the political precariousness of colonial rule because it was fundamentally unjust.

Civil-Military Rapport

The military ascent to politics was fraught with tensions and problems. The transfer of power to the military in policing, administering the native population, and rendering justice unleashed a series of structural problems centered on control over intelligence. As the military expanded its range of action, it sought increased freedom from residual civil constraints. A chronic tug of war ensued with civil authorities. From the military's perspective, management of intelligence, the speed of its collection and transmission, as well as population control were at stake in their interaction with civil authorities. Unlike the civil functionaries who defended their turf, officers fought for increasing theirs. Resistance—limited as it was, and primarily passive—to expanding military power sheds light on the inexorable manner in which the militarization of the state proceeded. Resistance took place primarily at the local level where a few political appointees evinced concern for their prerogatives in the administration of the population. It also developed in specific institutions such as prisons, or the various internment camps where issues of budget, expertise, or overcrowding crystallized for functionaries the burden of being subjected to a dual administration, and having to defer to the demands of the military.

At the beginning of the war, clashes between civil and military authorities were resolved by appointing a general as prefect and military commandant.[15] Subsequently, General Cherrière, Combined Arms commandant, instituted a *jumelage* (or matching, lit. "twinning") of military and civil authorities such that civil posts and the geographical areas under their jurisdiction were designated counterparts of military ranks and zones. He also assigned the new military prefect social tasks, including schooling and welfare, in addition to "keeping order." This decision may have been the beginning of the policy of "pacification."[16] Where the geography of military operations coincided with civil administrative districting, relations between the two authorities were deemed functional. However, this was not an ideal solution since not all generals were appointed prefects, thus leaving room for civil prefects with oversight (even if only nominally) over military chiefs. Officers frequently objected to the dual system of authority primarily because it made "coordination of action" difficult.[17] Recommendations were made that "generals holding a 'civil-military' command be entirely in charge of their zones before the resident minister-governor general, and free of the prefects' oversight."[18] At times, an inverted power struggle developed in which civil authorities wished to usurp military power by urging operations directly from the "highest authorities."[19]

The appointment of "civil-military" commandants reporting to the prefects on political and administrative matters, and to the general commanding operational zones for military matters, was a sort of transitional step before the army acquired hegemonic power as befit revolutionary-war theory. The formal authority that prefects were supposed to exercise over the military was undermined by the concordances established between administrative and military territorial spheres of action. The structure looked as follows before May 1958[20]:

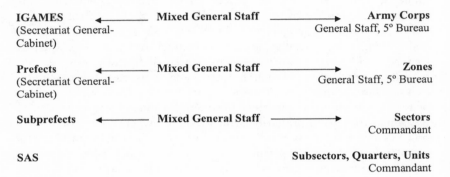

IGAMES ◄——————— Mixed General Staff ——————► Army Corps
(Secretariat General-   General Staff, 5° Bureau
Cabinet)

Prefects ◄——————— Mixed General Staff ——————► Zones
(Secretariat General-   General Staff, 5° Bureau
Cabinet)

Subprefects ◄——————— Mixed General Staff ——————► Sectors
                                                                         Commandant

SAS   Subsectors, Quarters, Units
                                                                         Commandant

If the commandant of a military division is "twinned" with the Inspecteur Général de l'Administration en Mission Extraordinaire (IGAME), and the subdivisional commandant with the prefect, there is no compelling reason why the military at each level would accept the supervision of a civil institution of equal "rank." Ultimately, it became clear that twinning could not work at all because of the absence of a civil counterpart to the general commanding the operational sector as standing rules required. It could not guarantee that cooperation at higher levels of the hierarchy would avail at lower levels. Military decisions, even when they concerned the civilian population, were taken on the basis of military strategy instead of sociopolitical considerations. The military was given charge of restoring "order" and "pacifying" the population. The formal supervisory function that the civil authority wished to establish was dictated less by a commitment to democracy than by a ritual need to preserve a civil façade to a state that had quickly moved in a military direction. It is important to note that the structural problems of coordination between authorities trained in different occupations was aggravated by dysfunction inherent in the overlapping hierarchical organization of the military itself.

For example, Colonel de Peyrelongue, commander of the 5th Light Infantry Group, identified as a serious problem the status of his unit that fell under three different military authorities located in different cities.[21]

The lack of coordination between civil and military authorities could be remedied only if a special prefect post was created. This would specifically help in the "search and transmission of intelligence as well as the elaboration and implementation of the pacification plan."[22] Civil institutions had their intelligence services; various military units had their own. Parallel sources of intelligence made for coordination difficulties that hampered the analysis and use of intelligence. The problem was especially acute for the new administrative structures, Sections Administratives Spécialisées which even though managed by military officers (often a new corps of Officiers des Affaires Algériennes) liaising with operational troops, were nevertheless under civil authority.[23] Again, the suggested solution was for the military officer of the SAS, working closely with the military command, to firmly take over the administration of "populations with whom the civil administration has completely lost contact." Bypassing the civil authority would result in the "direct transmission, from origin to destination, of military intelligence." Furthermore, the military suggested that the civil administrator (located in rural Algeria) should confine his functions to sustaining or permanently renewing contacts with the population in areas that had *already* been pacified, or those that had not been "spoiled [lit. "rotted"] by rebels' action."[24] Because the leading thread in this turf-based antagonism was a concern for intelligence and information-gathering, a good sign of civil-military cooperation resided in the degree to which civil authority shared intelligence with the army.[25] The solutions offered were consistent with this concern: The military ought to have control over intelligence; intelligence is a military affair. So, by implication, is the method of gathering it. The military autonomy claimed for the SAS, where interrogation with torture was practiced, shielded them from scrutiny. In the aftermath of May 13, 1958, the SAS were placed under direct command of sector commandants "for their political functions." They were also ordered to intensify their intelligence, as military action in "the human milieu" also increased.[26]

Parenthetically, the SAS was the instrument through which the 5ème Bureau, the successor to the Bureaux Psychologiques set up during the Vietnam War, carried out its psychological warfare.[27] The SAS mission was wide-ranging, its tasks including welfare, civil administration, systematic collection of intelligence, and justice, including "interrogations."[28] Conceived as the modern version of the nineteenth-century Arab Bureaus (1844–70), they purported to embody the notion of the soldier-administrator-builder-farmer so dear to Generals Bugeaud and Lyautey. The reputation of the SAS as an institution in which soldiers preferred to "help" the Algerian population, rather than engage in operations or torture, was undoubtedly erroneous, as the SAS, too, engaged in torture. Admittedly, there were SAS where the head officer perceived his job as a calling, and believed himself to be on a mission of genuine conversion of rural people to a positive conception of France and her military.[29]

As the sheer number of SAS increased, so did their role in the administration of the native population. By 1959, there were 600 of them comprised of 1,287 officers assisted by 661 NCOs, and 2,921 civilian specialists.[30] In fact, they became the military representatives of the government on the ground in a fulfillment of the governor's wish that they "bridge the gap" between the administration and the people. Rural areas were not the monopoly of the SAS. They also operated in urban areas, especially in neighborhoods inhabited by Algerians, under the name Sections Administratives Urbaines or SAU.

The crucial step that broke the stalemate between civil and military authorities was taken on January 7, 1957, by Serge Barret, Prefect IGAME who signed a law giving General Massu, commanding the 10th Paratrooper Division, police powers in addition to the restoration of "order" in the Department of Algiers.[31] The success of the "battle" of Algiers for which Massu achieved notoriety was (rightly) attributed to the civil government having given carte blanche to paratroopers to control an urban population (not a guerilla army), with no civil restraints on searches, arrests, torture, confinements, and summary executions. The symbolic significance of Massu's high-handed tactics made possible by the surrender of police power to the military cannot be minimized. It emboldened the military as a whole (by vindicating its claim to efficiency) to push for greater independence from civil authority. Torture could thrive only if the military secured for itself the greatest autonomy possible, and combined it with political control as demanded by revolutionary-war theory.

The constant concern for an independent intelligence-gathering capacity at the center of the push and pull between the army and the state was aggravated by another military concern: insufficient material means. An analysis of this issue falls beyond the scope of this book. However, the litany of complaints about inadequate or insufficient equipment, deficient renewal of basic tools such as pick handles, or at times the simple capacity for maintenance and repairs spoke of an institution that was in physical disarray, albeit not collapsing.[32] More important, this deficiency, whether real or exaggerated in reports, may have acted as one more grudge that the army, especially its key figures won to the antisubversive doctrine, had against the state. In order to carry out its counterguerilla warfare, the army needed to remedy what it perceived as the state's inability to elaborate and implement an uncompromising antisubversive policy. To do so, the army required a substantial budget, in addition to securing public acceptance of its military definition of a political situation.

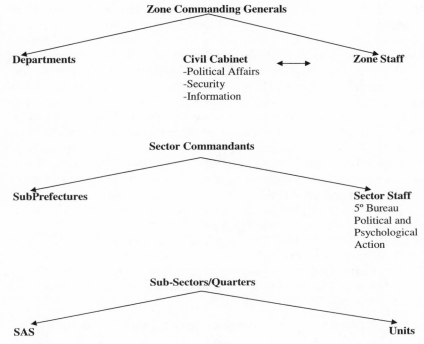

Fig. 2
Adapted from SHAT, 1H2403D1, "Report on the Role of the 6th Bureau and on the Civil and Military Organization before and after May 13, 1958," No. 638/ RM.10/6.SC, 4.

The problems created by the dual civil-military structure eased after May 13, 1958, as the new (Fifth) Republic gave the army control over civil authority as the following graph indicates:[33]

Military Power and Intelligence

Against this backdrop and armed with its special powers, the military set up an intelligence apparatus within which torture became routinized. The search for intelligence was the initial impetus behind torture before this practice acquired a life of its own, and played a role in social engineering. It led the military to abuse the power to confine "suspects," and to create a sprawling system of internment centers within which to detain them in violation of the April 3, 1955, law. Admittedly, intelligence is crucial in war. Within the Algerian context where the majority of the population spoke a different language and its loyalty was a stake in the war, intelligence acquired an even greater urgency. The intelligence infrastructure resembled an intricate machine operated by a staff imbued with a sense of specialness nurtured by the secrecy in which they worked. Often recruited among Indochina veterans, members were tied to one another by solidarity bonds, and generally perceived themselves as the true defenders of the values for which France stood. They saw themselves as the unsung heroes of a war, which they felt needed a strong sense of realism as well as commitment. The kind of work that the intelligence officers accomplished also gave them a sense of virility that they defensively contrasted with the weakness they attributed to others. The charge of being a "choir boy" or given to "sensitivities" (*sensibleries*) stereotypically associated with women was often leveled at those who objected to torture, or refused to engage in it when ordered to as discussed in chapter 5.[34]

General Salan emphasized that intelligence represented the administrative-judicial aspect of the war. He argued that the OPA could be destroyed with weapons other than "tanks, planes, machine guns, rifles." These other weapons were those that the military could now muster: "Codes, Laws, Decrees/Orders, and Instructions, which we are able to apply to our advantage." Instructions on how to conduct operations against "rebels and terrorism" were very clear:

> Any rebel using a weapon, seen with a weapon in his hand or committing an exaction will be shot on the spot.
> —A sighted [rebel] band will be fired on with all weapons available.
> —Food suupliers, accomplices and all other surviving and captured members of bands must be remanded to the Administrative Authority which will decide their future.
> —Any suspect trying to escape will be shot.[35]

However, instructions on how to wage an intelligence war were less explicit, but no less brutal. Smashing the FLN's OPA held responsible for the *pourrissement* of villages[36] took on the characteristics of a pervasive military phobia that grew in intensity as the war unfolded, justifying systematic torture as well as other abuses. The tool for destroying the OPA was the Détachement Opérationnel de Protection (or DOP). Initially, the DOP was a small part of a military counterespionage service, the Renseignement, Action et Protection (RAP), officially created in the aftermath of the Indochina war where it had been tried. Prior to the constitution of the RAP, at the end of World War II, the army had lost the management and control of counterespionage to a civil agency, the Direction de Surveillance du Territoire (or DST). With the RAP and its DOP units, the military was back in charge. The RAP was under the general interarmy commandant. Section P of the RAP spawned, and was responsible for, the DOP. Officially, the DOP was to assist the Deuxième Bureau (Intelligence

Office) in its task of dismantling the OPA. In reality the DOP acted as its surrogate.[37] They could bypass established procedures and laws for the sake of expediency and efficiency.

The DOP was a clandestine structure involved in not only "interrogating" suspects, civilians as well as combatants in uniform, but also arresting them. Once modeled after the organization of communist brigades in Vietnam, they copied the FLN organization in Algeria.

> There are six willayas [FLN military zones], so there were six general staffs of the DOP modeled after the willaya. A DOP was set up to correspond to an FLN *mintaqa* (about the same as a company in the French Army). In addition [DOP] sections were established in villages to combat the *nahia* (which were the equivalent of French military sections).[38]

They represented, in the words of a witness, "mobile interrogation brigades." The DOP could accompany troops during operations, and interrogate those captured on the spot with portable torture equipment. Section DOP was temporary, often put in place in order to do a specific job before moving elsewhere. Locally, in rural or urban military posts, the DOP was seen as a "parallel hierarchy" reporting only to the highest military authorities. Their staff enjoyed a broad range of freedoms, including "transporting under their responsibility and by any means of conveyance any civilian or military person whose identity they are not required to divulge."[39]

Their privileged status did not endear them to local commandants.[40] The secrecy of their existence combined with their status as a shadow organization made their methods elude scrutiny. In the etiology of state terrorism, they represent a major link in the chain that established terror as a tool of government. A former intelligence officer summarized the scope of the DOP's action as extending "from the small fund collector, to the ALN (Armée de Libération Nationale) officer who sneaks back home to kiss his mother, every civilian or military rebel must be caught in the web [of the intelligence structure] put in place."[41]

Generally recruited among screened draftees, although Vietnam veterans were its prized members, DOP staff was comprised of groups of ten officers per unit, operating in teams of two or three for a period of two months. Feeling above the law, DOP officers at times acted as warlords. One of them, in the southern city of Ghardaia, kept prisoners in his own home to interrogate at his leisure. A measure of the success of the DOP was their relatively large number, which doubled between 1957 (the year they were created) to twenty-four units and thirty-eight sections comprising a staff of 1,502 people. The DOP could not operate without a shield of secrecy. Hence the name change it underwent when its activities were uncovered. Officially (re)named Demi-Brigade de Recherche (Half Research Brigade), they continued to engage in what General Challe called "a genuine intelligence offensive." As a mobile institution in charge of intelligence, the DOP assisted other institutions that gathered information such as the Centre de Tri et de Transit (Triage and Transit Centers) or CTT. Often the DOP carried out the first triage at their own locale, sorting out the most promising suspects, before undertaking a second screening at the CTT.[42] The DOP also assisted other intelligence units specialized in storing and coordinating intelligence, such as the Centre de Renseignement et d'Action (Center for Intelligence and Action) or CRA.

In a cloak-and-dagger game, DOP and these other agencies shifted and swapped identities (and uniforms) as they moved in and out of their units.[43] The duplication and proliferation of intelligence services, their clandestine operations, the blurring of professional roles, the de facto resocialization of the police into the military worldview, and the acceptance of torture as a preferred tool of interrogation created a state of managed chaos that confused lines of responsibility. Accountability was no longer a goal in the discharge of one's functions. Whatever power the state retained was used, not to reign in the military, but to defend the military's methods of controlling the civilian population. Civil servants at all levels were supposed to go about their business following usual procedures except—and the exception became the rule—where these obstructed the actions of the military.

Triage and Internment Centers

In addition to the DOP, the military used the special powers it received to establish a network of detention and internment centers, institutional settings helped to routinize torture. These structures comprised Centers of Triage and Transit; concentration camps named Centres d'Hébergement (lit. sheltering centers) but commonly referred to as internment camps; Military Internment Camps (CMI); and the lesser known Re-education Centers (CRD) where brainwashing took place as discussed in chapter 6. The Exceptional Powers Decree gave the civil authority (the governor general, or the prefect) the power to confine suspects. Confinement (*assignation à résidence*) was a decision that compelled an individual "to remain in a given place without leaving it." The military felt that confinement was "the only legal way to keep a person in a given place whenever a judge has not issued an arrest warrant or order against him." The confinement procedure took place in two stages: First, the subject was taken to a Triage and Transit Center where he was "interrogated by the appropriate military [personnel], and by the gendarmerie or police." Thereafter, a confined person could be released, prosecuted by a tribunal, or kept in confinement. If maintained in confinement, the person was sent to a Centre d'Hébergement.[44] Subsequently, a list of all confined people was drawn up and forwarded in short order to the prefect, who would issue the confinement warrant. This manner of operating violated the procedure by confining individuals before the civil authority issued orders to that effect. Before his transfer to a CTT, the detained individual was interrogated "on the spot."[45] With the help of the DOP a decision was made about which detainees were kept in their cells for further interrogation, and which were turned over to the CTT. After completing their interrogation of a suspect, the DOP released him to the CTT where he was subjected to further interrogation by the intelligence officer. This means that torture, the preferred method of "interrogation," was inflicted at several points during the itinerary of a suspect from DOP to CTT to CMI and to prison. In a massive movement of population transfer, detainees were shuttled from DOP to CTT in cities and regions away from those in which they had been arrested.[46] While the CTT were publicly known, the DOP were not. In this sense, confinement was paired with internment; their link was torture. The longer detainees waited for transfer to a CTT, the more time intelligence officers had to decide where to send them on the basis of the volume and quality of information they extirpated from them.

General Salan put at "about eight days" the period of time within which to turn over "all rebels, whether terrorists guilty of exactions or made prisoner in combat, to the *Gendarmerie* which will take them to a military tribunal for trial without preliminary judicial inquiry."[47] Whenever this "accelerated procedure" could not be applied, Salan advised placing prisoners in a CTT. Theoretically, no person could be kept in a CTT longer than thirty days, yet this rule was largely violated. In fact a detainee could be kept for three months. Confident that no civil authority would oppose them, military commanders requested as many confinement warrants as they wished. However, one political appointee, Paul Teitgen, the police prefect for Algiers district, attempted to remedy the abusive use of confinement warrants by reforming the system. He insisted that confinement requests be made within twenty-four hours of an arrest to prevent the risk of a "disappearance." He also proposed that a police commissioner (*commissaire divisionnaire central*) be appointed to work alongside the colonel commanding the coastal sector of Algiers (Alger-Sahel) and be solely responsible for granting all confinement warrants needed by the military. The commissioner would also write a daily report to the prefect detailing not only the names of confined people, but also all incidents that occurred in the CTT, including "suicides," "attempted escapes," and "escapes."[48] In addition, Teitgen sought to limit the number of CTT to two per sector. He recommended that all detainees in CTT be legally "confined" for a maximum period of one month. Finally, Teitgen proposed that reports keep track daily of those who "disappeared," and note the time and place of their disappearance. As a former Dachau inmate, Teitgen worried about keeping silent in relation to blatant military abuse of the population.

Although essentially approved, Teitgen's reform was subverted by General Massu, who ordered his lieutenant-colonel Trinquier to refrain from divulging the names and numbers of the people arrested by paratroopers. In case of unfortunate incidents, the military would entrust an investigation to the gendarmerie. However, the resident-minister allowed the transfer of the power of confinement from the prefects to the military "during localized and important operations, and for a period that may stretch over several weeks, in accordance to Article 10 of the March 17, 1956, decree."[49] The decision was hailed by the military authorities as making official a common practice. The strained realionship between Teitgen, the military authorities, and the resident minister points to the slippery slope that led to greater military control of the colonial state. It also reveals how the military understood the legalistic game that civil authorities insisted on playing, and decided to ignore all attempts at curbing their own power. This made for parallel governments: one civil, very weak; the other military, very strong. In the end, Teitgen resigned, and Massu's paratroopers continued to do business as usual. The CTT became a holding pattern where men and women were kept for repeated interrogations— a sort of pool from which to pull out suspects and turn them into shades of guilty individuals, some deemed beyond the pale, others "recoverable," and still others presenting no value that would warrant their continued detention.

Just like the DOP, the CTT operated under the logic of information extraction. In addition to the officially known centers, there were clandestine or semiclandestine centers, some of which privately held, and mobile "tent"centers, set up during operations as "annexes" to fixed CTT.[50] General Salan had acknowledged the existence of illegal CTT and ordered them closed primarily for budgetary reasons.[51] Such places could be located in cities, as was the case with the Villa Sésini, in Algiers, or in the country, as with the Améziane Farm near the city of Constantine. There was a clandestine CTT in the barracks of Fort L'Empereur, near Algiers, allegedly unbeknownst to the commandant. The privatization of the law by the miliatry reached its climax in the discovery of a secret tribunal concealed in a villa in Les Sources, a suburb of Algiers.[52]

Although CTT and internment camps housed all sorts of individuals, generally on mere suspicion of guilt, a distinction was made between "rebels captured in action" who did not engage in acts of "terrorism" whose treatment could be "as close as possible to that of prisoners of war," and plain "terrorists." Salan thought of captured combatants as "bona fide rebels" who "in their error . . . have acted according to high principles and revealed above average human qualities." It would be unrealistic, he thought, to treat these men as ordinary felons. Their moral qualifications made them eminently suitable to psychological action resulting in "a moral reversal which will lead these prisoners to redeem themselves by taking up arms in the service of France." He had noted that many of these combatants fought to their death, and felt that to induce them to surrender he would transform some existing CTT into new structures, Military Internment Camps, within which prisoners would be subjected to intensive psychological action before being recruited in the regular army, or as higher-caliber Harka.[53] Salan reasoned that these Camps would signal to guerillas that, when captured, they would not be treated as common criminals, but more like war prisoners. Ultimately, this might encourage guerillas to surrender, which Salan knew they could not easily do since the French government did not apply to Algerian combatants the status of prisoners of war that would extend to them the protection of the Geneva convention.

About 100,000 individuals transited through the CTT every year before being turned over to military tribunals for trial and subsequent transfer to a Centre d'Hébergement (in effect France's version of concentration camps); a special military internment camp for combatants captured with their weapons (Prisonnier Pris les Armes à la Main, or PAM); a Reeducation Center; or a regular jail. The most notorious internment camps were those of Lambèse (Eastern Algeria) and Berrouaghia.[54]

The military was in control of the various camps except for the Centres d'Hébergement, to which it still retained the right to transfer detainees. Outside the camps, civil authority was in charge. Because confinement was the means by which torture, summary executions, and disappearances were effected, it soon attracted the attention of critics of the war.[55] Investigations were ordered regarding the conditions of detention as well as arrest procedures.[56] Inspections of camps were carried out annually by the International Red Cross as is customary in war situations. They were also carried out by the Commission for the Safeguard of Individual Rights and Liberties especially formed to look into allegations of torture. Finally, a Commission of Inspection of Administrative Detention Centers also looked into the issue.[57] Reports indicate a pattern of abuse of detainees,[58] including serial torture with the assistance of interpreters,[59] insufficient food given to PAM, harassment by guards,[60] lack of discipline and security in and around the camps, and forced labor.

The frenzied search for information took a life of its own, quickly leading to overcrowding in CTT and Centres d'Hébergement,[61] and contributing to a general state of lawlessness. Since guilt was not the motivation behind detention, charges against "suspects" were often vague or nonexistent.[62] Stopgap measures to deal with an overblown parallel penitentiary system followed the logic of intelligence-gathering, which was to create more camps. For example, General Vezinet, commandant of the Territorial Region and Army Corps of Algiers, nudged the inspector of the camps to *recommend* that Re-education Centers (CDR), of which there were ten for thirty-five CTT in his region, be expanded as a way of stemming overcrowding.[63] In addition, accelerating the pace of detainees' psychological reconditioning was proposed as a solution to overcrowding before it became necessary to simply free excess detainees. Thus, the military decided in July 1961 to free one thousand individuals detained in Military Internment Camps.[64] In addition, any prisoner who had served two thirds of a less than five-year-sentence before October 1961 was to be automatically released.[65]

Overcrowding highlighted the uneasy relationship between civil and military authorities without necessarily undermining the power of the military. The two quarreled over turf, "principles," and budget.[66] Nevertheless, overcrowding helped to shield the methods used by the military in the various centers just as they were also partially revealed by the various investigation commissions. On the one hand, the army could claim that only some misguided officers were responsible for abuse; on the other hand, business continued as usual with impunity for the army as the power in control. Furthermore, overcrowding had the unintended function of helping to expand the work of the OPA into detention centers and camps.[67] Special internment centers called camps "Zero" (such as Paul Cazelles, Bossuet, Djorf, and Berrouaghia), were turned into veritable "FLN seminars."[68] In reality, the FLN was active in all Centres d'Hébergement. The sheer mass of individuals coming from all parts of Algeria thrown together under harsh conditions made for an ideal situation for exchange of experiences, discussion of political, economic and social issues, and national identity crystallization.[69]

Military Justice

The intelligence apparatus set in place by the military could not fulfill its goal of smashing the OPA without the appropriate justice system. Since torture was illegal, civil courts could throw out confessions obtained under torture. The Exceptional Powers Decree allowed the military to hear a whole range of felonies and crimes normally under the jurisdiction of civil courts. Speed and efficiency (characteristics of "exemplary justice") made military justice a weapon of combat.[70] Gradually, military logic prevailed over due process, and civil courts became adjuncts to military tribunals. As Salan saw it "the military tribunal will generally avail itself of the right to claim from the civil tribunal all matters related to the rebellion."[71] By and large the military was helped in its task by civil magistrates of Pied-Noir origin who opposed the independence of Algeria, and thus did the military bidding.[72] Nevertheless, the dual civil-military system persisted even if in a formal fashion till the end of the war, and was fraught with tensions between the two justice systems due to different conceptions of proof, choice of methods of interrogation, and rules of procedures.[73] The resulting abuses such as unlimited detention of suspects, disappearances, interrogations by men other than intelligence officers led to a restructuring of military justice in 1960 (two years before he war ended) toward greater rationality and coherence ostensibly as a step to restoring civil control over the administration of justice.[74] The main features of this restructuring were the establishment of permanent military tribunals in each military zone headquarters and the appointment of a military prosecutor—a civil magistrate called to military duty—to oversee the handling of captured combatants and suspects. The goal was to simplify legal procedures; "guaranty respect for individual liberties at various levels of this procedure; strike down those guilty of attacks against public order in Algeria as quickly as possible, but in conformity with the prescriptions of the law."[75] Civil authorities were enjoined to cooperate more closely with the prosecutor to help him discharge his function with "all the necessary speed."[76] A culture of summary justice had developed among the military that made military tribunals difficult to reform.[77] In the end, although intended to restrict the scope of military justice, this effort contributed to increasing the power of military tribunals. According to Pierre Mesmer, the minister of defense, it made for an "effective repression of terrorism." He redefined the degree of gravity of offenses, thus clarifying what constitutes a "terrorist" act.[78] Mesmer wished to "limit the exceptional [scope of] competence of military jurisdiction to violations that have effectively given rebels help of tangible importance." Consequently, he ordered that permanent military tribunals continue to fight the OPA and ORU (Organisation Rurale-Urbaine), but "target individuals who have *habitually* served as liaisons between various rebels' structures, helped or assisted armed bands, collected *significant* funds, or instigated desertions." This interpretation was meant to restrict the power of the military tribunal to indiscriminately lump together as "rebels" or "terrorists" individuals who may have only occasionally provided support to the FLN, or may have done so unwillingly. Mesmer specifically added: "It appears necessary to verify the existence of duress that is or might be invoked by authors of *occasional* minor acts, such as paying dues, collecting funds in insignificant amounts, harboring and supplying [rebels]."[79] This definition essentially decriminalized the majority of economically marginal villagers, or low-income city dwellers who made irregular and insignificant contributions to the FLN without being members of the organization. Nor could they have refused to open their homes to passing "rebels."

Acts considered serious, such as murder, battery, bombing of public buildings or their destruction by fire, continued to be punished by military tribunals. However, hiding or supplying "rebels" fell under the penal code as did demonstrations and the distribution of leaflets (which was already covered by an 1881 law). Nevertheless, it is the very efficiency of the rationalized military justice that led to its opposite goal: a decriminalization of a number of acts previously deemed acts of "rebellion."[80]

However, the dual judicial and operational structure of investigation (i.e., interrogation) was maintained. Judicial interrogation was carried out by the military prosecutor, whereas operational interrogation was the domain of the intelligence officer. The army asserted that the two used "different methods of interrogation" adapted to their goals. Unlike operational investigation, which relies on speed of information extraction for setting up "fruitful" operations, judicial investigation relies on "proof," which takes longer to establish. Operational investigation must be "immediate and cannot waste time checking suspects' declarations."[108] Operational interrogation clearly privileged torture, and had precedence over judicial torture. The military held fast to the notion that "subversive war" makes judicial investigation lose its peace-time significance and becomes just another "form of combat which the Command will use, in combination with other military means, as befits efficiency."[81]

Techniques of Terror and the Militarized State

These elaborate intelligence, detention, and justice structures put in place by the army as it ascended to power helped the unbridled use of *techniques* of terror[82] designed to discipline the population qua war front. These techniques included summary executions, exposures of killed combatants' bodies, disappearances, and reprisals. Taken together, torture and these practices drew strength from one another, forming a terror matrix. Seemingly unrelated, the forced displacement and resettlement of over 2 million villagers kept under permanent surveillance spun torture and terror into the fabric of everyday life in rural areas. Terror so configured appeared random (and sometimes was) as well as chaotic. Yet it was structured, institutionalized, and informed by the military's assumption of knowledge of the native population. Military analysts often recommended the use of specific acts of terror against natives, as did Captain Amphyoxus, who advocated the decapitation of Algerians on the shaky anthropological assumption that it was the only form of death that "Arabs qua Muslims" feared.[83]

Summary Executions and Body Exposures

Summary executions completed the labor of torture. After a victim talked, intelligence officers often sent him for the *corvée de bois* (or "wood detail") outside the building where torture took place and had him shot. Ostensibly, the *corvée* was ordered primarily because the victim's body bore obvious marks of torture, although it happened according to the whim of the officer in charge. Summary executions took place in rural as well as urban environments. Algiers Harbor became notorious for the bodies of torture victims that were dumped at night, sometimes inside barrels. General Bigeard was known for this practice, which won his victims the derisive name *crevettes Bigeard*" (shrimp Bigeard).[84]

When kept secret, summary executions did not sink terror deeply enough into the collective mind of the native population unless they became public and bodies were exposed. Paul Delouvrier wrote to his friend, Hubert Beuve-Méry, editor of the daily *Le Monde*, about the public exposure for two hours of the body of a man, Maarouf Addi, who had been executed for a "terrorist" attack in the city of Tiaret, in southwestern Algeria, in February 1959. He noted that "the Muslim crowd was channeled to Maarouf's body," which bore a sign in two languages, French and Arabic. Public displays of bodies were common. Many such acts were reported to the daily *Le Monde* by eyewitnesses. A teacher wrote of a man who had been caught after a grenade exploded in a music and appliance store, was arrested, tortured, and killed. His body was exposed the following day with a sign reading "X . . . will not throw any more bombs." In another case that took place in Miliana and Affreville, three corpses were publicly exposed, "still bleeding," and paraded throughout the towns in military vehicles, "upside down, with their heads dangling in the air."[85] On the one hand, the French military used the bodies as mnemonic devices to remind the population that the power of life and death lay with France. On the other hand, exposure of the bodies also signified France's assault on and contempt for the culture of the native population. Like boomerangs, summary executions bounced off the victims and hit back the executioner, shattering his pretense at being the embodiment of civilization. It did more: it taught, effectively, history in action. Colonialism was laid bare, the Arabic word for it, *isti'mar*, rarely used before the war, entered the language of everyday life.

The fetishization of the bodies of men accused of terrorism reached the apex of its cultural infringement in the embalming of the bodies of nationalist leaders killed in combat. Amirouche, of *wilaya* II, and Si Haouès, of *wilaya* VI, both notable guerilla chiefs, were embalmed after being killed at the battle of Djebel Tsaneur on March 29, 1959, and publicly exposed to signal the death of the nationalist movement.[86] Once more, the notion that the death of a leader meant the end of a movement was transposed in a cultural milieu that understood that men do not embody ideas, but pass them on. The French military operated on two registers, one purely military, the other cultural. They also acted according to the unspoken Christian (cultural) idea that evil is embodied; the killing of the body removes the evil in it; the preservation of the dead body anchors the memory of evil. Admittedly, the death of a famous leader who had many times eluded capture was a blow to the FLN. But, to the villager who was not a member of the FLN, it was another desecrated body among many.

Disappearances

In 1959 Jacques Vergès, a Paris lawyer who acquired fame for defending women urban guerillas, issued a *Cahier Vert* (Green Notebook) with two of his colleagues, listing the disappearances of 175 Algerians in the Algiers area, drawn from various professions including medicine, teaching, and civil service. The *Cahier* provided detailed information about the identity of those who had disappeared, as well as testimonies from their relatives. The people on the list had been arrested by paratroopers, as well as at least four other units including the Foreign Legion (or Green Berets), Colonel Bigeard's men, and/or the internal secret service. Inquiries revealed "a tragic disorder" in the files of the civil as well as military administrations.[87] Families were sent redundant and contradictory form letters that could not trace disappearances at the hands of different military units.

Disappearances were an inevitable consequence of the secret modus operandi of the centers for Triage and transit and internment camps (Centres d'Hébergement).[88] They were facilitated by the use of confinement. Confinement as a method of preventive detention also gave the military the opportunity to envisage the preemptive elimination of potential leaders of an independent Algeria. For example, in December 1957, the Bar Association noted that fourteen lawyers had been confined, twelve of whom were prominent Algerians. The same incident also took place in Oran, which denoted a deliberate policy. The Bar Association protested the arrests, charging that these were arbitrary acts of sequestration. Subsequently, in an apparent frame-up, military officers "found" notes at the home of a man impugning the integrity of all fourteen lawyers. An investigation turned up no evidence for the allegation that the men collaborated with the FLN. General Pâris de Bollardière reported that he had been approached by an officer who intimated that he should give him access to some Algerian professionals so he could get rid of them, just in case Algeria became independent. Preventive arrests of individuals at their homes, at night, or at their workplace were an efficient method of terror, especially when there was no charge the confined could answer to and no single authority accountable.

Reprisals

Although executions inflict death, reprisals cause loss of shelter, diminished sustenance to an already impoverished rural population living on a subsistence economy, and decreased family stability. Reprisals were immediate, reflexive. After an ambush near the southern city of Biskra that killed a French-Senegalese soldier, the whole Senegalese company serving in the area walked into the city and burned down a native neighborhood, killing thirty-five people. A soldier, Jean-Luc Tahon, describes the logic behind the destruction of a hamlet:

> At dawn, we fanned out to take a *douar* (hamlet) of shacks made of reeds, branches and rusted sheets of corrugated iron. We were to look for weapons and ammunition, and check identity cards. . . . A few groups take position around the village; others move forward to check identity papers. The Arabs look with concern at the troops entering the alleyways. The village chief is brought in; he says he knows of no weapons in the village. The powerful men, machine guns under their arms, guns in hand, grenades at their belts, enter the shaky *gourbi*s with their low ceilings, and dark and smelly rooms. They overturn a plate or jar, kick frightened women to make them stand. They empty wooden trunks on the floor, walk on the scattered clothes, take a piece of jewelry as a "souvenir," run after the chickens, twist their necks, and slip them in their pockets. But all of this did not turn up any weapons. However, according to our captains' logic we must find something because this village is suspect. If it is suspect, there must be weapons in it. If we do not find them, it is because they have been well concealed. Therefore, the village must be punished not only for holding weapons, but also for hiding them. And then the *gourbis* started to burn like torches.[89]

Once a hamlet was surrounded, the expenditure of time and energy by the troops needed to be accounted for. But the fire consumed the arms that were supposedly hidden in the hamlet and, with them, the proof that the villagers had done anything wrong. Had weapons been found in the village, it would still have been burned down. Villagers were guilty for having been the objects of suspicion.

Mathieu, a former conscript, explains how thieving and pillaging were the real goals of village searches: "My pals and I were not searching for weapons; we were after money, interesting things like gold." Population-control operations were often used as opportunities for stealing "watches, gold coins (most Muslim women wear necklaces made out of Napoleon coins) . . . kitchen utensils, blankets." Another soldier who served near the eastern city of Guelma, recalls the time he had one hundred chickens at his camp. He gave some of them to his officers and their wives when they came to visit. He also sold wheat he took from rural people to the settlers.[90] The hunger for chickens layers the hunger for pieces of women's belongings conjuring up a surreal image of well-armed, well-dressed (and presumably well-fed) troops grabbing fowl and silver ornaments while the village burns at dawn, animated by a confounded desire to own things and their owners. This descent to the bottom of terror, mediated by powerless women and chickens, crystallizes the significance of the antisubversive war. Subversion is no longer an issue. Destroying, and reinscribing fear in the native is. Still there is something emblematic about stealing chickens, a custom that ties Algeria to Vietnam, one antisubversive war to another through a soldier's desire to eat fresh meat. During an operation against a Vietnamese village that had already been overrun by the Viet Minh, a soldier from a French commando seized a rooster, then lost it as the military operation ran into problems. The soldier waxed lyrical about the rooster with whom he felt a solidarity of sorts. After hearing the rooster sing, he reports,

> We immediately located it, surrounded it, and made it prisoner. It's a beautiful animal whose ancestors must have been on a tour [of duty?] in Europe where it was first found. We have a great deal of admiration for it, because we think that it was the only one capable of defending and preserving its freedom. And also, to be crude about it, we thought it would make an excellent meal. There is no such thing as freedom.[91]

The humorous tone allows history and identity to mix with the logic of plunder, and the more mundane desire to eat well. In French culture, the rooster is the symbol of old Gaul, the name by which contemporary France was known. In Algeria, the DOP appears to have been supplied with "hens, rabbits, and sheep," an ever increasing "war booty," kept by prisoners who also took care of the kitchen.[92]

The chickens episode, hardly unusual, weaves strands of reprisals by fiat—villagers had committed a crime against the troops by being innocent—with strands of normlessness, in a chain that links summary executions, public exposure of dead bodies, pillage, rape, and torture. The iconic picture of frightened women kicked into a standing position, and of equally frightened chickens being pursued by armed troops, harks back to the theorists of the "counterrevolutionary war." They had discoursed on the differences between a war fought by a regular army, and guerilla warfare. At last, the picture of women and chickens pursued by soldiers, like a mirror, reflects their own soldiers crossing the boundaries between the two wars. Regular French troops reveal themselves to be acting in bands engaged in a campaign of terror usually attributed to guerilla forces (as the theorists defined and described them), targeting the civilian population with no-holds-barred. This role reversal was not simply the result of wayward soldiers committing isolated mayhem. Such acts were systemic—implicitly condoned by military authorities despite occasional investigations—and benefited from the solidarity that tied recruits to one another, and to their superiors.[93]

Reprisals had a traumatic impact on villagers. Frantz Fanon left a record of the psychological problems experienced by one of his patients, a villager from the Constantine area. The patient had witnessed soldiers setting fire to houses

> while women who were trying to get a few clothes together or save some provisions were driven away with blows with rifle-butts. Some peasants took advantage of the general confusion to run away. The officer gave the order to bring together men who remained and had them brought out to near a watercourse where the killing began. Twenty-nine men were shot at point-blank range. S—— was wounded by two bullets which went through his right thigh and his left arm respectively.

S—— passed out and was rescued by an ALN group. The villager "demanded a gun, although he was helpless and a civilian, and refused to walk in front of anyone behind him. . . . He began by telling us that he was not dead yet and that he had played a dirty trick on the others. . . . During his stay in the hospital he attacked about eight patients with makeshift weapons." Fanon quoted excerpts from his daily interviews with the patient:

> God is with me . . . but he certainly is not with those who are dead. . . . In life you've got to kill so as not to be killed. . . . When I think that I knew nothing about all that business . . . There are Frenchmen in our midst. They disguise themselves as Arabs. They've got to be killed. Give me a machine-gun. All these so-called Algerians are really Frenchmen. . . . And they won't leave me alone. As soon as I want to sleep they come into my room. But now I know all about them. Everyone wants to kill me. But I'll defend myself. I'll kill them all, every single one of them.

Fanon diagnosed the survivor of reprisal as suffering from "undifferentiated homicidal impulsions."[94] How many individuals such as S—— suffered from such homicidal tendencies is not known. However, it is reasonable to conjecture that survivors who did not suffer disabling psychological trauma as S—— did, nevertheless may have also thought that they had to kill in order to survive. Gratuitous killing brings about more killing.

Reprisals, just like search operations, by their unbridled nature, were a source of exhilaration for troops born out of unlimited power. As a former soldier recalling a night operation put it, "a strange feeling of power washed over us."[95] Power found its materiality in uniforms, modern guns, tanks, and armored vehicles, but also in the mind, in the accepted idea of being on a mission to defend the French Empire against the primitivism of Algerians qua rebels and the barbarity of communism, the enemy by proxy.

Resettlement of Villages

The policy of massive resettlement of villages constituted terror by means other than summary executions and reprisals; it permitted torture to thrive behind barbed wire and established the military as the administrative authority ruling through the SAS. The resettlement policy was part of the antisubversive strategy to divide up the countryside into a grid of "forbidden zones" in which rural people were prohibited to live or circulate, and safe zones comprised of resettled villages, some of which were organized into "self-defense" villages. Estimates put the displaced at 2,350,000 in 1961,[96] representing 26.1 percent of a rural population of 6.9 million people. If the people classified as "absorbed"—a concept that glossed over the coercion at the root of their displacement—were added, the total uprooted population would reach 3,525,000, or 50 percent of the rural population.[97] Resettlements were an entirely military affair. Efforts made by civil authorities to integrate these masses of uprooted people into a rural development program foregrounding the construction of one thousand villages did not last long, as these development goals, no matter how unrealistic in times of war, clashed with the military objective of using the population as a strategic terrain.

Resettled villagers were set up as closed communities flung together often in jerry-built housing with very basic amenities, surrounded by barbed wire and watched over by the tower of a military post. The topography suited the panoptic power the military wished to project, and served as the setting for the work of the Sections Administratives Spécialisées. In resettlements, an estimated 200,000 people had no income at all; those who managed to earn a living still depended on assistance for 50 percent of their income provided by charities such as Secours Catholique or the protestant CIMADE (Comité Inter-Mouvements Auprès des Evacués). SAS officers distributed aid according to their conception of security, rewarding cooperative men willing to provide information or rally the army, and punishing the recalcitrant. Thus food became a weapon of "pacification" of rural people who had committed no crime. Each family received eleven kilos of barley per adult per month. Since children did not figure in the ration calculation, families had little food, prompting a military doctor to deplore the "pathological state of undernourishment of young children" as well as the 1,487 calories a day allocated to adults.[98]

Michel Rocard, a finance inspector who stumbled onto the dire circumstances of resettled people and first brought them to the attention of the civil administration, was able to determine that when a center reached 1,000 people, one child died every other day. In a center he visited in Ouarsenis (western Algeria), which gathered 1,100 people, 600 of whom were children, a third child had died in the preceding four days.[99] The much touted medical services provided by the SAS did not, and could not remedy a medical deficit that had existed for over a century.[100] Women were particularly affected by resettlement, and many kept returning to their old *douar* only to be trucked back to their resettlement.[101]

Perhaps loss of freedom and income were the worst for the nomadic and seminomadic populations who became generally confined to cramped quarters with their tents and their animals—a major source of revenue—drastically reduced in number.[102] A legionnaire reports in a German newspaper that in 1959, thirty-five nomads trying to salvage their belongings got separated from their people en route to a resettlement camp and were simply shot dead and buried in a common pit near Géryville (El Bayad). Although the miserable conditions under which the resettled people prompted some of them to become informers, and/or join the Harka, they also contributed to awakening a latent national consciousness. Furthermore, in spite of the tight surveillance, the FLN still operated in a number of resettlements at night.[103] The FLN also funneled help to resettled people whose relatives had died in combat. Yet, the resettlement policy was claimed to be successful.[104] Resettlements could easily be termed a proof of the incapacity of the army to exercise civil power effectively.

In sum, the onset of the Algerian War gave the military the chance to realize a major tenet of counterrevolutionary war doctrine: combine political as well as military power. The road to state terrorism began with a declaration of a state of emergency, a step that ushered in a series of laws that transferred civil control of the police to the army, and allowed the establishment of military tribunals. To help the military in its mission of "restoring order," the state suspended civil liberties in an apparently orderly process for the sake of preserving a legal façade to the military assumption of civil powers. However, militarization is not a simple military takeover of the state apparatus. It requires a series of complex and onerous adjustments of two organizations having different goals, managed by professionals with different orientations and priorities. Hence, the tug of war between political appointees at the local level and military officers was inevitable. Once entrusted with the powers that it craved, the military laid down the structural framework for waging counterrevolutionary war in and against the population, and in which torture loomed as a war weapon: a parallel and secret intelligence gathering capacity; centers for detaining and processing men and women deemed suspect and in which torture was practiced; internment camps (Centres d'Hébergement); special military camps; and reeducation centers. The structure was completed with military tribunals that favored operational investigation by intelligence officers over judiciary investigation by military prosecutors for a speedy and exemplary justice. Once established, military rule resulted in the application of techniques of terror that reinforced torture just as they drew power from it. Summary executions, public exposures of killed combatants, disappearances, and reprisals formed a terror matrix with torture at its core. Although they were not spelled out in the antisubversive war doctrine, these techniques were its logical consequence as it claimed the population as a war front. Hence, the SAS, ostensibly created to put a human and caring face on the war, could not dispense with torture and abuse of a captive population in resettled villages. It became another version of Centres d'Hébergement. The unceasing military demand to do away with civil control indicates that once given the opportunity to rule, the military cannot do so partially. Consequently, government efforts to curb the military's power resulted in reinforcing it.

The militarization process also created a relationship of dependency between the military and the civil authorities: the government was caught in a game of asserting its existence as a civil institution while empowering the military to carry out civil and social functions at the same time. The state thus had its dirty job done by the military, which it, when need arose, strategically and formally sought to restrain in the name of civil rights. Conversely, the military did its best to administer, control, and manage a civilian population in the name of the state, which it then blamed for its incompetence, and in a quid pro quo demanded silence regarding its methods of "pacification." In this sense, militarization enabled the state to violate its own legal safeguards by proxy, through the army, and the army to unleash repressive methods, which it justified as necessary correctives to the state's incompetence. In this situation torture thrived, unhindered, and military chiefs implemented their own methods of "pacification," including psychological action, as will be shown in the next two chapters.

Chapter 3

PSYCHOLOGICAL ACTION

ONE ASPECT OF TORTURE has eluded scrutiny: its use in facilitating mind alteration for the purpose of securing loyalty to colonial rule. Torture played a role in the psychological warfare waged parallel to military operations with the tools of applied psychology. Strategists of psychological warfare included the prominent Colonel Charles Lacheroy, member of Cité Catholique, and pioneer of revolutionary-war theory.[1] They distinguished *psychological action*, or propaganda aimed at boosting the troops' morale, from psychological warfare targeting combatants and native population in order to "control their attitudes and behavior."[2] Psychological warfare too used propaganda, but one of its critical goals was to "turn" captured combatants and selected native individuals. The most fundamental difference between the two categories of psychological warfare was the use of torture. However, in practice, the expression "psychological action" was also used to refer to methods of psychological warfare.

Torture always includes psychological techniques of various degrees of sophistication. But using physical pain as preparation for behavior modification is different from playing psychological games with victims or injecting them with Pentothal to break their resistance. As a rule, torture preceded sessions of brainwashing, just as it preceded interrogation. Torture formed the intermediate term between propaganda and brainwashing. This use of torture was facilitated by the definition of "psychological intelligence"—a wide-ranging collection of information about the enemy—as the foundation of psychological action strategies. The army viewed the interrogation of prisoners (as well as refugees) by military personnel about nonmilitary issues as a source of psychological intelligence.[3]

The use of torture in a program of psychological "conditioning" was the result of a reflection on the psychological methods used by the Viet Minh on their French captives, and conclusions drawn from theories of crowd and mass behavior formulated by Gustave le Bon and Serge Chakotin respectively. In addition, interest in Chakotin's work sparked psychological action experts to examine Goebbels's propaganda techniques,[4] as well as methods of collective psychoanalyis for mass manipulation used by the "American School,"[5] which they at times conflated with "behaviorism."[6] The function of torture as a facilitator of behavior modification appeared all the more appropriate as Algerians were believed to be *sous-hommes*, or lesser men, in need of (re)socialization into socially redemptive values and ideas. The necessity of this psychological engineering project was glimpsed as the colonial government had begun to contemplate reforms that culminated in 1959 in a reform program (Le Plan de Constantine) to alleviate socioeconomic inequities. The creation of "new men" to lead the "new" reformed Algeria under the French flag became a tantalizing idea. It resonated as a colonial echo of intellectual debates that took place in France in the 1930s and 1940s among professionals in the humanities and the sciences on the transforming effects on "Man" of technological advances, industrial capitalism, and increased division of labor. Methods for bringing about a "new humanism" in a "new order" with the use of psychological techniques were extensively discussed and evaluated. Chakotin happened to be a contributor to such debates on the side of one of the leaders of "scientific humanism," engineer Jean Coutrot.[7] This chapter explores the role played by torture in psychological warfare, and its consequences. For comparative purposes, it also examines the FLN psychological action techniques with the native population.

Psychology and Counterrevolution: Crowds and Masses

Crowds

The Cold War and the experience of French officers with brainwashing at the hands of their captors in Indochina formed the context within which Le Bon's and Chakotin's theories were received.[8] The concepts of crowd and mass connoted an amalgam of malleable yet fearsome groupings loathed by states.[9] Gustave Le Bon, the student of crowd behavior, whose ideas inspired Freud's conception of group psychology, belonged to a generation of French thinkers who were convinced that democracy ushered in the rule of the mob. Le Bon's theory was taught before World War II at the Ecole Supérieure de Guerre as a course entitled Crowd Psychology.[10] The relevance of his theory of crowd behavior for counterrevolution strategists resided in his reduction of revolutions to the expert manipulation of the psychological vulnerability of people brought together in situations of crisis. Using the French revolution as a case study, he examined the psychological mechanisms through which crowds are motivated to act. Referring to "crowd" interchangeably with "multitude" and "people," he emphasized its malleability and arationality. A crowd is but "an amorphous being which can do nothing, and will nothing, without a head to lead it." Even so, a crowd can be as powerful as "the shell that perforates an armor-plate by the momentum of a force it did not create." Being arational, crowds are characterized by "infinite credulity and exaggerated sensitivity, their short-sightedness, and their incapacity to respond to the influences of reason."[11] To induce crowds to act, revolutionary leaders must awaken their hopes by exposing the inequities of the political order while activating their *affective* and *mystical* logic. These mutually reinforcing forms of logic are unconscious and deeply grounded in emotions and beliefs, and therefore impervious to rational control.[12]

The specific psychological transformation that takes place in crowds was of special interest to antisubversive war theorists. They learned from an insightful aspect of Le Bon's work: his conception of the self or "ego," which he described as comprised of many "cellular egos," the "residues of ancestral personalities." In a stable environment, cellular egos combine into a balanced self. Under conditions of revolution, this equilibrium is broken, the cellular egos are sundered and must recombine into a new personality expressing itself in the same individual differently from the way it originally was. Drawing attention to the process that enables a different ego to emerge in situations of crisis, he explained that the best means to recompose a disaggregated personality is through "the inculcation of a strong belief,"[13] a factor that counterrevolution strategists grappled with throughout the war as *idée force*.

Le Bon's analysis was attractive to military strategists of psychological warfare because it was simple, based on a concrete historical case (the French Revolution), used the language of formal logic, and lent itself to the development of a *technique*. It gave officers, as men of action, a grasp on complex psychological dynamics by making these seem mere technical problems for refashioning the self. By equating "revolution" with "crowd," and stressing the *temporary* psychological transformations that crowds undergo, Le Bon's ideas enabled antisubversive war officers to think of the war as winnable through judicious psychological manipulation. More important, considering people anonymous, formless masses or crowds provided a shield against moral doubt and facilitated a mental attitude that would ultimately divorce torture from the pain and suffering inflicted on sentient beings.

Masses

Le Bon provided insights into the psychology of crowds in revolutions. But, Chakotin offered a technique of behavior modification. A physiologist, Serge Chakotin (Sergei Stepanovich Chakhotin) was a former Menshevik, enamored of Taylorism and an advocate of "scientific management." Expelled from Russia in 1902 for taking part in student activism at the University of Moscow, he was allowed to return in 1912 at the behest of I. P. Pavlov, who hired him as his assistant. In 1918 he founded the Department of Information and Agitation of the Army (or Osvag) based on his scientific management principles. Unsuccessful, this experiment cost him his job a year later. Subsequently he left Russia and, after a teaching stint in Zagreb, lived in exile in Germany where he became active in the German Social Democratic Party. With Carlo Mierendorf, a fellow social democrat and later a member of the anti-Nazi Kreisau Circle, he developed methods of political propaganda for mass mobilization against the Nazis in an attempt to prevent them from assuming power. After they did, he was arrested by the Gestapo and sent to a concentration camp. At the end of the war, he returned to Russia, pursuing his research at the Institute for Biophysics at the Academy of Sciences.[14]

In his book, *The Rape of the Masses*, Chakotin revealed that political behavior, like all other categories of human behavior, is based on four classes of instincts or "innate reactions." Extrapolating from Pavlov's experiments with cats and dogs, he argued that the instincts of struggle (or defense), nutrition, sexuality, and "maternity" form the foundation of "applied psychology." Accordingly, the manipulation of the right instincts yields the appropriate behavior through reflex conditioning. For example, the instinct of struggle is related to passive states such as fear and depression, as well as active states, which include the search for power and domination, whereas the nutrition instinct is related to material wants and rewards.[15] Chakotin believed that methods used by "counterrevolutionary" fascist movements that literally raped the masses could be adopted to bring about behavior reflecting peace, freedom, and equality among people.[16] He revealed techniques that overcome resistance in individuals and produce fear and obedience through expert use of symbols, speech, sounds (including music), and *pain*. For instance, resistance (also called inhibition) can be neutralized in an individual by shocking ("overexciting") his nervous system and causing a "deep emotion." Induced fatigue may also render the individual sleepy, a condition that weakens his resistance and makes him receptive to suggestion, as happens in hypnosis.[17]

Chakotin's work—taught at the Centre d'Instruction Pacification et Contre-Guérilla—inspired strategists to mount a "physical" and "moral" offensive to conquer the population. They saw the appropriateness of using "violent" methods of psychological action, including placing recalcitrants or "notorious rebels" in special moral rehabilitation camps (*camps de désendoctrinement*).[18] Chakotin sensitized psychological action experts in search of the proper methods of behavior modification to the use

of combinations of sound stimulants, especially music; images; and antici-
pation of pain. It also inspired the use of methods of propaganda that turn
fear into panic.[19] Furthermore, modulations of pain in the torture chambers were combined with reflex conditioning techniques between torture
sessions, calculated to induce detainees to talk. Some of the techniques included, besides constant and incongruous musical tunes, such things as
the sound of an electric shaver (that induced panic in detainees that had
already been tortured, or those waiting their turn); the waving of an ac-
cusatory finger at detainees before selecting one for torture as in a symbolic game of Russian roulette.[20] Such techniques were a part of "sociological terror" that used "the mysterious and violent eruption of an
unusual event" in a "zone of silence,"[21] such as a concentration camp, or
a waiting room in a torture center. Noteworthy is the odd use of "silence"
as a qualifier of camps in which torture was used to effectively break silence. However, psychological action officers strongly felt that silence was
a valued quality among natives.[22] Therefore, making prisoners break silence on the FLN while at the same time inducing them to silence their
thoughts and feelings about colonial rule and military methods of control
was seen as psychological action's goal no matter how paradoxical.

Experts developed psychological action handbooks that echoed Le Bon's
and Chakotin's ideas. They constructed a psychological profile for native
Algerians that transformed them into an approximation of the malleable
mass individual defined by Le Bon. The average Algerian was defined as
dominated by emotions and given to mood swings. A dreamer and a mys-
tic, he was fanatically attached to his religion and lacked a sense of irony
as a result. Although he could be intelligent, he was gullible and deficient
in the capacity for discernment[23] and critical, scientific thought. A creature
of his traditional past, he was proud, had a strong sense of honor and prestige, liked to show off, and was attracted to the military profession, which
required that he be handled by soldiers. He also displayed a strong sense of
dignity and justice—a condition that did not alert the experts to its systemic
roots.[24] Algerians thus emerged as a people living at a lower stage of psychological and social development than the French. Another version of this
profile depicted Algerians as being unable to adapt on their own to French
qua modern society. Their religion was seen as the primary cause of this
fundamental incapacity to adapt. At the same time, it was understood that
"Adaptation to the modern world does not mean the transformation of the
Muslim soul whom our western concepts have difficulty penetrating."
From this perspective being a Muslim could be a "quasi-indelible" mental
condition that gives rise to "a natural oppositional reflex."[25] Nevertheless,
with the proper techniques, Algerians' reflexes could be reconditioned
through a depth action that would "penetrate each individual." Like force,

such action was presumed to "answer a desire, a blocked need in the population."[26] In this sense, psychological action represented a form of strategic optimism turned against its own premises.

By contrast, the French personality profile revealed an individualist and a skeptical man with a sense of self and an appreciation of irony.[27] He had "a taste for moderation" and loved logic. A "latent patriotism" informed his deep "attachment to the soil." However, he too had a sense of honor, but as a commitment to himself. Appropriate psychological action strategies were devised targeting each personality characteristic among natives as well as troops.[28]

As psychological action became normalized, agents in the field used these profiles as templates to improve upon as they acquired more experience, with different consequences for Algerians. A significant outcome of the institutionalization of psychological action was its transforming the political issue of colonialism into a problem of individual psychology. Challenge to colonial rule was defined as "anticolonialism," which was reduced to a condition of (ressentiment), resulting from a personality built on negative values and emotions, principally "hatred."[29] Similarly, war could be turned into a struggle for peace since psychological action experts conjectured that the "Muslim mass" might be suffering from "mass drunkenness" stemming from the experts' understanding of war as a form of "recreation" for the masses.[30]

Pacifying French Troops: Propaganda without Torture

Before examining the use of torture as a psychological weapon, a preliminary discussion of psychological action without torture is required. Psychological action targeting French troops was a crucial component of the war, and a necessary condition for the systematization of the torture of Algerians. Conscripts from France were ambivalent about the war, being unclear about its purpose. Many had relatives who had fought in World War II or been in the Resistance, and thus were appalled by torture. Furthermore, the army strongly believed that troops from France had already been indoctrinated "by groups having common cause with our adversaries."[31] Consequently conscripts' morale was a source of constant concern, and their "moral education" a challenge.[32] Army-sponsored journals, such as *Bled*, and the radio were deemed insufficient for this task. Traveling intelligence officers were enlisted in the mission of reeducating troops, which featured "chats" with conscripts (and often officers) to "concretely reveal to native Frenchmen the legitimacy of the struggle in Algeria, as well as France's achievements,"[33] and to foster "love for the army."[34] However, the efficacy of "chats" with recruits was doubtful in the thick of the war. Hence suggestions were made to give conscripts a break and take them on carefully designed tours of France's achievements (such as public buildings). However, conspicuous economic inequities between Algerians and colonists (especially landowners) jeopardized the positive image of France that the army wished to convey,[35] as did the uneasy relationship between soldiers and colonists.[36] Nevertheless, contacts between the troops and the French colonists were encouraged and appreciated for their socialization function; they particularly impressed upon conscripts "the work that France has done over several generations."[37]

From Propaganda to Torture

The line between propaganda and torture was easily crossed when psychological action targeted the native population. In spite of its intensity, psychological action (in its propaganda form) without torture was inefficient when applied to natives. Chats could not take place meaningfully due to the language barrier, which required the use of interpreters with various degrees of fluency in Arabic.[38] Furthermore, the haste with which meetings with villagers were organized and the prevailing strategy of displaying power before them made "contacts"—crucial to intelligence—superficial as well as coercive. Usually men "were picked up during operations, workers from worksites, French-Muslims living around posts. They are then harangued by the intelligence officer, the SAS officer, or the administrator of the township. During operations, it is the women who are gathered and harangued by the intelligence officer."[39] Short of harangues, communication with the rural population was through tracts dropped from airplanes. A former FLN political commissar, Abdelhamid Benzine, left valuable comments in his war journal on some of these tracts dropped on the village where he operated. One bore a drawing of a *fellagha*'s head on the body of a cricket, with a text explaining that nationalists sowed devastation wherever they went just like the dreaded insects. Another tract cautioned villagers about the presence among them of "foreigners . . . sons of Satan," claiming to fight in the name of Islam. It exhorted villagers to report them to French authorities. Benzine bitterly notes, "Psychological action services continue to exercise their imagination."[40] In general, he depicts rural populations as unresponsive to French tracts. However, the comparison of nationalists to crickets was a cultural fauxpas given that Algerians use the imagery of crickets when referring to undesirable people in a derogatory not descriptive manner as the tracts did. Communication with tracts, often in poor Arabic translation—one translated FLN as Flahn which in Arabic means "so and so"[41]—came to symbolize the aloofness of the militarized state from the people it sought to administer. By and large, tracts depicted the wretchedness of the rural population as well as the severity of military repression.

Fig. 3.1.
Psychological action tract in French and Arabic (see Fig. 3.2). Source: SHAT, 1H2461D2.

Translation:

From left to right:
Rebels enter a *mechta*.
They help themselves to semolina and women, and slit the throats of some good peasants.
They take pictures of one another in winning poses.
Guided by a brave peasant, French soldiers arrive.
Rebels run away like jackals.
The nightmare ends for the people who stayed home and welcomed French troops.
Do the same, and help French troops. Do not run away.

Fig. 3.2.
Arabic text.

Fig. 3.3.
Psychological action tract. Source: SHAT, 1H2461D2.

Translation:

People of the Douars: What are you eating this winter?

Do you really believe that the fellagha will be able to supply your douar . . . and feed your children?

HABITANTS DE CE DOUAR

Vous avez reçu les rebelles
Vous leur avez donné votre argent et du ravitaillement
Vous les avez aidés par votre silence
Aussi complices de leurs crimes vous êtes traités comme tels

IL FAUT CHOISIR

La PAIX et la protection **OU** Les crimes et le
de la **FRANCE OU CHATIMENT**

Fig. 3.4.
Psychological action tract. Source: SHAT, 1H2461D2.

Translation:

People of this douar.

You have welcomed the rebels.
You have given them money and food.
You have helped them with your silence.
You have become their accomplices in crime and have been punished accordingly.

You must choose:
Either peace and the protection of FRANCE OR crime and PUNISHMENT.

Theoretically, intelligence was a function of "contact" with the population.[42] But, since the efficiency of tracts and gatherings with villagers was dubious, the most tangible means of communication was torture. As a method of "contact," torture took psychological action in a different direction from the mere gathering of intelligence. Psychological action was to be helped by physical force. The "treatment for the mind" was contingent upon the "physical conquest of the populations." As Colonel Fritsch argued, psychological action could not be dissociated from physical force understood both in operational and psychological terms. It could not be used alone as a privileged tool of control. Torture was the method best suited to making "contact" with the body as well as the mind. The strategy of "pacification" based as it was on "respect for force, and love for justice" could not be implemented without it.[43]

Within this context, psychological warfare specialists' definition of natives as fundamentally different beings opened up a number of possibilities: First, it meant that the natives' makeup had to be changed in order for the state reforms to be carried out successfully, and for a "new" Algeria to emerge. Second, in keeping with crowd and mass theories, changing natives' psychic makeup appeared feasible. Third, given the natives' assumed defective nature, the best method for altering their behavior was torture because it permitted an efficient use of force to weaken the body and prepare the mind for "conditioning." In this sense torture did not only transform muteness into speech or silence into complicity, it also transformed one modality of being into its opposite.

The Creation of New Men

Torture was used to screen "suspects" detained in CTT to determine those who were worthy of brainwashing and those who were expendable; it was also used to gauge the length of time that a detainee could be kept before being fully reconditioned.[44] The military used the CTT as incubators of new "pacified" men. In a note to the chief commandant of the armed forces, General Boyer Vidal, inspector general of internment centers, wrote of an important discovery of "groups of people, individuals, certain categories or fractions of the population [who] are taken to CTT, and held for various periods of time." These were different from the detainees usually picked up at random or suspected of terrorism. He specified that there was "no evidence of complicity with the rebels" that would justify this practice. In fact, the confinement had been initiated for "protection, regaining control, or political reeducation."[45] He requested that he be given further details on the practice in order for him to assess the extent of the problem. This remarkable note, written in 1960, sheds light on a top-secret directive, copies of which were restricted to fourteen, issued by General Salan in 1957, outlining a clandestine operation that may be linked to the objectives identified by Boyer-Vidal.

Salan had devised a "shock method which would lead to pacification," based on the erasure of the "ideological hold that rebels have on the population; the creation in the population of a new mindset favorable to our cause; and the establishment of the right infrastructure." This was an elaborate psychological scheme requiring the utilization of *special* psychological methods.[46] Salan cast doubt on the prevailing methods of psychological action that emphasized making "contacts" with the population. He wished to do a cleansing mental operation, followed by a refurnishing of the mind with new concepts. Echoing Pavlov and Chakotin, he strongly felt that "pacification" could not be "superimposed" on a mental domain that had not been emptied of its contents.

Salan's method was to proceed incrementally, from zone to zone until the whole country had been covered. The proposed organization was modeled after the FLN, with a political commissar and a commando operating underground. The instruments of this "pacification" program were to be the psychological action officers, including mobile officers, intelligence officers, and a trained corps of "political commissars." The last were to be selected by mobile officers in close cooperation with local authorities from the targeted zone. They were to be skillfully "kidnapped" (*enlevés*) and trained in "Special Secret Centers." After completion of their training, the "political commissars" would be "discreetly reintroduced into their *douars*, protected and controlled with extreme care." They in turn "will secretly recruit members for the new structure, organized in cells after the rebel model, and will form the kernels of future bands which we will later arm."[47] They would be introduced after the "cleansing" of the OPA and the establishment of a new infrastructure. They would bring about the ideological "conquest" of the population before being officially incorporated into the administration of their zone. At this phase, too, a "mobile self-defense" network would be created out of the bands that operated clandestinely. This "pacification" method was perceived as solid—it was based on a professional team of psychologically reconverted natives—as well as economical; its psychological reliability would help to reduce the number of troops. It is unclear how many people were picked up for no other reason than that they were deemed suitable for the task of being "reeducated" into the "new men" whom civil and military leaders often mentioned in their communications. This was a policy initiated at the highest levels of the military hierarchy, and carried out in secret, that targeted unsuspecting individuals for psychological engineering.

This mental cleansing operation implied a preliminary breaking of the will, with torture, of those kidnapped or arrested. It was part of Salan's larger plan of setting up a whole "third force," to counterbalance the FLN's and undertake antisubversive missions with subversive goals, with a staff recruited from the Harka, in addition to the kidnapped leaders.[48] Salan's directive appears to have been adapted by Battalion Chief Desgratoulet in the Warnier Quarter in Algiers Army Corps. Desgratoulet shared his experience with a number of officers. He created a "band" comprised of twenty-four Frenchmen and twelve Algerians, directed by an officer seconded by two Algerian political commissars, and mobile intelligence agents whose identity was kept secret. His method included subjecting the entire male population of the secured hamlet/village to "disintoxication training"—which essentially meant intense brainwashing—in a special camp, in batches of one hundred men every eight days.[49] This "totalitarian"[50] method, also included constant control checks of the population by day and night reinforced by "propaganda conferences" with villagers thus assembled for control. However, Desgratoulet's description remains silent on Salan's recommendation to kidnap key individuals and on the location of the camp he used for "disintoxication."

As a rule, military internment camps were the places in which prized combatants were kept in secret and subjected to psychological action. At the CMI of Hammam Bou Hadjar, in western Algeria, a secretary general of the Algerian Government in Exile (GPRA) and an ALN zone commandant had been held in "secret" for the previous two years despite Red Cross objections. One of the most noteworthy CMI was the camp at Ksar Thir in the Department of Sétif. Detainees spent an initial "waiting period" of four to six months at the end of which they were divided into two groups: "retrievable" (or salvageable) and "irretrievable." The former were placed in a special bloc and subjected to an eight-month "Instruction" period, after which they were subjected to an "End of Instruction," and "Imminent Liberation" period.[51] In this camp, there was "a rather large number of men with infirmities or with one limb," including one who lost both feet in an "accident at the Camp."[52] Brainwashing was a process that proceeded relentlessly all day long and focused on a closely watched individual whose ego was subjected to disintegration through the inducement of guilt and shame before his mind was refurnished with the proper thoughts through reindoctrination. This phase featured exposure to the French military interpretation of colonial history and the war. In due time, the victim was allowed to take part in discussions with groups of "turned" prisoners who "acted as an unfriendly superego towards recalcitrant inmates and which participated in the psychological campaign against the FLN beyond the barbed wire by writing propaganda letters to relatives and issuing manifestoes."[53] In this sense psychological action was a closed chain that looped together internment camp, individual, and family as befit a total war.

The Ksar Thir Camp served another purpose: "reeducating" young men, many of whom were adolescents from the Grande Kabylie, to think French, and enroll them in the Harka. Thousands of youth, labeled *fuyards* or runaways, had initially been kept in the overcrowded CTT of the town of Akbou in Grande Kabylie in the aftermath of the ferocious 1959 Opération Jumelles[54] that had caused them to seek refuge in mountain caves. This CTT carried out torture in a nearby farm equipped with two interrogation rooms and four isolation cells. Depending on the methods used, a young man was subjected for two months after his capture to "exploitation" or interrogation followed by observation. He subsequently underwent two additional months of preparatory reeducation training at the CTT or in Quarters for subjects deemed ready to become Harka. Finally a four- to five-month "training" at the reeducation center of Ksar Thir capped the cycle. This program was based on the twin notions of *dépaysement* (literally "decountrification" or estrangement-disorientation) and immersion in a new milieu.[55] By the end of the program the youth was deemed to have been sufficiently "estranged" from his familiar environment, and his mind reconditioned, to be returned to his village as a Harki.

It was not uncommon for young boys to be kidnapped by soldiers and inducted into the Harka corps. One such boy was Saïd Ferdi, who had been picked up on his way to school, kept in a military camp against his will, and made to tell his father who had managed to trace his whereabouts that he preferred the "protection" of the army to returning home. He found other teenagers in the camp. He was subjected to physical abuse routinely by one of the sergeants and forced to sleep in the same hall as older, career soldiers.[56] He became aware of the torture of other detainees among whom was a decorated Algerian veteran of World War II.

The psychological action staff played a crucial role in determining the extent to which a detainee had been morally reconditioned. Comprised of monitors (*moniteurs*) trained in military counterguerilla schools, the staff was loaned by the military to CTT. The best among them were used in the CMI. Many were simple soldiers, some functionally illiterate and assigned to Centres d'Hébergement after their release from duty.[57] The modest salary they received and the harshness of the surroundings in which they worked made their positions difficult to fill. Although they were not psychologists, monitors wielded enormous power over detainees, as their judgment could not be questioned.[58] However, they were often challenged by the Centres d'Hébergement, who resented their special status. Acting autonomously in his assigned center, each expert was in charge of one hundred detainees with whom he theoretically met at least once a month. In the CTT, the experts at times did no more than process the ever increasing flow of detainees who were required to have a psychological profile form filled out before they were admitted to internment camps. Although on occasion an inspector felt that the "systematic and rough interrogations made the possibility of any psychological action remote," it was also estimated that 10 percent of all CTT made a serious effort at the "civic retrieval of rebels."[59] In the hands of the better-trained psychological expert, torture could be used for behavior modification. The notorious Commando Georges headed by Colonel Bigeard, in the city of Saïda, was staffed with "turned" FLN combatants drawn from a nearby CTT and "rallied" men supplemented by native veterans of other French colonial wars.[60]

FLN Psychological Action

The FLN also had its own methods of psychological action. Although they shared some features with their French counterparts, they were fundamentally different. By and large, the FLN leadership had a better understanding of the population than the French military did. Many of the FLN leaders originated from small towns with close ties to the peasantry. This meant that they had witnessed pervasive poverty and understood the problems encountered by subsistence farmers. As Algerians, they also shared with peasants a pervasive discontent with unequal political and civil rights. Those among the leadership who had attended colonial schools may have been more keenly aware of the colonial double standard of an educational system that flaunted France's democratic ideals, but resulted in their being treated as second-class citizens all the same. Much has been written about the discriminatory policies taken by the colonial state, making their review here redundant. The FLN leadership, whether political or military, shared with the larger population an experience of discrimination. That this was a matter of degree goes without saying. There was clearly a difference between the frustrations experienced by a pharmacist such as Ferhat Abbas, who became the first president of the Gouvernement Provisoire de le République Algérienne, and Krim Belkacem, a regional FLN leader, who took to the mountains in the Grande Kabylie at an early age, years before the war started.

The FLN psychological action was not based on theories of crowd behavior, or clinical psychology. It was pragmatic, born out of experience with life in a colony. It was focused on convincing the people that taking up arms against the French state would lead to the overthrow of the colonial system. This was a tall order despite a popular yearning for change. The colonization of Algeria from 1830 to 1871 had been costly, as armed resistance resulted in land and other assets being irrevocably seized by the French government. Memory of the colonial past cut both ways: It could be a reminder that defeat was onerous, or that insurgency was better than the status quo. The FLN had to allay men's fear of leaving large families behind should they be arrested or killed. It also had to convince people that a powerful colonial army could be beaten. Finally, it had to persuade people that if they did not act to change the conditions under which they and their children lived, their unequal status would get worse. Ultimately, the FLN psychological action combined political consciousness-raising, empowerment, and impression management with harsh acts, some of which were particularly bloody and undermined its standing with the population. The FLN could tap into a rich fund of memories of colonial repressive methods of which May 8, 1945, was, at the time, the most recent. World events also helped in discussions of the necessity for Algerians to act considering that the French empire was waning. The FLN could list the loss of Madagascar and Indochina (where many Algerians served as enlisted men under the French flag), Morocco and Tunisia as evidence that the time had come for the Algerians to claim back their sovereignty.

But villagers were not easily convinced. Men would admit that they were miserable, but did not quite understand how independence would change things. Many were skeptical about the various shades of nationalist activism and wanted no part in it. Some of the methods used to overcome reticence combined a show of firmness, if not force, with a display of social justice and piety. This is how Azzedine, an FLN cadre, described a typical psychological scenario where showmanship was greater than substance. In a first stage, the FLN gathered information about the social composition of a village, or hamlet, its economic organization and distribution of income, as well as the nature of quarrels and enmities between families. In a second stage, fires were lit on ridges, and the village was surrounded by a group of guerillas. Two of them, selected for their demeanor, armed themselves to the teeth, and knocked at the door of the local notable. They identified themselves as members of the FLN, and ordered him to open his door. As soon as he did, he was asked to remit his hunting rifle and cartridges. Subsequently, he was asked point blank why he was collaborating with the French authorities. He was harangued about his frequent visits [whether real or invented] to the gendarmerie, which harmed "his brothers who [fought] for the liberation of his country." The notable denied working for the French authorities and after a back-and-forth exchange expressed the desire to serve his "brothers." He was thereupon enrolled as the person in charge of the village and asked to immediately assemble the men of the hamlet in the mosque with their rifles. Meanwhile, ten FLN soldiers paraded around the hamlet, carrying their weapons in an unending circle to give the impression that they were a large group of combatants. In a third stage, villagers gathered inside the mosque: "pulled out of their beds, their eyes thick with sleep, they crouch in silence." Those who made for the door came back upon noticing the fires on the ridge, thinking that they were surrounded by an army. To get the villagers' attention, the leader of the FLN group began his speech with a surah from the Quran on fighting for one's faith—which Azzedine did not identify by its number. The leader explained that he and his men had not come to steal:

> We are fighters and need you like the seed in the bosom of the earth needs water to germinate. You do not know us, but we know each one of you. You, Ibrahim, you own twenty sheep and a mule; you, Abdelhafid, you refused three years ago to return the money that your neighbor, Tayeb, lent you, and you are in litigation now; you, Saïd, you beat your wife.

Placing itself on a higher plane than these people with "petty" problems, the FLN leader asked a crucial question: "Will you join us?" . . . "Do you want to remain on the margin of the historical struggle we are waging? If you do, we'll just leave. As far as we are concerned, you are no longer Algerians." The villagers were made to feel small. Their pride stung, they remonstrated that they wanted to join the FLN. The leader went one step further, stressing, "You are good Muslims, ready to sacrifice your property, your sons, and your lives. We knew it. Do you agree to contribute to the liberation of Algeria?" Beating the iron while it was still hot, the FLN leader made them realize that they had just entered history: The notable had been appointed their representative by the FLN. They were told about, and thus made to bear witness to the notable's dallying with the gendarmerie. The FLN forgave him because his action had happened *before* he was made to see the light. He was now entrusted with a new redeeming function. Deftly, the FLN leader had activated a feeling of doubt about the efficacy of seeking the gendarmerie's help to solve villagers' problems. To do so would be to remain in the disreputable prerevolutionary past: "Yesterday, he [the notable] had no choice but to direct you to the colonial authorities. From now on, he has chosen to be your representative before the FLN." The fourth and last stage began with the villagers asking what they should do to help. Feigning restraint, the FLN leader asked "only" for a tenth of their "fortune," as befit the tradition of Muslim charity. He further suggested that a man without cash should sell his tenth sheep to fulfill his obligation. The leader informed his audience that an FLN member would meet them regularly: He would be their political commissar and would relay instructions to them and collect funds. The discussion ended with a symbolic return of the initiative to the audience: "In the meantime, do give this some thought, address your questions to the political commissar. We will see later what would be the best way for you to serve the revolution."[61] Each villager had to contribute two hundred francs a month. However, those who had no income were given a monthly allowance of three thousand francs from which they were expected to pay their dues. This was meant to instill a sense of individual as well as collective engagement in the nationalist movement.

Commandant Azzedine noted that the number of poor people was such that some villages were receiving more FLN aid than they contributed. Consequently, the FLN decided to increase the dues paid by more prosperous hamlets where people paid as much as five thousand francs per head. Because they were short of cash—a widespread problem in rural Algeria at the time—poorer villages made contributions in kind, mostly wheat, flour, and oil.[62] Surplus food obtained in one *wilaya* (or geographical zone) was exchanged for items such as clothing, electrical equipment, printing machines, or money, needed by another *wilaya*. There was a regular exchange of goods between *wilayas* that also included animals taken from settlers' farms. The confiscation of hunting rifles from villagers was proof of the FLN's limited state of preparedness for a protracted war.

There is no reason to doubt the accuracy of the FLN method of "penetration" of villages as described by Azzedine primarily because he wrote his memoirs at a time when a number of FLN leaders were still alive, making it difficult for him to tell tales. However, the same method of induction was not used in all zones, since conceptions of the war differed from *wilaya* to *wilaya*.[63] Nevertheless, the crudeness of the method is as remarkable as the style in which it is presented. Azzedine's frequent use of Arabic expressions transcribed in French makes his description superficial, detached from the nationalist spirit he asserted existed, and condescending. By comparison, Abdelhamid Benzine, a political commissar in the region of Tlemcen from 1955 to 1956, used transcribed Arabic terms only when their translation into French would not make sense to an Algerian audience because they referred to specific cultural situations. He would not use the term *fissa'* (which in Arabic means hurry up!) as Azzedine did.[64] It was French soldiers and some colonists who customarily peppered their language with badly pronounced Arabic terms in a vain display of knowledge of the local milieu.

The assumptions underlying the method of induction of a village into the nationalist movement are instructive: a shared past and solidarity among members of the same religious-cultural group. The past was left unspecified, and subsumed under the general term "history." The past was layered. It was a past that spoke alternately of Islamic civilization and Algerian defeat in the struggle against the French invasion of 1830. Rumor spread during the war for example that the Companions of Prophet Muhammad were fighting alongside the Moudjahidine, or combatants in the path of God, the Algerian name for the guerillas. The heroic period of Islam became one way of convincing people that struggle for independence was part of an unequal struggle in which God was on the side of the Algerians as he had been on Prophet Muhammad's. Yet this was not a religious war. It was not presented as the struggle of Islam against Christianity.

On many occasions, it was a struggle against local customs. There were instances when Azzedine was involved in combating superstitious beliefs among villagers. He harangued a group of villagers, women and men, carrying offerings to a sheikh whose exploits included "turning two men into statues of stone." The FLN leader ordered his men to search the sheikh's house. During the search the men destroyed stone drums, and gris-gris, and exposed before the villagers piles of sugar, coffee, cooking oil, new clothes, and boxes filled with money that the sheikh kept in his home. The FLN leader did not fail to compare the riches of the sheikh to the poverty of the villagers. He asked rhetorically why the sheikh did not turn his magical powers against the French army. Exposing the sheikh's riches and deriding his powers in this manner may not have diminished his popularity. This incident illustrates the FLN war against local popular sheikhs mistakenly referred to as marabouts (distortion of the Arabic *m'rabet*). These were the heads of religious orders accused (not entirely wrongly) of being French-supported sources of social quietism, who, from the FLN perspective, stood in the way of the political mobilization of the Algerian population. Yet regardless of their role in fostering superstitions, men like this sheikh filled an important function in rural villages. They generally could read and write Arabic although their level of literacy was limited. They also provided advice to women and men in situations of conflict, and attempted to alleviate various ailments by dispensing placebos. Exposing them as charlatans and thieves may not have had the intended effect of driving the population away from them. Commitment to the cause of independence, a laudable but uncertain prospect, was to replace the emotional comfort provided by the sheikhs, but did not obviate the need for it. It is highly possible that villagers, especially the women among them who frequently patronized sheikhs, felt offended. Azzedine noted that the "*fellah*s whispered, their heads bowed."[65]

Was it the realization that the FLN was getting involved in too complex a sociocultural task that prompted the author to muse: "The population liked us. But we sometimes made psychological mistakes against it that had grave consequences, and for which we paid dearly." Sociological mistakes were also bound to be made by young nationalists eager to make a tabula rasa of the traditions that comprised the rural way of life. This was only to be expected. When these young men joined the movement, they went through a ritual of shedding their old identity and acquiring a new one. Typically, a recruit destroyed his identity cards and assumed a different name. Before he took the name "Si Azzedine," Rabah Zerari was told, "When you go to the *maquis*, you'll become a new man."[66] The most powerful device was the reminder that history was calling upon Algerians to act, and in so doing to regain their full measure as men, and as Muslims. As men they were expected to transcend their internecine fights and embrace history. As Muslims, they were expected to show faith in the struggle for freedom from colonial domination and to help the nationalist movement. Seizing history, acting *in* history transforms subjects of political domination into makers of their own future. Action transcends the will of the people; it is imposed upon them as a historical duty. There is an existential philosophical echo to the FLN's appeal to history as choice, albeit constrained. To return to the method used by the FLN to elicit support from the rural people, the message was that the villagers had already chosen to participate in the decolonization movement by being Muslims and Algerians. They could not make any other choice. The implication was that the FLN was but a catalyst that helped villagers empower themselves to act as historical agents.

The FLN would still be judged by its action and invidiously compared to French troops. At times, especially in the village of Melouza, in May 1957, accused of support for the rival nationalist group, the MNA, the enormity of the crime, the massacre of an estimated three hundred males along with their dogs, was such that popular imagination was inclined to attribute it to French troops (known for destroying villages in reprisals), as the FLN wrongly intimated. It is sobering in retrospect to read Commandant Azzedine boast that in the sector of Zbar-Bar of which he was in charge, "I had the right of life and death on the whole population. In a revolution, one cannot have the luxury to leave dubious people free." He recalls an instance when he executed three men accused of treason, two of whom he thought were innocent. However, before the men were tried, a French commando with dogs came upon the FLN hideout. Azzeddine had his men execute the prisoners before the French soldiers captured them on grounds that their blindfolds having been removed, the prisoners could have given away the place where FLN military equipment was kept. This is not a convincing argument since French troops had already spotted the guerillas in the area, causing them to decamp, and probably would have found the cache anyway. Nevertheless, that Azzeddine mentioned this incident at all is an acknowledgment that justice had not been done in this instance, and men were killed without a trial, as he specifically says. In a moment of candor, or as a gesture to assuage a bad conscience, he wrote: "They did not deserve to be put to death. But, we had no jails; we had no free zones where we could send our prisoners. We could not jeopardize dozens of lives in our Zbar-Bar hamlet that was so important, politically and militarily."[67] The argument according to which executing or (for the French military) torturing prisoners saved the lives of many was a parallel and dubious justification, as will be discussed later.

Revolution imposed its murderous logic, just as French military repression did, although the former often sprang from desperate contingencies, the latter from deliberate acts of the will. Informers—threats to an underground movement—were defined as traitors to the cause, hunted down and killed. They initially were warned that they would be killed. Revolutionary justice too was quick and exemplary. There were two kinds of informers, those who did not hide their collaboration with the French authorities, and those who had infiltrated the FLN organization. The FLN found itself in a similar situation to the French military having to dismantle embedded informers as the French were determined to dismantle the OPA. Informers were typically shot on the side of a road leading to a village, and left there with a sign indicating that they had been condemned to death and executed by a revolutionary tribunal for the crime of treason. Unlike summary executions committed by the French military, the FLN standing procedure was to identify the individual's crime, and claim the execution.[68] However, the identification of informers relied on information from the population, which always left room for a false accusation. To minimize such an occurrence, a person making a false accusation incurred the death penalty. And the death penalty could be meted out to a combatant. Bellahcène Bali, who joined the *maquis* at the age of nineteen, recalls the execution of one his comrades for having wrongly (and without any trial) executed a man and a woman he had suspected of having informed the French military as to the whereabouts of a guerilla group in the city of Tlemcen. It fell to Bali to execute his comrade and friend. In spite of his objections, he had to comply. After giving the condemned man time to do his prayer, and hearing his last request that his children be taken care of after his death, Bali reports: "Ahmed offered his throat to me, and I swiftly cut it, thus putting an end to the life of a great warrior and a true patriot." Asking that his reader understand the context within which such executions took place, Bali explains that "Only blind obedience [to orders] could permit us to resist and deal blows to a powerful and ferocious enemy."[69] Trials were speedy: "There were no half measures and no pardon possible. Either a suspect was cleared, and went back home, or he was found guilty and immediately executed." Unlike Bali who was a "secretary" to a local FLN chief, Azzedine was in an authority position. He asserts that at times he was inclined to pardon men whose sentence was disproportionate to their crime. However, "experience and strict orders from the FLN prevented me from being as tolerant as I would have liked."[70] The author tempers his sense of the excessiveness of guerilla warfare by invoking his age, noting that he was twenty-one when he joined the *maquis*, and had little experience in resolving disputes between villagers that normally would have been taken to a French court.

Abdelhamid Benzine, recounts a hearing before a "tribunal" in his sector in the *douar* of Beni Ouazzane, near Tlemcen, where a man had appropriated equipment belonging to the FLN, and which he had refused to return. Another man had threatened to inform French authorities on the village's cooperation with the nationalists. The hearing was attended by the heads of FLN cells assembled for the occasion. The tribunal decided to give the two men a warning, and a fine. However, the group also took time to explain to the villagers that "we were obligated to render quick justice because of the war." Unlike Azzedine, Benzine evinced greater understanding of the rural people among whom he lived and worked. He expressed regret that at times some insufficiently trained FLN cadres had problems with the population: "They make threats and all too often use force. Because they could not or did not know how to explain themselves, they used the language of force." Nevertheless, he reports that when these cadres were made aware of their behavior, they displayed eagerness to learn better ways of communicating. Benzine remarked, "When approached as equals, our peasants understand the most complex political problems." He was also aware of the delicate nature of revolutionary justice. Rendering the most equitable judgments in inheritance and divorce cases was difficult given the circumstances of the war, yet crucial to retaining or losing the people's trust. Hence the FLN used the traditional *djema'a*, or assembly of elders and notables in the community, as a structure for its tribunals. Benzine mused, "Circumstances made us *cadis* [Islamic judges], mayors, police commissioners, judges, etc. Most of the time, we do better than the colonists. In spite of our exceptional circumstances, we strive to be as democratic as we can."[71] The difference between Benzine's and Azzedine's assessments of the relationship between the FLN and the rural population is in all likelihood one of education and political sophistication. Benzine was a journalist for the communist daily *Alger Républicain*, and an author. As a member of the Algerian Communist Party (a branch of the French Communist Party initially comprised mostly of Frenchmen living in Algeria), he had enjoyed formal political training. Azzedine, by contrast, had not finished high school when he joined the FLN. His engagement in the nationalist movement was born out of his special circumstances as a member of a working-class family with a tradition of resistance to colonial rule. Azzedine's profile was more typical of the average FLN sector leader.

The disproportionate nature of offense and punishment as identified by *Azzedine* was also evident in the policy of social cleansing the FLN was engaged in, as, for example, the maiming of tobacco smokers, drug and alcohol addicts, after the third warning to give up their habits. This prohibition was also enforced in jails by FLN members seeking to socialize inmates into a new social order. The rule against tobacco, however, did not result in physical harm to a group of guerilla offenders who had ingeniously hidden snuff tobacco in hollowed bullets. These guerillas, members of the elite FLN commando unit Ali Khodja, were transferred to the somewhat quieter *wilaya* VI in the south as punishment.[72] FLN justice was (ironically) based on its own "ten commandments" and classified crimes into simple (such as not paying dues), serious (as for example giving false testimony, or rape), and very serious (for instance, betrayal and surrender to the enemy). Revealing intelligence under torture was considered betrayal.[73] Azzedine reports an instance of attempted rape by a political commissar that came to the attention of the FLN upon complaints made by people in a hamlet in the Zbar-Bar area. The suspect was tied with a wire and a rope and placed under the watch of a group of militants among whom was a youth who objected to the culprit's treatment. The author decided to replace wire and rope with a turban. The knot made with the turban was not strong enough, permitting the suspect to escape. Subsequently, the suspect enrolled in the Harka in the rural town of Ain Bessem, where he apparently took revenge on civilians as well as guerillas, before being captured and finally executed.[74] Given the conditions under which the FLN operated, which became more difficult as French military repression intensified, it is remarkable that there would be any "tribunals" at all. But, no matter how summary their decisions were, these tribunals were deemed socially and politically necessary for the FLN to establish itself as a shadow administration. Their functions were to impress upon the population an alternative to established colonial tribunals, as well as to signify accountability for anti-FLN actions.

The FLN was eager to project an image of justice and concern for the welfare of people. Once a month it distributed fresh or preserved meat to poor villagers whose diet was deficient in animal protein. As Azzedine put it, "We established in the *maquis* a sort of minimum standard of living."[75] In addition, FLN teams taught rural men and women hygiene, and wherever they could, dispensed medical care as a parallel to the military's own use of doctors as tools of "pacification." However, wounded guerillas often used traditional medicine to care for their wounds, since establishing underground infirmaries was not always possible.

In sum, psychological warfare inevitably required the use of torture. Although it was theoretically distinct from military operations, psychological warfare was a genuine war for the conquest of minds. The unbridled search for intelligence was simply a step toward a greater project of psychological engineering, the possibility of which was glimpsed from the Vietnam War, and its feasibility from crowd behavior and mass mobilization theories. The concepts of crowd and mass deprived of rational thought fit in with the prevailing view of Algerians as *sous-hommes* who could be physically shocked into more suitable colonial beings. The systematic search for subjects to "retrieve" from the incessantly replenished pool of suspects enabled military strategists to seriously contemplate creating psychologically reconditioned "new men" to build a new colonial order. Under instructions from General Salan, men were kidnapped and placed in secret camps, just like captured combatants, where torture and psychological action combined to "empty" their minds before replenishing them with the appropriate social values and political ideals.

The incubators of the "new men" were, in order of importance, the CMI, CTT, and the Centres d'Hébergement. The strategic importance of psychological engineering was such that their staffs were generally trained in military counterguerilla war instruction centers and wielded power as a corps of experts over detainees often incommensurate with the skills of many of its members. A special population of detainees, teenage boys, was caught in this battle over the minds of the native population. They too were screened, "turned," and enlisted in the Harka. In these camps, direct "contact," a prerequisite for breaking the much dreaded "wall of silence," was made with the body and the mind of the detainee. And many detainees, after months of treatment, came out different men.

The distinction established between psychological action and psychological warfare merely reflected the thin line that separated propaganda from torture. That some of the methods used met with a measure of success is undeniable. There were combatants who became torturers, and French conscripts who presided over torture, as was the case at the CTT of Akbou. But the record is silent on the "new men" envisaged by Salan.

The FLN, whose structure and methods were theoretically copied by the French military, had its own psychological action strategy. However, its psychological action did not stem from racial and cultural superiority. Initially, from the perspective of the FLN, psychological action was synonymous with consciousness-raising, an awakening of latent pride in being a Muslim and an Algerian, and optimism about taking up arms against the colonial system in spite of its military superiority. Islam played a role in the appeal to solidarity and sacrificing one's life for one's country as one would for God. The living memory of the colonial system of domination helped to make villagers largely receptive to the FLN message. Algerians' colonial status was a facilitating factor in FLN political agitation. As military action grew more repressive, the FLN appeared as the representative of a tattered nation, unjustly occupied and abused by a foreign power. In the battle over minds, the inequities of the colonial system, which the military sought to explain away, played in favor of the FLN psychological action. The future without France could not be glimpsed in its details, but from the FLN point of view it could at least restore dignity through political sovereignty—a goal popular among Algerians. The language of freedom is far more powerful than the language of colonial rule, no matter the promise of reform. However, the FLN methods were also at times despicable and uncompromising. Their full range has yet to be documented.

In the end, antisubversive war strategy helped to expose the linkage between propaganda, brainwashing, and torture. Psychological action was inseparable from military strategists' conceptions of "pacification." The next chapter will analyze concrete modalities of "pacification," which wove in torture and psychological action.

Chapter 4

MODELS OF PACIFICATION:

FROM NIETZSCHE TO SUN TZU

En Algérie, nous n'avons eu qu'un seul ennemi: nous-mêmes.
—Jean-Claude Racinet, *Les Capitaines d'Avril*

THE BLURRING OF THE boundaries between people and masses/ crowds, or propaganda and torture reflected a degree of indeterminacy at the heart of psychological warfare. Antisubversive war doctrine had assigned psychological warfare a pacifying role. However, in practice, "pacification" suffered from the same lack of specificity as psychological warfare. As General de Bollardière pointed out, the army had failed "to define what it [the word "pacification"] meant. An army can be broken by leaving the definition of its mission so ambiguous."[1] Techniques inspired from Le Bon's and Chakotin's ideas were the domain of psychological-action officers honing their skills in torture chambers and the 5ème Bureau's written and oral propaganda. But concrete instances of "pacification" at sector level put into play political and philosophical conceptions of colonial rule held by individuals in command. Officers understood that counterrevolutionary war required, in addition to military operations, the destruction of the enemy "OPA" and its replacement by a new one. However, the doctrine did not codify "pacification" or provide safeguards against it becoming an end in itself. Since there was no precise definition of the concrete relationship between "pacification," operations, and psychological action, officers at the sector level felt free to fill the gaps according to their own political ideals,[2] moulding terror, torture, and psychological action into a single war weapon. The implementation of the antisubversive war doctrine was the task of lieutenants, captains,[3] and at times colonels, whose zeal and commitment to *guerre révolutionnaire* as a theory took on personal interpretations as a doctrine. These men often brushed off principles of psychological warfare as taught by mobile psychological officers.[4] Consequently, their actions did not reflect anarchy within the military; they were tactical imperatives: It was the unified military and political command within which "pacification" was to evolve, and that they held in their hands, that gave these "young committed chiefs" freedom of action.[5]

This chapter explores four concrete modalities of "pacification" adopted by three different officers: Colonel Antoine Argoud, Squadron Chief Jean Pouget (credited with a successful "pacification" method), and Captain Jean-Claude Racinet. All three men were fervently committted to keeping Algeria French. They all believed in subordinating civil to military power. Two of them (Pouget and Racinet) were graduates of Saint-Cyr Military Academy. They knew one another and had actively participated in the May 13, 1958, movement that brought General de Gaulle to power before they turned against him when his Algerian policy proved disappointing to them. Argoud had been a student of Charles Lacheroy in Rabat, Morocco, who taught him observation flying.[6] Argoud and Racinet had been active in the April 1961 putsch. Subsequently, Argoud became a leading figure in the OAS underground. Sought by the army, he found refuge in Spain and Germany before his capture in Munich by the Barbouzes, the French secret police. Taken back to France, he was tried and condemned to life in prison, but ultimately benefited from the pardon de Gaulle extended to rebellious officers in 1968. The tactics employed by these officers ranged from brute force to culturally nuanced coercion, and made routine use of torture. They all displayed various degrees of Christian commitment to the war. Argoud and Pouget may be termed National-Socialists[7] who felt that international capitalism was as much to blame as international communism for social strife in the colonies. Racinet approximated the National-Catholic ideological orientation.[8] All three were convinced that socioeconomic reforms were necessary to sustain military victory over the FLN. However, they differed from one another in the degree of terror they were willing to use in "pacifying" the native population. I am also discussing Henry Descombin, an intelligence officer assigned to the 5ème Bureau in 1958–60 to highlight a different aspect of pacification that did not feature torture, but reinforced the ideological assumptions underlying the methods used by the other officers.

Argoud: A Self-Styled Ataturk

Colonel Argoud's "pacification" methods focused on the unrestrained use of brute force as a form of psychological action. From Argoud's perspective, successful "pacification" was measured by the number of Algerians enrolled in the auxiliary corps of the Harka, and the number of villages organized into "self-defense" against the FLN. To achieve his objective as encapsulated in the formula "Protection, Engagement, Control," he combined operations against the OPA with torture and terror. Protection meant extirpating the enemy from the population through "intelligence and punishment." Engagement of the population essentially meant a psychological offensive mounted against that same population in which "guilty" individuals were publicly executed without trial. Control was to be "permanent" to prevent a return of the guerillas to villages. To justify terror, Argoud agreed with the psychological action officers' definition of Algerians as people that only understood force. He convinced himself that "Muslims will not talk as long as they are not totally protected, as long as we do not inflict acts of violence on them. . . . They will rally our camp only if it [justice] responds to their respect and thirst for authority." Aware of the harshness of his methods, Argoud wondered whether "a certain form of torture and public executions are contrary to the demands of a Christian conscience?" Against this stirring of conscience, he invoked Clausewitz's principle that "war is an act of violence that has no limit," stressing that "From our perspective, torture and capital executions are acts of war. Now, war is an act of violence aimed at compelling the enemy to execute our will, and violence is the means [by which to do it]. The end is to impose our will on the enemy." Might makes right. Any expression of Christian "goodness of the soul" would be a "mortal error" in war. Addressing military opponents of torture, like General de Bolladière, he invoked antisubversive realism "to attack the guerilla through the population."[9] Terror aimed at bringing forth intelligence was a tool of behavior modification. From Argoud's perspective, the mistake made by opponents of torture such as General de Bollardière was to judge "Muslim mentality" after their own, when Muslims called for a completely different standard. Inevitably, such a view placed the burden of torture and terror squarely on the victims' shoulders.

According to Serge Chakotin, political action is "a form of biological behavior."[10] Argoud easily crossed the line between politics and biology as he turned military strategy into a tool for taming Algerians seen as "primitives with savage impulses." Considering that "there is a one-thousand-year lag" between their "civilization" and the French, Algerians were eminently suitable for terror tactics. In fact, they called for them; their nature needed them. However, despite their closeness to a natural state of being, Algerians preserved qualities that the French had ostensibly lost. Paradoxically, Argoud admired Algerians for risking their lives, whereas the French colonists sought to preserve theirs. The idea of risking one's life— a narrow interpretation of Hegel's lordship and bondage metaphor, echoes Argoud's equation of war with virility, patriotism with empire. It also helped him to explain decolonization struggles in psychological terms, thereby exonerating colonial rule in spite of his awareness of its inequities. By extolling Algerians' risk-taking, he wished to criticize France for its assumed "decadence"—a notion common among advocates of counterrevolutionary war. He asserted that whereas colonized peoples kept their energy intact, colonizers have become soft because of the increase in their standard of living, comfort, and easy life. They are more and more reluctant to risk their lives. They find a hundred reasons, some of which highly moral, to justify their cowardice. In so doing, they reinforce among the defeated of yesteryear the will to recover their freedom, and risk losing their positions by defending them so poorly.

In a parody of Nietzsche's "will to power," Argoud established an inverse relationship between colonizers' "weakening of the will" and the "vital energy of the Muslim community." One diminishes as the other rises. Moreover, the colonizers' lack of vigor emboldens their subjects, whose nature it is to be restrained by force. Thus for the colonized,

> To accept being dominated by a virile people [in French, *mâle*] capable of conquest and victory is a lesser evil; they may even see in this the hand of God. But, to be subjected to the yolk of an effeminate people [in French, *femelle*], defeated ten times over, is an unbearable insult for the Muslim soul, even if this yolk is accompanied by expressions of civility and generosity.

Argoud's presumption to understand the "Muslim soul" was a mere justification for the use of force, even against his compatriots, when necessary. He once sent a message to General Bigeard, equally a hard-liner, demanding that he refrain from "hunting" nationalists in his sector or risk being shot at with a 75mm gun. To intimate that their colonel meant business, Argoud's men ambushed Bigeard's.[11]

For practical purposes, Argoud's presumptive knowledge of native Algerians was open to an inverted revision. He was once visited by a White Father from Maison Carrée, a suburb of Algiers, in search of his driver who had been picked up by Argoud's men and never heard from again. In the course of the discussion that took place with the priest, Argoud expounded on his view of natives' propensity to obey force. The White Father replied, "Yes, Muslims respect force, especially when it is unjust." Taken aback by this comment, Argoud mused: "They viscerally respect force. But pure force is unjust force. If they pretend to rebel against injustice, it is because they know our western ethic and hope it might get them some redress."[12] Missing the priest's point, Argoud turned it into yet another argument for continuing to use "pure force." His knowledge of native Algerians was categorical, leaving no room for an uncertainty that might have allowed for correction.

Argoud approved of the routine use of torture by paratroopers, arguing that

> torture is an act of violence just like the bullet shot from a gun, the [cannon] shell, the flame-thrower, the bomb, napalm, or gas. Where does torture really start, with a blow with the fist, the threat of reprisal, or electricity? Tor-

ture is different from other methods in that it is not anonymous. The shell, the bomb, gas are often blind. Torture brings the torturer and his victim face-to-face. The torturer at least has the merit of operating in the open. It is true that with torture the victim is disarmed, but so are the inhabitants of a city being bombed, aren't they?

Argoud's analogical reasoning lumps together Nazi methods of extermination of defenseless people with the violence characteristic of a war between well-armed forces. If torture is different from other war acts, it must be an "act of justice insofar as it strikes the guilty whereas other acts of war, under the guise of legitimate defense, are often no more than collective reprisals—blind, yet immoral."[13] Thus the normalization of torture requires its interpretation as an instrument of justice.

From this perspective, gassing people during World War II was also an act of justice. However, in this defense of torture Argoud stumbles on the factor that distinguishes torture from other acts of violence: Torture is inflicted upon individuals who cannot escape or seek shelter as inhabitants of a bombed city might. It places an individual (not a group) at the absolute mercy of his torturer, who may inflict pain on his victim in any manner that he wishes, as long as he wishes, or until death occurs. In addition to symbolizing the powerlessness of an individual placed in a situation in which he cannot fight back, torture also aims at humiliating and dehumanizing its victim by forcing him into a state of absolute abjection. Argoud's argument presents another flaw: Torture cannot be an act of justice as well as an act of war. Justice evokes laws, and courts to uphold them. It also provides for the accused to defend himself.

In the end, Argoud's defense of the justness of torture was also a defense of related unjust practices:

> It is my choice. I will carry out public executions. I'll shoot those absolutely guilty. Justice will therefore be just. It will thus conform to the first criterion of Christian justice. I'll expose their corpses to the public just as Mustapha Kemal did, not out of some sadist feeling, but to enhance the virtue of exemplary justice.[14]

Argoud once more mixes arguments by playing on several registers. Terror, beginning with torture, is but the implementation of canon law. Thus "Christian law" is applied to Algerians who may or may not be caught in flagrante delicto. But their punishment is also in keeping with what the leader of a Muslim country, Kemal Ataturk, did to the Turkish people. Reference to Mustapha Kemal was meant to neutralize the invocation of Christianity. However, Ataturk was not any Muslim: He had declared his own kind of war on Islam through the use of coercive methods of secularization. Argoud intended to indicate that his actions were neither inordinately violent, nor biased against Algerians qua Muslims. Like their Turkish counterparts who were coerced by Ataturk, Algerians can also be forced to accept Argoud's law: Rally France or die.

Although critical of the use of force alone in *doing* "pacification," Argoud nevertheless used it for its psychological effect. Force was used to intimidate. Argoud described his method of operation in the village of Melouza (near the city of M'sila), ironically the site of a massacre by the FLN in 1957. After an empty school had been nearly destroyed by guerillas, he assembled a group of about fifty men on the public square, demanding that they give information about the attackers. Receiving no answer, he decided to shock the men into talking:

> I brought in the armored car, and made the fifty men lie face down in front of it. I point the cannon and destroy two *mechtas* [rural houses with enclosures] that belonged to two notable *fellaghas* wanted by the gendarmerie: The shells—a dozen of them—whiz by, barely one meter over the men's heads. Once the operation was over, I order them to get up. I line them up in a single row, review them, and make them shout "Vive la France!"

After a subsequent air-land operation that he likened to "slaughter," he writes:

> To the great astonishment of my men, I then decided to bring the corpses back to M'sila to expose them to the population. I piled them up in sacks and transported them to Melouza where we arrived in the evening. The following day, I had the sacks loaded on the shuttle bus to M'sila. I ordered the driver to unload them in M'sila on the main square."

However, the driver was reluctant to drop the corpses off in a public place and kept driving in circles instead. Apprised of the situation, Argoud threatened the driver with death if he did not obey his order. Despite a phone call from the civil administrator indicating the illegality of the procedure, Argoud left the corpses exposed for twenty-four hours before allowing their burial. As is customary with accounts justifying terror, Argoud ended his narration like a fairy tale: "When we left, the ambiance had completely changed. No more attacks, and the population, initially mute, opened up, and information began to pour out."[15] Argoud's message was that terror works; it is the best method to untie tongues. The psychology of terror differs from the psychology of propaganda advocated by the psychological action experts. However, because it was based on the same conception of the nature of Algerians, Argoud's method was but psychological action stretched to its logical extremes.

Argoud's methods were known to his superiors. Hard-liners such as Generals Massu and Salan, ostensibly disapproved of them, and asked him to stop. General Allard specifically ordered him in person to stop executing Algerians. Argoud asked the general whether he was not simply objecting to the public character of his executions. The general answered affirmatively. Argoud's response was: "Well! Then, I propose to shoot the guilty in the mountain [in L'Arbaa-Rovigo-Rivet sector] over ridge 300 for example (L'Arbaa, Rovigo, Rivet are at 80 meters altitude)." The general reportedly gave his agreement. However, Argoud still had the last word: "From then on, terrorists were executed in the mountain, but still in public, for I transported spectators to them in trucks."[16] Executions of the "guilty," whose guilt could not be ascertained in a court of law, was a form of theater. The psychology of terror rests on an audience. People had to see with their own eyes pure force in action. Yet, despite the ritual display of force, if a suspect does not know anything, he will have nothing to say, as was the case with the fifty men at Melouza. Even then, the group was its own audience witnessing the flaunting of force. In terror, pure force is blind: It does not seek to punish the guilty as Argoud tirelessly claims; it seeks psychological shock. In an inverted manner, it uses the Pavlovian principle of stimulus and response to instill fear in the heart of every villager. However, it assumes that fear will automatically result in compliance, though clearly fear did not prevent an attack on Argoud himself. To show that his method bore fruit, he boasted having gathered together a force of three hundred Harki.

Racinet: Nietzsche in the Orient

The second paradigmatic attitude toward "pacification" was represented by Captain Jean Claude Racinet. After a "pacification" stint in the city of Constantine in 1958 that won him an unwelcome transfer to France, he was reassigned to the Paratroop Commando Group in the southern town of Géryville. Keenly aware of his working-class background, Racinet thought of himself as an antibourgeois "Titiste" (or sympathizer of Marshal Tito's ideas) who could admire the Egyptian leader Nasser for asserting his independence against Western powers, and even appreciate Muslim culture. Unlike Argoud, he retained the basic outline of "pacification" doctrine, which he referred to as "structuration." Taking a critical look at the pacification method used in Algiers in 1957, he felt that the parallel hierarchies created by strategist Sirvent had been deficient in the "Verb" by which he meant a galvanizing political formula. What was needed was "a philosophy, key words. I proposed to speak and to speak more of revolution than integration." The concept of *Verb* indicates Racinet's commitment to the right-wing Cité Catholique's view of the war. Racinet appointed himself to a religious mission of sorts in which Algerians, when subjected to the proper treatment, would actively, on their own power, act out their support for France like neophytes seek to display their newborn zeal. Unlike many of his contemporaries, he evinced a degree of understanding of Islam that enabled him to discount it as an impediment to his mission. He found the simplicity of Islam "more compelling and more democratic than ours." He further noted, "It is not true to pretend that one cannot discuss religion with a Muslim. . . . I found in them [Muslims] more culture than fanaticism."[17] He used this more enlightened understanding of Muslims to adapt the "pacification" strategy implemented during the Battle of Algiers.

Finding a new meaning to "pacification," he believed that France ought to "fulfill the Algerian revolution at the home of the FLN, in its place, and against it," before expanding it to France. He argued that the definition of colonialism as the domination of one society by another was an invention of the European Left that obscured colonized people's consent to what amounted to a colonial pact. The point was to breathe new life into French colonial political culture. As he explained:

> We wanted the Algerian population to do its revolution. We made the revolution ours. We felt we were the direct cousins of the wayward men among them [the FLN] who were our present enemies, but whom we wanted to rally to us through the power of the Verb, or combat through mass action. . . . our France had the look of 1792.

This configuration of history, religious identity, and repression gave Racinet's view a distinctive character. The French Empire could be saved by saving France from its political lack of will. Algeria was the center of gravity of (imperial) French identity. Since the Algerian Revolution was inevitable, with or without the FLN, it might as well be France that spearheaded it by endorsing its ideals. The new French revolution began in Algeria: "Algeria was there to be taken like a woman."[18] Once Algeria was taken by the antisubversive officers, France would follow.

The revolution so conceived combined religious imagery with the cult of the great man, the opposite of the Algerian sous-homme. Racinet shared with Argoud the cult of the great man, the great leader, exemplified by his superior, Robin, when both served in Constantine: "The army has always manufactured supermen: Robin was one of them. Physically and morally he was Frederic Nietzsche's Uberman, the man who never ceases to transcend himself. He filled us with religious awe."[19] Unlike Argoud, however, Racinet sought to use the figure of an idealized leader as a tool of social mobilization of Algerians. He candidly described his ideological construction: "I relied on the archetype of the Father that's much more alive in the collective unconscious of oriental crowds than in ours. I idealized de Gaulle before my audiences. . . . I had no choice. We needed a great man." Racinet's presumed knowledge of Islam floundered on the military imperative to win the war. Muslims do not believe that God could be a father, or that de Gaulle would be his representative on earth as Racinet's image manipulation intimated. Unaware of his cultural faux-pas, he commissioned the 5ème Bureau to do "a naïve-looking portrait of General de Gaulle, exactly in the oriental style. We had them posted in all the houses [in Géryville]." The irony of plastering a holy-looking de Gaulle in Muslim homes was lost on Racinet even when he felt disenchanted by de Gaulle's Algerian policy: "And as in a nightmare, the icon that I had hung to the *gourbis*'s walls started to speak more and more loudly. But its mass will not be mine." The garbling of geography coincided with the forcing of Christian dogma onto Islam. In its twilight the empire was one blurry space. Images of Father de Gaulle also expressed Racinet's view that: "Just like a snail recoiling when poked by a twig, the Muslim man would withdraw in his shell if we tried to persuade him with speeches and logic."

Racinet's "pacification" strategy followed General Allard's goal to "destroy first, build next," and "break the *fellagha*." Using the experience acquired when he "pacified" Constantine, he set up a *quadrillage*, which he entrusted to one hundred soldiers that became known as "La Centaine" (the One Hundred). A census of the population followed, at night, when paratroopers were sure to find people in their homes. At the same time, teams of paratroopers, flanked by interpreters, walked among the population in search of men who might be used in the structuration program as "island leaders," or heads of groups of houses in a given neighborhood. Once appointed, "island leaders"—there were 750 of them in Géryville—met with a military team biweekly to report on the state of their neighborhood and theoretically communicate people's needs. They worked together with a number of committees organized around such tasks as sanitation and policing. They were to form the core of a tight surveillance plan aimed at "denouncing, unmasking, tracking down and chasing away the adversary," the embryos of "self-defense," the ultimate goal of "pacification." The last stage of the method focused on the "indoctrination" of the population, now thoroughly isolated. Racinet's plan was in effect a restructuring of the population that took place under conditions approximating a laboratory situation to achieve an "in-vitro effect." Totalitarian psychological techniques were used at these meetings to ferret out dormant FLN militants. As an experiment, Racinet used one of these meetings to induce guilt in an innocent island leader. He called out his name and, pointing an accusing finger at him, charged him with being too "soft" as well as a "traitor" unfit for "our cause." After this dramatic accusation, Racinet proceeded to expel the victim from the room. Racinet claims that the man, named Soudani, visited him in his office for two consecutive weeks to obtain his "rehabilitation," which he could not give him without appearing "soft" in the eyes of the other island leaders, and because he knew that the victim had committed no crime. As Racinet saw it, structuration meant unlimited psychological manipulation of the Algerian population. Admitting that he took an unhealthy pleasure in humiliating Soudani, Racinet thought that he could have made anything of him, even "prostitute him." He observed that "terror, when it is handled well, that is to say, somewhat as it is in Peking rather than in Chicago, is the ultimate weapon." Oblivious of the gratuitous pain he caused Soudani, Racinet concluded: "But we did not belong to that race of men [the Chinese]. We firmly maintained Soudani's expulsion."[20]

For Racinet, the structuration method, as he applied it, was the only alternative to torture. He argued that "torture is efficient only if it is handled right, and if the subject has something to say." He denounced the inadequacy of the conventional method of gathering intelligence by rounding up people, arresting them, and torturing them. He noted that this led to gross abuses imputable to the intelligence services' lack of understanding of the native population. He described one instance of abuse involving a man with the very common name of Mohammed Ben Ahmed. This man was arrested and tortured four times. Yet his crime was that he shared a name with a thousand other men. This error could have been avoided had the gendarmes known about the commonality of the victim's name and also checked the first name of his father to determine whether he was the right man. The method of structuration, helped by Racinet's quasi-anthropological knowledge provided total control of the population so that "any enemy agent would be rejected just like a foreign body is expelled from a living organism by its immune system."[21] After the paratroopers were convinced that the community was "pacified," they would relax curfew hours and have the people symbolically remove the barbed wire themselves.

On the face of it, there was nothing wrong with a method that shunned torture and sought to bring some normalcy to everyday life through a relaxation of curfew hours and the removal of barbed wire. However, coercion was still present; commando operations were ongoing around Géryville. Using General Lyautey's dictum about the deterrent value of a show of force, Racinet wished to first "intimidate" the population. Since he, too, gathered intelligence, he coordinated activities with the Centre de Renseignment et d'Action, one of the incarnations of the DOP. His conception of structuration was also based on a stereotypical conception of Algerians, which ultimately did not differ much from the view that served as a justification for torture. He thought that other officers had failed the task of "pacification" "because they did not understand that secrecy, duality, ambiguity are the golden keys to the Oriental's mind. For the Oriental, only two things are certain: that God exists, and that we will die some day. To be certain of anything in any domain is a Western atti-tude."[22] Thus Algerians were defined as the absolute other that could be subjected to psychological terror inherent in the structuration method, without any qualm.

Racinet's psychological manipulation was also used as a shallow pal-liative to concrete economic problems. Armed with the notion that rebel-lions are manifestations of neurosis rooted in fear, contempt, or pain, he had his assistant organize meetings in various places, including coffee shops. His interventions at these meetings were calculated, through care-fully phrased questions, to make the audience talk about unemployment and poverty, issues of great concern to them, as a psychiatrist would let his patient talk. However, at the end of the session, Racinet's assistant would lead the audience to think that both economic problems would only be aggravated should Algeria become independent. Through this "psychoanalytic treatment . . . a man who came in without a job or hope, would still, unfortunately, leave without a job but not without hope. He will have found someone to listen to him; he will have for a moment ex-perienced a feeling of brotherliness." Racinet was convinced that the com-bination of surveillance and psychoanalytic benevolence would squash one revolution by another. As he put it, "by enlightening the Arab about his revolt, I help him to move away from the obscure domain of feeling, of Pan-Arabism, of half religious truths." How long this experiment with a captive society could have gone on without backfiring will never be known. But while Racinet was experimenting with structuration, re-peated occurrences of rape by paratroopers that went unpunished in spite of Racinet's complaint cast doubt on his "pacification" plan. Further-more, every year that Racinet was at Géryville, thirty young Algerians left the town to join the FLN.[23]

Jean Pouget: From Mao and T. E. Lawrence to Sun Tzu

Jean Pouget, squadron chief, best known for having brought discipline to a particularly unruly 228th Batallion at Bordj de l'Agha, a small southern rural community, represents another attitude toward "pacification." He kept a *journal de marche* that was incorporated into a book in which he narrates his experiences through a fictitious character named Jean-Marie. Whether this literary device helped him be more objective with himself, or simply detach himself from some of the disreputable acts he commit-ted cannot be ascertained here. After the French defeat at Dien Bien Phu, he pondered the reasons for which Clausewitz's war theory had not been borne out in Indochina. He read Engels, Lenin, T. E. Lawrence, Mao, and Giap and concluded, as other revolutionary-war theorists had done before him, but more crudely, that: "The final goal of a revolutionary war is the control of the population by all means, including military, political, economic, propaganda and terror. Convince or Coerce." He frequently reminded himself that: "In revolutionary war, the population is at once the objective, friend and enemy." The leitmotif "objective-friend-enemy" guided his actions throughout the war. The challenge was to turn the population from enemy to friend, using all means necessary. When he took up his post, he looked up his terms of reference and found that they could be summed up in five words: "maintenance of order, and pacification." He felt that these words meant "everything and nothing" but gave the quarter commandant "full powers and freedom of action," as long as he was willing to exercise them,[24] which he was.

Pouget shared with Argoud a sovereign disdain for civil justice, as well as the conviction that his mission included setting the course of the war on track even against the will of other officers. Frequent references to Christianity in his narrative give his hard-line stance an aura of righteousness, and his actions the inevitability of a calling. For example, he recounts in quasi-mystical terms the appearance of a young boy of ten at the gates of his camp, on Christmas eve, to seek medical care for an otitis:

> There arrived, on the day before Christmas, the small nomad dressed in rags and dignity, with large Semitic eyes, long hair peppered with sand, and this air of imperial gravity when he spoke of his father's rheima [sic] [the correct word is kheima] just like the other one, the child of Nazareth, spoke of his father's Kingdom.[25]

The situational romanticism of the soldier on duty in the desert is triggered by an unspoken nostalgia for a Christian Algeria that many nineteenth-century French figures too had bemoaned.

Pouget's actions were guided by his critique of the military's "pacification" strategy. He rightly noted that "contact" with the population was a recurring theme in the Joint Chiefs of Staff's documents: "'search for contact, contact intelligence, line of contact, etc.' This line of contact on the ground, the Joint Chiefs of Staff represented it on the map in a double underline: red for the enemy, blue for the friend. . . . Where on earth is this devilish contact located, elusive like the enemy in an unnamable war?" He argued that in revolutionary war, line of contact is not to be found on the ground, but at the military quarter, in the hands of the commanding officer who is in touch with the "population-objective-friend-enemy." Pouget, perhaps the most theoretically guided officer, reasoned that in order "to reach the population-objective, with the help of the population-friend against the population-enemy," the quarter commandant needed to have "the political powers belonging to civil [authorities]." As

Pouget saw it, "pacification" required him to seize civil powers in accordance with revolutionary-war theory. In order to get them, he decided to stage what he called a "military coup." He called a meeting of the lieutenants in charge of two Sections Administratives Spécialisées one at Bordj de l'Agha, the other at Ben S'rour nearby. He knew that the two SAS officers were deficient in their understanding of their mission and decided to announce his intention to take over the management of the Ben S'rour SAS. He ordered his men to escort the unhappy and remonstrative lieutenant to the road leading to the nearest city of Bou Saada, the administrative center of the Sous-Prefecture. Pouget's men were also ordered to "execute" the lieutenant should he resist. Technically, only the civil authority, in this case the Sous-Préfet, could remove the head of a SAS. Pouget's approach was in principle right insofar as he correctly noted that the local civil administration, just like the SAS officers, misunderstood "pacification." Theirs was a traditional colonial custom of exacting taxes from an impoverished population unable to pay them. In fact the administration was willing to compel local villagers to pay back taxes they had been unable to pay *as part of* the strategy of rallying the population. Pouget opposed the Sous-Préfet of Bou Saâda, declaring him a "cause of disorder." He also prohibited him from entering his SAS territory, which by law fell under the Sous-Préfet's jurisdiction.[26]

Once in possession of military and political powers, Pouget proceeded to make contact with the population. The standard contact method was to do a census. Pouget wished to go about it in a more civil fashion. He ordered his men to refrain from the customarily rough entry into people's homes, instructing them instead to "gently knock on the door, and wait until you are asked to enter the house, otherwise you will speak from the threshold." The contact makers were to find out from the population the nature of the problems that it encountered in dealing with the administration and the military, among other things. They were enjoined to discuss any topic except "taxes, and the rebellion." The new rules of military civility were aimed at giving the population confidence in the army. However, habits die hard judging by the soldier, a Dubois, who made a pass at the daughter of an Algerian man who had invited the military team to tea. The girl screamed, alerting her father and the rest of her family. This was an enormous affront to the father and to the girl, and a mockery of the "pacification" goals ostensibly upheld by the commandant. As Pouget describes the incident, the daughter was wearing a shirt that was too tight for her budding breasts which the soldier could not resist groping on his way out. Both Pouget and his man had concluded that because the girl was not "veiled," she was a servant and thus could be groped with impunity. Reflecting on the incident, Pouget felt, "At the Place de la Bastille or on the Champs Elysées the incident would have been trivial.

For a French soldier, in operation to boot, to gently jostle (*bousculer*) a girl has never been a crime; it is the phallocratic side of the warrior that the MLF denounces." Clearly there is a difference between a woman who is teased or harassed on the Champs Elysées, and a young girl whose breasts are groped by a soldier in uniform in her own house. But Pouget understood the power of desire, having had an affair himself with a captured female combatant, Fatia, in Algiers in 1958 that he claims caused him to fall out of Salan's grace.[27] Poking fun at the French women's movement (the Movement de Libération des Femmes) while seeking to justify a boorish act that violated hospitality rules (that exist even in Parisian homes) is an assertion of the right that Pouget, a military officer, claimed for his soldiers: To seek pleasure where they could get it and even on duty, during an experiment with "pacification."

Nevertheless, the incident was exploited for its public-relations value: Dubois was divested of his weapon and confined to isolation at the camp between details. However, Pouget felt badly about punishing a soldier for an act that he did not find reprehensible and decided to give him gloves to protect his hands from the cold while he swept the yard. He also bought him a used piano—Dubois was a pianist in civil life—that was set up at a military club. The girl's father received two hundred kilos of barley "to increase the girl's dowry." This may have been a gratuitous comment, as in Algeria a girl does not customarily bring a dowry to her husband. Pouget was quite satisfied with the dissemination of the news of the settlement among villagers. It helped establish a reputation of fairness and righting wrongs committed by the military against the native population.

Pouget's experiment with "pacification" combined a more civil approach to the population with firmness. He learned from Sun Tzu, a fourth-century-B.C. Chinese military theorist, that "To win one hundred victories in one hundred battles is not evidence of know-how. . . . To capture the enemy is better than to destroy him. Therefore, experts in the art of war, subdue the enemy army without combat."[28] Hence, at a meeting with the Algerian mayor of a small village, Ain Melah, in the area of Bou Saâda, whom he suspected of collusion with the FLN, Pouget made the mayor understand that, despite his denial of any FLN activity in his town, the army was aware of what "he was doing," but still offered him a medical doctor to care for his community on condition that he guarantee his safety. Pouget also offered to build an irrigation canal with experts brought in from Algiers. These were offers that the mayor could not refuse. Once accepted, they made him an active participant in the social-development component of "pacification." For the military, acceptance of medical care was a sure sign of the success of "pacification," an error in understanding the sentiment of a rural native population long deprived of access to health care. Once the doctor established a practice in the village, he was approached by the mayor to tend to a wounded FLN combatant. The doctor agreed but did not report the incident to Pouget. Yet Pouget, too, acted in a manner similar to the doctor's by letting a young FLN member go free after interrogating him. This was a student from an Algerian immigrant family in France, where he had been recruited by the FLN. Pouget detected in him more ambivalence and disenchantment with the war than commitment to a cause, and so instead of remanding him to civil courts, he claims to have given him a pass and money before releasing him. He noted, however, the anti-intellectual character of his interrogator-interpreter Gonzales, who made fun of the student and took the student's brand-new hiking boots, which he exchanged for his old shoes, a common practice among French soldiers when they captured a well-dressed combatant. Pouget knew of Gonzales's racism but appreciated the torturer's propensity to sharing a meal with one of his victims, or tending to the wounds he inflicted upon them.[29]

This "pacification" method was inspired by Sun Tzu's dicta that "The art of war is based on duplicity," and "those experts in the art of war subdue the enemy without combat." However, it was not coercion-free. In reality, Pouget hunted down FLN combatants or members of the OPA. He allowed his own young informant to be killed and presided over numerous torture sessions. He was denounced by an FLN leader, Si Haouès, who operated in Pouget's sector, for his systematic use of torture at Bordj de l'Agha, the model of "pacification." Like Argoud, Pouget justified torture. He distinguished between "*La Question*," the medieval ordeal, which he felt was not practiced in his sector, and torture by other means. Invoking the example of half wild pigs driven to eating their own testicles, he argued that people are attracted by the "bestiality" that torture unleashes. Torture resides in human nature. In a narrative typical of officers in Algeria, he first claimed he disapproved of torture. Nevertheless, he felt that "in war, the measured use of violence is neither pure nor simple. It is a mixture of the horrible and the sublime, of ambiguity and contradiction in the image of men. In each one of us, there is the Meteor [his torturer in Vietnam], the lurking beast, and the cook [the compassionate Vietnamese who brought him food], the angel." By upholding a religious view of a dual human nature, evil and good, and assuming that it is universally accepted, Pouget relativized his use of torture. Besides, since torture is located in an organic, human nature, he was absolved of any guilt. He admitted to being complicit in torture "each time in my battalion, a man, disarmed, was brutalized."[30] He also admitted to inflicting torture on two prisoners whom he executed on the public square.

Under Pouget, torture sessions followed a standard pattern with a few modifications. The suspect was stripped naked except for his underwear, and made to kneel down. He was then whipped until he screamed with pain in order to snatch from him the "smallest bit of information." As the victim's face became distorted with pain, which Pouget read as hatred, he wondered if his own face, too, was at that moment distorted by hatred. In the small torture chamber "the smell of sweat mixed with the smell of suffering was nauseating." All the while Pouget, using his split-personality literary device tells himself, and has the narrator say about him,

> when you are alone tonight in your room, you'll be ashamed of yourself. Tonight, when you are face to face with God, you won't be able to pray. . . . He [Jean Marie] has become an abstract character, unreachable; a man of bronze that cannot be moved. . . . *Houach* [the torturer] is the arm that inflicts suffering. Jean Marie [Pouget's alias] is the master of suffering.

Continuing to speak of himself in the third person, Pouget qua Jean Marie writes: "He does not feel the slightest pity. He observes coldly, he analyzes lucidly the condition of the prisoner to determine the moment when he is ripe. . . . A purely technical problem." Pouget's enlightened view of "pacification" resulted in making formerly tortured suspects in turn torture other prisoners under the supervision of Gonzales, the Pied Noir torturer-overseer.[31] However, Pouget kept his men from watching torture sessions or entering the torture chamber known as the "interpreter's room," a name connoting that torture was a tool for breaking the language barrier with the victim by breaking his silence. Seeking to be fair to the last, Pouget promised two prisoners to spare their lives if they gave the name of the FLN leader who had ordered the killing of his intelligence officer. However, after they broke, they had nowhere to go except to enlist in the Harka, but he made sure they would not be admitted. Knowing that the men would be killed by FLN operatives should they return to their community, he released them to their death.

Pouget's version of "pacification" was no less and no more abusive than that of Argoud's. For him, as for his contemporaries, "pacification" was not only a part of the war; it was a war in its own right. His conception however was based on a rejection of the ideology of "French Algeria" as the moving force behind "pacification." He rightly felt that this was precisely the ideology that caused the "revolt." The only way "to open the road to constitutional reform that would enable the government to conceive and implement a realistic policy, and for the army to adjust to such a policy as well as carry out useful operations, is to blow up the system like a rock that obstructs a path."[32] Like Racinet, Pouget objected to those in the military and civil administration whom he felt were not keen on reforms. However, judging by the coercion that both officers exercised or condoned, doubt can be cast on how different their views really were from those they criticized. For reforms to be initiated sucessfully, the military had to give up guns and uniforms: It had to become a civil force.

Pouget still felt that given the proper number of troops (about a thousand), he would have locked the population in his sector into surveillance such that no FLN combatant would have been able to function and no villager would have joined the FLN. This was tantamount to saying that every individual in the sector would have been kept prisoner in his/her home.

Pacification Hollywood Style at the 5ème Bureau

Unlike the preceding theorists and practitioners of pacification who focused on the psychology of force, Henry Descombin created reality. He was assigned to the "pacification" section of the 5ème Bureau located in the Châteauneuf neighborhood in Oran. A second section, located in downtown Oran, focused on reports sent to the military, tracts, speeches, and articles for the military morale-boosting paper, *Le Bled*. The Bureau's reality fabrication included making up sociological studies for various journals as well as for "official reports." Descombin reconstructs his year at the Bureau from a brief diary written on his way back to France at the end of his assignment in 1960. Like the previous officers, Descombin blamed the top brass for not believing in the revolutionary-war theory that they had elaborated. He felt that the Bureau, a factory of military and at times civilian propaganda, suffered from a lack of direction: "Each unit acted as it pleased. The sector acted differently with different constituencies; at the command level, the chief called the shots." Descombin was aware of the centrality of torture, emphatically noting that

> about torture, when I became a reporter for the 5ème Bureau, wherever I went, everywhere, I inquired about it discreetly with trustworthy people. And almost everywhere, at least at the sector level, I heard the same generalities, or saw the same nondescript construction set a bit apart. I no longer see the need to challenge anyone to support or prove the contrary.[33]

Descombin's statement speaks to a generalized use of torture with its recognizable, albeit innocuous-looking chambers. Descombin's role as an intelligence officer doing propaganda makes his story insightful on two counts: First, it depicts a Bureau largely left to its own devices, with a staff that mocked the top brass as a pastime, or on occasion discussed the future of Algeria with a prisoner. Second, it documents the propaganda war that the French military waged against its own troops.

Descombin's description of the Bureau's ineptitude corroborates Albdelhamid Benzine's evaluation of the tracts that were dropped in the *maquis* near Tlemcen. An incident illustrates the manner in which work was carried out at the Bureau. A reckless mistake once created a social incident in Oran when a sack full of fake francs destined for action against the ALN, and bearing information about how to surrender, was ripped open by passersby who rushed to stores to use the bills as payment for merchandise. This caused the army to reimburse the hapless merchants who could not refuse to honor military bills, false or genuine. When it did not fake studies, the Bureau did carry out surveys on demand. One of these, focused on morale, angered officers for telling an unexpected story about soldiers being neither "enthusiastic, nor revolted, but either resigned or indifferent, waiting to go home."[34]

Descombin's major achievement was a propaganda film entitled *Fraternité*, entirely staged, using a burned-out farm as a setting, grenades thrown by soldiers, and officers playing their roles as actors, reading lines from a script under the direction of the Bureau's staff. In an uncanny way, it prefigured the film *The Battle of Algiers*. There was a surreal aspect to a documentary about a real war when cameramen were barred from big battles with the ALN. The film was "a false reconstitution of a military operation" in which role reversals between Bureau's staff directing, with barely contained delight, commissioned officers to act as officers in an operation. The subtext was the real conflict within the military between various ranks and categories of men that unfolded in the open under the guise of acting and directing. The Bureau was rent by the same conflicts that opposed career and enlisted soldiers, officers and the rank and file. It was however, mostly staffed by noncommissioned officers. That officers would take time to act in a film destined to be seen by their peers as well as the public connotes a somewhat intriguing sense of the real. That the war itself had to be staged represents a degree of detachment that conveys levity rather than sense of purpose. This episode illustrates the recurring complaint among conscripts as well as many officers about the lack of clarity of the meaning and direction of the war. The staged "attack" on a farm with live grenades, and the ensuing fire were expected to bring out the inhabitants of a surrounding hamlet. However, being used to such events, none of them showed up. The Bureau interpreted this as a sure sign that the strategy of "pacification" was really working.[35] The direction and production of *Fraternité* epitomize the French imagination of the war where the real and the fictitious, the past and a desired present, intersected in a complex dreamlike configuration. Staging a military operation on the theater of war with expectations that real villagers would show up as spectators-actors, extras in a film about them, but without them, and against them, spun threads of fantasy around the concrete reality of the villagers ensconced in the folds of a massive material history awaiting its own resolution.

Descombin, the producer-director, recounts that his interpreter took him to his hamlet and showed him the land that had been taken away from his fellow villagers under King Louis Philippe and Napoleon. This was a case of tangible imperial history, grounded in the topography of land and memory, dwarfing the fictitious war of French Hollywood. To add another twist to this battle between image and reality, history and fantasy, Descombin came up with the idea of using, out of context, a quotation from Emir Abd-El-Kader, the first hero of the Algerian resistance to the French invasion of 1830, on the benefits that might result from a rapprochement between French qua Christians and Algerians qua Muslims. A French voice substitutes itself for the Emir's, seeking to be the voice of peace but signaling a second defeat of the Emir's. This conjuring up of the ghost of the Emir in a region where he had reigned symbolized a French desire for a defeat of the FLN/ALN coded as the Emir's modern heir.

Playing with history in staging visual propaganda creates its own counterpropaganda. By invoking the figure of the Emir, mimicking his voice, and disembedding his words, the film was a call to war for the Algerians. The symbolic boomerang effect was neither discussed nor anticipated. With this film the strategy of "pacification" took on a new twist: It no longer aimed at some cultural caution in the manner of Pouget, but stirred up the memory of one defeat in order to bring about another. In this sense, the film represented not only the liberties that French propagandists took with the meaning of the past for the Algerian population, but also a remarkably arrogant, if not inept, use of the history of colonization to salvage its continuation in time. To the Emir's quotation spoken in French and reembedded in the context of French propaganda, the Algerians could easily invoke the Emir's other quote: "Algeria is Arab and shall remain Arab." However, for the young men at the Bureau, their mission was to "show why French presence in Algeria was necessary as well as the achievements made by the army for the benefit of the population now and in the future." Furthermore, since the war had been defined as a "reconquest," it made sense to summon up the ghost of the Emir to impress upon the Algerians the notion that theirs was a lost struggle, and that France was unbeatable.

Finally, Descombin, an image manipulator, was not sure that the war was really a war: "Algerians called this a war; they exaggerated a great deal [because] of their Mediterranean temperament." Another twist in the saga of the revolutionary-war theory occurred after Descombin returned to France, a disillusioned man. He found use for the theory in an unlikely terrain: the theater. He helped to design a program to use the theater as a medium for the development of culture among the public in East Paris in 1963. As he explains: "For eighteen months, I became exceptionally interested in an information operation of *quadrillage*, parallel hierarchical structuring, mobilization, ultra sensitization of public as well as private institutions, and minutely designed inundation and saturation programs on the eve of the performance."[36] The transition from the theater of war to the "real" theater was made without a hitch. From Descombin's perspective, revolutionary-war doctrine had peaceful application: It called for agitation and mobilization. Culture, especially its spread among the masses, meant warfare. The most remarkable aspect of this transfer of military strategy lay in its new geographical field of application: France. Just as the Algerian War spread to France where torture, arrests, and antiwar demonstrations took place, the "pacification" doctrine was also exported, albeit in a cultural domain. Symbolically, this represented a deterritorialization and reterritorialization of the antisubversive doctrine paralleling the disembedding and reimbedding of Emir Abd-El-Kader's quotation. More important, it was a continuation of an unsatisfying war at home. What happened to this new cultural propaganda for the sake of culture is not told, but my suspicion is that it was short-lived.

This chapter demonstrates the extent to which the "pacification" military doctrine, when left indeterminate and ambiguous, allowed for the interchangeability of operations and psychological action. In spite of the various methods used, "pacification" was psychological action by other means. The door was open for officers at the sector level to carry out "pacification" according to their own political commitments while upholding the doctrine's basic principles. The men experimenting with "pacification" methods used totalitarian techniques of population control calculated to instill terror in their sectors. They found inspiration in an eclectic and ill-digested assortment of ideas originating in Hegel, Sun Tzu, Kemal Ataturk, and T. E. Lawrence, in addition to Mao, Lenin, and Giap. Various cultural and political images served as a constantly floating background to experimentations with "pacification"—a sign that officers desperately searched for an ideological anchor to the war outside of justifications of the Empire in terms of itself. The cult of the "great man," a sort of uberman who risked his life, merged with the idealization of political figures flaunted for their toughness.

Colonel Argoud's method was the most extreme and the clearest in its conception: Unbridled physical force "pacifies" the mind; torture is its bedrock. It is in Argoud's practice of "pacification" that the role of torture can best be delineated. He avoided the "it saves lives" argument, falling back instead on the most normalizing of all justifications: It is in the nature of man to torture. With him, the torture chamber lost its confined space and merged with the theater of operations, thus becoming an operational environment. Racinet's and Pouget's methods attempted to humanize "pacification" by indulging in a military version of cultural anthropology. But the military use of the natives' culture only confronted these officers with their own cultural identity fastened to the colonial system they defended. Hence Racinet found it appropriate to use Christian doctrinal themes to "pacify" Muslims. His method additionally exemplifies the ideological appropriation of the concept of decolonization turned into a "revolution" to salvage colonial rule. And Pouget made amends for the sexual misbehavior of his subordinate à contre-coeur. Yet, torture and psychological coercion were inescapably at the core of this rehabilitation of colonialism through the manipulation of the culture of the colonized.

Algeria's identity constantly shifted in the military's imagination: French, Oriental, Muslim, revolutionary, primitive. In this sense, there were many wars going on in Algeria—as many as the images of Algeria that officers held in their minds. In the end, "pacification" was indistinguishable from fiction as shown in the staging of war scenes with live officers acting their own roles. For the villagers held virtually prisoner in their homes, the theater was dead serious. It is instructive that three out of the four officers raised questions of conscience albeit that they answered them in a presumably realist military fashion. The next chapter will explore in greater detail the banality of torture made possible by the pacifying realism of the military.

PART II

ETHNOGRAPHY OF TORTURE

Chapter 5

DOING TORTURE

Understand? It [torture] is the only way we can learn something.
—(A recalled soldier), G.M. Mattéi, "Jours kabyles," *Les Temps Modernes*

FROM THE END OF 1956 onward, torture was rationalized, professionalized, and systematized under the leadership of committed generals, the most notorious being Jacques Massu, Maurice Challe, and Raoul Salan. Torture became a standard method for screening individuals picked up during roundups, identity checks, or operations. It was not only inflicted to get confessions, but also to obtain information of any kind. Any suspected nationalist activity, no matter how inconsequential, was grounds for subjecting a suspect to torture. Furthermore, torture served an important social-psychological function: It was used to overcome the psychological obstacle that cultural difference created for the military. In this sense, torture was also an instrument of resocialization of prisoners into obedience and, through proper psychological action, collaboration. However, within the framework of the counterrevolutionary war doctrine, torture turned out to be the link between the subversive and antisubversive war. While military battle usually destroys the body, torture disturbs it, dismantles it in order to reach the mind, open it, and pave the way for its rearranging. Yet, torture did not sit well with the French civil authorities' notion of decorum. It thus led a double life as a crucial weapon of the counterrevolutionary war, and as an elusive practice semantically hiding behind various euphemisms that sought to protect its existence. It was known to be practiced routinely, yet it was just as routinely denied. This chapter attempts an ethnography of torture, the core of the terror matrix without which counterrevolutionary strategy could not be implemented.

Speaking Terror

A distinguishing feature of state terror as managed by the military was the special language in which it was spoken—a vocabulary developed to code the meaning of terror-inducing methods. Coding was a method of justification carried out through concepts, such as "pacification," that evoked a state contrary to what happened in real life. It was supplemented by the frequent use of euphemisms. This special vocabulary helped, among other things, to create a psychological distance between the practitioners of terror and their practices. Two different tongues were spoken, one by officials, the other by the practitioners of torture. Officials developed a grammar of torture that connoted the existence of a state of terror. Recurring terms such as "exactions" evoked a collection of actions ranging from torture to the destruction of people and property. Their use indicated that the speaker was aware that something was wrong with the prosecution of the war without specifying what it was. Concepts such as "cruelty" were more precise. Yet in the original language, *sévices* could also mean "brutality"—an imprecise term. The grammar of euphemisms contained torture by sinking it below the level of consciousness, repressing its disturbing intrusion on the oft displayed stage of France's "civilizing mission." It released torture from its special status as an uncivilized method and floated it as one of many anonymous "exactions," reflecting the namelessness of the war itself. French officials and the press alike referred to the war as "Algeria's incidents" (*événements d' Algérie*).[1] The French word *événements* is also synonymous with "events" and "happenings." Algeria was thus eventful, but not at war. Similarly, nationalists were dismissed as "rebels" to be eliminated or indigenized as *fellagha*, an Arabic term (meaning "head-splitters") borrowed from the Tunisian nationalist struggle. Tangled up in this orgiastic name-fixing was the French unease with acknowledging Algerians' identity. A French department (Algeria's official status) was inhabited by *French* people. But every French person knew that Algerians were not quite French, yet they needed to be thought of as such for France's own sense of identity. As Prime Minister Pierre Mendès-France put it in 1976:

> The often repeated phrase, "Algeria is France" must be understood in the context of what I said at the time. When we held discussions [for independence] with Tunisia—since this is the precedent that I had set—or with Indochina, we had protagonists. In Indochina, it was Ho Chi Minh with whom we negotiated in Geneva. In Tunisia, there was the Bey to whom I made the Carthage offer to form a government with whom I could negotiate. In Algeria, there was none of this, no counterpart, no notable families, no military chiefs, nothing. We had destroyed them one after the other for generations. Juridically and practically, Algeria was France.[2]

This imperious act of self-assertion erased Algeria's political identity. That Mendès-France's view was incorrect is less important than the amnesia that it connotes. Algeria could not have a nationalist leadership—even though it did—because all the men capable of it had been killed long before. Algeria was juridically French because it was socially dead. The act of summoning up another France out of the ashes of the old Algeria cancels the intrusive, as it were, acknowledgment of the existence of a pre-French Algeria.

The euphemistic grammatical code wove together imprecise words and loaded others that gave the listener the opportunity to choose his/her meaning. Robert Lacoste, a onetime resident minister in Algeria, spoke of "alleged atrocities."[3] Vaujour writes of "pressures and brutality (*sévices*) or of "cleansing" (*nettoyage*). In his 455-page book, the word "torture" appears on p. 356. In seeking to explain away the practice, he strenuously takes issue with critics of torture who compared the French military methods to those used by the Gestapo. He argues that "the French Army does not occupy a foreign territory as the Wehrmacht held France under its toe, stole her resources, and plundered the little wealth she had at the time. And the Gestapo—that of Hitler's [*sic*]—hunted down citizens, deported and often murdered members of the resistance." Vaujour's statement typifies the personal and political amnesic space occupied by Algeria in the French collective psyche. This amnesia expressed itself as denial and dismissal even when the facts of torture were incontrovertibly known to the authority in charge, as was Vaujour. He notes that torture may have happened, but it could not have happened intentionally. As he puts it

> There was no perversion, but occasional lack of judgment; there was no deliberate decision to dig a chasm between two communities [native and colonial French], only revolt at undignified acts committed by both sides; there was no gratuitous will to deal out suffering, only a pressing desire to get information in order to save lives; there was no hatred, only fear.[4]

In seeking to reduce torture to an incidental act born of a genuine desire to save lives, Vaujour is willing to share responsibility for it with the FLN, which he obliquely refers to under the anonymous concept of community. French troops could not inflict torture as part of a military strategy as the Nazis did during the occupation. Any such undignified act that might have been committed was not planned deliberately. It was an instinctive act of self-preservation, of protection of life. Beyond this, torture was used for the sake of knowledge. Other officials, such as Paul Delouvrier, asked for the control of "repressive methods."[5] Prime Minister Guy Mollet, who ultimately had to admit to knowing about torture, still used the vocabulary preferred by authorities all the while justifying the practice:

> Regrettable facts must have taken place at the end of a struggle that can only be understood by those who took part in combat. As for others, I ask them to keep quiet! In a situation such as this, it is not the man who made a mistake who should be punished. Rather, it is the struggle itself that should be

held in contempt. What we condemn is not the struggle, but the fact that prisoners who had been arrested in accordance to the reinstated laws were, without any apparent justification, tortured subsequent to their arrest.[6]

The confused nature of this statement need not be pointed out. It speaks however to the fumbling resulting from the prime minister's reluctance to admit that torture was routinely used in violation of the law.

General Massu, who used torture systematically during the Battle of Algiers in 1957, recommended "coercive methods." The varied vocabulary of euphemism also included "professional errors," and "certain methods peculiar to Intelligence services." The Church (whose views on torture are discussed in chapter 8) developed its own torture vocabulary, referring to "methods that do not respect the other" or "intrinsically bad methods."[7] The concept of cleansing was often supplemented by that of *dégrossissage*, or exploratory torture to determine if the information provided by a suspect was worthy enough to preclude further interrogation. The term *dégrossissage*, means to trim, to rough-hew, which fits well with the notion of Algerians being "primitive," lacking the refinement of French civilization. The indirect and euphemistic language used to discuss torture symbolized a struggle between two views of this drastic method of conducting the antisubversive war: realism and humanism. The tension between these two perspectives was resolved in the Subversive War Training Center (Centre d'Entraînement à la Guerre Subversive)[8] of Camp Jeanne D'Arc in Philippeville where officers were taught "humane torture."[9] Established in May 1958, this center was transformed into a Center for Advanced Training of Infantry Officers (Centre de Perfectionnement des Cadres de L'Infanterie) the following year. According to the notes taken by a trainee, this kind of torture must:

(1) [be] clean; (2) . . . not take place in presence of young [soldiers]; (3) . . . not take place in the presence of sadists; (4) . . . not [be] inflicted by an officer or a person of rank; (5) and must especially be "humane" that is to say, it must end as soon as the guy has talked, and mostly that it does not leave any trace. Considering which, in conclusion, you had the right to use water and electricity. This I have noted down as he [the instructing captain] spoke.[10]

There was another Centre d'Instruction Pacification et Contre-Guérilla at Arzew, which undoubtedly taught torture.

Cornélius, a frequent contributor to *Verbe*, distinguished between "vindictive" or punitive torture, and "medicinal," or investigative torture.[11] Thus language had ceased to convey meaning, and became instead a means of obfuscation. Syntactically, the language used in the Algerian War did away with rules that normally ensure clarity and relate the signifier to the signified to avoid contradiction. To attach the qualifier "humane" to the noun "torture" in the context of pain and suffering meant more than giving this practice acceptance. It emptied it of its political meaning and transformed it into an act of charity. The Intelligence officer qua torturer is allowed a semantic space that sanctifies a politically motivated act of repression by relocating it in the religious domain. This deterritorializing of torture from the context of war also represents its transubstantiation into punishment for sin. As punishment, torture holds the promise of redemption. This tour de force achieved by the Camp Jeanne d'Arc Training School, helped to assuage the intelligence officer qua torturer's occasional guilt, or misgivings. He could now join hands with Father Louis Delarue, a chaplain assigned to the 1st REP in general Massu's division, who provided torturers with the spiritual justification for doing their job. He permitted the fractured consciousness of some of the torturers who disliked torture, but engaged in it nevertheless, to find comfort in the notion that torture was good for the suspect: It rehabilitates him spiritually, and reconciles him with France qua repository of the idea of the good.[12] Father Delarue's thoughts on torture will be discussed in detail in chapter 8.

Intelligence officers in charge of torture developed their own vernacular. It too relinked with France's past in an unbroken chain of memory harking back to medieval times. A victim that had to be eliminated after being "exploited" or "treated" was "sent for wood" (corvée de bois, or wood detail), an expression referring to the obligatory wood-collecting chore that serfs had to do for the lord of the manor.[13] Embedding torture in medieval France succeeds in estranging the torturer-executioner from his act. A salutary psychological distance is created between torturer-executioner and torture-execution enabling a sort of historical alter ego to nudge the existential self to the sidelines at the moment when torture or murder is committed.

Practitioners of torture supplemented the historical vocabulary with the euphemistic terms used by officials, referring to torture as "vigorous interrogation" appropriately described as musclé (lit. muscled), summoning up the image of a torturer exercising his muscles on a victim. Torture was alternately described as "tight" (interrogatoire serré).[14] The adjectival register of interrogations was a means of denying that torture was practiced at all. Information muscled or tightly squeezed out of a victim fell short of torture only if it took place without the use of any of the instruments routinely used by the experts in interrogation. In reality, "muscles" softened the victim as a prelude to torture, which included slicing through the victim's own muscles with a blade, and scorching his chest and arms with a blow torch. The arsenal of euphemistic terms included "coercive interrogation," which in the French language surreptitiously inserts doubt as to whether it is not the torturer, rather than the victim, who was coerced into interrogation. The phrase *interrogatoire sous contrainte* (or literally "interrogation under constraint") implies that the act (and thus the actor) is the subject *sous* (under) the "constraint" of interrogation. Since interrogation is always coercive—no one likes to be interrogated—constrained (coerced) interrogation loses any objective meaning other than one born out of the substitution of the interrogator for the interrogated. This deliberate semantic confounding of the practitioner of torture with his victim allows a shift of responsibility for pain and suffering from one to the other. It signals a working through of the logic of the absurd where the torturer is declared the victim of torture. Captain Joseph Estoup, testifying on August 1, 1962, on behalf of Lieutenant Daniel Godot at his trial for crimes committed when he was a member of the colonists' counterterrorist group, Organisation de l'Armée Secrète asserted that: "I know the rape committed on the officer who is ordered to implement this [order to torture]." The grammar of torture does not fix, but floats meaning in search of a peg from which to dangle it momentarily. Captain Estoup best describes this process in his testimony:

> Mr. President, in military language we say we "do intelligence"; in polite language we say we "press with questions"; in plain French we say we "torture." I declare under oath that Lieutenant Godot, like hundreds of his comrades, received the order to torture to obtain information.

Estoup's candor clearly identified the social adaptability of the coded grammar of torture. It was designed to suit various audiences from the civilian, decorum-minded social class, to the class of bureaucrats in need of semantic cover, and the rough-and-tumble military officers whose commitment to the war required no special linguistic legerdemain. True to revolutionary-war theory, officers committing torture often explained that their goal was to "conquer" the native population. This peculiar notion of conquest was predicated on "the conquest of reams of information . . . by all means necessary."[15] What was a preliminary step soon became the main step as "doing intelligence" was transformed into an end in itself. The conquest of information substituted itself for the conquest of the population.

The Setting: Of Villas, Farms, Candy Factories, and Wineries

The settings where torture was practiced by the French in Algeria were remarkable for their variety. Villa Sésini[16] on the heights of Algiers in the residential neighborhood of El Biar; an apartment building still under construction, also in a residential area of the city; a farm a few miles away from the city of Constantine; an abandoned candy factory and old wine storehouses in Western Algeria; a racetrack; basements of public build-ings; stadiums, cafés; schools (the most notable was Ecole Sarouy in the Casbah in Algiers);[17] and a Turkish bath,[18] when extra space was needed. It is not only that torturers needed to be in places where victims could not be heard when they screamed from pain or that torturers required free-dom to act without being seen. They needed to be estranged from their ordinary environments, to descend into the depth of another physical uni-verse as a sort of conditioning before entering the battle of wills. Their work required dark and secret places, arenas for discharging duties that fascinated and repelled at the same time.

The torture chambers were generally small, stark, and unclean as was some of the equipment used. Henri Alleg, a French communist journalist arrested and tortured for aiding the FLN, reports that he was attached to a "black board, streaked with humidity, and soiled with sticky vomit un-doubtedly left over by other 'clients.'" In some cases where the torturer was not the officer who did the interrogation, the sight of blood smeared on the face of the victim was discomforting. Alleg recounts a scene where his interrogator, Charbonnier, exclaimed "Watch it! He is going to spit! . . . I don't like it. It is not sanitary."[19] Similarly, a torturer operating in Paris on an Algerian student ordered him to "take your handkerchief and wipe off these bloodstains; I don't want to see them."[20] The odd feeling of revulsion at the sight of blood and spit slices through the consciousness of the torturer/interrogator as an incongruous mishap in a scene of pain and suffering. It is a sort of coup de théâtre, an out-of-character admis-sion that the professional role played is unsettling, and the task distaste-ful. The weakness usually attributed to the victim at his breaking point contagiously and unexpectedly reappears in the interrogator's revulsion at the sight of the blood and spit. The torturer is taken aback by the in-terrogator's request. Alleg remembers his torturer, Erulin, responding: "So what?"[21] It would be tempting to make a case for the humanity of the in-terrogator, assaulted by the inhumanity of the pain inflicted under his command and repulsed by the product of his own acts. But this was an-other, more confused, emotion that was triggered in the interrogator: cleanliness and tidiness in the midst of gore and filth. A job well done must be clean. A man about to be asked questions must be presentable so as not to offend the dignity of the interrogating officer. Interrogation, os-tensibly the aim of torture, had to proceed as though torture had not taken place. At the heart of torture is its denial.

The stage where torture was performed was usually at the end of a cor-ridor or below ground. A torturer describes his as a cellar accessed through a "wooden trap and a ladder, dimly lit by a small bulb . . . with one tiny transom, 50 cm large, that lets in a little bit of air." In the bowels of the earth, twelve cells, two-by-three meters, were built in two rows of six each, resembling "cages." The cells were windowless, their floors made of cement, walls covered with breeze block, and their thick wooden doors secured with large bolts.[22] Henri Alleg's cell was similar, with no light except from a small transom.[23] Prisoners were not allowed "to communicate with one another, sing, or pray in a loud voice." The chamber was equipped with two water pitchers, one field telephone, and a funnel: "everything to inspire a salutary panic [in the prisoner]."[24] The geography of torture settings and chambers reflected the professional soldier's convoluted perception of his job. Soldiers doing intelligence do torture. They do not fight in the mountains, tracking down guerillas; they fight in the recesses of urban and rural spaces, extracting every bit of information possible to consign to files, usually kept in a space adjoining the torture site.[25]

Often the torture space, instead of torture, kills the prisoner in a graphic instance of the unconscious wish for death becoming material. A number of these deaths occurred in old wine storehouses—windowless constructions—where prisoners were left overnight, in an atmosphere saturated with sulfuric gas accumulated from the remnants of fermented alcohol. The religious motif ran through these deaths like filigree, calling out the crusader in the torturer who snuffs out the lives of the prisoners without dirtying his hands, simply by allowing alcohol, the object of a Muslim taboo, to work its invisible magic on the Muslim body. Deaths by asphyxiation in wine storehouses occurred too many times to be the outcome of mere chance, or dereliction of duty. These incidents were reported by the Commission for the Safeguard of Individual Rights and Liberties in July 1957. The first incident took place at Ain Isser, near Tlemcen, in western Algeria, on March 14–15, 1957, where 101 "suspects" were locked in four wine storehouses that had been abandoned in 1942, measuring 3m × 3.50m × 3m, with an air capacity of 30 m³ each. The men were introduced into them from a hole at the bottom. Air was supposed to flow from a small opening at the top. On the morning of March 15, twenty-four men were found dead in one storehouse, seventeen in another. Survivors felt ill, and told of having tried in vain to call for help by making noise. The lieutenant in charge, a Curutchet, covered up his crime by transporting the dead bodies to a "forbidden zone" (or no-man's-land) and dumping them in bushes, apparently in an effort to pass them off as dead guerilas. The second incident took place in Mercier-Lacombe, near the city of Mascara, also in western Algeria, a wine-producing region, on April 16, 1957. Twenty-three villagers had been rounded up after a military operation and locked in a wine storehouse on orders from an intelligence officer, Sub-Lieutenant Lefebvre, in punishment for "their arrogant attitude." The following morning all the suspects were found dead of asphyxiation from SO_2. The third incident occurred in *Mouzaiaville*, near the city of *Blida*, southwest of Algiers, where twenty one "suspects" also died of asphyxiation in a wine storehouse on June 27, 1957.[26]

The repetition of these peculiar incidents caught the attention of military authorities who discussed them in their correspondence. Death by gas emanating from wine fermentation encapsulated attacks on religion and race in a double and troubling imagery: Islam was disrespected and sullied; the mimicry of Nazism snuck in like a cutaway in a film where flashbacks to the past settle the past in the present in the blink of an eye, as if the past had always been there. The memory of Nazism was alive on both sides of the war: among those who supported its excesses, and those who did not. But the amateurish (albeit deadly) mimicry of one of the most unsavory Nazi methods intruded buffoonlike on the consciousness of all who heard about it. The FLN was naturally sensitized to the repetition and mimicry of Nazi methods when, in another context, it accused the military torturers of engaging in forced sterilization of prisoners. Deaths by asphyxiation had occurred in less historically laden circumstances, with a mere wet handkerchief applied to the face of a victim tied to a chair.[27]

Nevertheless, in a December 1957 report, the Commission for the Safeguard of Individual Rights and Liberties (whose charge it was to investigate allegations of wrongdoing) described the problem of the deaths in wine storehouses—but refrained from detailing others—"because it will undoubtedly be brought up at the United Nations." However, the Commission quoted extensively from the report on the wine-storage deaths written by one of its members, Governor General Delavignette, who found the cover-up by the guilty officer disturbing. He was also disturbed by the silence of the Algerian population in the town of Ain Isser. He worried that such silence might be indicative of a feeling of terror or lack of confidence in the government. Nevertheless, he excused the deaths and their cover-up as due to the youthfulness of the officers, whose ages ranged from twenty-two to twenty-six. Remarkably, the governor took this opportunity to express his own resentment of a "system that is vitiating everything. What system is this? A system in which our own authorities are struggling, in the midst of a confusion of powers, a confusion which resulted, among other things, in the Muslim population not knowing whom to trust." He subsequently derided the Army Corps in Oran for dismissing the deaths at Ain Isser as an "error" and issuing a toothless note merely prohibiting the use of old wine storehouses for the detention of suspects.

The Practitioners of Torture

The Algerian War was a vast socialization agent for the 500,000 soldiers, most of whom came from France. Despite the large number of troops involved, military authorities constantly complained of being shorthanded, insufficiently equipped, and/or inadequately trained to fight a counter-subversive war. Did this logistical situation explain troops' cavalier attitudes toward torture? At any rate, explanations of the systematization of torture, and the wanton disregard for life evinced by French troops, have often focused on the young age of the soldiers, and/or their lack of experience, which prompted them to engage in repugnant behavior. Yet, the inclusion of torture in training curricula and its subsequent professionalization did not diminish the brutality of the practice or its indiscriminate use; nor did it improve the attitude of the torturer toward his victim.

In theory, torture was the domain of the intelligence officer. In reality, men other than intelligence officers took a hand in it. No matter what the method was, torturers were generally young men in their early to mid-twenties, more often with the rank of captain, enlisted or conscripted. As indicated in chapter 2, many of them were also veterans of the Vietnam War who had been prisoners, tortured or subjected to psychological action to convince them of the justness of the Viet Minh cause. Torturers included Pied-Noir conscripts, with an ax to grind against the native population, as well as Algerian rural men armed by the military to fight alongside the French: the Harka (sing. Harki). Some of these had been captured by the military, tortured and subjected to psychological indoctrination.

Torturers' social profiles varied greatly, and do not appear to be determining factors in their behavior. One soldier who found himself a vocation as an efficient torturer had started out in life as an average French citizen with a ninth grade education, married, and the father of a little girl. When he was sent to Algeria, he had requested work in a Section Administrative Spécialisée, but was assigned to a DOP, under the most secret conditions, to become an intelligence officer. He honed his skills as a torturer by trial and error, innovating on occasion. The captain of his team, who had been a prisoner in Vietnam, thought that they were "pioneers" in the field. The captain also believed that their job was "to convince the *fellagha* that our cause is just. The Vietnam experience will help us."[28] Torture was the means by which to *convince* Algerian nationalists that French colonialism was a just "cause."

The young French torturer with the ninth-grade education was interviewed extensively after the war by a journalist-historian who published his testimonial in a book that the French government initially banned. The torturer wished to remain anonymous, and for the sake of clarity, I will refer to him as Aldop. His description of the organization of the DOP in which torture was practiced invoked a painstaking attempt to capture information in the same way as a spider "patiently weaves its threads in a very tight web." The intelligence officer qua torturer saw himself at the center of a task that was bigger than himself, but essentially began with him. The intelligence that he extracted from detainees was to "be disseminated immediately to all levels at the same time that it is immediately exploited." Aldop further points out that "without it [interrogation], no information, therefore no more arrests, and renewed FLN activity." Since the adversary was but a "fly that could not be crushed with a bulldozer," torture was the most appropriate mode of fighting men-flies; it was the foundation of the "counterrevolutionary war."[29] The imagery of the fly fits in well with that of the spider web woven by the DOP. Torture transforms people into insects that can be caught *naturally* and done away with. In this way, it diminishes the danger that they pose, the fear that they provoke among the troops.

Other torturers were less reflective than Aldop about the role of their work in the war; they were wrapped up in their racial prejudice and locked in a contest of wills with their victims. Sergeant-Major Murly, when faced with a prisoner, immediately "tightens his fists. . . . He evinces a total lack of psychology combined with an unacceptable raw brutality that makes him unsuited for an interrogation mission."[30] Confessions and diaries of former torturers are replete with descriptions of men that resemble Murly, for whom the exercise of muscle was more important than the ultimate purpose of getting information.[31]

Training in torture methods theoretically remedied the missing skills. Nevertheless, the professionalization of torture conveyed the message of its acceptance as a war weapon on a par with training in shooting, disabling an adversary, or crawling under barbed wire. Professionalizing torture caused it to become routinized. Torturers exchanged information about what technique worked best, shared innovative ways of doing their work in order to refine their skills. Torture was thus pulled out of the shadowy semantic domain in which it lived, and thrust into the forefront of the everyday life and world of the professional intelligence officer. It was inserted into the lives of soldiers whom it tied to one another in a chain of solidarity that transcended the usual fraternity born out of serving in the army. In this sense, torture functioned as more than an instrument of government: It reached deep into the military body, which it tied to the political system in a way that supplemented the esprit de corps that normally characterizes the army. Torture was the source of social integration that melded the political and the military, and consumed the structural transformation of the state into a militaristic institution.

Torturers were not mere sadists. They ran the gamut from ordinary (like Aldop) to highly educated men. General Paul Aussaresses, General Massu's right arm, and torture practitioner, was writing a dissertation on Virgil when he started his career in intelligence. Nor were torturers monsters devoid of feelings. Officer Aldop could feel revulsion at the sight of a gazelle he hunted, deciding to never hunt again. He described his experience in vivid terms:

I shot at the gazelle with my revolver, almost point blank. . . . We stopped the jeep and ran to the animal struggling to get back on her legs. I moved the barrel of the revolver close to her, and saw her beseeching eyes staring at me intensely. Her delicate head rolled back and forth, her legs kicking in the air. She would not survive. I knew it. I know when death approaches. Nevertheless I could not pull the trigger. Then the gazelle moaned like a wounded man.[32]

Whether Aldop was reading in the animal the pain he inflicted on men in his torture chamber I cannot tell. He had feelings for an animal, although he did not have them for the men he tortured. Aldop's hunting experience denotes another dimension in the job of torturing: relaxing and appreciating the beauty of Algerian scenery, just like tourists do.

Doing Torture

The career trajectory of a torturer begins with initiation by observation. Learning by watching is a prelude to learning by doing. A professional recounts his encounter with torture: "For the first time, I watch a torture session. Volunteers are not in short supply. Kicks, fists rain on the prisoner. Everyone shouts 'are you going to talk?' Officers calmly watch the interrogation, ready to receive the confession. I am standing apart, slightly nauseated, but unable to move; finally, the prisoner talks." As a hardened captain put it to his team, "The first time, it is always difficult. But think of the results."[33] The main purpose was to shorten the length of the war in a mental operation that configured the war as an economy of pain. The more unsustainable pain is, the greater the likelihood the mind will crack and information be obtained.

The first time a soldier engages in torture is also remembered well. It is the direct encounter with the prisoner that unlocks the door to its routinization. Two men face each other for the first time: "The first prisoner is looked at almost timidly. We know very little about him, only that he had run at the sight of an approaching patrol, a charge sufficient to establish presumption of guilt." The first time torture is performed also fixes details about the victim: "He was about twenty-five years old, short. He looks at us with terror in his eyes, and we observe him, a bit embarrassed. We wonder how we should convince him to talk when we did not even know how the prevailing techniques were supposed to be applied." The chamber looks "sinister." "Our shadows draw ominous silhouettes on the sweaty walls."[34] The gloomy atmosphere is buttressed by the torture equipment ready to be used. What goes on in the torture chamber is only one aspect of the torture situation, which includes a series of interlocking

acts calculated to sustain a climate of fear and uncertainty, absolute powerlessness and dependence on the whims of the guards, incrementally
weakening the tormented body with hunger, unsanitary conditions, and
insufficient or lack of care. In an illegal CTT, fear was induced in detainees
by having a torturer hurriedly enter their room every twenty minutes and
haphazardly point to the next one of them to follow him to the torture
chamber. Hearing the screams of the tortured partially drowned by dance
music already filled detainees with dread. Fear was also sustained by the
frequent visits of a hooded torture victim from outside the CTT brought
in to identify more "suspects."[35]

Sexy-ing Torture

The first order is in every session—evocatively called in French *séance*, a
term associated with psychoanalysis—the technique that leads the patient
to *talk* about his life, revealing the secrets locked in his unconscious mind
to strip. Another meaning of the word *séance* evokes the occult, the para-
normal, thus adding another layer to the extraordinary nature of what
goes on in a torture situation, and the voyeuristic impulse it triggers. The
prisoner must strip, and strip fast as the *séance* must begin immediately
to prevent any symbolic equality of exchange from taking place between
prisoner and torturer. Stripping before men still fully clothed is the first
step toward weakening the prisoner's psychological defense. Although
this technique is generally used with all prisoners regardless of culture (as
was also the case in Nazi Germany), the French torturer views it as "the
most terrible of humiliations for an Arab whose prudishness is well
known."[36] Torture in Algeria was turned into a weapon for fighting native culture. Stripping kills two birds with one stone: It tears up the prisoner's cultural garb, and assaults him with exposure to French culture assumed to be compatible with (the torture of) nakedness. The torturer's
comment cuts through the political-military meaning of torture to expose
its actual function as a tool of resocialization, even if momentary, of the
native qua Arab into the ways of the colonizer. But stripping is also sexually laden. It transposes sexual gestures, acts, and innuendo from a strip
club to the torture chamber. Thus sex is always present in the torture
chamber whether the victim is a man or a woman. The sexing of torture
is deeply grounded in the recesses of the torturer's psyche. He either lets
his fantasy loose by coercing his victim into sexual positions, and by
touching him, or prefers to contain it, gazing, ogling, instead. The sexing
of torture is also charged with the traditional conception of gender that
inferiorizes women. In the torture chamber women as well as men must
strip. Like a woman, the man is exposed to the gaze of other men who ag-
gressively survey his anatomy with their eyes or their hands.

Although the torture chamber was the preferred setting for stripping, prisoners were also stripped during military operations, out in the open, in full view of curious soldiers eager to see how torture was practiced. On occasion, an officer would step forward and try his hand at torturing the publicly exposed flesh. Aldop, who resented being denied a tent for doing his job privately, without distraction, recounts his experience during a military operation, just as an ambush of the FLN yielded a few prisoners: "I grabbed the first man by the lapel of his uniform jacket, pushed him against a tree menacingly. . . . Strip, quick! He obeyed and fell to the ground in pulling his pants down. I heard the imbeciles [French soldiers] gathered in a semi circle behind me laugh. Tie him to the tree! I take a few steps back, pointing my gun at him." The intrusion of onlookers who did not belong to the DOP, as well as the open-air setting changed the dynamics of torture, and aborted its ritual simulacrum of sex. It caused the torturer to lose his touch. "I lose my patience; I garble my questions giving the prisoner time to slowly regain his confidence." Right there, in the field, he decides "to use the field telephone," which provided electrical current. The crowd around the naked prisoner gets larger and more vociferous: "Look! He's putting the wire to his tail," says an onlooker. Aldop depicts another scene he witnessed in the DOP unit he worked for in western Algeria where masculine identity is used as a tool of confession against an FLN man who had infiltrated the DOP unit and had not cracked under torture. Warrant Officer Tarle, in charge of torture, threatened the victim with "crushing your balls and you will never be able to fuck. Do you hear me? Never again. You like women, don't you? It's normal; I do too. When I am finished with you, you will no longer be able to jump them. You don't know how I am going to castrate you." He subsequently ordered his coworkers to "separate his balls." The soldier simply pulled on the electrical cord that was still wired to the victim's testicles. Tarle wanted to "smash them with one bullet." Taking his time, he aims carefully and shoots. By design or accident he missed his target. He cocked his gun a second time, dead serious. The victim, against whom no torture method had worked, finally cracked, "dripping with sweat."[37]

This episode graphically exposes male understanding of masculinity, and its use in war. The presence of women in men's imaginary mediates their relation to one another at the exclusion of ethnicity or race. The insertion of women at the core of masculine potency, and the threat of their elimination, anoints the *couilles* (French slang for balls) with a power that torture by all sorts of devices fails to achieve. Castration by smashing the *couilles* released the victim's tongue. A man-to-man suggestion about women's place in the male imaginary did the trick.

Abused men seldom describe their sexual humiliation and manipulation under torture. Torturers are understandably more forthcoming with information, although they too shrink from recounting the marks of sexual difference that set them and their victims apart, and which they no doubt sought to expose. Native men are circumcised, and this must have figured in the sexual handling of torture. An Algerian student, Benaissa Souami, recounted his torture in a Paris police station in these terms: "They forced me to sit on one of the bottles. I screamed all night. . . . In the morning, he [the torturer] had found a new method: hit me on my sexual organ with a wooden ruler."[38] *Sitting* prisoners on bottles was an old torture method used against the Viet Minh. The bottle perforates the intestines often causing death. The French text uses the word "sex" for "sexual organ," connoting the invasive and totalitarian nature of sexual torture. From the standpoint of the victim, his whole sexed being was not only on display, but played with. His identity as a male was violated. To be "forced" to sit on bottles connotes an unsettling image of a man who is embarrassed to say that he was raped with bottles. Another student, Moussa Khebaili, recounted that "electrodes were applied everywhere on my body even in my mouth, anus, and my heart. . . . I still have scars today . . . around my anus, on my sexual parts, on my left breast, and on the inner side of my forefingers." After passing out several times, he was made to kneel, and was taunted by a policeman who told him, as he put his foot to his lips, "I just came out of the john: I am going to give you a taste of French shit." The student does not explain whether the policeman acted on his threat, although he mentions that he was still kept naked. A third student, Khider Seghir, tortured in the same place as the previous two, angrily wrote: "Then, they kicked me and punched me, and grabbed me and twisted my arms and legs. They even shoved their fingers in my behind."[39] These are rare moments when men were willing to describe, even if in evasive language, the sexual core of torture. These manual methods of sexual gratification-degradation were more common than is realized.

The late Abdelhamid Benzine, recorded a testimonial detailing a gruesome and powerfully evocative scene of the rape of a male prisoner, from one of his former fellow inmates of Lambèse Internment Camp, notorious for its abuse of detainees. Prisoner Amor had been accused of passing to another prisoner a small piece of cigarette paper containing scribbled news about the outside world:

> Guard Dem . . . brought the irons and chains. Other guards fastened them to Amor's arms with his wrists pinned behind his back. The same Dem . . . wrapped the chain around Amor's arms and pulled it with force. Amor lost his balance, but guard Fra . . . straightened him up by grabbing his testicles. He squeezed his parts with both hands, twisted them and pulled on them as if he wanted to unscrew them. With a violent tug at the chain, Dem . . . caused Amor to fall down. Fra . . . kept unscrewing his testicles. Another

guard brought a broomstick, and forced it in Amor's anus. He pushed it as far as he could. The other guards entered the fray with their clubs and their feet.

Stripping was routine at Lambèse as was the deliberate humiliation of arranging the toilet holes in such a way that prisoners had their genitals exposed to one another when relieving themselves. As soon as a group of detainees was brought in, the first act of degradation was to make them strip in the prison yard and walk though a gauntlet of guards who pummeled them along the way. Assembly would take place in the camp main yard, with prisoners standing naked in snowy or scorching hot weather. Observing prisoners naked was only one part of the degradation ceremonial. The camp chief guard, a Pied-Noir who spoke broken French, would announce: "You're in Lambèse. Here, no more men, only broads; here, only one John. It's me! . . . Here you're the women, we are the men." While hitting a prisoner, a guard would taunt him about his sexuality: "Fag! Say it! Say you're a fag! I'll show you how I'll f— you. Sissy! Fag! Coward!"[40] The sexual content of torture and of the general physical abuse of prisoners was aggravated by the social background of the guards, many of whom were first- or second-generation working-class immigrants from southern Europe. They shared with settlers a common contempt for native Algerians. Although social class is not necessarily a predictor of the use of torture, it sheds light on the mixture of anxiety, fear, and defensiveness that guards experienced when faced with natives challenging their colonial privileges no matter how limited these may have been in relation to the wealthier settlers.[41]

Electricity is the best known of the torture methods used during the Algerian War. Electrodes were applied on the right ear and left testicle before current coursed through the body jerking it, at times flipping it in the air, while the victim screams, in a forced simulation of the orgasm. Sometimes, a captain urges his team to crack a "recalcitrant" prisoner by pointing out, "He has to have a weak point. Find it!"[42] Where better than in the simulation of sex to find the weak point? Other methods included immersion in a bathtub to near suffocation, forced ingurgitation of water with a funnel (and at times a hose), sleep deprivation, exposure to the sun with no water or food, often in a hole dug in the ground in which the victim was buried up to his neck, or the "tourniquet," a violent whirling of the victim tied to a tire hanging from ropes fastened to the ceiling.[43]

Torturers do not write about their own sexual feelings, which they conceal behind jokes and project onto their prisoners to whom they attribute a perverse enjoyment of their sexual torture. They may, on occasion, talk among themselves about the sexual nature of interrogation. In helping a comrade improve his torture skills, one intelligence officer said:

An interrogation is like making love. An essential rule is to take your time, know how to hold yourself long enough till you reach the crucial moment, keep up pain till it reaches its climax. Most of all do not go beyond this threshold or your partner will die on you. If you can motivate him, he'll talk. Well, you know, orgasm. Otherwise, he'll pass out. If you love women, lieutenant, you should understand.

Imagining the victim as a sex partner permits the torturer to "feel the exact moment when the prisoner will crack."[44] The hackneyed notion that the torturers were sadists does not capture the full meaning of the relationship between sex and torture. Reenactment of sex in the torture chamber also goes far beyond a simple, albeit real, gratification of sexual fantasy. It enables the torturer vicariously, through sight more than touch, to reassert his masculinity as he coerces another man's body to mimic sexual pleasure-agony. A naked male body evokes a narcissistic satisfaction of maleness. Subjecting the naked male body to the electrically induced throes of simulated sex with orgasmlike vibrations and ejection of fluids qua erections from the mouth as well as the anus and the penis fulfills a function similar to that of male impersonators. A man watching another man forced into an impersonation of other men participates in a staged celebration of the phallus. The torture chamber is often crowded with other men, all watching and partaking in this small "world of penises."[45] However, the colonial situation intrudes on sexual torture as a source of surplus perverse pleasure. The native man is a politically despised subject: a "rebel," and a member of a culture held in contempt. He also exists in the mythifying consciousness of the colonizer as a sexually potent male who fathers an infinite number of children and often appeals to many a French woman.

The imagery of sex and electricity wired men's minds with the fear of impotence.[46] Native men expected to be rendered impotent; soldiers watched how or whether that might happen. The painful simulation of sex the native man is subjected to does more than degrade him, or humiliate the man in him. It desexes him. And it is this paradoxical situation in which the narcissism of maleness is enmeshed with a deep-seated contempt for the colonized man that gives the torture chamber its complex sexual texture. The performance of the simulation of sex for an audience of soldiers binds them in the all-gratifying brotherhood of narcissistic men as much as it flatters their sense of power over men reduced to sexual objects of both desire and contempt. The narcissistic core of the torture-chamber-strip-club ties torturers-gazers to the tortured in an unspoken consumption of (homo)sexuality. The aggressive sexual torturer crosses the line from gazing, gawking, to thrusting his hand, not an object, into the victim's anus. He is in direct contact with the inside of the victim's sexualized-desexualized body. He turns him into *his* sexual *object*, his eunuch. An excess of simulated sex penetrates and eradicates sex in the native's mind but arouses it in the torturer's.

A similar situation prevailed in Nazi camps where prisoners were whipped at the post, naked, and urged to scream with each whipping. The alteration of the color of the buttocks, their flinching and twitching reminiscent of "coital" movement excited torturers and guards who often masturbated while beholding the spectacle of pain. The screams of the victim were found to increase the intensity of the sexual arousal of the torturer and his acolytes. Klaus Theweleit suggests that screams under torture whipping were welcomed by torturers and their superiors as they fulfilled two functions: On the one hand, torturers and watchers fancied their victims' screams to be their own as they masturbated; on the other hand, they perceived such screams as the victims' reexperiencing (on command) past sexual pleasures that they now stole from them and made theirs.[47] The public nature of this display of sexual excitement, and the private nature of masturbation are not contradictory. Rather, they signal the absolute power of the torturer to destroy the privacy of the victim, and his triumphant will to discharge himself of sexual desire by experiencing it in himself as he destroys it in the victim publicly. His interior and his exterior become one. The power of scopophilia and the torturer's power to make it happen, turn it on and off, whip and stop whipping, set electricity to the victim's genitals and feel its sexual current coursing through himself as the pain courses through the victim is as mesmerizing as it is unbound. It is not that the torturer is necessarily sexually repressed, although he might be. The torture *séance* creates its own dynamics; the reenactment and mimicry of sex creates its own fascination. Voyeurism, the excitement of a sexual spectacle on command, and sheer curiosity, combine to make torture an event to look forward to in spite of everything.

Tools of simulated and reenacted sex include electricity produced during military operations with a field telephone and called in slang *gégène*, bottles, the hand, wooden rulers, metal bars, chains, whips, clubs, and anointments. The students referred to above, who had been arrested and tortured in Paris in 1959, were subjected to the "skewer" (*la broche*), a term that suggest roasting a chicken, or a lamb. The victim's hands and feet are tied together and a metal rod is slipped through the knots so that his trussed body hangs down. The rod is placed on a table. In this position, electrodes are placed on the victim's genitals. A police officer doing torture explains to the victim, "We are going to take your blood pressure before fucking you."[48] There is also reference to the use of Dolpic, an analgesic pomade used in France in sports injuries to stimulate the blood circulation through the release of heat. Directions for its use warn against its application to soft tissues as it can cause severe burns. Cheap French pornographic stories allude to its capacity to cause heightened pain/pleasure when used on the anus.

It is not clear from the student who angrily mentioned that "they even shoved their fingers in my behind" whether this was done by policemen acting together or severally. Allusions have been made to guards entering the tiny cells of selected prisoners and sexually abusing them. Moments of candor as those displayed by the group of students are hard to come by. An Algerian auxiliary of the French military, a Harki, reportedly said to a member of the ALN just captured in a mountain village, "You're lucky I just got married, otherwise I would have sodomized you."[49] The homoerotic dimension of torture by whipping or electricity does not necessarily mean that all torturers or their acolytes are homosexual. Although (repressed) homosexuality is an important component of torture, especially under conditions of fascism, it is not the only explanation of the systematic infliction of torture. Just like their counterparts in Nazi prisons, the Frenchmen who engaged in torture in detention camps knew there were no limits to what they could do to their prisoners. They operated in a milieu that set the tone for abusing prisoners, and took advantage of their freedom to act as they wished. That they indulged their sexual fantasies goes without saying. That many of them derived sadistic pleasure from the pain they inflicted on their victims is also incontrovertible. It does not make all of them clinically sadists. Sadism as an explanation, plausible as it is when a blowtorch is set to a naked chest,[50] only excuses generalized acts of cruelty that are politically motivated. Where military authority prevailed, and the goal was to win the war by all means necessary, torture provided the means to satisfy the goal, and some.

Attraction to the native man's body must have been diffuse as it surreptitiously escaped the bounds of the torture chamber. Desire was barely contained in a conscripted seminary student, Alain Maillard de la Morandais's description of the physical appearance of a group of young Algerian men, members of Commando Georges, who fought on the side of the French: "Fit, tall, their leopard camouflage trellis tightly hugging their bodies, their knives hanging at their hips, they exude a male self-assurance; they look handsome and ominous. They must make girls and petits-bourgeois shudder with excitement."[51] Reference to the masculine petits-bourgeois remains pregnant with sexual meaning that the author does not take time to explicate.

The former FLN combatant Louisette Ighilahriz describes in a manner similar to the male students' that a bottle was thrust into her, but does not acknowledge it as rape. The stigma attached to rape for women as well as men, the shame it connotes, the indignity of public exposure compound the painful memory of it and act as so many gags on the victims. However, on occasion, where sexual torture alters the genital functions, men are ready to talk about it, as was the case with the young man I mentioned earlier, who, years ago, told me angrily, "The French broke my testicles." He felt that this was too high a price to pay for what he received in return after the war ended. Considering the systematic nature of torture, there are surely thousands of men and women who were so deeply affected by sexual torture as to be dysfunctional in one way or another. The torture chamber was the great gender equalizer. Not only were women raped in the same manner as men, with objects, but the body parts that the torturers targeted were the same: breasts and genitals. Nevertheless, more than men, women's bodies were subjected to greater indignity inside as well as outside the torture chamber. The rarely reported practice of forcing members of the same family or the same sex[52] to have intercourse with one another compounded the humiliation.

Although torture was discussed in the media, and civil as well as military authorities were also willing to address it, rape was not. The notion that French soldiers could rape women embarrassed French authorities more than torture did. Rape was not seen as part of torture, as torture. Presumably, torture was justifiable by the requirements of the "counter-revolutionary war," but rape seemed more gratuitous, and thus more perverted. Besides, troops had their *bordels de campagne* (country bordellos) and should not have had to rape women. However, rape was seen by its perpetrators as punishment, as reprisal on women's bodies, a humiliation of both women *and* the men in their families. Rape was in reality a method of torture as will be discussed in the next chapter.

Body Parts

Genitals, the material of sex, were not the only targets of torture. The morphology of torture included vital organs such as the liver, the heart to which electrodes were often attached, the stomach, the face, especially the eyes, hit with ropes. There were cases of death from a burst liver.[53] Ironically, the liver holds symbolic significance in Algerian lore. Called *kebda* in Arabic, it represents the locus of affection for close relatives, especially children. The torturer calculated his blow, with his fist or a kick, to hit the liver several times causing excruciating pain. The liver was also a central part of French medical practice as small ailments were often attributed to a dysfunctional liver. The anatomy of the body was thus surveyed with the same precision as a surgeon's outlining with a pencil the spot where he should cut. On the surface of it, slaps could not be termed torture. Yet when administered with the full force of the hands of two large soldiers, standing on either side of the victim, slaps deafened the victim momentarily, disoriented him, and could cause him to fall, provoking more damage. Like slaps, kicks and punches constantly rained on the naked prisoner. He was kicked and punched in the office of the officer overseeing the "interrogation," on his way to the torture chamber, after he was released from electrical treatment, on his way to his cell, and on his way to being transferred to another locale. Kicks and punches are meant to sustain pain, to prevent it from abating, to keep pressure on the prisoner's body. Kicking an open wound, punching an already swollen eye *after* the victim has been subjected to torture by electricity, immersion in a bathtub or basin filled with water, forced water ingurgitation with a funnel that swells up the body beyond recognition are more like the coup de grace than just inconsequential physical violence. Slapping, kicking, and punching also accompany and compound the disorientation suffered by solitary confinement, blindfolding, and near starvation.

By analogy, hitting a victim in the stomach, also referred to as "the belly" in French, coincides semantically with expelling information qua food. It was illustrated by the colloquialism used by a policeman/torturer with a prisoner: "Throw up everything you have in your belly."[54] Often body parts are possessed as trophies, or talismans linking the proverbial "savage" to the antisubversive warrior. Jacques Puchu, a former conscript, described one comrade among many, "wearing a *fellagha*'s ear as a fetish, dangling ostensibly on his chest."[55] Algerian body parts formed an organic chain extending from the nineteenth century (when French troops collected the ears and heads of their victims) to the 1950s.[56]

Where the body refused to release the information that the torturer searched for—and this happened with many nationalists—experimentation with truth serum was attempted in order to quickly access the mind. However, the same simulation that gave sexual torture its stagelike quality, overlay the properly called truth serum *séance* with acting drama, expectant voyeurism, and coup de théâtre. After being injected with Pentothal, the patient-prisoner "recounts in detail an extraordinary attack that had taken place in Algiers a few weeks earlier, killing twenty soldiers and destroying a [military] post." However, upon verification, it turned out that the "patient" had invented the attacks. This victim may have been faking the "truth" effects of Pentothal as he continued to speak of numerous bloody attacks in which he took part. Interestingly, the narrator attributed the dissembling to Pentothal having unexpectedly—this was an experiment—opened up the gates of the prisoners' dreams of aggression against the French. The truth sought about the FLN by injection released the far more lethal truth buried in the unconscious mind of the colonized man qua prisoner. As the narrator put it, in a different context, there are times when torture reaches its limits and "our technique fails against the patriotic convictions of the [FLN] militant."[57]

Witnessing Torture

The grammar of torture is as rich as it is specialized. Not only does it provide semantic rules of protection for the practice; it also evokes images that connect the animal domain to the human, in smell and sound. Witnesses report shrieking screams that reminded them of a "pig being slaughtered," or the howl of a savage beast. Torture released the beast in the man, on both sides of its divide: The torturer is immune to the sight of suffering; the terrorized victim can no longer retain the sound of his exploding pain. Although the sight of the victim excites the curiosity of the witness, the smell of pain repels him. Witnesses depict a strong smell "characteristic of tortured bodies"[58] that combines sweat with the dampness of the chamber. Most certainly blood and the live electrical wires released odors that mixed with the smell of sweat, urine, and so forth. The torturer sweated as much as the tortured, a smell originating from the exercise of muscles and shouts. Besides, the torture chamber was usually small, dark, and poorly ventilated, causing smell to linger and stick to men and things. And it was dirty. It was cleaned once in a while when there was a lull in interrogations—for there was a queue for torture, as for checking out of a store—with *crésyl* (a cleansing liquid antiseptic) poured in the area where the board was located, or in the middle of the chamber so that the liquid spread in all directions, making cleaning easier.

The torture *séance* usually takes place at night to enhance its gloom and foreboding. For a prisoner expecting to be tortured, the night fills her/him with additional fear of things that might go wrong under cover of darkness. Torturing at night ensures discretion and catches the prisoner "at his most vulnerable." A man

> pulled from his first stage of sleep at around 11 P.M. is already in a state of inferiority. As soon as he arrives [in the torture chamber] we ask him to strip. . . . Our presence terrifies him even more [than the chamber]. There we are, standing squarely on our feet, with our sleeves rolled up, sure of our power.[59]

Torturers do not sleep. One of the images used by torturers evokes labor pains preceding the birth of a child, an image at odds with the gender of its users who, in the Algerian War, happen to all be men. Nevertheless, in their minds, their actions facilitate the release of information. A prisoner is subjected to extreme pain, just like a pregnant woman must endure labor pains as she gives birth to a child. The body of the prisoner must be worked over, and worked through. The imagery used by the torturer helps him to appropriate the ownership of the information he seeks to get. Because it is he who inflicts pain and suffering, and makes the prisoner "labor," *he* has *produced* the information. The pregnancy metaphor enables the torturer to look upon his actions as producing life. After all he is involved in a life-giving process that marks the familiar justification of torture: It saves lives. The metaphor also denotes a trivialization of the prisoner and the information he is assumed to carry in the recesses of his being. The prisoner is but a vessel through which the torturer works. For a long time, women were also seen as mere carriers of the infants implanted in them by their husbands. When stretched to its extreme, this metaphor results in a routinized conception of torture in which information loses its value altogether. After doing his job, the torturer expects *any* information, good or trivial, from his victim. Torture becomes a ritual that prisoners must undergo, a rite of passage to death or incarceration, releases from the DOP being few and far between.

The ritual is solemn enough to impress its witnesses. After shouts, screams, howls, screeches of the mechanical lever of the *magnéto* (or generator) sending electricity through the body of the prisoner, and lulls during which the prisoner passes out, the ritual comes to an end when the prisoner breaks down and decides to talk. Silence ensues. No one speaks. Everyone seems to be dumbfounded. "Suddenly all that can be heard is the oppressed breath of the man who just delivered his secret, and who undoubtedly hates himself."[60] The victim at times breaks into tears. The threat of death that hovers over the torture chamber as in a game of Russian roulette dissipates. At least for the moment, life prevailed, the child is born. Then, the questions begin, and more answers are written down.

A competing metaphor used by torturers imagines torture as an exercise in cleansing the prisoner of his anti-French actions. It rests on Pascal's notion that gestures of worship pave the way to conversion and faith. Similarly, repetition during torture of expressions of regret for anticolonial acts was meant to anchor guilt in the flesh. Pain is a way to political redemption. For this to work, the prisoner must first and foremost be made to feel guilty. Furthermore, he must be convinced that the colonial system treated him well. Torture, in this sense, undermined the very basis on which it stood: that the prisoner was presumed guilty and thus, as a real or potential enemy, he could be subjected to pain and suffering. The very language in which the torturer spoke to the prisoner set the stage for resistance: The prisoner, no matter his age, was addressed as *tu* (instead of *vous*), a familiar and demeaning form of address when used with strangers. The personal pronoun imprisoned the torturer in his presumptive superiority, just as it locked the prisoner who understood the French language well enough—and this type of man was a crucial figure to be rallied to the French side—in his struggle for dignity and recognition as an equal.

To return to screams, torture was meant to beat the "primitive" out of the failed Frenchness of the victim. The Algerian was seen as having been created by France, but failing to become French. Torture was meant to remake him into an obedient French colonial subject. An echo of this endeavor is found in the French lore of the werewolf. A nobleman, Bisclavret, metamorphoses into a wolf after losing his clothes as well as his capacity to speak.[61] His howling when in his animal state resembled the screaming of the tortured. Torturers and their acolytes were seldom bothered by the screams of their victims. Although habit may have dulled their senses, screams also formed an important part of their job. They were more fulfilling than the musical and dialogue sounds of the movies shown to paratroopers in the field, some of whom preferred to go torture a few prisoners than sit passively before a screen.[62] Screams were the most tangible sign that a person resembled a beast. By implication the beast was being beaten out of the person. Just like Bisclavret had been naked before becoming a werewolf, the victim is naked in undergoing torture and screaming to make it stop. Before Bisclavret could return to his human shape he had to find his clothes. The tortured regained his clothes only after he broke, and breaking him also often meant turning him into a collaborator-traitor. He did not regain his full human dignity, but a lesser personhood, neither French nor Algerian. Unlike Bisclavret who regained his humanity and avenged himself on his treacherous wife, the tortured person was returned to a virtual animal state of tamed quiescence.

A constant feature of torture *séances* was the *laughter* they generated among their audiences. Men witnessing a man being tortured laugh or jeer. Obscenities were hurled at the victim, naked and posed in often ludicrous positions. Crowds also laughed and jeered at men about to be hanged on the town square in medieval times. However they did not when a man was subjected to torture. For this was a solemn ritual carried out by the Church, and precluded laughter. Presumably, there are many reasons for laughing at others' misfortunes, one of which is the unconscious desire to relieve the tension caused by the sight of torture. Laughing also renders the torture *séance* banal, empties it of its pain, and transforms it into a spectacle. In Paris, some torturers referred to the serial kicking and punching of their prisoners as "soccer." Watching the *séance* was akin to watching a soccer match. Torture is sport.

Torture exhausts the couple, tortured and torturer. Pauses are often taken to allow the torturer time to rest and carry out routine talk about sports, forthcoming furlough, to take a smoke and ritually drink some beer with a comrade. Torture must not rend the fabric of the mundane, the normal. Torture makes itself anew. It fascinates and repulses; tantalizes and appalls. Each onlooker wonders when the prisoner will crack or die, how painful is the electrical shock, or the blow to the genitals. When the *séance* is brought to an end, the onlooker needs time to collect his wits as if he had just watched an engrossing movie before going back to his world, free of torture. A number of soldiers took pictures of torture *séances* not just to send home as mementos, but also to prove that they happened. This prompted the state to prohibit mailing all war pictures outside of Algeria.[63]

Dialectic of Torture: Culture, Identity, and Memory

The man who "does torture" also witnesses its severity and effects. However, the spectacle of pain as such does not move him. His experience has hardened him. As a torture practitioner put it: "We have long lost any sensitivity to moral or physical suffering. This was a requirement of our occupation." He compares himself to a surgeon who "enters the operating room whistling, amputates the patient, and leaves without a care." After having "interrogated" 250 people, Aldop concluded,

> To accept torture, to acknowledge [its necessity], to approve it, and even to inflict it on others is finally not difficult. It's a matter of convincing one's self that the cause is just, that torture is indispensable, and that the end justifies the means. No one is born a torturer.

Nevertheless, he believes that his experience with torture gave him "the right to hate violence."[64]

The encounter between the torturer and his victim lends itself to the Hegelian lordship and bondage metaphor. Where the victim is an active militant, with a strong sense of the justice of his cause, the situation is a heightened contest of wills: the torturer desires the nationalist to bend, the nationalist is determined to resist to death. At some point, pain becomes habit-forming so that the torturer reaches diminishing returns. To break the victim, a number of techniques are used. Then "suddenly, we improvise, we try to break his [prisoner's] vacillating resistance by using some precise information we had kept secret, or by arranging a damning confrontation. The man who wants to talk gets discouraged and reveals everything."[65] When the militant is unshakable, making believe that he is going to be castrated might work. In one instance, the intelligence officer who had watched the torture of a prisoner stepped in, removed the Pied-Noir interpreter (who had interfered with the *séance* by interjecting his own opinion and abuse), and faked a civilized conversation with the prisoner about children and family. He shared a smoke with him, and left him alone on and off to get him to appreciate the lull in pain. The efficiency attributed to this technique of making a prisoner who had resisted severe torture meet the intelligence officer, who had not physically abused him, but pretended to act as an ally against the torturer, might not have worked in all situations. For one thing, intelligence officers often were the torturers. Furthermore, the DOP could barely keep up with the large number of suspects they processed, making it difficult for intelligence officers to take the time necessary to sweet-talk their victims. However, the hot and cold treatment, alternating blows, threats, or simulated executions, with nicely formulated questions was a standard technique of "interrogation." The moments of faked kindness at the end of torture included giving a beer to the prisoner after he talked.

Breaking a committed FLN activist, especially the urban guerilla, was not easy. The intelligence officer needed to work on the suspect as soon as he was captured ostensibly because the FLN had instructed its operatives to resist torture for twenty-four hours, if captured, in order to give the teams with whom they worked time to disperse. But in the DOP torture was a swift and mobile institution. Torturers took turns working vigorously on their suspects day and night, "innovating, perfecting methods to build momentum in questioning as well as inflicting pain."[66]

Resistance to torture evoked different feelings and reactions from the torturers and their teams depending on whether the suspect was a Frenchman or an Algerian. Henri Alleg drew the admiration of young soldiers when his torturers could not break him and gave up as a result. He was however allowed to live. A young Algerian nationalist who also did not break was less lucky. His torturer, a captain, was locked in an endless contest of wills with him, found his defiance unbearable, and decided to execute him outside the DOP locale, in a wooded area. He had him buried in a hole dug in the ground. Since the execution took place in the presence of two of his team members, the captain called his subordinates to his office to explain away his action, arguing that he had had no choice: "This guy did not talk, and without proof, what could we do? We couldn't keep him prisoner. Yet we know he was a killer. I take full responsibility for what happened tonight, and ask that you erase it from your memory. Don't ever talk about it, even among yourselves."[67] Turning the suspect over to justice was felt to be a sure way of getting him released.

Torturers classified their victims according to their degree of education and capacity to sustain pain, the two presumed to be related. A suspect who did not speak French appeared to his torturer as rough or crude—a man manipulated by the FLN to do specific tasks but kept in the dark about the workings of the organization and/or its planned operations. The combatant "hardened by two or three years in the underground" was deemed resistant to torture but breakable. As Aldop put it: He "never talks at the first entreaty. Even when I sense that he is on the verge of confessing, I prefer to let him weigh the pros and cons. Either he will open up totally, or he'll decide to resist to the end. He will not stop half way." In this intense struggle, the prisoner is said in French to "deliver himself totally" (*il se livrera totalement*) or undergo torture with the possibility of death. Deliverance of the self must be whole, entire. In offering the bargain, the intelligence officer must, in his words, "act in good faith" and even make believe that he feels "genuine empathy" for his prisoner: "I am not asking you to betray your brothers [in arms], only to confirm information that we already possess. You are hesitant, and I understand that. However, if I were you, I would allow myself to be convinced. Aren't you afraid of death? Think of your wife, your children."[68] The keying in of the term "brother" that belongs to the nationalists' vocabulary was calculated to overwhelm the nationalist with the *knowledge* that the Frenchman qua intelligence officer possessed. The call to the nationalist to fear death implicitly dismisses his goal, which is to precisely brave death in order to free his country from France. At any rate, escaping torture did not mean freedom. Often the nationalist who talked was not sent to an internment camp. Rather he was "rallied" to the French military through in-depth psychological action and served in the auxiliary troop of the Harka, frequently engaging in torture.

The more educated suspect or experienced FLN cadre, referred to as the "intellectual," caused a particular psychological problem for the torturer. They shared a language that created a closeness of sorts, but the culture sustaining it set them apart. The cultural narcissism that framed the torturer's view of the colonized was challenged by the "intellectual's" rejection of colonial France embodied in his nationalism. Torturers had been familiar with rejection of colonial policies in Algeria by their own: the communists. However, they understood communists to be acting according to the party line, for which they despised them as much as they did Algerian nationalists. In the torture situation, the French torturer encounters a man he perceives as having been *produced* by his own culture, but who stands now as his accuser, often using the language of the Enlightenment against him, discoursing about the rights of man, and justice. Haranguing an Algerian student before torturing him, a police officer in Paris reminded him: "You're going to see what France is all about, bunch of slaves. We taught you how to shit in a hole." The "intellectual" was the subversive man par excellence. At times, he aroused class resentment in his torturer. As the Paris police officer put it: "Go ahead and laugh. I know, I am only a cop, and you, you're an intellectual. Ha! Ha! But that's the old story. Today, *I* am in charge. The reign of the cops has begun." Class also intersected with race as can be gathered from the police officer's outburst mixing anger with inchoate fear. "I hate your race just as I do niggers."[69] To the more professional torturer, the "intellectual" was doubly dangerous: as a revolutionary, and as the symbol of a failed French "civilization" project.

With the "intellectual," the torture *séance* acquires supplemental meaning, and becomes a game of one-upmanship. It is a contest of wits, a duel, where history, culture, and power interlace and separate as ghosts of the past come and go. Winning is the goal, but it is not a private, personal victory that's at stake. The winner redeems the collective history that grounds him; the loser, if it is the "intellectual," loses the fight that gives meaning to his life. He may also lose his own life. This is a struggle to the finish, but with unequal weapons, and where the "intellectual's" mind and body coalesce in a defense of his collective historical community. In the words of a less educated, but efficient and professional torturer:

> They ["intellectuals"] know that they can defeat us as long as they dominate us intellectually. In general, their interrogation begins with a preliminary observation of the other, each keeping his distance and trying to gauge the strength of the other. Skillfully, they try to mislead us by giving us some worthless information to make out what we already know. As soon as the interrogation begins, they speak a lot, give names of dead people or fugitive militants, or tell of an old cache in which we only find useless documents. At times, we ignore the bait hoping the fish will get caught in its own game. With these prisoners, there is only one method: to play a tight game, and never lose sight of the ball. We do not always win the intelligence combat that opposes us to them.[70]

The best way to "pressure" them is to subject them to "depth interrogation" (*interrogatoire poussé*).

In the hands of the intelligence officer who does not respect "intellectuals" as the more psychologically oriented officer does, "depth interrogation" may yield good results. Sustained bodily pain was calculated to break the capacity of the mind to think coherently and thus resist answering questions. Depth interrogation disrupts the organization of thought and shocks the mind out of its secrets. It is the torturer's tool of effectuating the anti-Cartesian operation of relating, connecting body and mind as befits an unconventional war. Death can ensue as it did for one of the "intellectual" leaders of the FLN in Algiers, Larbi Ben M'hidi, who officially died in 1957 by "hanging himself," after several days of interrogation featuring truth serum.[71] Torturers knew that FLN militants wondered about their own capacity to sustain torture without cracking. The *séance* enabled intelligence officers to test the limits of these men's resistance, and break them at the same time. This did not prevent torturers or their superiors from admitting that they had respect for their stalwart victims. By the same token, pushing a depth interrogation of an "intellectual" to the death point eradicated the failed *product* of the French "civilizing mission," and dealt a severe blow to the "subversion." For the nationalist, death without talking sealed his commitment to his cause and to his comrades in arms. Not only had he given them time to alter course, and/or disperse, but he had also defeated his enemy, their methods, and their assumed knowledge of his being. The sense of being familiar with the "intellectual" that the intelligence officer assumed, mediated by the colonial situation, laid a trap for him, which he glimpsed each time he lost one of his prized victims. An intelligence officer could not suspect or understand how the nationalist's culture and experience of colonial rule had shaped the *culture* that French education sought to impart to its subjects. What the intelligence officer *knew* of the "intellectual's" mind was the product of *his* imagination of the dissolving, universalistic power of French culture that, he was convinced, rent asunder all identities, ground them into a pulp, and remade them in its own image. Each "intellectual's" death proved anew that the meaning of French *culture* was subverted from within the colonial system by the torturer who called out in the tortured nationalist the very resistance he sought to overcome. In this sense, torture transforms the body into history that it destroys or remakes.

This is not a simple confrontation between two beings seeking recognition from each other in a Hegelian fashion. Rather, it is a far more complex confrontation between being-in-action and being-in-thought. The nationalist *knows* the Frenchman from his actions, past and present. The Frenchman is sure of what the colonized man essentially *is*. He thinks he made him, even if he has an inkling that his *product* has misfired; he also has dismissed as redundant and inconsequential the colonized man's culture. He perceives the colonized man qua nationalist as an imperfect copy of himself. Torture, bodily pain, will adjust the copy; "rallying" France would be the result of the adjustment of the copy. The confrontation between the "intellectual" nationalist and the intelligence officer, the being-in-action, and the being-in-thought, is unstable. Torture stabilizes it and grounds it in the tormented flesh. However, the "intellectual" nationalist holds a special interest for the thinking intelligence officer. The officer is intrigued by him, the *product* of French civilization gone awry. The interplay of closeness and distance, sameness and difference, may excite the officer's curiosity. The confrontation may turn into a meeting of minds for the sake of self-discovery. The officer qua torturer seeks to understand how a failed copy of himself functions. What if he will find himself, his true self in the copy? The nationalist "brother" may become the French officer's alter ego. France in Algeria, Algeria in France at the heart of the DOP.

Aldop read the diary of a captured combatant whom he had "interrogated." After mining the diary for information about the enemy's morale, he became interested in the man behind the combatant. He was particularly taken by the wistful notes the combatant had written about his female comrade, his long and tiring marches, and his imagining an independent Algeria. All of it written in French when it could have been written in Arabic, which the prisoner knew very well. The prisoner's knowledge of Arabic had been used by Aldop to translate captured FLN documents. Wanting to *know* more about the prisoner, the officer held nightly interrogations-conversations with him in the basement of the DOP building where torture chamber and prisoners' cells were located. He discovered that the two of them could discuss Montesquieu, Verlaine, and Lamartine. Before long, Aldop realized that both of them dreamt of a future of Algeria "free of capitalists." Soon, Rabah, the prisoner, sowed doubt in the torturer's mind. The officer mused: "I no longer believed so strongly in my cause. Consequently, the suffering I inflicted to get confessions appeared to me to be less necessary. All the Algerians I tortured reminded me a little of my friend. I started becoming less efficient."[72] One day, Rabah told his interrogator that the translation work he had been ordered to do for him was worthless as he would never translate a valuable document. This was an act of subversion at the heart of the DOP. But the officer had now crossed over to the side of his victim. The psychology he used against the "intellectual" nationalist boomeranged. In-depth interrogation of an "intellectual" nationalist brought the officer back to the basement, night after night, like Shahriar to Shaherazad in the One Thousand and One Nights, to come face-to-face with his ALN uniformed prisoner qua himself. This identification with the prisoner turns the age-old identification of the captive with his captor on its head, thus completing the consummation of the cultural narcissism of the officer qua defender of French "civilization." Were it not for the discovery and analysis of the *French*-written diary, none of this would have happened. The language of the diary revealed the humanity of the "intellectual" nationalist, and seduced the intelligence officer, as the image of Narcissus reflected back his love for himself. However, the conversion led to the intelligence officer "question-(ing) the cause that I defend." His superiors began to suspect him. And as was customary at the DOP, he was transferred without any explanation to another DOP some distance away. Before leaving, he and his prisoner memorized each other's addresses and promised to write each other at war's end. In a tradition of the military gathering souvenirs, Aldop asked his prisoner to autograph his diary. Interestingly, he was allowed to leave his DOP with the diary that should have remained in the prisoner's file.

Perhaps this was an inevitable (albeit temporary) end to the career of a torturer who took his job seriously, and did it efficiently. His expertise and experience were such that he claimed he could tell exactly when a victim would break, or recognize the torture method used just by listening to the pitch of screams. Intimate *knowledge* of the effect of pain and suffering may, under some circumstances, bring the torturer so uncomfortably close to his victim that he starts identifying with him/her. The process evolves

in stages, ranging from the officer engaging in the predictable police interrogation game of simulating anger, telling the prisoner that associates
have already talked, arranging a confrontation, to playing at being an empathic officer who understands the rules of the nationalist military. Entering the logic of revolutionary action during interrogation may backfire
at the point when the intelligence officer takes a human interest in his prisoner. The doubt that the officer started to experience about the meaning
of his actions occurred after he read his victim's diary, and placed himself,
during interrogation, in the role akin to that of a therapist listening to his
patient. Interrogation finally acquired its full French meaning of a *séance*,
a special one, at that, with the therapist learning about himself by listening to his patient. It was as if the interrogator had fallen in love with his
victim. Transference of desire, a splitting up of the self—the French word
dédoublement, doubling up, is more accurate—into torturer and victim,
and the exotic estrangement of being a native while remaining grounded
in French culture, combined to shake the certainty of Aldop's view of his
role in the war. This outcome is all the more noteworthy since the officer
had often wondered whether a bond could develop between torturer and
tortured. He had seen some of his victims come back after their release to
see him, or bring offerings of dates for his visiting daughter.[73] His identification with Rabah was also made possible by the interest he evinced in
the culture of the colonized. He had made the effort of studying Arabic
and claims to have made friends among the local population. Aussaresses,
too, felt a (cultural) commitment to bury the 134 bodies of men killed in
the aftermath of an FLN attack against a mine at El Halia, near Philippeville (Skikda), according to the Muslim ritual, with their faces turned toward Mecca.[74]

The cognitive dissonance created in Aldop by torturing and witnessing
death, yet nurturing friendship among people similar to his victims was
the occasion for a number of rationalizations. Torturing was made necessary ostensibly to "save lives." As torture became routinized, and thus
divorced from the immediate concern of saving lives, Aldop found himself arguing that the institution to which he belonged, the DOP, in effect
saved the lives of prisoners who would otherwise be brutally tortured by
less professional torturers.[75] It is evident that all intelligence officers did
not necessarily question their duties or doubt their mission to the point of
identifying with their victims. Those who opposed torture were not its former practitioners. General Paul Aussaresses, a professional of torture who
caused the deaths of many men and women, defended the practice and
did not regret it several decades after he had engaged in it.[76] And torture
can become habit-forming, hardening a man's heart and turning him into
a pain-producing machine, making the case of the officer who started
doubting his mission all the more remarkable. To avoid addiction to tor-

ture, Aldop recommended that a torturer not do this kind of assignment for more than one year "or risk becoming a sadist."[77] In other words, he felt that enjoying the pain of others was the result of practice, not an emotional condition.

There is something about Aldop's view of degrees of expertise in the practice of torture that rings true. A simple brute going after the flesh of the prisoner may get some results, but hardly understands the meaning that his victim may attach to what he/she has revealed. Nor does the unsophisticated torturer understand the political context that informs the significance of the intelligence he collects. For the latter, his job is to make the prisoner crack and answer questions, any questions. One such torturer made a young Algerian talk, asking him to confirm that a café owner was a nationalist. The prisoner acquiesced, to the delight of the torturer, who knew that the café owner was an undercover agent working for the French intelligence services. The torturer laughed, secure in the notion that torture works. This episode is testimonial to the banality of torture, which delinks its use from any search for intelligence.

The relationship between torturer and tortured presents itself in different modes and varies with the "expertise" of the intelligence officer. However, it is always laden with memory and history as they shape identity. In general, the prisoner faces the torturer with massive difference: he speaks a different language, desires an Algeria without France, and may even think differently. Each sees the other as the antithesis of himself. Some Algerian prisoners were reported to repeat consecrated Muslim formulas on their way to the torture chamber, or when facing their torturers. On the other side of the torture divide, the history of France is conjured up as pain it inflicted on the Algerian body. General Aussaresses had the Battle of Valmy, which took place in 1793, in the back of his mind while torturing an Algerian in 1956. An intelligence officer recalls Nazi Germany where he had been tortured as he prepares to torture an Algerian student. At times, the memory of the Resistance is invoked in an inconsequential thought that wonders whether the FLN was comparable. This means that the prisoner rarely appears as a man or woman except perhaps when electrodes are applied to his genitals to simulate "sex." Even in this case, his man-hood or her woman-hood is less important than his maleness, or her femaleness. His sexed body, electrically prodded is stimulated for pain. The prisoner is a being overlaid with historical significations: A colonized man, he signifies the reach of France's empire, across the Mediterranean, across cultures and religions. There is a thrill in being on a mission to observe, break, and remake the human material of the Empire.

Outside the torture chamber, Frenchness is omnipresent. Prisoners walking in a DOP yard trigger comparisons with the French in the minds of the staff. Rabah, the ALN prisoner, "had fine features that exuded intelligence. His uniform was clean, denoting a sense of hygiene uncommon among prisoners."[78] This comment resonates with psychological warfare methods that included hygiene lessons as part of the process of brainwashing. The reconfiguring of the Algerian rebel's mind began with the cleansing of the body in *the French manner*. Techniques of the body, the French way of treating the body, began with reconditioning the rebel body with torture. After the edges of rebellion were rounded, and the ideas of revolution washed away in blood and tears, the body was ready for new methods of hygiene as a precondition to *thinking French*, thinking of the colonial war as a counterrevolution, as well as a new revolution, as will be discussed in chapter 6.

The preceding has shown that torture was widespread, systematic, and mobile, taking place during operations. It also reveals that sex, including rape, is at the core of torture. The use of portable generators to provide electrical current anywhere—on the battlefield, during operations—underscores the significance of sex and sexuality to the intelligence officer qua torturer. Was it absolutely necessary to strip combatants during operations and set electrical current to their genitals? There were other methods that could have been used. But the essence of torture is sexual. Sex was understood to be the fundamental, most efficient way of making a combatant or suspect talk. The sexual component of torture in the hands of a professional torturer such as Aldop was no more and no less than a routine aspect of a method of interrogation. In the torture situation, in an enclosed setting, however, the ritualized simulation-performance of sex with the stripping of suspects, attachment of electrodes to their genitals, rape, and the frequent smashing of testicles raise a number of issues. First, torture satisfied the conscious or unconscious male torturers' voyeuristic-narcissistic desire to watch the male body simulate real sex. Second, the simulation-stimulation of sex was predictably calculated to humiliate as well as desex the Algerian man's or woman's body through electrical shocks that represented a paroxysm of excess sex. In the hands of the most determined torturer, the victim's body was to become unsexed. Third, in the torture situation, cultural identity, memory, and history coalesced around pain and suffering. In this sense, torture assumed a resocializing function. In torture, more than pain is taking place: A lot is said by the torturer and the audience as members of a dominant culture to the victim, and a lot is not said that is nevertheless pregnant with meaning. Breaking the silence of the victim was the first step toward rebuilding him as a "rallied" man. Torture helped to condition the mind for brainwashing after it traumatized the body, as was shown in chapter 3. Torturers' attitudes varied according to their victims' degree of education. The "intellectual" combatant or militant was the object of scorn as well as cultural fascination. His existence brought out intelligence officers' desire for cultural estrangement as well as inchoate self-discovery. The risk was that the officer as torturer could lose commitment to his task, and begin to see torture with the eyes of his victim. The Lacanian insight into the psychology of the self and the other, expressed as "Why can't you be like me" transforms itself into "You are like me; I am like you." Such occurrences may have been rare, but that they took place at all speaks of the limited capacity of torture to sustain itself indefinitely without some identity resolution. It is true that Aldop, after an ebb in his activities, reverted to torturing in his new assignment. However, the moral of his story was that torture does not entirely eradicate doubts about its legitimacy in the very mind of the torturer.

Chapter 6

WOMEN: BETWEEN TORTURE

AND MILITARY FEMINISM

When I endured the pain from my torturers' blows,
I was sure that we no longer belonged to the human species.
—Djamila Boupacha, *Djamila Boupacha*

She takes herself for Joan of Arc. . . .
She wants Algeria's independence!
—Maurice Patin, *Djamila Boupacha*

REVOLUTIONARY-WAR theory did not disaggregate "population," a crucial element in its structure, by gender. In 1957 military strategists filled this gap as they became increasingly aware of the active participation of women in the war on the side of the FLN[1] as exemplified by the arrests of female urban guerillas in Algiers. They found in the ideology of "women's emancipation" a weapon of choice and an opportunity to open a new psychological and political front that expanded their "pacification" doctrine. Targeting the Algerian family, they initiated a campaign that brought a quasi-feminist military ideology to *douars*, resettled villages as well as city homes.[2]

Military feminism adjusted antisubversive techniques of psychological action to focus on women as the molecular units of the population friend-enemy. In its fundamentals, the military gender strategy sought to use women as its Trojan horse to do its bidding in the intimacy of the family under the banner of a "new" Algeria. Bringing about a new woman was to complement General Salan's project of engineering a new man as discussed in chapter 3.

The rhetoric of "women's emancipation" purported to liberate women (from their cultural norms deemed beyond the pale) just as it sought to "protect" them from the FLN. The overwrought colonial theme of the "oppression" of Algerian women that preceded the war facilitated the military's strategic interest in women, and obscured the fact that the war was a defining moment for women.

This chapter examines the dual and internally contradictory antisubversive war strategy subjecting women to terror tactics on the one hand, and, on the other, targeting them for a military version of feminism aimed at changing their lifestyles as proof of their commitment to continued colonial rule.

Women as Antisubversive Allies

The army's strategic interest in women stemmed from its assessment that the FLN was having a positive impact on the Algerian family, especially in matters of marriage, and was thus changing gender relations in the right direction for women, but not with France as a sponsor.[3] The discovery in 1957 of an FLN document detailing a plan elaborated by Zohra Drif,[4] a captured militant, to organize an underground women's network made these incipient changes ominous, and convinced the military of the importance of its counter offensive to redirect any such changes to suit the goals of the war to keep Algeria French.[5] With the help of monographs on the Algerian family as well as Islam, military strategists sought to target women. Faced with the prospect of a "possible renaissance" of the Algerian population,[6] the army found it necessary to revise the colonial stereotypical conception of women's roles in the family for tactical reasons. At the same time, it upheld the view that the Algerian family needed changing to approximate an idealized French family. Military instructions warned that "the absolute subjugation of the wife is but a fable for the benefit of those foreign to the family."[7] The point was to "expand" women's influence from the family to the larger society, but in accordance with "pacification" objectives. The discovery of this strategic significance of women was informed by the prevailing military quasi anthropology, taught at the Centre d'Instruction Pacification et Contre-Guérilla, that "due to their lack of contact with foreigners," women had given Algerian society its social coherence by preserving its core values steeped in a common Berber cultural heritage.[8] Therefore, targeting "women's society" was akin to a genuine conquest, as well as an attack on the very foundation of Algerian society. Some realists in the military felt that this was probably the time to reform native family law, but their suggestions were timid, and did not quite fit it into the "pacification" strategy, which was military in essence, but used social change as a ploy.[9]

The military gender strategy followed the outline of the antisubversive war doctrine. The conquest of women was the "intermediate stage" between military destruction of the OPA and return to civil life.[10] It called for a corps of women drawn from both army and society gathered together under the name of Equipes Médico-Sociales Itinérantes (Mobile

Socio-Medical Teams), EMSI. Teams were theoretically comprised of one medical doctor and three female social workers, one French, two Algerian, however it was not always the case that all teams had a doctor, or native women. Although military women were included as a way of ensuring that the new corps was military in nature, the majority of the women comprising this corps were drawn from civil life. Initially recruited in France, among women with a grade school diploma, they were appointed and paid by civil authorities in Algiers who placed them at the service of the military. Specifically known as Adjointes Sociales Sanitaires Rurales Auxiliaires (Auxiliary Rural Social and Health Workers), or ASSRA, these women were subjected to military rules of conduct and received detailed instructions on how to discharge their functions from the military sectors or quarters in which they served. They were assigned up to three "protected" *douars* or "centers of interest" at a time, selected for their multiplier effect, with a population of 1,500 to 3,000 women in which they spent one or two days a week each. The army reasoned that with a female target population of 2 million and 300 ASSRA, sustained action and follow-up dictated that each ASSRA concentrate on thirty to fifty women aged fourteen to thirty.[11]

The mission of the EMSI was not sociomedical assistance, as the title of this corps intimated, although free medical care was provided by a military doctor where available. The military command frequently explained that the "real objective" was to use sociomedical assistance as a medium through which to "make contact with women," that is to say, "to know, inform, educate, organize and guide them" in preparation for their acceptance of the "most French solution to the Algerian problem." The EMSI were warned against empathy for a poor and "miserable" population (especially in resettled villages) that might cause them to lose sight of the ultimate purpose of their mission.[12] Sociomedical assistance was a means for the EMSI to collect information on their subjects, identify potential allies, disseminate government directives, and sell colonial ideology through a critique of the role of women in native society. Guided military feminism thus used rural women's thirst for sociomedical assistance as a reward for their acceptance of a definition of their role in their society as inferior to that of French women. The message was that only if the FLN were defeated could Algerian women become (like) French women, a goal left empty of concrete content but full of promises for the future— as promises were "a fundamental concept in psychological warfare."[13] In its response to this strategy, the FLN pointed out that the military propaganda reduced "emancipation" to Frenchness.[14] However, having initially been reluctant to accept women as full-fledged combatants in its ranks,[15] the FLN failed to appreciate the hollowness of military feminism, feeling threatened by it instead. It was compelled to reveal its own prejudices while assessing and glorifying the role of women in the war.[16] Thus, the FLN claimed that customs had atrophied women's "sense of initiative," but nevertheless women were naturally committed to the anticolonial war: "She [woman] gives and will always give moral support to combatants in cities and rural areas." Furthermore, since women revealed themselves to be worthy of "increased trust," the FLN felt confident that they would in all likelihood take over the struggle should all Algerian male fighters be "exterminated."[17] In other words, the FLN discovered women's commitment just as the French military did—an acknowledgment of the FLN's own prior misgivings about half of the population it was ostensibly fighting for. The FLN response confirmed French military strategists that their targeting women was the right thing to do as it caused concern among their enemy, in addition to tapping into an emergent gender situation.

Carefully planned by the command, the method used by the EMSI during their "meetings" with women combined thematic lessons on topics such as hygiene, child rearing, and housekeeping (while listening to music) as entry points for propagandist discussions of key political issues focused on the military conception of the war. For example, lessons on body hygiene[18] (seen as easily achieved because "a bar of soap is not expensive") included discussions of the "myth of Algeria's independence," France's achievements in Algeria, her benevolence, and civic rights—all of which were contrasted with a description of gender inequality among native society. Using a system of punishment and rewards, the ASSRA withheld children's clothes and other enticements from women deemed unclean and thus unreceptive to French norms. The strategy equated acceptance of continued colonial rule with adoption of French customs and lifestyles.

To increase the efficiency of the lessons, and give them a home-grown flavor, they were peppered with references to local proverbs and even the Quran.[19] In villages and towns, the ASSRA were given step-by-step instructions on how to make women remove their veils.[20] Fighting veils was on a par with getting rid of "flies," "ticks," and "lice."[21] These vermin were associated by their semantic contiguity with the "bad shepherds" and "demons" (of the FLN) who were leading the people astray, and away from France. In a gesture of magnanimity, women who had "a husband, son, or brother in the *maquis*" were asked to convince them to come back to the fold.

To win native men to the "emancipation" campaign, military strategists recommended that the ASSRA avoid pitting women against their husbands too obviously, but deftly nudge them instead to stand up to them on their own. This monumental task of cultural engineering carried out by a staff with limited education sometimes resulted in an occasional ASSRA calling her subjects "dummies"[22] (the French word *bourriques*

conveys the idea of being an "ass") just as a handbook unabashedly defined Algerian women as "beasts of burden."[23]

The campaign aimed at breaking down the "homogeneity" of Algerians despite their social and ethnic differences, which it attributed to Islam.
Consequently, unveiling women—and this was the most significant part
of the campaign—was seen as the most effective means to this end. It was
assumed that shedding the veil would pry women away from family and
community; a new "solidarity" (a term frequently used among gender
strategists) would subsequently be built for them within colonial society,
in accordance with the antisubversive principle of restructuring the population after destructuring it. Some military sectors were presumed to be
more suitable than others for such a destructuring-restructuring action.
One such sector was Azazga in Grande Kabylie. It was proposed as ideal
for EMSI action because there were "practically no males" left in it: Some
had emigrated to France, others had joined the *maquis*. Because the
women were deemed psychologically "vulnerable," it was thought they
could be easily convinced to help the military secure the surrender of their
male relatives still in the *maquis*.[24]

Within the framework of the gender strategy, making "contact" involved more than just holding propaganda sessions with women: It included setting up "circles" anywhere, including in the "shade of an olive
tree,"[25] and training the most promising among them to take over the task
of indoctrinating others in their native tongue.[26] The strategy was supplemented by regular radio-talks (entitled *Woman's Magazine*, everyday
Sunday at 3 P.M.), in Arabic, on women's issues, including the veil. Some
of the letters written by listeners to the radio host, an Algerian woman,
were relayed to the military as were any declarations made by native religious figures regarding "women's emancipation."[27]

The EMSI overlapped with a corps of Women Auxiliaries to Algerian
Affairs (Attachées Féminines des Affaires Algériennes), which supplemented the staff of the SAS and SAU, dispensing to women guidance in
health, hygiene, child rearing, and the like in order to "foster among
women a need to change their daily life."[28] The military gender strategy
was also supplemented by civil institutions such as the Centres Sociaux
(Social Centers), which targeted youth of both sexes for "mass education," and voluntary associations, including the Mouvement de Solidar-
ité Féminine (MSF).[29]

Mrs. Salan was a leading figure in the MSF. She traveled throughout the
country in support of the military's interest in women, and to foster "solidarity" among native and French women while visiting or creating local
"circles." Her trips were planned, and relied on the "demonstration technique" with "warmed-up" audiences shouting "Yes" at key points in her
speeches.[30] Mrs. Massu engaged in a similar public-relations task, fore-

grounding Algerian and French women get-togethers for socializing and soft propaganda, and teaching Algerian women domestic skills, with music playing in the background.[31] Yet, the success of this well-orchestrated campaign targeting women was dubious. The women's "circles" sponsored by the EMSI reported that the women they attracted preferred romantic movies to propaganda films about the war they were told to watch. The women also demanded to "sing in Arabic, and when they did, they sang *fellagha* songs!"[32] The military also pointed to a backlash, as some women were killed by men it assumed to be members of the FLN.[33] The military feminist campaign was in full swing at a time—the late 1950s, after the collapse of the Zone Autonome of Algiers—when the FLN needed women's participation, and increased social support to close ranks against determined antisubversive war strategists. Nevertheless, the FLN worry about the French military "women's emancipation" campaign may have been exaggerated, but it made strategic sense in a war that was played out amid the population.

The crowning achievement of the EMSI's dogged campaign against the veil took place on May 16, 1958, as colonial generals led by Raoul Salan brought the French government down, asserting their determination to keep Algeria French. Unveiling ceremonies of Algerian women in major cities took place before the international press, the most noteworthy being held in the capital city. The military had given orders to "encourage participation of unveiled Muslim women with applause and expressions of sympathy."[34] A woman in Constantine, Monique Améziane, reports that at the time, she was an eighteen-year-old student, living in a dorm, at the Lycée Lapérière. She was coerced by the military to show up at an official unveiling ceremony planned in the city, wearing a veil she had never worn before, and instructed to unveil herself publicly on the official podium. Had she refused, her brother, in detention at the notorious Améziane (torture) farm—a property of the family's—would have been executed.[35]

The unveiling ceremonies hid the atrocities committed against female activists, some of whom were also French. At the same time, it starkly brought into the open what was buried deep in the French collective unconscious: exposing what they felt native men had hidden away from their gaze. This was a battle of the veils, material and psychological. It was also an assertion, steeped in gender prejudice, that women, regardless of their nationality, represent the nation. Therefore, taking them, appropriating them, signifies the taking and appropriation of their nation. The fall of the veil was the symbolic fall of the nation the nationalists were fighting for. Nevertheless, the fact that this ceremony took place at all is an intriguing psychological question. Ostensibly, some media event had to be staged in order to publicize the benefits of the "antisubversive" war. The point was to drive the message home that Algeria was truly and genuinely French. Differences of customs as exemplified by the veil were simply a vestige of a past that the FLN was allegedly fighting to maintain. They could be removed symbolically by the public unveiling of a few women.

How some of these women must have felt has not been told, but can be glimpsed from Monique Améziane's account. She remembers crying as she was dressed in blue and red to give her "the look of Marianne," the female representation of the French republic.[36] Monique Améziane was distressed at being coerced to act out a role in a massive propaganda event. Having never worn the veil, she had to fake liberation from a "tradition" that colonial generals wished to at once reify and jettison for the sake of dramatizing the triumph of modern France over archaic Algeria—the dawn of a new colonial era. How many of the women who appeared in these staged public events had actually worn the veil before May 16, 1958? In analyzing these unveiling ceremonies, Frantz Fanon argued that some of them (at least in Algiers) had been maids rounded up by their employers to play their part.[37] Archival pictures of these women indicate that some in Algiers were dressed in poor to modest "traditional" clothes (thus supporting Fanon's view); others appear to have been be well groomed for the occasion.[38] Whatever the case may be, it is not easy for a woman unaccustomed to appearing before a crowd at a ceremonial event to shed her veil.

But, the real issue was the unveiling of the French (colonial) mind, and its veiling at the same time. By singling out the veil for its symbolic significance, and thinking of it as a gesture that dissolved local culture and ushered in an all-French French Algeria, the military exposed a degree of cultural illiteracy among its strategists. They imbued a taken-for-granted cultural custom with an absolutist and totalitarian meaning that it did not have. Women in rural areas, for example, never wore veils. There were already young Algerian women in lycées who also did not wear them, but started donning them after May 16, 1958. Some of the women who had been arrested for depositing, or having attempted to deposit, bombs in public places had not worn veils.

The political use of the veil in the hands of the military when decoded militarily could also have meant that the battle against the FLN was not won, as was touted. The military still needed to prove that it had won the war for the hearts and minds of the native population. It was a tactical error to subject the veil, a custom grounded in religion—albeit questionably so—to the psychological war waged against the FLN. Religious customs were beyond FLN control, and attacking them frontally, in the manner that the military did, in the thick of the war, was counterproductive. In the end, the symbolic message that the military attempted to convey resonated more with colonists and French people in France. In this sense, the military may have been speaking to itself about the native culture objectified by the veil. For, native women and men saw the fetishization of the veil as one more act of colonial evasion of the fundamental problem posed by colonial rule: domination. Still, the official unveiling spectacle was one of historic significance: Anxious woman and triumphant general, standing side by side, two iconic figures of empire, one compelled to expose herself, the other reveling in his power to summon up a "new" albeit fleeting reality.

Women during Operations

Military feminism coincided with the subjection of rural women to unbridled terror. Being generally illiterate, they have inevitably remained silent on their painful war experiences. Their plight was unique: They depended for their livelihood on subsistence farming and economic solidarity with their kin. When a village was burned down, and men escaped to the *maquis* or were killed or arrested, women's capacity to sustain themselves and feed their families was severely damaged, if not destroyed. Those among them who could walk to the nearest village to seek help from relatives fared better than those who had nowhere to go, and whose kin's village had also been destroyed. Descriptions of women crying in despair over their destroyed dwellings, animals, and meager personal belongings are common among former soldiers'memoirs. Unlike men, rural women, hobbled by infants, generally could not easily escape to the mountains before paratroopers marching into their villages, and when they did, they had to return to their homes, or remnants thereof, more quickly than their husbands, and thus were exposed to more brutality.

Frequently, women were the targets of thefts by soldiers who, beside jewelry, searched for rural women's other prized possession: chickens. Expecting to be robbed, women developed strategies to protect their property. Captain Ladhuie reports an incident during the search of the village of Ait Irzer in the Grande Kabylie. He noticed that the women's behavior was curious. They were gathered in groups, one of which had children who appeared to cry on cue. Ladhuie and his men found out that the women whose children would not stop crying were sitting on a cache of chickens! The captain does not say how he felt about this discovery, except that he or his men bought two of the chickens. Yet, he also mused that "But I must also add that searching a village thoroughly makes it uninhabitable for a while."[39] Was the village burned down? The captain's musing cast a shadow of doubt on his assertion that he bought two chickens from the women who so ingenuously sought to hide their property. Troops had been under orders to "acquire the Lord of the Manor complex towards the population, and possess the 'punch' that imposes respect and fear, and ends combat decisively."[40] When applied to women, the "Lord of the Manor" complex connotes sexual aggressiveness and proprietorship of women in the medieval manner. Since women were known to be the lookouts that informed combatants of approaching troops, they were particularly watched during searches. Their body movements and facial expressions were scrutinized as Ladhuie intimated.

Some, captured during operations, stood up to their captors' demeaning behavior. Leulliette recounts a scene he witnessed between two young women who were discovered in a cabin in the woods, at Maillot, near Palestro, thanks to a nursing manual they had unwittingly dropped at the foot of an oak tree:

Interrogation. The Arab interpreter doesn't like women in men's clothes. He searches them brutally, with an ugly look, rips their pockets, almost tears their blouses. But they have no papers on them, not a thing. The interpreter is furious. He starts all over again, practically strips the two women naked in front of us. Still nothing, nor is there anything feminine about them now but their bodies, so hard their faces have become. There begins a furious dialogue in Arabic. But the women are not "talking." They have recovered all their presence of mind and they are speaking haughtily to the man even insolently. He translates: "They say they're prisoners of war, and that they won't say a thing, and that they will complain." But they are saying a good deal more than that. To these women, the interpreter is an abject traitor. They would kill him like a dog if they could, and he knows it, and shows that he knows it. They even revile him in French: "Traitor, coward, traitor!" The wretched man's face darkens, fills with bad blood of mingled rage and shame.

Our little second lieutenant doesn't know what to do. He would like to take his chance to show himself a leader. But how. . . . An idea! He goes up to the two who have been ignoring him, and drawing himself up very straight, he slaps them both in the face, first one and then the other. Just like that. To show who's boss.

We look at each other in astonishment, horribly embarrassed. The two women have turned to statues, petrified. Their pale faces go from grayish yellow to ghastly white. Two round red spots slowly grow on their tense cheeks. Fury, shame and fury. Finally, one of them, with perfect naturalness, walks straight forward into tragedy. She seizes by the collar the man who slapped her and who, she well know, holds her life in his hands. She seizes him, and she slaps him, as he slapped her. The interpreter tries to intervene, but too late. A woman's hand is printed in red on the lieutenant's cheek. . . . Silence.

"Tuez la" Mais tuez-la donc!" our officer screams at the Arab in a choking voice. Why can't he kill her himself? But the interpreter does not hesitate. He throws the woman to the ground and holds her down with his foot. The little lieutenant, red with rage, never stops shouting: "Tue-la! Mais tue-la donc!" He seems to have lost his mind. Without batting an eye, the interpreter cocks his rifle, and fires five bullets one right after the other into the woman's body that lies crushed under his foot. First two bullets in the breast, and then three in the stomach. She dies without a cry. We are dumbfounded. Then, gun in hand, the man starts toward the other woman, standing silent, motionless, with closed eyes. Again he cocks his rifle, which is still hot. But now, it's he that's seized by the waist—by us, determined, this time to prevent him. The lieutenant, who's waiting without saying anything, does not dare insist. He gives vague orders: "Get on up there. There are more rebels."[41]

This episode illustrates the delicacy of women's situation in a war where many male compatriots collaborated with enemy troops, and where compassion could come from the enemy instead of the expected natural ally.[42] Confusion reigned where a paratrooper could be, alternately, occasional savior and frequent rapist. In the end, one woman was ordered killed without trial, for having stood up for her dignity. Leulliette asserts that the victim haunted him. He went back to see her dead body:

> But war for me now is her full breast, bloodstained like crushed grapes, her short frizzled black hair in disorder around her pale face. War is that body I am still ashamed not to have defended, that young Algerian woman who might have been loved by a fine young man. . . . War is that woman torn and mangled for refusing to believe that men are always vile when they have power. The fixed gaze of her dark eyes that we forgot to close haunted me for a long time.[43]

That some soldiers were able to note women's despair is a testimonial to the mixed feelings generated by a war that moved some men in the military to describe it in merciless detail. As Benoit Rey wrote: "We received the order to 'scorch' [in French, *cramer*], burn everything." Through his spy glasses he could observe the actions of part of his commando and see

> women screaming, dragging or carrying children, fleeing towards us. An old man remained on the threshold of his home. A soldier slits his throat. Another one hangs his body to the central beam of his roof. . . . When the whole village is in flame, women are collected. . . . The women cry, and tear up their faces as the children scream. To make them stop, a few soldiers shoot at mules. Shots always have an effect on people.[44]

Scenes such as this one were common in rural areas, as was rape. For rural women, the notion of the militarized, women-emancipating, state faded into one of absolute terror.

Rape as Military Strategy

The veil masquerade obscured the reality of women's rape on the ground. Rape as violation was already inscribed in the conception of military op-

erations. The military strategic discourse was studded with rape as a figure of speech. Psychological action officers, imbued with Chakotin's
ideas, were wont to refer to "psychological rape."[45] The "flooding" of
Kabyle villages with military forces was assumed to have a beneficial psychological impact on regions that had been "inviolate."[46] Penetrating a
region was thus symbolically synonymous with rape. On occasion, some
publications in support of the war, written by men with professional cre-
dentials, sought to justify the rape of Algerian women by trivializing it:
They flatly asserted its alleged routine occurrence at the hands of Algerian
men.[47]

Although at times random, rape by troops was systematic in rural villages and scattered hamlets where the population was defenseless. Jacques
Zéo, an enlisted officer at the age of eighteen, serving as mountain soldier
in the Grande Kabylie, emphasized the frequency of rape, not only during reprisals, but also as part of routine search operations. In describing
reprisals for the killing of a French officer of native affairs, he pointed out
that "Well, let's not talk about rape, during the 15 days [of reprisals] the
men helped themselves freely." He noted that rape was so common that
women expected it, and "were so scared that they lay down immediately
[upon the entrance of the paratroopers into their homes]."[48] There is no
way to ascertain whether women's response to rape really took on the
Pavlovian character that Zéo describes. It is possible that this, deflecting
responsibility onto the women, was Zéo's manner of exculpating himself
and his comrades in arms. He nevertheless provides evidence of rape as a
tool of military "pacification."

An Algerian, Rachid Abdelli, who enlisted at the age of seventeen in the
auxiliary (Harka) corps, also in the Grande Kabylie, witnessed a serial
raping of a young woman by French troops as well as Harka during an
operation in a mountain village. Upon noticing him watching the scene
from the roof, the woman cried for his help, which he felt he could not
give her, noting that "everyone closed their eyes on it."[49] Esméralda, a
Berber-Jewish victim of torture, noted that when Legionnaire paratroopers took over the management of the CTT where she was detained, they
asked "Are there pregnant women here?"[50] an indication that they knew
about routine rape. The Algerian writer Mouloud Feraoun, who had kept
a diary during the war, relays, on January 8, 1957, a description made by
a colleague of his—whose story he checked out—of the manner in which
rape was carried out during reprisals against the villages of the Ouadhias
tribe in Grande Kabylie:

> The first village was simply emptied out of its inhabitants. In the other vil-
> lages all the men were picked up and locked up together for fifteen days. . . .
> The women remained in the villages, in their homes. They were ordered to

keep their doors open and to stay in separate rooms in their houses. The *douar* was thus transformed into a populous BMC [Bordel Militaire de Campagne] for the Alpine chasseurs company or other legionnaires who were released to go in. One hundred and fifty young women were able to find refuge at the White Sisters' or Brothers'. . . . No trace was found of a few others.[51]

Feraoun wistfully noted the seriousness of the crime of rape for his honor-conscious community, and asked "What will the Ouadhias do? They will not slit the throats of their dishonored daughters; certainly not. What will they do? They will wait." Feraoun remarks that rape is common in war and was committed by German and Russian troops when they invaded enemy countries. However, in Algeria, it was happening in the context of France's claim to modernize Algerian society. He points out sarcastically that the Kabyles, not being German, Russian, or French, do not accept

> the idea that their women can be raped with impunity, because they consider this the most heinous of crimes. From time immemorial, the Kabyles' customs, laws, and raison d'être have centered on the prohibition of rape, and the sacred respect for the preservation of woman's virtue."[52]

It is precisely the violation of Algerians' social organization that the army sought to achieve above and beyond providing for the sexual gratification of the troops. Reprisals, when they affected the private lives of Algerians, were a method that helped to make a tabula rasa of existing institutions that had survived the nineteenth-century destruction. Feraoun further notes that after soldiers descended at night on the village of Ait Idir, "twelve women only admitted having been raped. At Taourirt M spent three nights as in a free bordello. In a village of the Beni Ouacif, forty-six bastards were born. Here, the majority of the pretty women have endured rape from the soldiers."[53] He adds that a woman he knew, Fatma, had witnessed the rape of her own daughters and a daughter-in-law. It was the rape of three young girls by soldiers near the town of Aumale, at Ben Shaba, where his post was set up, that convinced Ahmed Bencherif, an Algerian officer serving in the French army, to take a long-postponed decision to defect to the FLN.[54] Pierre Leulliette, writes about his incursions into the Kabyle village of El Merba, among the Beni Belaid, which was turned into a "heap of uninhabitable ruins." Hungry women and old men carrying white flags and chanting religious hymns were allowed to return to the village. The resulting destitution of the villagers was turned to the sexual advantage of the paratroopers who exchanged biscuits and cans of beef for the "seductive charms" of the women.

This forced prostitution of hungry women was so frequent that every night, with sentinels guarding them, "the whole platoon would descend on the *mechtas* [rural dwellings] one by one." One of these, Bernard, a comrade of Leulliette's, recounts how he went searching for a pretty woman he had spotted the day before:

> I struck a match. Nobody was asleep. I saw the girl. In the dark, she looked like a ghost. There were other women there, all very old and huddled together in their rags. They gave me a funny look. Right away I gave them the food I'd brought, and they took it. Then I took my girl's hand and started for a dark corner. She followed me without a word.[55]

The narrator proceeded to boast about being loved by the girl who allegedly said things to him in Arabic (it could also have been Berber), a language he did not understand, which he nevertheless thought could only have meant "I love you!" Whatever the woman said or felt may not be consequential, given the context within which it occurred. Yet, Jauffret, neglecting this context, refers to the incident as a case of "half consensual" rape.[56] What he failed to appreciate was the structural transformation of young women and girls into sex objects to be had at will. Without the food, the armed paratrooper could still have compelled the woman to acquiesce to his sexual demand. A soldier may also act alone in seeking to rape a woman. Leulliette recounts the short-lived and unauthorized foray of one of his comrades into a hamlet. Upon hearing women's laughter, the soldier scaled the wall of a house, and surprised two young females in the middle of washing their faces. He was spotted and shot at by the women's father. This happened in 1954, when presumably a soldier on operation who overstepped the limits of his duties by harassing the civilian population could be punished. The hapless man, who felt unable "to have two weeks without seeing a woman," received a two-week jail sentence.[57] Nevertheless, as Feraoun bitterly writes, there were a few rare cases of women who found rape "pleasurable to the point of following the conqueror." He adds that pride and nationalism prevented people from talking about such occurrences, to avoid giving the enemy the feeling that he had struck at the "raw core of the Kabyle soul." Feraoun also reports that in Tizi-Hibel, the troops allowed their local "guides," or collaborators to "chase" women in nearby villages. The women in the Grande Kabylie (as in other mountain villages) were caught between the soldiers' use of rape or torture, and the guerillas' strict (and equally murderous) code of behavior, if they collaborated with the enemy. At Tizi-Mokrane, a woman was shot dead by a guerilla. She was known to be of "loose morals," and had taken to visiting the French soldiers stationed in a school. It was feared that she might bring women to the conscripts.[58]

Feraoun expressed his disappointment at the social numbing generated by the banalization of rape in the villages. He noted that the FLN, clearly worried by unpredictable reactions from men to the frequency of rape committed by French soldiers, sought to explain it away (or make it more bearable) on religious grounds: In a situation of war, women should accept rape, endure it as part of the struggle. At the same time, men appeared to Feraoun as tacitly accepting the rape of wives and daughters during the numerous searches that the soldiers did in the villages by acting as if it had not occurred when they knew it had. Feraoun wondered how these men who once thought their "honor buried in [the woman's] vagina like the most precious of treasures, now prefer to hang on to life more than to the vagina."[59] This apparent evolution toward an assumed "Western" model in the social mores of his community clearly unsettled Feraoun. Yet, where rape is routinized, and men are powerless, pretending that it does not occur is a coping mechanism.

Despite his own bruised sense of honor, and his stereotypical understanding of the role of sex in Western societies, Feraoun glimpsed an essential element of the routinization of rape: Like torture, rape has the effect of resocializing women and men into the war culture, and disciplining men by debasing their gender-based value system. Was he also implying that through rape women were being resocialized into a looser or freer conception of sex? It is unlikely, although he also points out that the nationalists, just like the soldiers, "sleep with the most beautiful girls and give bastards to unmarried women and widows. As for married women, thank God, they are spared such accidents."[60] From his perspective, the violation of a married woman did not qualify as rape since she was no longer a virgin. Nevertheless, the author reports in his usual tongue-in-cheek manner that there was a consensus among villagers that the FLN was more respectful than French troops of local customs and human dignity. The rape of a married woman in the presence of her husband bound husband and wife in a mutual degradation and helplessness. In instances when a husband was able to strike back at a soldier who raped his wife, military retaliation against the recalcitrant's own mother and father was as swift as it was gruesome.[61] Rape against women crystallizes the stakes and clearly draws the lines between occupier and occupied, compelling people to act as one in opposing the military order. In small village communities, those who did not understand the situation usually paid with their lives.

Rape evoked a consensus among the Algerians as well as the French: It was considered abhorrent. Witnesses to rape, or those who heard about it, seem to express unease, a sign of the complex emotions that the excesses of the war triggered in soldiers. But, despite the official rhetoric about rallying women to the cause of French Algeria, women were perceived as native men's wards. Raping a woman was, like raping a man, an assault on her dignity. The effect of rape on a woman was seldom imagined. For rural women, rape was a violation and a degradation compounded by the pain of losing one's husband or children, and watching one's home burn. When left homeless after the destruction of their hamlets many women turned into wandering figures of a new war nomadism; they were told that "it was in their best interest to leave the region and settle near to one of our posts."[62] Whether they were subsequently turned into prostitutes servicing the military, as an alternative to the mobile rural bordellos, is not always clear.[63] This apparent induction of women into forced prostitution is not without precedent. A tradition had been established during the nineteenth century among French military authorities of putting pressure on native notables to do the bidding of the colonial authorities or risk having a daughter spirited away to an urban whorehouse.[64]

It is nevertheless instructive that a language of rape developed among soldiers: Rape sessions were called "strip tease"; rapists committing collective rape "go through" the victims as through a field, or "play." A former paratrooper distinguished between rape as a tool of torture for securing intelligence, and "rape for comfort." Clearly for the victim the distinction was meaningless. In the various urban torture centers women were routinely raped, especially at the famed Villa Sésini in Algiers. The women who survived the war use the code word "torture" among themselves to mean "rape," a term that covers all degrading experiences, as they continue to feel the trauma of having been violated but are unable to come to terms with it, not only because of shame and fear of opprobrium,[65] but also because of the everlasting and indelible memory. It was not infrequent that women were picked up during roundups for the purpose of being raped and were selected according to their looks and age.[66]

The arrest of a group of young women (among whom Djamila Bouazza, Djamila Boupacha, and Djamila Bouhired) in 1957 in Algiers, after bombs exploded in a number of public spots, their subsequent torture, rape, and trial dramatized the issue of rape in detention. Rape brought along with it the risk of pregnancy, causing logistical problems for the military administration. A historian reports the case of a woman who was pregnant when she was captured by a DOP, and subsequently released because she would have caused difficulty for the Center of Triage and Transit in which she would have been placed. Many of the women arrested were detained in special sections of the CTT. However, not all CTT had quarters reserved for women. At times, as was the case in the CTT of Sétif, eastern Algeria, women were forced to share cells with men.[67]

It is not so much routine rape presumably committed in violation of the army's rules of engagement as rape under arrest that exposes the state's view of women, who had been objectified as the most telling pieces of material evidence against the assumed backwardness of Islam—the tangible, palpable difference between French "civilization" and the "primitiveness" of the culture that informed *guerre révolutionnaire*. However, as soon as women displayed the consciousness and will to actively undo the colonial system, they became enemies to be fought with the same ferocity as men.

The interest in torture generated in France in recent years has also spurred curiosity about rape. A journalist, Florence Beaugé, reports having been urged by former soldiers to "dig" into the issue of rape. Her interviews with these soldiers reveal disquieting and titillating depictions of how women were raped, albeit presented as an unburdening of conscience. Descriptions mix with justifications thriving on stereotypes rendered familiar by various narratives of the war. It is as if talking about rape brings with it its own *pleasure* born of breaking a taboo. However, the thrill of describing the rape of women in the embrace of the French Empire comes across as a more powerful sentiment than the pursuit of knowledge about the relationship between rape, conscience, French culture, and the politics of war. The search for rape testimonials—not for the reason of bringing culprits to trial, but for exorcizing the seamy side of empire for the benefit of its reluctant heirs—may be a cruel exercise in voyeurism for Algerian victims. Getting women to talk about their rape has entered the orgiastic discourse of the Algerian War as a complement to confessing to torture. In this context, Algerian survivors of war rape often refrain from discussing their ordeal, as for many, this would be akin to being raped anew.

Torture as Rape

The "pacification" of the female population included the use of torture as a tool of resocialization into the colonial social project. Although rape could take place without torture, torture seldom took place without rape. When rape occurs under torture, it compounds the pain and humiliation suffered by the victim as she is also penetrated by objects of various sizes in addition to being subjected to the electricity or water techniques. When a woman was taken prisoner, the sexual nature of torture was a matter of fact. It was borne by her gendered body. She had to strip like her male counterpart. Her body, perceived as that of the generic female, was imbued with sexual desire. And in a military organization such as the rural DOP, where few women worked except for the occasional typist, the female prisoner's body acquired even more sexual significance.

Aldop describes a scene of preparation of a woman for torture by electrical means, which he witnessed. The woman had been caught carrying a message intended for a man, and was assumed to be an FLN liaison agent. The officer asked her point blank "Are you a virgin? You won't be anymore." After she took her clothes off but kept her slip and bra on, he barked "I said naked" (in French, *à poil*, meaning down to your hairs), tore off her bra, and slid her slip down her legs. She curled up instinctively in a vain attempt at covering her breasts and genitals. The officer describes her as being "tied to the bed"—probably a camp bed since usually in the torture chamber there is no bed, but a board. She sobs as "her legs were spread. Her tears fell on her long black hair. We introduce one wire into her vagina; the other is curled around her ear. The *séance* begins."[68] The woman broke and her confession allegedly helped the DOP uncover an all-female underground. Some of the women were arrested in their homes with their babies in their arms. It is unclear what these women were charged with. Since they were housewives and mothers of young children, they may have had little time to be active in the nationalist movement except to provide occasional shelter, relay messages, or favor Algeria's independence. But all of these were crimes against the security of the state.

Louisette Ighilahriz, a combatant, was wounded and captured by paratroopers during an ambush in 1957 near the town of Chebli. While lying in bed at Mustapha Hospital in Algiers, in a cast, she was injected with Pentothal. The truth serum had little effect on her, causing her to think that her "psychological training" in the *maquis* had been effective. She was transferred to a torture center on the heights of Algiers, where she was visited by a number of paratroopers who either stared at her in silence, curious to see a female combatant, or derided her for being a *fellagha*. Still recovering from her wounds, she was unable to move, and compelled to urinate and defecate in her bed. She was fed soup once a day, and sometimes a cup of coffee. On many occasions she heard men in adjoining rooms scream and moan from torture. Her torturer, Captain Graziani, followed the usual procedure before subjecting her to torture: insults, gender-based sarcasm, such as "a girl who wants to play the *fellaga*," and threats. Let's see who will play the longest!" Graziani tried to saw off her cast, but preferred to poke under it with a sharp instrument to cause pain in the still raw wounds around the bullet-shattered bones. She remembered that on one occasion, he used a bayonet to cut her bandages.[69] As she did not talk, Graziani switched to slaps and blows, and finally raped her with "all sorts of objects."

While at the torture center, she reports having been visited by Generals Massu and Bigeard. However, her torturer did not know that a male medical attendant had told her of the death of all the combatants in her group, which meant that she did not have to worry about being brought face-to-face with any one of her comrades as was standard procedure during interrogation to coerce prisoners into talking. The threat of confrontation, which Graziani used against her, was thus useless. Ighilahriz's ordeal was ended when a medical doctor entered her room by mistake, and discovered her lying in filth. She was immediately sent to a hospital. Subsequently she was tried and imprisoned in Algiers before being transferred to France, and finally to the island of Corsica. She managed to escape from her Corsican jail, just before the independence of Algeria.

Ighilahriz's story is instructive for several reasons. It is a firsthand account of the itinerary of a young woman's engagement in the nationalist struggle, and her experience of the inequities and prejudices of colonial society in Algiers, which informed her joining the FLN. Furthermore, it reveals the long-lasting psychological (in addition to physical) scars that torture leaves in its victims. It took Ighilahriz thirty-nine years after the independence of Algeria before she could describe her torture and rape in writing. She had felt out of phase with the world after recovering her freedom, and perhaps in an attempt to come to terms with her posttraumatic experiences undertook to study psychology. More important, her account of her arrest and torture decades after they occurred reveals blind spots and a rare sensitivity undoubtedly found in people who have not broken silence. She had empathy for the paratroopers who came to take a look at her as an object of curiosity while she lay in her camp bed "swimming in my shit, in the dried blood from my menses, with no tears in my eyes, and aching all over." Grateful that they did not "touch" her, she thought of them as "the poor men who were following orders [not to help her], and did not wish to get involved."[70]

Ighilahriz did not think that she had been raped, although she explained that various objects had been thrust into her vagina. The abhorrence of rape for women as well as men is such that its victims do not perceive it as rape unless it is carried out with a male organ. Finally, in the middle of her ordeal, Ighilahriz noticed that her torturer, Graziani, had "beautiful teeth and beautiful green eyes."[71] Inchoate subterranean desire suffuses the torture situation, investing it with a psychologically destabilizing meaning that transcends pain and suffering. In the end, when she decided to write her story, she had been eager to search for the army doctor, Officer Richaud, who had saved her from a sure death.

Her book created a stir in France among high ranking officers, veterans of the Algerian War. General Massu could not remember her, but identified the army doctor who helped her, and who had since passed away. Richaud's surviving daughters were not keen on establishing contact with Ighilahriz. As for Bigeard, he denied ever meeting her, or knowing about her torture.[72] General Schmitt, who has been identified by a number of Algerians as having directed their torture, sued her for libel. Journalist Françoise Beaugé, did not believe Ighilahriz story until it was confirmed to her by a veteran of the Algerian War, Raymond Cloarec.[73]

The trauma of being raped with bottles and other objects leaves young women who had had no sexual activity before being arrested bewildered and confused. Djamila Boupacha asked her lawyer whether having never had intercourse, she could still be a virgin since she had suffered rape-torture with a beer bottle not a penis. She said, "I do not know if I am still a virgin. . . . You understand? I passed out, and I was bleeding when they took me down to the cell."[74] She had been given "the second degree": rape with a beer bottle on the floor of the torture chamber.[75] The denial of rape-torture by civil and military authorities added a layer of humiliation to victims who insisted that their condition be acknowledged. Djamila Boupacha was examined by a team of five doctors in France, who, after many hesitations, concluded that she might have suffered "traumatic deflowering."[76] Furthermore, Dr. Hélène Michel-Wolfron, who reported on the psychological condition of the victim, concluded that "her psychic make-up corresponds to that of a virgin." Boupacha's court-ordered doctor in Algiers wrote that she exhibited "problems associated with her menses."[77] However, he also testified that he did not perform a gynecological exam on her because "she did not complain of sexual maltreatment [in French, sévices]. Besides, such examinations are somewhat "humiliating." Overlooking the cigarette burns on her body and her broken ribs, the doctor concluded that she exhibited "no partial permanent incapacitation."[78] Boupacha's case highlights the institutional imbalance between a woman insisting on making her torture known, and the state's effort to discredit her in order to cover up the practice. The court, the doctor, the police, the paratroopers presented a united front to impugn the victim's integrity and cast doubt on her mental stability. As a militant she was assumed to be guilty. The president of the Commission for the Safeguard of Individual Rights and Liberties found her "not nice," noting that she and her family "do not like France!"[79] Besides rape with various objects, the torture of women (including those pregnant) featured "slapping" their breasts, a particularly painful method, or electrical shock not only to the nipples and vagina, but also to the gums.[80] Between torture sessions, women were often groped.[81] Many survived torture maimed.

However, Algerian women were not the only victims of torture. As were Frenchmen who sympathized with the nationalist movement, French women too were tortured. Some of the women, such as Gaby Jiménez, a Pied-Noir of Spanish descent, had experienced torture years before the Algerian War started, in 1941, after being arrested for membership in the banned Algerian Communist Party (PCA) and conspiracy to "dismember the French territory."[82] She was subjected to torture with electricity, whipping, and bludgeoning. After her liberation and the revival of the PCA, she was arrested again for supporting the nationalist movement and tortured at the "Hotel Victoria" in Oran, this time by drowning in a bathtub. She was made to watch, with a hood on her head, the torture of her friends, males and females. She remembers the name of her torturer, Ciaca Upa—the "Corsican"—working under the orders of Lieutenant Charbonnier who later tortured Henri Alleg.

A number of these women had been school teachers in small towns, and had experienced shock at discovering extreme poverty among the rural population, and defacto racial segregation in classes. They had also discovered that Algerian children were deliberately prevented from attending school. One of the women, Miriam Ben, who identified herself as a Berber-Jew, realized that she understood the meaning of "apartheid" through her years teaching. Jacqueline Guerroudj, another jailed militant, had come to a similar realization.[83] It is the discovery of poverty and racism that led these women to join or support the FLN. Similarly, it was the spectacle of a group of soldiers kicking a pregnant Algerian woman already spread out on a sidewalk in the Châteauneuf neighborhood in Algiers that caused young Louisette Ighilahriz to get a gun kept in her father's bakery, walk up to the sentinel outside the barracks to shoot him in revenge. What saved the sentinel from Ighilahriz's finally killing him was his young age and his good looks.[84]

After a woman broke under torture, psychological action by other means began: She was often taken to the mess to eat with officers,[85] or driven around in a jeep with an officer for all to see. On occasion, she was courted by one of the officers as Pouget did with Fatia (Fatiha).

On a lighter note, the victim in a torture chamber could on a rare occasion arouse unusual emotions in her interrogator. An intelligence officer became emotionally invested in his female prisoner in a manner similar to Aldop with his male prisoner. In one DOP, an intelligence officer fell short of interrogating a captured ALN nurse. As he was pressed by his superior for her confession, he stalled, arguing that he needed more time to not only break her, but also to rally her to the cause of French Algeria. But intelligence work in the DOP rested on suspicion of all, including the staff. Aldop reports that a listening device was placed in the torture chamber in which this officer interrogated his female prisoner, and it was discovered that he was in love with her, begged her to give him some information to relay to his team, and even proposed to her.[86] The officer was transferred to another DOP thereafter.

Sex, Sexing the Body, and Pacification

The frequency of rape during the war[87] was facilitated by the legal vacuum that surrounded the implementation of the antisubversive doctrine. But it was enabled by the military-ordered practice of examining women's genitals for sexual activity with suspected relatives, and/or making gender identification. A chief master sergeant stripped a woman of her clothes, beat her on the head, pointing to her shaved pubic area as evidence of her contact with her wanted husband. The implication was that shaving her pubic hair meant (according to the army's assumed knowledge of Algerian culture) that she was sexually active with her husband, who must have been around, or was expected to come for a visit.[88] As Jauffret put it crudely: "Some 'specialists' can tell, by touching or just looking at the length of pubic hair, how many days the husband, who joined the *maquis*, had last been around."[89]

A military circular recommended that a woman's gender be ascertained by a doctor if necessary.[90] Ordering soldiers, for whom sex was a constant preoccupation, to verify the sexual identity of Algerian women was incitement to rape. Whether the medical requirement was implemented or not is less important than the notion that a woman's body was another war "terrain" in the counterrevolutionary war. Admittedly, women's veils, and thus clothing, were equated with disguises. A male FLN operative (again as shown in the movie the *Battle of Algiers*) could conceivably disguise himself as a woman by wearing a veil. But checking women's genitals for gender identification overstepped the bounds of military security by assuming that gender differences are not visible with the naked eye. At any rate, former soldiers (who were not doctors) took advantage of the gender circular to grope women, and at times rape them. Using the derogatory and generic word *fatmas* to refer to Algerian women, a soldier described how he ascertained their gender:

> We had to touch them to see if they were really women. . . . I must admit that it was a little . . . I am sure the young conscripts who had gotten used to that milieu [of violence] . . . Well, it was quite horrible. We had to . . . The soldiers had to look, to touch the genitals [*sexe* in French] of the *fatmas*. . . . That order to touch the genitals of the *fatmas*, it was a precise instruction. So, you can imagine how terrible it must have been for the Algerian women.[91]

The culture of the women intruded on the narrator's commiseration as both an unspoken desire and a satisfaction of having broken a taboo by virtue of an order. The mythology to which Algerian customs had been subjected comes across in the former soldier's instant cultural expertise encapsulated in one sententious line, "Naturally, in relation to men, the Algerian woman is very, very . . . The man who is not her husband cannot see her." But, *he*, the military man, is ordered to "see" her, although he knows that he should not "see" her most intimate self. Any other woman, regardless of her culture, would have felt violated. Being ordered to "see" women, with fingers, no doubt carried with it the thrill of breaking another man's taboo by "touching" his woman's body. In the former soldier's account, the Algerian woman was pitiful not because of the symbolic and physical rape she was subjected to, but because of her culture. Even if the act of rape with a penis had not occurred, this was still rape with the hands.

The war thus began to penetrate deeper into the female body. Breasts and muscles were no longer enough to distinguish a woman from a man; a medical expert or a conscript's hands, if not penis, were necessary to ascertain the real thing. Rape became the ultimate test of sex identification. It is unlikely that all the DOP had a medical doctor on hand, or whether one was needed at all, given that searches of women's genitals were part of identity checks in villages, on the street, and during house searches.

There was a time, immediately before the Battle of Algiers in 1957, when the military still felt that women should be searched by other— French—women. On the night of May 26–27, 1956, eighty social workers on the staff of the governor general were summoned to Algiers' main hospital, Hôpital Mustapha, by the public-health director. He had them driven in military vehicles to police headquarters, where they were divided up into ten groups of eight and transported to the Casbah. Once there, they were ordered to get out and "search under women's veils to see if they were not men." In reality they were to search women in their homes, while the husbands were removed during a midnight joint police-military operation.[92] During the Battle of Algiers, armed paratroopers stormed houses in the Casbah, raped women in their homes, and tortured men and children also in their homes. They also stormed Turkish baths (*hammamat*)[93] in the city and regaled themselves with the spectacle of naked women washing themselves in the steamrooms. Leulliette described this oft repeated incident as having been planned, and not the result of a mistake, as was claimed by the military.[94] It is not clear whether any of the women in the *hammamat* were raped.

In spite of its frequency and its centrality to the antisubversive war, rape did not cause the same outcry as torture. The victims' understandable silence does not explain the silence of the media, the military authorities who were aware of the occurrence of rape, or religious figures. Judging by the complicity that tied military and civil institutions in a collective denial of torture, let alone rape, there was little that women, in particular rural women, could do against their rapists, some of whom were also their torturers. Soldiers who engaged in rape benefited from the solidarity of their comrades, who, even when they disapproved, felt obligated to keep silent. Perpetrators were also at times protected by their own superiors who looked the other way, but were mostly shielded by a general acceptance of rape as a war weapon that also affected some French women, who on occasion "urged the troop to rape and kill Muslim women" as happened in the village of Aïn Abid (Constantine) in the aftermath of the killing of a French couple by the FLN in 1955, and the subsequent ransacking of the village by the army.[95]

A former soldier describes how a *commando de chasse* included rape as part of the devastation it wrought on a small village near Texenna. After setting dwellings on fire and killing mules, the commando was told by their midshipman, Prévost, "you can rape, but do it discreetly." The narrator adds "That evening, on the way back I learned that a fifteen year old Muslim girl had been raped by seven soldiers, another one, aged thirteen, by three other men."[96] Aldop reports the rape of a child by one of his comrades, a chief master sergeant who bragged about it at the mess: "I had me an eight-year-old *bougnoule* [racist term used against North Africans]. It's so tender at that age, you have no idea."[97] This caused an officer to leave the dining table after dressing down the braggard. Presumably, rape is common in wartime, and its occurrence in Algeria should come as no surprise. However, in the Algerian case, the state claimed to save native women from wayward Algerian men. So the question is, why did it not protect them from its own presumably wayward troops? In reality, rape was an essential part of state terror, the most efficient part of it.

Alongside the women who participated in the war for nationalist ideals, there were those who were caught up in it for different reasons. Bellahcène Bali recounts instances of women who worked as informants for either the French military or police and who had been condemned to death by the FLN. One of these was a Bent El Hamasse whom Bali shot in the belly with the intent to kill, but she survived the attack. Another woman, Bent El Djadarmi, was found in her bed with a naked man identified as married to another woman. The FLN chief of the commando, Si Khaled, ordered the execution of the man for "adultery" on the spot, in addition to the woman. The woman's jewelry was laid on her dead body as reminder that the FLN did not steal from people, men or women. Yet Bali noticed on one occasion that an executioner wore a gold ring that had belonged to the male informant he had executed.[98]

In sum, interest in women enabled the military to refine revolutionary-war theory, and adjust its antisubversive strategy accordingly. But it also starkly exposed the paradox of the gender strategy. On the one hand, women were subjected to torture, rape, routine search of their genitals, and displacement from their homes. On the other hand, they were targeted for an "emancipation" campaign carried out under near-laboratory conditions, in "liberated" areas, aimed at turning them into active antisubversive war agents. The cynicism behind military feminism was masked by an ideology of women's liberation made to fit the reductive view that equated colonialism with progress, and decolonization with retrogression. The propagandistic core of the military use of "emancipation" can be measured by its failure to provide the material means (other than teaching young girls home economics, and a fuzzy project to develop handicrafts) that would sustain women's "emancipation" from family and community. It can also be gauged by the military's selective focus on women aged fourteen to thirty, assumed to be more receptive to its propaganda. The job of "emancipating" Algerian women was entrusted to Frenchwomen whose level of education and low qualifications bespoke a society in which women were still in need of emancipation. Nevertheless, these women could only feel empowered by their position as agents of psychological warfare.

The socioeconomic context within which "emancipation" was carried out with the help of monographs on Islam and Algerian culture revealed the abstractness of military feminism and undermined the credibility the army felt it had. In 1957 there were 116,340 Algerian girls in grade school, and 1,558 in high school—for a female population of 4,024,800 (2,062,000 of whom were less than twenty years old).[99]

Yet the military's confidence that with women it seized on the perfect *tactical idea*[100] cannot be discounted. The formal goals set for women invoked an ideal that human beings value regardless of their gender: freedom as expressed in agency. However, military feminism was based on a conflation of women's "emancipation" with a rejection of their culture, family, and community in time of war. In the hands of the military, women's "emancipation" was but another tactical weapon in the psychological warfare it waged against the population friend-enemy. It aimed at breaking down existing networks of solidarity mediated by women. However, the military had no mechanism through which to replace broken solidarities. Nothing was proposed to women except a vague promise of satisfaction born of shedding the veil and wearing "European" clothes. The manipulative character of the military campaign (at once for and against women) emptied it of meaningful content, although it opened up a debate among some (urban) women on their position with regard to religion and the veil during troubled times.

Women's participation in the war was an act of emancipation of the political will, no matter how the woman question evolved after the war. The French authorities' decision to crush this momentous event, and its minimization by the FLN subsequent to the independence of Algeria, are testimonials to the difficulties women experience in gaining acceptance as autonomous beings in times of crisis. Women were deprived of the most essential element that any man gets when taking up arms against injustice and lack of freedom: recognition as a self-willed human being fighting for a cause he strongly believes in.

The history of Algerian women's lives during the war will remain in-

complete because it does not include the standpoint of rural women—
prime targets of military action. Many have died, and others will follow,
taking their memories of serial rape, torture, displacement from their villages, hunger, and pain to the grave. They were caught between military
repression and their desire to be part of a national movement, or often
simply their right to be. That many of them were punished by both sides
in the war only compounds their unhappy historical situation. But on the
whole they had as many reasons as men, if not more, to participate in the
movement. On occasion I come upon the yellowed picture of an older village woman poorly dressed, with tattoos marking her lined face, her
frayed shawl tightly wrapped around her head, and holding a gun. She
looks determined to not allow a soldier to turn her jars of olive oil upside
down, to rape her daughter, and to kill her husband and son. I suspect she
knows why the war is raging: She has suffered the greatest injustice; she
has been deprived of her dignity and the sanctity of her home.

PART III

IDEOLOGY OF TORTURE

Chapter 7

CONSCIENCE, IMPERIAL

IDENTITY, AND TORTURE

To lose an empire is to lose one's self.
—General Raoul Salan, *Mémoires*

MANAGEMENT OF conscience was essential to the troops' tolerance of torture and to related acts of terror. The modality of conscience management was a function of the degree to which an imperial identity was assumed or questioned. Psychological action targeting troops could not alone account for diffuse tolerance. Clearly, not all soldiers in the French army were torturers. That torture presented some of them with a *crise de conscience* cannot be overlooked. Many, who felt shock and revulsion at the sight of torture, recorded it in their diaries or took pictures to preserve its memory. Even though the military code of silence smothered stirrings of conscience, there were men, such as General de Bollardière, who spoke out against torture. However, there was no shortage of soldiers who committed it, including many conscripts (frequently seen as innocent)[1] as well as enlisted men. Diaries, confessions, and other war narratives reveal a plasticity of conscience in their authors that requires elucidation. Consciousness of wrongdoing coexisted well with the commission or quiescent observation of acts of terror. Admittedly, wars are not fought according to what conscience dictates, but to what strategy requires. And despite the hue and cry about them, torture and terror continued until the end of the war. Using retrospective narratives of the war, this chapter seeks to understand the role played by imperial identity, real or imagined, in the management of conscience in relation to torture and the war, as individuals assessed their past actions and attitudes.

Imperial Identity and Torture

For many conscripts tolerance or acceptance of torture, reprisals, summary executions, and rape (even when passive) was grounded as much in military solidarity as in identification with an imperial republic. Patriotism is occasionally invoked as having been at the root of the manifold abuses committed by troops. Yet few soldiers were really convinced that Algeria was French in the sense that France was French, or that Algeria was an organic part of France. Conscripts knew that Algeria was a colony with a special status. But many felt pride in being citizens of a country with an empire. As a teacher who served in the war put it, "We couldn't really imagine losing the colonies. It was the school, secular and republican, that hammered it in our heads that France was France because it had a colonial empire." At times consciousness of the nation collided with that of the empire producing an implicit acknowledgment of the non-French identity of Algeria that did not rise to the level of awareness. School again was invoked as the cause of this political amnesia: "They stuffed it in our heads. . . . Every Frenchman knew that Algeria was French, that it was a French territory. . . . And then when the rebellion began, we knew that it was for independence, for detaching the three departments from the national territory, from the territory of the Republic as it were."[2] Alternatively, imperial identity expressed itself in terms of a moral mission. A second-lieutenant asserted that giving Algerians "the honor of being French citizens was after all a fantastic humanitarian achievement." Those among the troops who felt Algeria would give them the opportunity to correct the mistakes made in Vietnam, as did a graduate of the military academy of Saint-Cyr, claimed to have been moved by a "missionary spirit." He recalled that he and his peers seldom thought of "colonialism as a mode of exploitation." Instead, they felt, "'France has colonies,' and we had to fight in order to defend them and keep them." His cohort—that came of age after the defeat in Vietnam—strongly believed, "'we will be the first ones to win.'"[3] The concrete reality of the colonial war—weapons, death, and torture—were silenced and subsumed under the traumatic loss of Vietnam. Algeria will redeem Dien Bien Phu, and the soldier-missionary will fight with guns and citizenship. The Algerians' identity was seldom posed as an issue in its own right. It was not spoken, as if Algerians occupied a blank space in the minds of the narrators. Thus fighting for imperial identity was predicated upon the suppression of the identity of the empire's subjects. Torture was the tool of the suppression.

In Algeria, troops discovered a new country, with different peoples and customs. It was not only Algerians who were new to them, but also the Pieds-Noirs. Despite their French citizenship, these were mostly perceived as quasi alien: "They were guys with names that ended in 'o' or 'i,' many of them of Italian, foreign, or Spanish descent."[4] Similarly, the discovery of dire poverty among Algerians came as a shock to conscripts who had imagined the Empire as an extension of France. Being part of this diversity but also separate from it, and having to do a military duty, gave rise to numerous permutations and expressions of imagined imperial identity moving across a political-cultural as well as physical field.

Geography of Imperial Identity

An odd but psychologically telling expression, "nomadization" (used by the military to refer to the strategy of sending small commandos on rapid and frequent operations to hunt down guerillas), compared soldiers to nomads, carrying their belongings with them, roaming over a vast territory. The term connoted an exotic desire to go native, although by outnomading the nomads. Playing at being a nomad was also a pastime for some. Alain Maillard de la Morandais, a conscripted intelligence officer, took to donning a burnous, mounting his horse with the help of two Algerian aides, and galloping in a safe perimeter around the SAS he had been assigned to in the High Plateau of Géryville. He imagined himself as free as the nomads had been who were now regrouped in tents under his surveillance. This helped him to divorce himself from the tedious task of filing names and wondering about the legitimacy of torture.[5] Louis Delarue, a chaplain with paratroopers of the 1st REP, and an apologist for torture, found time to take in the quaint beauty of a mountain village in the Grande Kabylie during one of the best-known and deadliest paratroopers' operations, Opération Jumelles (Spyglasses). He delighted in the description of his walks through

> poetic Kabyle villages, along the paths that thread them to one another. I would unexpectedly discover at the foot of the naked hills crisscrossed with ravines, along the *oued* [river, in Arabic], shady orchards with bright green fig trees, and trellised vines—idyllic islands of illusory peace with water gurgling away—Ah! To walk through the mountain at my leisure, to be able to listen, oblivious to danger or time, to turtledoves and nightingales in chirruping duets, to seek the vantage point from which the village would look its best![6]

The physical beauty of Algeria anchored imperial identity in a tangible space implicitly deemed worth fighting for. Topography acted as a means of assimilating Algeria to France. Algeria as a country, her geography, was frequently compared to regions in France. The northern plains were likened to the Midi; the eastern mountains were said to be just like elevated parts of France. Only the high plateaux and desert could not be assimilated to the familiar in France. But then the specialness of the desert lent to it the mystique of the south, in which Morandais and Aldop indulged. Sometimes the people of Algeria, especially children, appeared to be specimens of a different race of people. A former conscript described a seven-year-old boy as "a little Arab, a handsome kid. . . . He had distinctive, typical Arab features [*typé*, in French], very typical."[7]

In combat zones, Algeria merged with Vietnam, and Algerians were at times referred to as Viets. An officer was reported to have announced at the mess the death of a "Viet." As the narrator put it: "There was a sort of equation of the situation in Algeria with our lived experience in Vietnam, of the '*fellagha*' with the '*Viet*.' In the end, we 'bashed the *fellagha*' just as we 'bashed the Viet' in military operations." The expression was frequently used, and the substitution of Vietnam for Algeria was so widespread in the minds of the troops that General Noiret, commandant of the Constantine and Eastern Division, disseminated a circular on May 31, 1956, to make his troops aware of the problem: "It has been noted that often officers have, by way of reminiscence, used the term 'Viet' to refer to our current adversary. This term no longer corresponds to reality, and risks offending the French-Muslims who remain faithful to us, as well as harm[ing] our pacification action." He ordered the commandants of his zone "to cross out [the term] from the current language as well as official vocabulary"[8] In reality, the politically hazardous linguistic confusion that the general sought to correct transcended "reminiscences." The problem was not simply that in all wars protagonists call one another by derogatory names, as, for example, French troops calling the Germans the *boches* during World War II. In Algeria, French troops already had names for the nationalists, whom they referred to as *fells*, *fellouzes*, or *felloches*. The referent "Viets" went to the heart of the complexity of imperial identity in times of crisis. If the Empire, the grounds of identity, is crumbling, it is conceivable that individuals will no longer distinguish their enemies from one another; fighting a Vietnamese becomes the same as fighting an Algerian. Yet any soldier who fought in both colonial wars, Algerian and Vietnamese, could in conversations identify specific villages where he operated and know full well where exactly he had served. General Chabannes knew the "big difference between Viets and *fellaghas*: [is that] the former were really political men; the latter were mere terrorists, who only understood force."[9] This was not a matter of mistaking Algeria for Vietnam in a moment of absentmindedness. It shook the psychological security that the Empire provided, and is best encapsulated in the phrase "from Tamanrasset to Dunkirk."

The possible loss of Algeria, imagined as the safest of all colonies, stalked the troops at a time when the defeat at Dien Bien Phu weighed on all of them, veterans of Vietnam and conscripts. Referring to an Algerian nationalist as a "Viet" was more than a mere *lapsus* that betrayed a social unconscious saturated with fear, foreboding, and anxiety. It was an anticipatory reenacting of a forthcoming defeat that at the same time conjured it away. By fighting the new "Viets" better than the old, troops exorcized defeat with the hope of achieving victory. But fighting a colonial war, a guerilla war, robs troops of the possibility of a clear win that rests on military prowess alone. The last fulcrum for sustaining imperial identity was in perpetual challenge; Algeria might fall just as had Vietnam, "the pearl of the Empire."[10]

Life without an empire meant a recomposition of identity. As long as fighting in Algeria was imagined to take place in Vietnam, Algeria, the last bastion of France's empire, was wishfully thought to be still secure, and so was imperial identity. General Noiret's reminder to his troops that the word "Viet" no longer corresponded to "reality" addressed the dreamlike world that the troops constructed for themselves to protect their identity. But dreams and imaginary constructions of self do not obey military orders. The circular brought to the surface the irony of reminding troops, whose task it was to know their maps and how to orient themselves, that they were in Algeria and not in Vietnam. General Noiret was compelled to invoke the reality principle as opposed to fancy, and to reiterate the difference between past and present. Ultimately, General Noiret was asking the impossible of his troops: Do not imagine, he seemed to imply, defeat in Algeria, and do not think of success in Vietnam; get your calendar straight, and find your linguistic bearings or we might lose Algerians faithful to us. But the troops were concerned about their *own* loss of self, and the dubious faithfulness of the Empire to *them*. Could it be that the survival of the derogatory label "Viet" enabled the troops to express their racist as well as anticommunist feelings?[11] It is true that according to the precepts of the counterrevolutionary war, Algerian nationalism was merely communism by proxy. It is also true that race played an important role in the abuses of Algerians. However, there was more to the substitution of the Vietnam War for the Algerian War, of the "Viet" to the *fellagha*. The substitution was repetitious as well as spontaneous, denoting a supplemental meaning that lay in the very constitution of imperial identity. It bespoke the unfolding of a crisis of self. It mirrored the opposite process occurring among nationalists. The Algerians who joined the FLN, at least in the early years of the war, experienced a heightened sense of self, discovered meaning in their lives that they had not experienced before. The meaning of the Empire to the soldier's sense of self is best expressed by General Raoul Salan, who presided over the withdrawal of France from Vietnam: "It is the loss of Indochina that sapped the foundations of the Empire. To lose an empire is to lose one's self; it is to remove all meaning from a man's life, the life of a builder."[12] Echoing Salan, Colonel Lacheroy explained the impetus behind his elaboration of counterrevolutionary war theory as "my love for empire," which, in his estimation, included "one twelfth of the globe with [troops of] 40,000 men"—the stuff of "dreams."[13]

Terror as Force

The mythical colonial notion on which counterrevolutionary strategy rested—that force was the only language native Algerians could understand—was largely accepted by soldiers serving in Algeria. As Aldop, the confessed torturer encountered earlier, mused: "What were we defending in Algeria? How did I come to think that some men could live on 300 francs a day? How could I have believed racist arguments such as 'They only understand force; they don't like to work; they are cowards'?" Once the myth of the self-evident legitimacy of force against native Algerians was exploded, the person who had accepted it as an article of faith was at a loss to explain its crudeness. Officer Aldop's surprise at his past gullibility did not materialize until he left Algeria and started reflecting about his actions. However, his focus on the myth reveals the ideological role it played in his prosecution of torture. But the myth by itself could not rise to the level of an ideology that helped motivate soldiers to win the war. It lacked a moral-philosophical grounding for which Aldop found a substitute in racial difference. He argued that racism was "the principal reason for the use of torture on a grand scale . . . and for the ease with which torturers were recruited. Only people considered inferior are tortured systematically." Undoubtedly race played a significant role in the brutal treatment of native Algerians by the army and the police. However, the torture of Maurice Audin to death, or of Henri Alleg among others, was just as exacting as that of native Algerians. Algerians were subjected to different and racist verbal abuse than their French counterparts whose torment centered on their political beliefs. Thus, torture as a tool of government transcends race or ethnicity.

The ideology of racial difference as encapsulated in the myth of force was reinforced by the unshakable reality of Algerians as a defeated people brought under colonial control. As a result, torture appeared as part of the natural order of things colonial. Aldop's discovery of the racial dimension of torture was no doubt a realization, after the fact, of the immorality of his acts, and a milestone in a process of self-understanding. Yet, he had been unwilling to go along with the torture of Pieds-Noirs, members of the OAS, should he have been so ordered. He found the prospect of a Frenchman torturing another Frenchman repulsive and intolerable. Ultimately, he laid responsibility for his function as a torturer on psychologial action: He had been "conditioned" to inflict torture on native Algerians. In other words, he was a victim of the army: "So, I realize that the institution that employed me for nearly five years had also wanted all the others to keep a good conscience: A few thousand men [to sacrifice] in order to save a few millions. Unfortunately, I was one of the few thousands."[14] From his perspective, torturer and tortured were both victims of the army. This reluctance to assume responsibility for torture, and the realization that one was manipulated by the army was not peculiar to Aldop. It was also found among other veterans[15] and used as an exculpatory argument in a few trials. It helped torturers come to terms with their past and avoid experiencing a futile sense of guilt, which, as Aldop pointed out, when taken to its logical conclusion would result in his suicide. But he enjoyed being a grandfather and could not entertain the thought of killing himself. Besides, he also found solace in helping occasional Algerian immigrants in France whenever they had to negotiate the French bureaucracy.

When invoked retrospectively, torture for a self-confessed former intelligence officer was considered a "method" to help distinguish good from bad Algerians. When a bomb exploded, "anyone was a suspect. If you asked me at that point which Algerians were for or against the FLN, I would have found it difficult to answer you. . . . There had to be a 'method' to identify the culprits." However, this exculpatory function of torture in situations of urban attacks was belied by the officer's treatment of men who did not throw bombs, but were part of the OPA as collectors of funds. They too were subjected to "vigorous interrogation." Like Aldop, the narrator also invoked "efficiency" in describing his work, a manner of rehabilitating torture by wrapping it in the garb of professionalism. He too distinguished himself from amateurs or sadists who found pleasure in inflicting pain, taking pride in doing "police interrogation work." He saw his job as applying the method to get specific results regardless of time, place, or person. As a professional, he claims to have released an "old Arab man . . . who lost his voice" and thus gave no information. Under normal circumstances the man would have been sent to "fetch wood." Seeing torture as a profession with a method informed by efficiency helped to sever the practice from any moral entanglement. Paradoxically, conscience got garbled, as the severity of the method called for an extra-professional justification. Even though the narrator asserted, "I am not ashamed of what I did to people," he added: "I was young and had had no training." He left the responsibility for the nature of his acts hanging between youth and inexperience, thus evading guilt without claiming innocence. Yet, there was a point at which he could draw the line and take a stand: He would *not* torture other Frenchmen, members of the OAS, fellow Pieds-Noirs, who might fall in his hands. As Aldop did, the narrator argued that it was hard enough to torture "Arabs," some of whom he knew. But he simply would not do the same to Frenchmen. Ironically, he was one of the first officers to be arrested by the French government crackdown on the OAS. In an unexpected role reversal, he was now asked to name names, although he was not tortured, but received blows to his ribs with a machine gun. He was subsequently sent to an internment camp among native Algerians for two months where he lived in fear of being recognized by some inmates he had tortured. He was ultimately released in May 1958. His experience failed to help him understand the pain he inflicted on others. Instead it triggered in him a greater awareness of his identity as a Pied-Noir who spoke "with an accent." His loss of power and reversal of fortune prompted a short-lived revenge.[16]

Unlike professional torturers, witnesses subsume the practice under the unbridled violence of the war using words such as "massacres," which in colloquial French may mean "demolishing" without connoting torment. However, knowledge that torture existed gives rise to a moral gymnastics aimed at assuaging guilt by association. Bertrand, from a village in the Vosges, remembered, "It wasn't war anymore; it was a massacre. When we killed people, we didn't just kill them, we massacred them on the day when an ambush occurred." A former teacher wondered whether the remains of seven men "massacred" by a torturer and buried in the garden of a school in the town of "K" near the western city of Oran had been found. He had thought of divulging this incident but asked rhetorically, "To whom could I write?" Shifting to others responsibility for the commission of acts of torture, reprisals, or summary executions helps to evade or conceal complicity. Speaking of an Algerian prisoner who had been taken out of his cell and killed with spades and picks in a vengeful act, a former conscript recalled, "The poor guy, he was a man like us. . . . We made him dig a grave and we buried him almost alive." Managing the consciousness of the severity of acts committed against Algerians reaches beyond the perpetrators of torture and at times affects those who listen to their accounts. The social scientist who carried out interviews with veterans categorically states, even though she is aware of the systemic nature of violence during the war, that torture, rape, summary executions (which she refers to as "extra-judicial executions") were committed by a "small minority of soldiers only."[17] Although statistics are not, and may never be available since much of the violence was not recorded, these abuses were far more widespread than she intimates.

The memory of having witnessed torture at times collides with images of France's occupation by German troops in 1940 and the Resistance. A former conscript who was woken up by the screams of tortured men questioned his own role in the military: "The picture that haunts me is that with my helmet and my uniform, I looked more like a German soldier than a partisan."[18] He had visited the "shack" where torture took place and felt outraged that "the armies of the Republic could commit such atrocities." However, he did not think that the rape of the women whom he helped to round up and "park" in camps behind barbed wire partook of the same logic as torture. He saw the event as a police operation conducted by military men. The passage of time gives the comparison with Nazi Germany a poignant relevance. Twelve years after he had ordered the summary execution of three Algerian men in a mountain village in the Grande Kabylie, a second lieutenant went back to find the spot, a clump of olive trees now surrounding a memorial stone, where the executions took place. He remembered how he had gone to the third man who survived the fusillade, and killed him point blank with his gun. He could still see in his mind's eye the supplicating eyes of his young victim pleading for mercy. He fell to the ground, as he remembered having watched on television the German chancellor Willy Brandt do at Auschwitz sometime earlier, and knelt before the memorial stone, thinking that in Algeria, *he* was the German.[19] Whereas Willy Brandt paid his respects to the memory of the victims of Nazism as a contrite German who had not committed the crimes he condemned, this French officer returned to the place of the crime he had committed in Algeria, not to show sorrow publicly, but as a private pilgrimage. He did so with impunity, with no fear of arrest from the Algerian state, and without identifying himself to the surviving relatives of his victim. The memory of World War II and the Resistance cut both ways. However, it added a complicating dimension to the crisis of self. It paradoxically sowed doubt in the minds of those who fought hard to keep Algeria French, just as it helped them to assuage any guilt for wrongdoing. Doubts were temporarily quelled on the grounds that Germany *occupied* France, whereas Algeria *was* France.

The conflicting memories of World War II and Vietnam rested on the silencing of the meaning of colonialism for the Algerians. Imagining France as the purveyor of progress and civilization also meant thinking of the dire poverty of the majority of the Algerian population as a personal, if not cultural, choice. The sight of the miserable conditions under which rural Algerians lived, shocked many a conscript, as it did Morandais: "They were very poor. They were French too, but lived less well than we do in France. They were a bit like beggars." Being French could not be reconciled with poverty in the colony being fought for. Hence a denial among some: "They were poor, but they were not unhappy. The way they lived was different from ours. This was the way they chose to live, and they were happy to live like that."[20] And although some found in the discovery of Algerian poverty a cause for the war, many accepted it as a rejection of progress, and a result of an assumed laziness. This interpretation of poverty had an anesthetic effect on the mind, helping to preserve the wholeness of imperial identity.

Imperial Identity: Full and Blank

Although, in objective terms, imperial identity depended for its sustenance on the suppression of a distinct native identity in the Empire, it required duplicating itself in colonial subjects without losing its integrity. General Noiret's reference to the "faithful" Algerians who would be offended if called "*Viets*," the enemies of the Empire, conjures up the formation of an identity among native Algerians based on faithfulness in and to the Empire. The Algerian qua rebel, the Algerian civilian qua suspect, the Algerian qua poor all represented failures of the installation of an imperial self on the periphery of metropolitan France. The failure was at times perceived as a result of the inadequacy of the human material at hand. A conscript noted, "They [Algerians] were all presumed to be born on. . . . They did not have birth dates; they had nothing." He further remarked that they were known by the phrase "without a surname" (sans nom patronymique, or SNP, in French).[21] The generalization aside, the narrator was right. But knowledge of the history of the colonization of Algeria would have alerted him to the French policy in the nineteenth century of registering people under inaccurate names, transcribing Arabic and Berber names improperly, and referring to some as "having no surname," or SNP. He also was unaware of one of the modalities of resistance to the French Empire: Traditionally, rural people in Algeria frequently refused to register their children when they were born, thus significantly confounding the military task of registering and accounting for every Algerian. But for this narrator, Algerians could not be made French, because they lacked even the basics of human identity, names to be called by; their existence could not be accounted for since they had no birth dates. Yet it was the Empire that had created new names for people who already had one or left names blank. The decision to brand people with the label SNP constituted an act of ultimate identity erasure as well as the attribution of a virtual identity. The colonial state thereby asserted its will to create anonymity out of presence, and subsume being under nothingness. The narrator pointed to an essential part of the imperial manufacture of identity beginning with naming. The identity so constructed was alien to the narrator, although it was the flip side of his own, the imperial blank on which his own identity was forged.

That an imperial self might have already been created on the periphery but in ways that differed from its center was not glimpsed at the time. Yet this was what Fanon attempted to address not only in *Black Skin, White Masks*, but also in the *Wretched of the Earth* by calling for a "new man" who severs the trappings of colonial subjectivization that reach deep into the colonized person's psyche. The manufacturing of identity was necessary to maintain the imperial order's functioning. But in a situation of crisis, it was also a source of challenge. Fear of the Algerian, any Algerian, since he was a suspect par excellence, worked in various ways: It could be caused by the mere existence of the colonized person. Soldiers were never sure whether they would be attacked by apparently unarmed native civilians. The stereotype of the deceitful, murderous Arab who would stab a Frenchman in the back was present in the soldier's mind when he was off base, or traveling on a boat filled with Algerians. Although guerilla warfare understandably fostered such fear, it was also embedded in images of native Algerians that preceded the war. There was the irrational fear of being poisoned by villagers from whom coffee and homemade bread was demanded as war booty. Finally there was the fear of not recognizing the enemy, who might speak good French, be dressed in French military uniform, and possibly look French. The French Empire, like the other European empires, was an endless source of exotic sights, people, customs, and costumes. Paratroopers often wore *shesh* (long turbans) just like native Algerian men; other soldiers at times posed for the usual souvenir photo in turbans and blankets imitating the traditional burnous.[22] The language of the soldier, whether he was a metropolitan French man or a Pied-Noir, was studded with (badly transcribed) Arabic words, many of which were learned from survival handbooks handed out to conscripts.

Colonial warfare dramatizes the instability and plasticity of identity formation as well as its elusiveness. By establishing a colonial *culture* of subjection to, and glorification of the French nation, colonial France found comfort in the thought that the route to being French for an Algerian was to speak French and adopt French ways. It thus equated appearing with being, pretense with truth, acting like with plain acting. Arguably, France did not care whether her colonial subjects felt French or not. It was concerned with keeping them in line since it did not give them the political and economic means to be French. However, colonial schools and the systemic denigration of Algerian culture were aimed at undermining the integrity of Algerian identity. Yet the identity game foisted on Algerians, especially the urban among them, was just that, a game. In the real world of everyday life in the colony, appearing French was never confused with being French, and being French played itself out on the colonizer side of the fence. Nevertheless, the "acting like" in the identity-production game is always perilous: One can be taken in by the game, confuse the role with the real thing. Blaise Pascal suggested that the first step toward acquiring faith begins with the body ritual of kneeling down and joining the hands together in a gesture of prayer. Belief, much like identity, is not a given; it is a process. Although unstable and resisting fixity, identity is not a free-floating peg that one hangs a self to. The colonial situation demonstrates the complexity of the process through which identities cross over into one another, collide, become submerged or assert themselves. And torture as the modulation of pain can inflect the outcome. In this, the colonized person had an edge on the colonizer; the nationalist on the defender of the Empire. The former generally knew from experience how to navigate competing identities; the other had to allow himself to learn that imperial identity was neither fixed nor coterminous with national identity. More important, he had to learn that his imperial identity was inculcated in him just as it was, in a different form, in the colonized person. His identity *prise de conscience* was the flip side of the nationalist's. They were both creations of the Empire. A conscript from a working-class background, who had never set foot in Algeria before the war, and who found himself committing atrocities in the name of an empire he, as an individual, did little to build or manage, was as much a creation of the Empire as the Algerian who fought against it. The war, as mediated by torture, helped a few men ascertain who they were and examine what they fought for. The memory of the war for many French soldiers, whether expressed immediately upon discharge, or years later, is often accompanied with unease about the legitimacy of the fight, which is tied to questioning who one was/is, given the appeal made by the colonial government to the patriotism of the conscripts. Yet those who kept diaries detailing the war and the abuses they committed were predominantly enlisted men. I do not know why this is, except that they went into the Army by *choice* and thus knew more or less clearly the reasons why they fought. Their disenchantment with the army may have been more intensely experienced than the conscripts'.

As might be expected, the men who led the war, colonels and generals, did not question the legitimacy of the methods they used. On the contrary, they found more and better reasons for having waged the war in the manner they did. Speaking in his defense on May 29, 1961, General Challe, who led the putsch, claimed to have opposed the French government policy of ending the war because it was not adapted to the "Algerian reality," which he purported to know intimately. He claimed, among other things, to know how the "Muslims" thought of the future of their country. He defined the "Muslim conception" of the choice between self-determination and continued colonization as being "different from the European conception of things. When a Muslim chooses, he chooses a leader and therefore a destiny." Consequently, the French government's decision to ask Algerians by a second referendum (in 1961) whether they would seek self-determination was ill advised, according to Challe, because Algerians had already voted in a referendum on de Gaulle in 1958. He argued that Algerians qua Muslims had thus chosen to remain colonized, and felt obligated to defend their choice. Having spent two years overseeing their "pacification," he was confident he understood their needs. From his perspective, Algerians were one colonized people among many whom, in his view, France had promised to defend against nationalists, but ended up abandoning. Challe had in mind specific groups of people who had identified with the Empire, such as the "Catholics of Tonkin, the Tais, the Meos, a tremendous number of Vietnamese, the Berbers of Morocco, very many Arabs, Tunisians, and today the Algerians." Thus the putsch was justified on the twin grounds of an assumed specialized knowledge of native Algerians and a sense of duty toward all the colonial people deemed faithful to France. Nevertheless, the general's language betrayed ambivalence toward native Algerians. On the one hand, he referred to them as "French," on the other hand, he characterized them as fundamentally different people. The cultural difference he sought to subsume under the French flag for which he fought erupted out of his discourse to subvert it: His struggle was not to protect Algerians, but to keep Algeria French. This sentiment was best expressed by his accomplice in the putsch, General Zeller, in explaining why he rebelled: "purely and simply to keep Algeria under French sovereignty."[23] For Zeller, the colonial war was also waged for his self-preservation as a self-appointed carrier of the Empire.

Destabilizing Imperial Identity

Unlike the insurgent military chiefs, General Jacques Pâris de Bollardière—commanding the eastern sector of Blida near Algiers—was an opponent of torture and differentiated between a narrowly defined imperial identity that could not separate itself from possession of an empire, and one that was grounded in "the moral values of our French civilization."[24] Bollardière uncoupled civilization from empire, while the insurgent generals equated the two as one and the same grounding of identity. In rejecting torture and repression, General de Bollardière opted for a gentler approach to keeping Algeria French. He preferred a morally clean loss of Algeria, to winning with dishonor. Although aware of abuses in wartime, military men such as Bolladière also knew of the importance of respecting rules of engagement. In the end, honor is as elusive a reason for fighting and torturing as it is for going against the grain.

For segments of the French population the war provided the opportunity to reflect on what it meant for them to be French: members of the Communist Party who refused to torture (and not all did), those who decided to actively help the nationalists, or religious figures who felt that

Christian ethics compelled them to reject violence. These and other individuals who simply could not shoot at a defenseless old man, or execute an unarmed and wounded man in cold blood wondered about their presence in the army, the meaning of war, and, most important, the meaning of patriotism. From their perspective, acting patriotic meant acting against their conscience as Frenchmen brought up to value freedom, democracy, and human dignity. The army dismissed these men's misgivings as stirred by Communist agitation, or a "conscience" incompatible with military duty. Yet, conscience was one aspect of a larger identity crisis triggered by the war. One of these men was André Monjardet, who refused to shoot at an unarmed group of three peasants in Zémourah, which resulted in his demotion and imprisonment. It was also the case of soldier Jean-Denis Bennet, who allowed a civilian to approach the post in one of the forbidden zones to seek help for his wife in labor. The wife was subsequently taken by helicopter to a nearby hospital. Although the soldier was credited by his comrades with saving two lives, he was nevertheless disciplined and spent thirty days in jail. There were to be sure a number of such acts of resistance to orders to shoot and kill.

A leitmotif in many barracks, camps, and posts was this sense of instability in a war that was increasingly fought outside the law. Jean Faure who, after the war, became a member of the French senate wrote, for example, "Today I killed a man running at a distance, purposely, I the conscientious objector. He was innocent, and an old man too! 'You must kill lucidly, coldly.' This is what the captain told me." In such a state of anomie, imperial identity for those who came from France either crystallized, freeing the individual soldier from qualms of conscience, or gave way to national identity defined in moral terms. The "problems of conscience" (états d'âme in French, or "states of the soul") were intimately linked to how one defined France, what it stood for, or one's role in it. Among those who talked about their war experiences to various researchers, there is a constant amazement about the tolerance of acts that would have been immoral had they taken place in France. Former soldier turned priest, Jean-Paul Bouland notes: "It is when I came back that I became ashamed of having had to see what I saw. . . . One can only talk about things that can be fathomed. But for most Frenchmen, it was unthinkable that France would do that [i.e., atrocities]. So, they did not want to, and could not hear. And so, we didn't tell them."[25] The unfathomable, the unthinkable, also could not be spoken independently of whether others were willing to listen. It could not be heard because the perpetrators would not say it. And they would not say it because it did not square with French people's self-image.

Those intellectuals who opposed torture invoked not only moral values, but also French honor. René Capitant, upon hearing of the death by "suicide" of a former Algerian student of his, Ali Boumendjel, who had been tortured, wrote to the French minister of education. He pointed out that he failed to understand how "such practices," which had not even been used by the French against their German prisoners during World War II, could be "prescribed and tolerated by the government of my own country." Such practices could only risk "dishonoring France."[26] Honor held different meanings for different people. Capitant perceived it as the opposite of the shame derived from inflicting cruel and unusual punishment on prisoners. For François Mauriac, a literary figure, honor lay in spiritual strength. In 1957 he hoped for a "transmutation of the will to power into a will to love," which France, despite her loss of prestige, could have performed because it "miraculously still held a spiritual preeminence."[27] For Alban Liechti, a conscientious objector, refusing to fight in Algeria was motivated by a concern for "the honor of my country."[28] It cost him two years in jail at the end of which he received two more years for still refusing to fight. The authors of the putsch understood honor to mean the French flag continuing to fly over the colonies, and winning counterrevolutionary wars.

Imperial Identity Misfires: Children and Paratroopers

The manner in which imperial identity is induced or misfires is best studied in children. Former conscripts have pointed out, time and again, how schools had socialized them into French imperial culture. How empire on the wane socializes native children is equally instructive. As the war unfolded, it fashioned a counterimperial identity among Algerian children attending French schools. Views expressed by grade-school children illustrate how far the repression reached into their minds. On June 22, 1957 (when the paratroopers' assault on Algiers was ending), a teacher asked a class of ten- to fourteen-year-olds to write a French composition answering the following question: "What would you do if you were invisible?" Responses revealed anger at paratroopers and French politicians, as well as a general sympathy for the FLN: "I would kill all the French soldiers." "I'll free prisoners." "I will place a bomb at the Milk Bar [where a real one had been placed in 1956]; I'll attack Massu's paras [paratroopers]. I'll go all the way to Guy Mollet [then prime minister] and Robert Lacoste [the governor general], and I'll kill them." "I'll go to the Aurès mountain and encourage our brothers, the glorious Moudjahidine [combatants] I'll find there, and I'll toss grenades at paras." "I'll free my three brothers held prisoner by the soldiers; I'll massacre all the French people, young and old, on the way." "If I had a gun, I'd kill the Bouché-nachas [informers]; if I had a rifle, I would be a *fellagha*." "If I was invisible, I would go into a barracks, kill all the soldiers, and throw a bomb in there. Then I would go to the paras and kill them like dogs. I'd go to police stations and throw bombs; then I'd kill the CRS [riot police] and go to the Aurès Mountains and kill all those who are tracking the rebels down. God bless the Arabs! God bless the FLN!" "I'd strike all those who do harm; I'll kill all the paras because they do harm . . . and I'll free all the prisoners in Barberousse [notorious jail]." "I'd kill the paras who torture men like Indians. . . . I'd attack arms supply convoys, and give them to the men in Paul Cazelles [an internment camp]." "I'd steal French women's jewelry as Massu's men do; they take pictures of women to give to the men. They cannot take Algiers. It belongs to Arabs." "I'd take a cord and strangle the last of the paras on patrol in the tunnel in my neighborhood. . . . And if they dared do what they usually do, I'd torture them and some, before I kill them. And I'll have a job like my teacher; I'd buy a villa . . . and be a Sultan of the whole world but not France."

These composition excerpts that the Committee for Peace in Algeria reproduced ring true. They are studded with children's flights of fancy about stealing bicycles and lumps of sugar from a mother, holding up a bank to give money to old people, or dreams of the poor becoming rich and the rich poor.[29] Importantly, they reflect the extent to which war was the framework within which Algiers children were socialized. Additionally, these compositions reveal how families in the Casbah were affected by the war and the Battle of Algiers. Of significance is the geography of the war as narrated by children: Aurès Mountains, Barberousse Jail, Paul Cazelles Internment Camp, and the tunnels of the Casbah, narrow alleyways running under roofs and balconies that meet overhead as ceilings of sorts. Similarly, major politicians were known by their names, as was the most notorious general in Algiers, Massu. The sexual component of paratroopers' actions was retained not so much in the form of rape, but as something that was morally offensive: taking pictures of women and passing them to men. Paratroopers were also lumped together with informers as people who do harm and need to be punished. Beyond the larger issue of children's war involvement, directly or indirectly, these compositions go to the heart of military repression on the Algerian population, which helped to make role models of the very people it combated. One of the children wrote that *he* had killed Ali Chekkal, an Algerian politician who supported the French government and whom the FLN had killed in France as he came out of a stadium in May 1957. Arguably, these children lived in the Casbah, a neighborhood that had ostensibly supported the FLN, and thus could not be representative of sympathies in other places. In reality the war drew Algerians and French people apart, and loyalties generally followed the colonizer and colonized divide. Children felt that pull.

The film *The Battle of Algiers*[30] portrays children harassing a drunkard on a street in Algiers prior to the encirclement of the Casbah by Massu's men, in an illustration of the determination of the FLN to cleanse Algerian society of all the presumably French-induced social ills. When organized or condoned by the state, terror backfires and unravels the trappings of imperial identity by bolstering a national(ist) identity. A leader of the FLN in the Casbah, Saadi Yacef, noted the transformative effect on the Algerian population of the bombing—by a group of French ultras, with police complicity—of a row of houses on Rue de Thèbes on August 10, 1956. After this attack, the FLN emerged as a legitimate authority. Streets were policed by its members, who established their own curfew and issued passwords to individuals circulating after hours. Yacef pointed to the indiscriminate nature of state terror as contrasted with the initial FLN attacks (before they became random) that targeted individual Frenchmen who had committed heinous acts against Algerians, as well as Algerian informers. One of these was a former subprefect, Achiary, whom the FLN charged with killing children in Guelma, eastern Algeria, during the May 8, 1945, massacres.[31] This concrete illustration of the power of the memory of past events in guiding present political acts ran parallel to French military officers' memory not only of previous colonial wars, but also of the more remote French history. In many ways, the Algerian War was the battleground of memories that reached as far back as the eighteenth century and rebuilt themselves as the war unfolded.

The preceding has shown that torture and other acts of terror were the channels through which imperial identity either crystallized or became destabilized. Imperial identity overshadowed stirrings of conscience among professional torturers or helped to quell guilt. The many modalities of the interface between identity and tolerance of terror illustrate the plasticity of conscience as a formal, discursive capacity for shifting responsibility onto others, evading guilt, or concealing complicity. Awareness of the unsavory character of torture, as well as of the pain that it causes, was neither a necessary, nor a sufficient condition for not engaging in it. Imperial identity loomed large in the widespread use and routinization of torture. Where imperial identity was delinked from national identity, rejection of torture became possible; it left room for a refashioning of the self on an idealization of the nation and the values it stood for. The memory of torture experienced under Nazism did not necessarily lead to a rejection of the practice. Nor did it necessarily act as an impediment to engaging in torture. Yet when reflected upon after the fact, acts of torture and terror were mostly seen as having been not only immoral, but also inefficient. Conscience appears to be extremely malleable: It could find comfort in myths that dehumanize others, blame atrocities on the youthfulness of the perpetrators, and help the torturer feel like a victim. In the end, the workings of conscience in the context of a war of decolonization are mediated by identity.

The Church and the men whose job it is to speak to conscience had an important role to play in the rejection or tolerance of torture and in establishing a common ground on which to build military and political solidarity, as will be discussed in the next chapter.

Chapter 8

THE CHRISTIAN CHURCH

AND ANTISUBVERSIVE WAR

THE ANTISUBVERSIVE war strategy required more than propaganda to make torture morally acceptable to the troops as well as the public. Revolutionary-war theory stressed the importance of ideology, or a cause, in securing commitment to the revolution. By contrast, the counterrevolutionary doctrine did not formulate a compelling (counter-) cause except for the political-cultural ideology of empire. Consequently, religion, a traditional source of social solidarity, appealed to the military, eager to shore up its hackneyed defense of colonial rule, and buttress its anticommunist stance. The army was served by the Church's own misgivings about the process of decolonization, just as it welcomed the relentless activism of the religious right.

The Algerian War was saturated with religion: Torture and other acts of repression generated support or criticism in the Christian press, among Christian associations and individual priests, ordained or lay. The role played by religion (as used by the Church and private Christian groups) in justifications of torture and the war needs examination as does the FLN's handling of Islam.

Religious symbolism was attached to the very name of the war: it was often called the war of the Toussaint, or All Souls' Day War, because it coincided with the Catholic celebration of that day (November 1).[1] I have found only one reference indicating that Prophet Muhammad's birthday, Mawlad Ennabawi (in Algerian Arabic, Mouloud), in 1954 fell on that day too.[2] Given the lunar calendar, Muslim connotation of the war, as it proceeded, was spurious. Nevertheless, the Algerian War began under an ironically ecumenical sign, one marking death, and the other life. The invasion of Algeria in July, 1830, had been hailed as a Christian victory. After Algiers was taken, a Te Deum of grace and a mass were said at Notre Dame Cathedral in Paris and in the Casbah on July 11, 1830. Addressing the chaplains, the commandant in chief of the expedition declared: "You have just opened with us the door to Christianity in Africa. Let's hope it will soon rekindle the civilization that had been extinguished." A few days later, a Te Deum was also sung in celebration of the "resurrection of the

African Church" by the pope in St. Peters basilica in Rome.[3] One of the first acts of sovereignty taken by invading troops was to turn Ketchaoua Mosque at the heart of the Casbah into a cathedral. It remained so until independence in 1962.[4]

Christian Church and Colonial Interests

Throughout the colonial era religion played a significant role in the administration of the native population. Laws were constructed on the premise that Islam was incompatible with the extension of full civil and political rights to Algerians, who were predominantly Muslim.[5] Within this context, a question is inescapable: Was the systematic use of torture grounded in the religious factor? There were a number of functions that the perceived divide between Islam and Christianity played in the conduct of the war. First, the tradition of equating Christianity with civilization in French thought magnified the cultural differences between colonizers and colonized, and delegitimized any claim made by the latter for self-rule since by definition they were incapacitated by their culture-religion. Second, Islam was understood to be a source of solidarity with and support for the FLN among newly independent countries such as Egypt, Pakistan, Indonesia, and neighboring Morocco and Tunisia and thus a cause of political concern. Finally, the fear—real or imagined—of Islam as an old foe, and loathing for it as a culture,[6] meant that the defense of Christian values could be used by military authorities as a motivating force to make repressive methods acceptable to the troops.

However, these factors acquire meaning only within the framework of the historical relationship between Church, state, and the society of colonists. The Church's silence on the conduct of the war (and the process of decolonization) in spite of occasional condemnations of torture by key figures, such as Monsignor Duval, archbishop of Algiers, must be understood in light of a number of historically specific conditions: Unlike other African colonies, there was no critical mass of native converts to Christianity, and no indigenous Christian clergy in Algeria. This means that the Church ministered primarily to French settlers of whom there were over 1 million in 1954. And the Church's primary obligation was to her constituency.[7] This relative isolation of the Church from the native population facilitated the development of prejudices among priests. Recruited from France and trained in a theological tradition that denigrated Islam, they tended to identify with their constituents and to share their views of the native population. Eloi Laget, the president of the Catholic Action Diocese Committee for Algiers, bluntly admitted, "We sometimes have a superiority reflex that runs the gamut from the contemptuous use of *tu*, to degrading comments, unsavory jokes, and false pity."[8] Endemic prejudice was reinforced by sheer ignorance: Few priests spoke Arabic (apart from the White Fathers) or had sufficient knowledge of Islam.

There was a commonality of interests between Church and state: Keeping Algeria French meant keeping a relatively large Christian Church undisturbed. Besides, were Algeria to become independent, the Church would have to return the mosques that had been converted to churches; it would also have to return the property of mosques that had been seized by the colonial government. Consequently, the Church had historical-spiritual, as well as material interests to defend in Algeria. On an equally mundane level, as a colonial institution, the Church benefited from the Patronat, an outcome of the 1492 Bull by which the Vatican gave colonizing states the power to select religious personnel and establish the ecclesiastical structures necessary for evangelical action on condition that they take charge of the upkeep of churches, as well as the payment of stipends to priests.[9] Therefore, unlike their metropolitan counterparts, the clergy received subsidies in Algeria in violation of the 1905 law on the separation of state and Church.[10] This could not but make the Church dependent on the state for its material survival, and thus curtail its freedom to oppose state/military repressive policies.

To these considerations must be added a purposely noncommittal and at best ambiguous attitude of the Vatican toward the Algerian War. Part of the Vatican's posture was a function of the pope's propensity to speak in general terms about issues such as colonialism, decolonization, racial discrimination, and the like until events on the ground could no longer be ignored without cost to the Church. For example, Pius XII did not clearly condemn the manner in which the military conducted the war, or the war itself. Nor did he come out in favor of the independence of Algeria. Yet, an ambiguous statement he made about the rights of indigenous peoples to seek sovereignty in an orderly manner was invoked by those who opposed repressive methods, and those who justified them as well. His successor, Jean XXIII, kept the tradition of silence until he could no longer.

Catholic responses to torture and the war invite three observations: their sheer volume, especially in France; their diversity; and their espousal of the main political divisions, left, right and liberal.[11] They also expressed the complexity of the relationship between the local (Algerian) Church and the Church in France on the one hand, and between the local Church and the chaplaincy on the other. The chaplaincy was entirely independent of the local Church. It operated under the aegis of the military and reported to the vicar of the army, the archbishop of Paris, Cardinal Feltin. The vicar was assisted by two directors, one in Algiers, the other in Paris. Chaplains received a stipend by the Ministry of Defense, making them salaried personnel of the army. This dual institutional structure accounted for occasional divergent opinions voiced by men of the cloth in addressing torture and psychological action, among others. Individual priests' attitudes varied according to conscience, exposure to military abusive actions, and/or ties established with native Algerians. Nevertheless, on the whole, individual condemnations of torture and related abuses rarely addressed the root cause of the war: the colonial system of government.

Catholic Church and Anticolonial War

Monsignor Duval condemned torture early in the war, followed by the head of the Reform Church. Nevertheless, both men kept silent on the legitimacy of the war or soldiers' conscientious objection to it. Furthermore, condemnations of torture and psychological action were not initially made in the name of a common humanity that needed to be protected, but as violations of judicial norms. Monsignor Duval, whose liberal views earned him the nicknames Mohammed Duval, Duval l'Arabe, and Le Petit Fellagha, wrote: "The seriousness and dignity of justice as well as public authority demand that strict judicial norms be observed when a suspect is arrested and interrogated." He added: "Judicial procedure must exclude physical and psychological torture as well as 'narco-analysis,' firstly because they violate natural right, even if the accused is really guilty, and secondly because all too often they give erroneous results." Monsignor Duval's moral statement, valuable as it was, fell short of a categorical condemnation of torture and related abuses. Telling the army why torture is not advisable is different from condemning the army for engaging in such a practice, and/or declaring torture a violation of Christian ethics. The FLN was critical of Monsignor Duval for not going far enough in his condemnation of "violence" and "terrorism," and in discussing the causes of the Algerian revolution. In others words, the FLN wanted the Church to acknowledge the legitimacy of its struggle by condemning the colonial system as a source of violence. The FLN was eager to see the Church disassociate itself from the colonial system and become "ready to adjust to life in the new order of independent Algeria as it did in Tunisia and Morocco."[12] Later, in 1961, the FLN would send a memorandum to the bishops of Algeria politely asking them to give up all the mosques that had been turned into churches, and to consider returning to the future Algerian state all the property given to them by the colonial authorities.[13]

Major statements against torture included a letter signed by the bishops of Algeria on September 15, 1955, entitled "Christians and Peace in Algeria." The bishops emphasized the common good on which states should make decisions concerning the "dignity and destiny" of human beings, under the guidance of moral law and faith in God.[14] They also called for equal rights for Algerians, access to civil service, and "free expression of the legitimate aspirations of peoples."[15] This was a generally timid response to a more decisive declaration made earlier on June 3, 1955, by the Theological Committee of the city of Lyon stating, "We cannot deny from a moral and Christian standpoint the legitimacy of the Algerian people's aspirations to independence."[16] The colonial clergy's avoidance of the issue of decolonization meant that it could not question the legitimacy of the war, which made opposition to torture a formal moral act.

There were differences in attitudes toward the war between bishops. Unlike Monsignor Duval's, Monsignor Lacaste, bishop of Oran, ceaselessly defended the military as the sole guarantor of a French Algeria, and extolled the "sacred union"of the army, the state, and the Church. He expounded, before a civil-military audience, on the joint actions of "religious colonization" and "other forms of colonization." Lacaste's hard line also radically differed from Monsignor Mercier's, the bishop of the southern city of Laghouat, and cosigner of the bishops' letter. Mercier apprised General de Gaulle of torture practiced in an intelligence center housed in Villa les Oiseaux, in Laghouat,[17] and ceaselessy drew attention to poverty among Algerians. The Christian community, just like the society at large, was thus either split over the issue of torture, or ambivalent. However, the most remarkable support for torture came from within the chaplaincy.

Military Chaplaincy

Chaplains were nominated by the chief vicar to the army, the archbishop of Paris, and approved by the Ministry of Defense. The chief chaplain of the 10th Military Region (which covered Algeria) was in charge of the various religious centers but was under the control of the commanding general whose approval was needed for the appointments of chaplains to the various military units.[18] The Chaplaincy (which included Jews but no Muslims) acted as the spiritual arm of the military, anticipating recruits' stirrings of conscience and dispelling them for political reasons. Monsignor Badré, chief chaplain, exemplified this role: "I hear that some of you would like us to discuss the Algerian War, torture and the . . . To these I say: You have plenty of time to think about this when you are there. For the moment, it is here [in France] that you should live as Christians."[19] The Chaplaincy's eschewing discussions of torture and related methods was ostensibly motivated by its fear that doing otherwise would play into the hands of the FLN. In other words, the Chaplaincy considered itself an active part of the countersubversive war instead of a religious group that catered to the problems of conscience posed to some of the troops. It supplemented the Action Psychologique of the 5ème Bureau by helping to still the pangs of conscience that disturbed some soldiers.

The chief chaplain in Algiers, Father de L'Espinay, singled out seminarians (who numbered 1,450 with conscripted priests) as recalcitrants:

> The seminarian is easily a troublemaker, a potential organizer, and a rebel against authority. . . . More important, it must be noted that his presence in Algeria is a tragedy for him. He cannot be insensitive to what he sees and hears. He asks himself questions, and is upset by the horrors of the war, inevitable as they might be, and even more so by the others. Being an absolutist, he does not understand that "pacification" means "repression." All this hurts him very deeply. Because of his spiritual avocation, he suffers more than others.

Yet, some seminarians were respected as "Christian Marabouts [spiritual/ holy men] by the Algerians they came in contact with, causing them to feel that they had to own up to the dignity of their new status.[20]

The Chaplaincy's politically motivated conscience management left it open to the accusation of deliberately suppressing letters written by soldiers discussing torture, racism, and poverty that had been intended for publication in the *Letter to the Seminarians and Priests-Soldiers,* a monthly review with a section, "Free Tribune," devoted to soldiers' correspondence. Subordinating the spiritual to the temporal, Cardinal Feltin advised troops,

> The pacification orders you receive cannot make your conscience object to them in light of the things you are witnessing, because they emanate from a legitimate government, and have been sanctioned by a majority of elected officials. These orders are not anti-Christian because, above all, they aim at establishing peace, and political, administrative, social, and economic reforms.

He also reminded the troops of God's command "to love one's country as one loves one's mother, and to sacrifice one's life for love of her."[21] In 1957 Feltin acknowledged "executions and tortures," but felt that reports were exaggerated. Repeating the army's classification of the population into enemy, friend, and neutral, he underscored the complexity and "positive" aspects of "pacification," which among other things educated the "little Muslims."[22] Feltin's remarks revealed the Church's awareness and acceptance of the excesses of the war. Within this context, a vigorous defense of torture was formulated by Father Delarue in March 1957, and leaked to the press on June 21, 1957.

Father Delarue: Between Two Evils

Father Delarue was a former missionary in British Columbia. Drafted in 1940, he did not have a chance to fight, having been captured by German troops six days after he arrived in France. He became a member of the military chaplaincy in 1941 and volunteered for the Indochina War, but again arrived too late, six days before the defeat at Dien Bien Phu.[23] He served eighteen months in Indochina before joining the 1st REP, the notorious unit of Massu's 10th Division where torture was used routinely. After a stint in Port Said, Egypt, he returned to his regiment.

When he took up his functions in the Division, Delarue was asked by a second-lieutenant whether he knew the "work we do here? . . . We, we don't ask questions, but do we have the right to do things like this?"[24] Initially, Delarue felt too "cowardly to dare inform myself" about the use of torture. But a question about the morality of torture he was asked publicly at the end of a mass by a reserve officer compelled him to seek an answer. He claims he researched the few theology books he could find in his camp:

> We did not exactly have a library in the *djebel* [mountain]. . . . The research I did for writing the text, I did it with the fear that it [torture] might not be permissible in which case my second fear was that I would be compelled to refuse to cover up this sort of thing and resign.[25]

Delarue claimed he had not read St. Thomas of Aquinas's writing on the "question," or Monsignor Duval's protests against torture. He also maintained that he was unaware at the time of the Cité Catholique publication, *Verbe*, widely read among the army, which condoned torture. Purportedly, Delarue only consulted other chaplains who chose to remain silent on the issue.

It is therefore on a flimsy research foundation that Delarue wrote a twelve-page memorandum entitled "Reflections of a Priest on Urban Terrorism," justifying and condoning the use of torture by paratroopers.[26] It could also be construed as an angry response to the Catholic priests who had given active support to FLN combatants. Nevertheless, this momentous act lent the spiritual power attached to the status of chaplain to a practice that caused pain, suffering, and often death. In its essentials, Delarue's essay claimed that torture was a legitimate act of self-defense[27] of a society beset by acts of terrorism, no different from the death penalty, which rids society of its criminals without causing any guilt or misgivings.[28] The logic of Delarue's defense of torture flowed directly from his acceptance of revolutionary-war theory. In this sense, Delarue's contribution was to have clearly established a link between military antisubversive doctrine, torture, and religion. He reasoned that revolutionary war called for new methods of combat as well as "a real obligation to see that justice is done." Since the adversary was not a regular army but an organized network of "bandits" and "international troublemakers," bent upon the destruction of life, an "army of policemen, of soldier-policemen" was needed to annihilate him.[29] Quoting a 1953 speech made by Pius XII, he asserted "the right of society to protect itself from those who violate the law," and the necessity to punish the guilty.[30] Doing otherwise would be capitulating for the sake of peace at all cost; upholding Christian charity would likewise be a "pretext" for "disloyalty and abject cowardice, " and a sign of emasculation." Furthermore, the Bible makes allowance for reprisals against the guilty. Since the Quran bears traces of "biblical culture," Algerians, as Muslims, are more inclined to accept religiously prescribed punishment than "our fledgling justice, which in their eyes is hopelessly weak and ineffective." Since the French penal code was designed for "civilized people," it could not be applied to "primitives" for whom the "penal code of the Bible is more appropriate."[31] In other words, Algerians needed and welcomed the use of torture.

On the whole, Delarue's justification of torture espoused the military's lines of argument. It foregrounded information as crucial to fighting terrorism. The clandestine nature of the enemy makes it inevitable to acquire intelligence "by other methods." In order to save lives, and for the "common interest," it is imperative "to make those we are lucky to capture talk." Not only did Delarue recommend torture, he also warned paratroopers that they might have to engage in it wherever the judicial police are in operations. Like Joan of Arc who did not shy away from shedding blood for the sake of her ideals, they, too, should be convinced that "efficacious justice is a duty of charity." Implicitly, torture was a weapon with which to fight terrorism. Aware of the consequences of the generalized use of torture, Delarue recommended "avoidance of arbitrariness." He made six recommendations, some of which elliptically referred to common abuses: interrogation should not be carried out by underlings but by "the chief in charge assisted by two colleagues he deems competent and indispensable"; torture must not be inflicted to assuage anger; it is permitted that torturers be "tough" with a guilty man known to possess information;[32] it is not permitted to use violence against a man picked up at random to get him to confess to a crime in the absence of any proof; it is acceptable to "inflict occasional suffering on a bandit caught in the act." The sixth recommendation gave notoriety to Delarue's essay, as it was expressed in a sweeping and sententious tone:

> Between two evils: on the one hand, to inflict occasional suffering on a bandit caught in the act—and who in fact deserves to die—in order to overcome

his criminal resistance with a tough [*obstiné* in French] and relentless interrogation, and, on the other hand, to allow the massacre of innocent people who could be saved by the destruction of the criminal's gang thanks to his revelations, we must without hesitation choose the lesser evil, that is an efficient interrogation without sadism.

Torture can be applied to a man "even if it is acknowledged that he is not a killer, but is certain to know those guilty, has witnessed a crime, or has deliberately given refuge to some bandit, and refuses to reveal freely and spontaneously what he knows." He added that "the goal of justice is to punish the guilty man and discourage those who would be tempted to imitate him."[33]

Delarue wrote as a soldier committed to the war, using his priestly status as grounds to legitimize torture. His argument rested on the familiar principle that the ends justify the means. However, his view falters on a conception of guilt so broad as to encompass individuals who did not commit any act of "terrorism," but simply happened to be at a place where such occurred. Delarue used a regressive expository method that proceeded from an observation of paratroopers' acts of repression, and ended with using such acts as standards by which to measure the guilt of suspects. Yet guilt was not an overriding issue in inflicting torture. Nor was the degree of seriousness of the crime committed. In reality, the systematic use of torture was not the lesser of two evils, but the greater evil, as it resulted in the death or maiming of the innocent just as terrorist acts did.[34] A feature of Delarue's essay that had not been noted by his critics was his claim to address "urban terrorism" when in reality he was mostly on operations during which he had ample opportunity to observe paratroopers' abuses of the rural populations, especially in the Grande Kabylie region where he served. In the end, Delarue denounced terrorism when committed by the FLN, but condoned it when undertaken by paratroopers.

When placed in the historical context of the medieval Church involvement in torture, Delarue's essay appears singularly short-sighted and his argument shallow. The comparison of torture to the death penalty overlooks the legal process that gives the accused a chance at defending himself before he is condemned to death.[35] Considering that the individuals tortured were primarily "Muslims," Delarue's essay also symbolized by implication the Church's assessment that torture was a morally appropriate method for fighting "terrorists" qua Muslims.

The cooperation between the chaplaincy and the military was best illustrated by the manner in which Delarue's essay was disseminated. Massu, whom Delarue may have initially consulted, had the essay duplicated and circulated.[36] Subsequently, Delarue decided to speak to his chief chaplain, Father Vaugarni, known for his pro-French Algeria stance, to obtain his authorization to widely disseminate the essay among the troops as had been requested by Massu. Vaugarny suggested minor changes and gave his approval.

Delarue's justification of torture caused an uproar in the media, prompting Monsignor Badré, the chief chaplain in Paris, to write to each one of his bishops, explaining that Delarue simply wished to "see clearly and enlighten the conscience of those in his charge," and was guilty of nothing more than "recklessness for having shown [his notes] to General Massu" before submitting them to the chief chaplain. In an attempt to minimize the issue, Badré characterized it as "inconsequential." Nevertheless, Badré felt obligated to point out that revolutionary war (not decolonization) posed new problems, which theologians had yet to clarify and resolve.[37] He depicted Delarue as an unfortunate victim of the press. More important, at a retreat in September 1957, Cardinal Feltin told Delarue that he had written "a good paper," "serious and well researched." This meant that Delarue's opinion had satisfied both the military and the Chaplaincy. Any objections raised in the press would be criticized by the Chaplaincy. This had already happened as early as March 1957, when the ACA (Assembly of Cardinals and Archbishops) published a statement condemning "intrinsically bad means" to achieve "a cause even when good." The Chaplaincy responded by defending the good name of the army against all its alleged detractors. And closing the stable after the horses had fled, a questionnaire was sent to chaplains inquiring about their moral problems as well as the effectiveness of the methods used by the army.[38]

Realizing that the initiative taken by Delarue revealed a moral vacuum, Monsignor Badré asked Abbot François Casta, chaplain at the 25th DP, to do a study of the moral problems caused by revolutionary war. In March 1958, a year after Delarue's views became public, Casta submitted a sixty-four-page typewritten report entitled "Morale Chrétienne et Guerre Révolutionnaire." Casta was a veteran of Indochina and through his work in the 25th DP, most likely familiar with the use of torture in his elite paratrooper regiment. In his report, more nuanced than Delarue's essay, he acknowledged the use of torture but, predictably, minimized its scale, and attributed it to "pathological cases." Furthermore, in an argument common among advocates of antisubversive war, he blamed "abuses" on the civil authorities, which, unable to carry out their functions, caused the military to be overburdened with new responsibilities. In this view, military abuses were due to a lack of civil leadership compounded by the failure of the Church to provide moral guidance. Casta did not fail to address Delarue's notion of "the lesser evil," arguing that, although objectionable in theory, it was acceptable under special circumstances. For good measure, he noted the relative efficacy of torture, but failed to answer the problem of conscience raised by seminarians and others: He merely suggested that the Chaplaincy emphasize moral values and leave it up to each soldier to try and implement them. As a chaplain, Casta had to seek the military's opinion. General La Chapelle obliged and countered Casta's "new casuistry"of letting soldiers decide how to implement moral principles, with a "kind of stayed [*figée* in French] casuistry of the subversive war" that would condone a whole list of methods.[39] In other words, despite its defense of torture, the Chaplaincy was still not measuring up to the military's expectations of a blanket support for the manner in which it conducted the antisubversive war. The uproar that Delarue's essay caused came at a time when public opinion in France had been alerted to the letters that Jean Muller, a conscript and member of the Catholic Equipe Nationale de la Route Scouts de France, killed in a military engagement, had sent to his family in France, detailing atrocities he had witnessed. After his death, his family published his letters, thus exposing the army's actions in the poignant pen of a soldier killed in the line of duty. His brother had sought out soldiers who corroborated Jean Muller's descriptions.[40]

Delarue's essay was a defining moment for those inside and outside the military, supporters as well as critics of the war. In 1958 the respected Catholic paper *La Croix*, generally seen as the mouthpiece for the French Church published a series of articles by its reporter Jacques Duquesne discussing the coercive methods used by the military. The chaplaincy responded in its usual manner, admonishing journalists to mind their business and refrain from maligning the army.[41]

Whereas Delarue condoned torture, a conscripted seminarian ordered a man tortured and watched him suffer. Alain Mallard de la Morandais was an intelligence officer assigned to the SAS of Oum Djerane, near Saida in 1960. He had known about the widespread use of torture before going to Algeria. He had also discussed torture on numerous occasions with priests as well as servicemen. Wishing that the war had been fought for "Christian values," he was critical of the army for its "secular liberalism," which he thought generated little galvanizing power. Although he felt some sympathy for the plight of the 2,500 seminomadic people who had been resettled (with their tents) at Oum Djerane, he still considered them "primitive" remnants of a bygone era who needed to be brought into the modern world with, as a first step, their forced resettlement in houses they had to "volunteer" to build on the grounds of the SAS. His meditations on torture invoked the difference between "situational morality" that justifies means by their ends, and "objective morality" that upholds human rights. Yet, one day, without much proof, he decided that one of the men in the resettlement was suspicious and could be working for the FLN. He handed him over to a native torturer with the recommendation that he interrogate him "gently." As he watched the "suspect" writhe, bleed, and scream like "an animal," he was filled with disgust but did nothing to stop the torture *séance*. Armed with this voyeuristic and vicarious experience, he pondered what might be the best course of action to denounce torture. He opted against resignation and writing to the press, and decided instead to speak to a medical doctor who occasionally visited the resettled people. At times, he accepted the prevailing justification of torture as a method that saves lives even though in his SAS, torture was inflicted to get information about whether some sheep and wheat belonged to FLN militants:

> Last evening, I saw one of the two men lying on his back, all naked, panting and foaming at the mouth like a bottle of beer at its neck. . . . When I saw him yesterday I surmounted my pity for him. My disgust, my feeling of horror, thinking, well he is a *rais nahia* [head of an FLN sector]. These hours of suffering will save innocent lives. He is paying; it's justice! And now I hear that he was innocent!

When he caught sight of the innocent man talking to his torturer (also an Algerian rallied to the army), he wondered whether torture was not appropriate for Algerians: "Is it possible that this coercive method should not be judged by our standards? It seems certain that they [Algerians] understand it better than we do, because between them the only standard is force."[42] Faced with the brutal fact that torture did not help to establish proof of guilt, Morandais fell back on the stereotypes against natives that he had found objectionable in the Pieds-Noirs. A seminarian with an abstract moral sense, Morandais proved Father L'Espinay wrong.

Father Peninou: Diversity and Christian Love

Abbot Henri Peninou was a chaplain serving, like Casta, in the 25 DP. In 1959 he wrote an essay addressed to his soldiers, the publication of which was approved by Monsignor Badré despite its condemnation of atrocities committed by the army. Within two years of the Delarue incident, the chaplaincy became more tolerant of criticism of army practices. Undoubtedly, it wished to counterbalance Delarue's radical defense of torture with a more lucid opinion. Peninou's essay stands out for its focus on two issues that the Chaplaincy had failed to address: diversity and intolerance within the army, noting racism against Senegalese troops serving during the war, against Muslims, or against "animists," whose cultures and beliefs should be respected, for they "could be led to Christ" by example. In addition, Peninou broke new ground in the chaplaincy by describing the abuses committed by the troops, which the military had at the time denied. His method was to identify and describe prejudice and abuses, often repeating racial slurs as he heard them, without fixing blame on anyone in particular, but stressing instead the brutalizing effects of the harshness of life in the military, which ostensibly limited soldiers' moral horizons and led them to alcohol and bordellos as palliatives.[43]

Peninou's goal was to remoralize soldiers' behavior by evoking the tragic element in Christ's life, which by analogy was reenacted in the war, and describing for them the morally reprehensible acts they committed. These included summary executions and reprisals; forced resettlements of villagers; the public exposure, desecration, mutilation and robbing of corpses; rape; thefts of property, especially vital tools for artisans such as bodkins; and falsification of reports inflating the number of enemy combatants killed. Falsified reports were part of a larger conflict between various paratrooper regiments engaged in competition with one another over prowess, rank, and insignias such as the color of one's beret. He reminded his soldiers that revolutionary war was fought over the "Muslim population," and thus represented "a human confrontation rather than [a mere application] of different technical methods."[44]

Peninou condemned "the violation of human conscience, even if it is guilty . . . torments by *magnéto* [electricity] or bathtub [torture by drowning in bathtub], and violations of sexual organs." Nevertheless, he suggested that stepped-up military action might bring about better results than interrogation under torture. After noting that the West owed much to "Arab achievements" in science and philosophy, he hailed the return of Christianity to Algeria with colonization, although he understood Muslims "had escaped it almost entirely." Wistfully observing that "Christ, however, died for all men . . ." he exhorted his soldiers to think of certain sites as the setting of the New Testament, and to envision Christ and the Virgin Mary in places such as Bir Al-Ater, or El Ma El Abiod, instead of talking about rural military bordellos. He concluded anticlimactically with a colonial cliché, invoking "the low status of many Muslim women" in comparison to Mary, as if to call out in his soldiers the prejudices he had denounced: "Pray to her [Mary] so that [Muslim women] like her also know dignity and the joy of a genuine motherhood."[45] This incongruous pity for Algerian women reduced to a generic Muslim type, some of whom were among the guerillas whom Peninou's soldiers were fighting, fed into the ideology of cultural superiority that the essay purportedly sought to dispel. In this sense, Peninou, like the Church, remained squarely within the bounds of the colonial system, which he was unable to transcend, sharing with it nostalgia for a bygone African Church, and a strong sense of the universal vocation of Christianity.

Nevertheless, Peninou's essay reflected an apparent shift in the Chaplaincy's attitude toward the war. The outspoken supporter of the military,

Chief Chaplain Vaugarni, had been recalled in 1958, and replaced by his deputy, the more circumspect Father de L'Espinay. At a time when OAS attacks against Algerians were in full swing, L'Espinay acknowledged that "racism is innate in us."[46] Under his tenure, the Chaplaincy began to ponder the moral implications of the antisubversive war. These were developed in the Green Document of 1959; a letter written by Monsignor Badré condemning torture in response to a letter denouncing torture, psychological action, and other atrocities, addressed to their bishops by thirty (or thirty-five) recalled priest officers in April 1959;[47] and in response to Cardinal Feltin's 1960 pastoral letter.[48] The Green Document enunciated principles radically opposed to those defended by Delarue in both their universal reach and their content. Echoing Peninou, the Green Document asserted the "transcendence of moral law" and the "paramount dignity of the human person." It stressed the wholeness of the person as both physical and spiritual, as well as its inviolability regardless of social and moral circumstances. It cast doubt on the prevailing "morality of efficiency," noting, "Men may be killed; but ideas do not die."[49]

The Green Document also condemned "situational morality" using an argument made by Pierre-Henri Simon, a Catholic opponent of torture, and cast doubt on the logic according to which the ends justify the means. It noted the indivisibility of the good, pointing out that good intention and ends cannot serve to legitimize bad methods. However, the document did not reject torture but classified it in three categories: *sadist* or vindictive; *repressive* or punitive; and *investigative*. The last is dehumanizing since it aims at "inflicting suffering on the other in order to deprive him of self-possession, and inner freedom—part of human essence. It [seeks to] break his will to force him to confess or give secret information he does not wish to reveal."[50] Investigative torture was condemned for humanistic reasons that pointed to its effects not only on the victim, but also on the torturer, on those who "benefit from the results obtained under torture," and on the human community at large. The analytical distinction made between the three types of torture obscured the fact that in reality, torture, as practiced, included aspects of all three types outlined by the Document. In addition, it ignored exploratory torture, a most common occurrence, against individuals who had no secret information to reveal, but were tortured anyway.

The Document, excerpts of which leaked to the press without the Chaplaincy's approval,[51] exhibited an unusual degree of realism in seeking to describe torture and its effects. "It [inflicts] a degree of pain that stretches the limits of what an even courageous man can bear, literally spins its victim out of his mind, and transforms him into a frightened and exhausted animal." The Document further described some of the most common methods of torture, noting their sexual component:

Methods are often degrading and bestial; sexual areas are targeted, and torments are customarily accompanied by techniques of social and moral humiliation the purpose of which is solely to degrade the patient [sic]. . . . Finally, it sometimes happens that those who were badly mutilated are executed in cold blood.[52]

On the face of it, this was an important step taken by the Chaplaincy since it appeared to criticize the military, the institution to which it was attached and that paid a stipend to its staff. However, the Document fell short of categorically condemning torture. It remarked that, under exceptional circumstances and strict control, a man can be subjected to pain and corporal "deprivations" if it is known with certainty that "he possesses unjust secrets that he refuses to divulge." Nevertheless, since a definition of a "just secret" lies with the torturer, there is no foolproof way of avoiding torture. Furthermore, once permitted torture becomes routinized, and thus escapes control. Aware of the paradoxical nature of their position, the authors of the provision acknowledged that it would not be possible to "limit physical constraints."[53]

Barely two years before the independence of Algeria, Cardinal Feltin unambiguously condemned torture, stating:

In this domain even for the protection of human lives in immediate danger, God's absolute law takes precedence over this duty no matter how vital. We are dealing here with faith. . . . Upholding Christian and divine values, even if difficult, and [requiring] heroic [strength], is ultimately more efficient than the brutal search for immediate results.[54]

Coming full circle, Cardinal Feltin finally put to rest, religiously, six years into the war, the "ticking bomb" scenario often used as an argument for condoning torture.

Like the Catholic Church, the "reform church" too had trouble categorically condemning the military methods of conducting the war. It too was divided over the issue of Algeria's independence, and could not transcend its colonial character. However, it focused on bringing substantial relief to Algerians held in internment camps as well as those living in shantytowns; it also helped draw attention to the plight of resettled villagers.[55]

Missionary groups such as Mission de France and the White Fathers acted according to their conscience, providing medical care or sanctuary to FLN militants, or helping to print and copy FLN tracts. Mission de France was often in the limelight for the liberal views of its priests, the most notable of whom were Father Scotto, Declercq (a chaplain at the famed Barberousse jail), and Joseph Kerlan.[56]

Cité Catholique and Revolutionary War

A complicating yet crucial factor in explaining the role played by religion in the conduct of the war lies in the underground action of the Cité Catholique, a radical fundamentalist movement established in 1946. The military in Algeria needed the unconditional support of a religious organization that could also provide it with a *doctrinal* justification for its unorthodox methods of fighting the war. It found both in Cité Catholique.[57] There was a convergence of views between the army and Cité Catholique: They both believed in engaging in politics; they both sought a "new" social order. Cité Catholique aimed at "enlightening, fostering, and encouraging the promotion of a Catholic renaissance in the temporal order specifically through doctrinal action."[58] Unlike other groups involved in Catholic Action, Cité Catholique claimed that the "Church has the right to be interested in politics as in anything else,"[59] as it was engaged in a "counterrevolutionary struggle and the defense of the motherland."[60] Cité Catholique therefore combined features of religious fundamentalism with a secular concern for political engagement to bring about a new order based on the traditional Catholic values that undergird conservative nationalism. It did not aim at being a mass movement. Rather, it targeted members of the professions and high-ranking officials as it sought to influence the course of national and world events. A number of notable military figures, including Marshal Juin and General Ely, chairman of the Joint Chiefs of Staff, as well as a number of key players in the antisubversive war had either participated in its activities or supported them.[61] In 1959 there were an estimated four hundred to five hundred military members in one hundred cells[62] in Algeria, comprised of five to eight members each, and there were four thousand subscriptions to the journal *Verbe*.[63] More important, Cité Catholique played a significant role in spreading justifications of antisubversive doctrine abroad through the creation of branches in Europe, Morocco, and Argentina, and in arranging refuge for rebellious officers and members of the OAS after 1961.[64]

By 1955 the army, which was prohibited by law from engaging in religious activism, asked Cité Catholique to begin organizing within its ranks. Using the "flexible, capillary methods" of infiltration based on small group chats, secret cells were set up to indoctrinate troops and disseminate information meant to quell their doubts about the war and convert them to the ideology of the "Catholic counterrevolution." The main publication of Cité Catholique, *Verbe*, was frequently discussed at the army *popotes* (or mess halls).[65] Although it was not a church, Cité Catholique claimed its teaching was "under the strict supervision of a regularly designated canonical censor."[66] Both Cité Catholique and the military knew very well that in Algeria they were fighting a primarily Muslim population—a fact that points to a subtext rich in implications. The Algerian War posed no specific moral problem for Cité Catholique, since it was perceived as a revolutionary war masterminded by international communism: "We have made our choice! By fighting the rebellion in Algeria, we are aware that we are at the vanguard of the struggle against the global revolutionary movement; we are conscious of fulfilling our duty as Frenchmen and Christians, and serving humanity as a whole."[67] In Algeria Cité Catholique could fight a "just crusade" against Islam.[68]

Eager to "counter doctrine [i.e., communism] with doctrine," Cité Catholique focused on the psychological aspect of indoctrination, albeit not on brainwashing. But supplemental advocacy of psychological action came from Georges Sauge, a leading right-wing Catholic, and a former communist, who had opened a Centre d'Etudes Supérieures de Psychologie Sociale in Paris to study, among other things, communist ideology and methods of organizing, in addition to the uses of the Church's doctrine in stemming a perceived communist tide. The Centre was a sort of school for counterrevolution and fit neatly into the army's conception of anti-subversive war. Sauge lectured extensively in military schools. Not surprisingly, the 5ème Bureau (specializing in psychological action) was staffed with officers (including Colonels Goussault and Gardes, Lieutenant-Colonel Feaugas, and Commandant Cogniet) who were all members of the Cité and used its method of indoctrination with troops. It was particularly gratifying to the army to find in Cité Catholique an advocate of techniques of politically motivated civic action qua propaganda. In the name of counterrevolution, and in order to save the Catholic Nation, adherents to Cité Catholique were to become "troops of order."[69] Their leader, Jean Ousset, a former associate of Charles Maurras and founder of Cité Catholique, made a trip to Algiers on May 12, 1958,[70] the eve of the demonstrations orchestrated by the proponents of Algérie-Française, which had been hailed by Sauge-inspired psychological-action officers as a success in the use of their methods. Within this context, Ousset found justifications for torture. He distinguished between "a priori torture," and "a posteriori torture." He condemned the former, synonymous with "investigative torture," as "illicit." He found "a posteriori torture," permissible *after* the suspect had been found guilty. Preventive torture, named "medicinal," was deemed appropriate to save lives in immediate danger.

Other right-wing Catholic groups reinforced the teachings of the Cité's publication *Verbe*, including reviews such as *Itinéraires* and *La Pensée Catholique*. The editor of *La Pensée Catholique*, Abbot Luc J. Lefèvre, noted in 1958 how in North Africa, "The struggle today is between the Cross and the Crescent tossed on the line of fire by the master of the red star, the hammer and the sickle."[71] Two years into the war, *Itinéraires* argued for the "legitimacy of repression . . . against the panthers that sow death,"[72] and wished to give the army "the moral means to carry out necessary repression."[73] Warning that "France was the first country to be targeted by the Muslim peril," authors depicted a "clash of civilizations pitting Christ against Mahomet . . . [a man] incapable of doing anything against sin."[74]

Thus "all reprisals are not morally forbidden."[75] Liberal intellectuals were denounced for "arabophilia," and actress Brigitte Bardot blamed for distracting the public from the Islamo-communist threat to the nation.[76] What make these views notable are not their contents since many of them originated from officers writing under the pseudonym Cornelius, who were already either committing torture or witnessing it. Rather, it is their publication, and general endorsement by groups that claimed Catholicism as their faith and sought to inject a Catholic morality into their society.[77]

Right-wing Catholics could not be simply dismissed as believing in a religious "retrogressive utopia." Their originality did not lie in their religious views, but in doing political battle under the banner of religion. It was their political understanding of Catholicism that necessarily led to their justification of torture and other abuses.[78] Considering the general silence of the organized Church, notwithstanding episodic declarations condemning this and that abuse without much vigor, right-wing Catholics had the merit of revealing the interface between Christianity, politics, and the torture of Muslims in the modern age.[79] It is symptomatic of this relationship that it took its doctrinal foundation from the writings of St. Thomas Aquinas, a religious figure notable for his negative views of Islam. Conversely, the right-wing Catholics also brought out into the open what was downplayed by civil authorities: that the war was against a predominantly Muslim people whose religion had been used for political aims throughout the colonial era.

Left-Wing Religious Activism

Left-wing individual priests spoke out against torture and the war primarily in France. In Algeria one of the most principled positions was adopted by Abbot Berenguer, a Pied-Noir. In 1945 he had run afoul of the colonial police for organizing a Boy Scout movement that included children from all three religions—Christianity, Islam, and Judaism. In his parish of Montagnac (near Tlemcen), he became conscious of poverty among Algerians, as well as the spread of nationalist sentiments. In January 1956 he published in the daily *Oran Républicain* a controversial article (that coincided with an anticolonial demonstration in Tlemcen), "A Christian Look at Algeria," exhorting colonists to face up to the nationalist factor, and change their attitudes toward Algerians before it was too late. He denounced ignorance and racial prejudice among local priests as well as the collusion of the Church with the state. Anticipating his critics, he dispelled the notion that priests were prohibited by the colonial state to evangelize, and thus could not penetrate the Muslim milieu in order to know it better. He called for an enlightened clergy recruited among Pieds-Noirs to improve the work of the Church. His was not a theology of liberation as had emerged in West Africa, Cameroon, Togo, and Madagascar, but a theology of cultural understanding and charitable services. Berenguer was deported to France for his ideas and harassed by the police, which in the end caused him to join the Red Crescent, becoming its representative for Latin America. He subsequently became an advocate of the independence of Algeria.[80] Berenguer was a member of a very small minority of Pieds-Noirs critical of colonial rule. Among lay Catholic Pied-Noirs, Dr. Pierre Chaulet and his wife stood out. They claimed an *Algerian* identity in their opposition to the war and support for the FLN and independence, thereby breaking the colonists' racialist-nationalist consensus on the war.[81]

André Mandouze, a former professor at the University of Algiers and editor of *Consciences Maghrébines*, who tirelessly denounced military abuses throughout the war, wondered in 1988 about the real impact of left-wing Catholics' activism against torture, and in support of the independence of Algeria. He concluded, "All those conscientious positions, all our papers, all our bulletins, they did not weigh much in bringing about an earlier and less bloody resolution to the Algerian war. . . . 'A religious conscience': It's a difficult [thing]; I believe that we should be very modest in this affair."[82] Mandouze hit upon an important aspect of the struggle that Catholic men and women of conscience waged for many years: Was the opposition to the atrocities committed by the military shared by the majority of Catholics? Did it have an echo among the French people? Who read the reviews and newspapers put out by men like Mandouze? It is difficult to tell how the majority of French people in France felt about torture and other atrocities, or about the legitimacy of the war, at least until the early 1960s. There were, however, audiences for the various publications, left, right or liberal Catholic. In addition, youth organizations such as the Boy Scouts also took positions on religious grounds. Nevertheless, except for left-wing Catholics, outrage about torture, although real, was generally subdued, since the causes of the war were elided because raising them would have meant taking a political stand against the government and the military. Thus the consequences of the war posed a moral problem, and its causes a political problem. The resolution of this situation was found in a common attitude: Express surprise and moral outrage, hope that all parties to the war come to their senses, and wait and see how the war develops before finally stating that independence is inevitable and necessary.

FLN and Religion

Until 1958 Algerians' identity was defined by law as "Muslim-French"—a political use of religion initiated by the colonial government. The FLN named its underground paper *El Moudjahid*, the holy fighter, and its combatants often attacked French troops to the cry of "God is great!" Was then the Algerian War a religious war for the FLN? It was not, in the sense that it was not motivated by religious factors.[83]

On the Algerian side, Islam did not generally play a role different than it had prior to the war. Islam had been selected by the colonial government as the marker of difference between the colonizer and the colonized. Therefore, the FLN did not have to appeal to the history of the Crusades in order to galvanize people into action. It could simply point to Algerians' unequal status *because* they were Muslims. Nevertheless, for propaganda purposes, nationalist groups spread the rumor in the larger population that combatants were helped by Suhaba, or companions of Prophet Muhammad, who had come back to fight among them. The combatants knew well enough that they faced the French army alone, and their cry of "God is great" cannot be easily equated with a jihad in its restrictive sense of a holy war. In the Algerian tradition, reference to the greatness of God is an expression that bolsters one's courage to face a serious situation with equanimity. That a combatant might have felt, at the point of entering a battle, like a companion of the Prophet was not impossible. But the very choice of the Suhaba evoked a complex imagery. These were men who at the dawn of Islam fought against persecution with limited means, and were equated in the local lore with the underdog. Therefore reference to Suhaba was meant to boost the morale of the Algerian population and stem doubt about the capacity of the FLN to measure up to a more powerful professional army. That the Suhaba also fought against pagan, Christian *Arabs* as well as Jews cannot be ignored. However, it is the valiant and nearly invincible character of the Suhaba, as well as the reverence that their memory inspires, that was emphasized rather than the people they fought. At any rate, it is not clear to me to what extent the rumor concerning the Suhaba was used or believed. But it is noteworthy that it spread among the Algerian population; I cannot gauge the extent to which it mattered among combatants. As General Salan noted, many combatants fought hard, till death, because, among other things, they knew that when captured they would be tortured and killed.

Discrimination on religious grounds was experienced by native Algerians as part of the colonial system of inequality. Nevertheless, since Islam also informs a social and legal order, it was used by the FLN as a way of delegitimizing colonial institutions such as family courts (even colonial-controlled *shari'a* courts), courts of small claims, or police stations. The point was to provide the native population, especially in rural areas, with noncolonial institutions foreshadowing an independent state. In addition, these measures were aimed at eliding colonial history by relinking a re-constructed present with a legal order that predated the French invasion. As I mentioned above, villagers respected priests in uniforms, calling them *mrabtin*, one of the signs of areligious perception of the war among the rural poor. In the end, there was no counterpart in FLN publications of the virulent articles written in the various military journals and the right-wing Catholic reviews about Islam. While Algerians pointed to economic and political inequality, the generals evoked the specter of fanaticism, Pan-Islamism and Pan-Arabism. That the generals were manipulating re-ligious sentiments among the colonists is demonstrated by the secular outlook of all postindependence governments in Algeria. But perhaps the story of the religious motivation behind the French military decision to fight the war as long as they did, and with such ferocity, has yet to be told.

In sum, religion played an immeasurable role in keeping a moral lid on the army's antisubversive strategy. The justification of torture and other atrocities mounted by the religious right (whose support was enlisted by the military) and the Chaplaincy turned the immorality of torture into a political question. As Cornelius, writing in *Verbe*, wrote: "It [repression] is not a moral problem; if there is a Hierarchy [the name by which the Church is called] to which we must turn, it is the military hierarchy and the government that empowered it."[84] One hierarchy's justification of tor-ture by another's also revealed the eminently political-ideological charac-ter of the war as understood by both army and Church. Paradoxically, lib-eral and left-wing Catholics did the opposite of the right: They turned a political problem into a moral one. The shifting grounds for defending an opposing torture by the various religious institutions with differing polit-ical views helped the army to do its work with the blessings of Christian doctrine instead of against it.

However, a consequence of Christian declarations and publications for or against military methods lay in publicizing abuses. As Mandouze notes, the war continued, and so did abuses—until the end. Does this mean that right-wing Catholics were more successful than others in their use of re-ligious doctrine to further the aims of the military? Or that the silent French majority was, for whatever reasons, unmoved by the war until it was brought home? The structure of the colonial militarized state pro-vides an answer: From 1955 it had suspended civil liberties and curtailed freedom of the press. Although such measures were technically applica-ble to France proper, they were mostly used in Algeria. However, as soon as civic repression began to be felt in France, a generally aloof public was able to take notice. But these considerations may be academic. For, vocal and well-structured political minorities may wield more influence than large, unorganized crowds. All the military needed was justification of its morally unsustainable methods by professionals of morality. And it got it.

The local Church's silence was an expression of its commitment to a colonial system that had guaranteed the Church's structural viability. Whether Catholic or Reformed, the Church could not question the legitimacy of the war without questioning colonial rule. It did not do so until it became clear that independence was the only viable solution to the war. It is symptomatic that the Church and the Christian right adopted the military's view of *guerre révolutionnaire*, thereby dismissing the colonial nature of the war. The Vatican, which theoretically supported the "political autonomy of the people presently considered colonial," nurtured ambiguity. In an eloquent historic faux-pas, Jean XXIII, eager to see Algeria remain French, prematurely congratulated rebellious generals on April 26, 1961.[85]

The Catholic Church typically made statements of a general nature, leaving it to its bishops and priests to speak their conscience as individuals,[86] which they did in various ways, for or against the war and its methods.

A major thread running through Christian responses to torture and the war of decolonization was fear of Islam should Algeria become independent. The fear seems to have been as profound as knowledge of Islam was tendentious. Clearly the Catholic Church had much to lose materially since it would have to return property belonging to mosques. Also, problematic for the Church was the symbolism of a possible FLN victory. Images of the Crusades invoked by some Catholic groups blended with a diffuse sense of failure among priests and seminarians at the Church who could not establish an indigenous clergy, giving the prospect of Algeria's independence the outlook of a religious defeat, a lost Crusade. A second common feature of Christian responses resided in differing conceptions of the nation. Torture and colonial rule were opposed because individual Catholics had a vision of the nation as standing for freedom, liberty, and the respect for human dignity. Conversely, torture and colonialism were defended because Catholic groups identified nation and empire, and felt compelled for patriotic reasons to save the nation from a perceived international communist conspiracy acting by proxy. Yet the communist-conspiracy ploy fades before the fear of Islam, embedded as it was/is in a Catholic history of its own holy wars. As I mentioned in chapter 2, General Massu, a Catholic advocate of torture, who nevertheless was received by the pope, asserted that no one in the army believed in the communist conspiracy, "We could not care less!"[87]

Chapter 9

FANON, SARTRE, AND CAMUS

T HE CENTRALITY OF TORTURE to the antisubversive war was
not only a catalyst for identity crystallization among its perpetrators, but also a trigger to a broader search for the meaning and purpose of the violence unleashed by the war. Torture in Algeria was a watershed for French intellectuals.[1] It compelled them to pause and examine
French political history, as well as the role that the French Empire played
in reshaping their society's value system. Among the intellectuals who
condemned torture in their writings were, Jean-Paul Sartre and Simone de
Beauvoir, François Mauriac, Raymond Aron, Pierre-Henri Simon, Henri
Alleg, Pierre Vidal-Naquet, and Albert Camus. In so doing, some of them
shed light on the philosophical-psychological springs of torture and terror as they traced the consequences of the original act of colonization.

This chapter focuses on three politically engaged intellectuals' attempts
at making sense of torture: Sartre, Fanon, and Camus. Jean-Paul Sartre
was a French-born existentialist philosopher and relentless critic of the
corrupting effect of the Empire on France's political system; Albert Camus
was a Pied-Noir committed to a French Algeria; Frantz Fanon was a psychiatrist from Martinique who became the FLN roving ambassador.
Fanon was also a theorist of the Algerian Revolution, and the first professional to treat torture victims as well as their torturers.

Sartre on Henri Alleg's Torture

Henri Alleg, the editor of the communist paper, *Alger Républicain*, was
arrested and tortured in a secret torture center in the residential neighborhood of El Biar in Algiers in 1957. His torturers demanded that he give
information on a group of French individuals, members of the Algerian
communist party who opposed the war. Alleg's book, *La Question*,
banned but sold underground, provided Sartre, and the French public,
with a firsthand account of torture. In his analysis of Alleg's ordeal, Sartre
argued that the colonial situation formed the material and existential conditions out of which torture emerged. Natives had already been dispossessed of their sovereignty, land, and even language; they had been re-

duced to the condition of *sous-hommes*. Torture completes their inferiority by reconfiguring their bodies through pain, penetrating their flesh and bones, remolding them into disfigured forms and warped psyches. In the colonial situation, the torturer represents the settler whose sense of self and humanity is contingent upon the dehumanization of the native. The two are locked in a dialectical relationship reminiscent of the master-slave dynamics studied by Hegel. Although torture is inflicted on individual men and women, its significance reaches into the community to which the victim belongs: Every victim was made to represent the community of Algerians. Nevertheless, the effect of torture is not confined to the victim's community alone; it does not merely express the colonist's hatred for the native: It stands for contempt for humanity at large.

From Sartre's perspective, torture assaults the human-universal in all people. The torture of an Algerian holds in abeyance the torture of any person in Paris or in New York. This existential humanism seeks to break down the psychological and emotional barriers that are usually raised between self and other whenever torture is discussed, since these barriers traditionally allow for the acceptance of torture as either deserved by others for actions they might have committed, or deserved because the so-called otherness of the tortured reflects a special (e.g., "primitive") nature that invites and/or warrants the infliction of pain. Therefore, when a victim such as Henri Alleg does not break, refuses to talk, he represents the triumph of all people, of humanity against the forces of inhumanity and degradation: He denies his torturers the power to transform a resister into a traitor, a man into a *sous-homme*, a free mind into a mound of mortified and bleeding flesh pleading for mercy. This heroic resistance to extreme pain may not always be sustainable in the torture chamber. Nevertheless, Henri Alleg did not break. He also refused to commit suicide as his torturers nudged him to do in an attempt to prevent him from making his torture public should he be released.

However, a detail escaped Sartre: that in the thick of pain and suffering, as he was mercilessly tortured, Alleg thought "I felt proud of holding a place among them [Muslim detainees] because I was a European."[2] It is not that Alleg wanted to suffer just like his Algerian friends did, but that torture separated him from his fellow Frenchmen who were now treating him as an enemy, as if he were a native Algerian. In a sense, he was glad that he was (mis)treated like a native Algerian. He perceived his torture as demonstrating that his French torturers, with whom he shared a nationality, inhabited a different France from his. Torture thus helped to separate him from this fellow Frenchmen qua torturers, and at the same time brought him closer to Algerians whose (denied) humanity he shared.

Alleg's triumph over torture was also a triumph over racism. Because he had been tortured as a Frenchman, his resistance to torture perpetrated by other Frenchmen broke the other psychological barrier on the Algerian side where all Frenchmen might have appeared as torturers. Alleg chose the human-universal over the French-particular, asserting his humanity over his Frenchness. As for the torturer, he seeks to smother his awareness of the abjection he inflicts on his victim (and that reflects back to him the image of his inhumanity) with increased pain.[3] After obliterating the humanity of one Algerian, the torturer needs to be reassured that he has done the same to all Algerians. He is thus impelled to start his work anew, with every prisoner brought to him. Torture exhausts itself in the resistance, death, or breakdown of its victim. Like Sisyphus, the torturer's task must be repeated each day. Sartre is careful to remind his reader that not all torturers are settlers and that settlers are not necessarily torturers.

This conception of torture as the necessary outcome of the special material conditions of colonialism that pit colonizer against colonized in deadly combat runs into a theoretical difficulty as soon as Sartre points out that many torturers were young Frenchmen, draftees, who had never lived in Algeria and thus had never had any contact with Algerians. Yet they adopted the racist practices common among settlers and engaged blithely in torture. It was young French soldiers from France who jeered at Alleg while he was being tortured. Some of these young men looked in on him at the end of his ordeal and congratulated him on his courage in the manner they would have employed for a winning boxer. Sartre identified the actions of these men as "this hatred of man that took hold of them [torturers] without their consent, and which has remolded them." It is "a sort of floating and anonymous hatred, a radical hatred of man that befalls torturer and victim to degrade one by the other."[4] This odd explanation acknowledges the freedom of the victim to choose his humanity against abjection through resistance, yet refuses a similar freedom to the torturer to choose to be such. By subjecting the torturer to an inescapable political-economic determinism, Sartre lumps together the social-psychological motivation for torture and its political functions. Clearly, in the torture situation, torturer and victim are locked in a battle where individual psychology, identity, history, and memory play a significant part in determining the intensity of pain and the capacity to withstand it. And yes, fear and hatred, especially racial hatred, are features of the torture situation. However, since torture exhausts itself in each victim, so might fear and hatred. While fear and hatred may account for a Pied-Noir intelligence officer finding solace in the daily torture of native Algerians, these emotions shed little light on the behavior of conscripts from France. Sartre felt that these young men had been drawn into hatred's "magnetic field [and] that [this] traversed them, corroded them, and enslaved them."

Torture neither determines nor sustains itself out of fear and hatred alone. In fact, Sartre gave an inkling of what the full psychological mechanism behind torture might be. He argued that torture is a function of the will to freedom, the hallmark of the century. "It is that man can make himself." An individual's fundamental desire to be free from domination by another is met by the other's strong desire to suppress that freedom. But the ontology of freedom transcends the contingency of unbridled power as well as the mythologies surrounding it. It is true that the settler had turned the Algerian into a "native" and sustained his creation with myths about the native's natural inferiority. Consequently, the settler felt betrayed when the "native" asserted his freedom from and against him. As Sartre put it, "At first, the European rules: He has already lost but he does not know it; he does not know yet that the natives are false natives; he says he hurts them in order to repress the evil that lurks in them. . . . He does not realize [the power of] human memory, of memories that cannot be erased."[5]

The existence of the guerilla, the FLN militant, is evidence in the settler's view that the object of his myth is quite different from what he thought he was, or wanted him to be. The settler needs confirmation that he has not been wrong, and since he cannot get it without the use of force, he will use torture to refashion the Algerian prisoner in the very manner that he had mythified him, as an abject, animal-like creature. Torture then becomes a (psychological) method for remaking a man through pain and suffering, and turning him into a wrecked body and a mind that speaks what it is told.

As Sartre was aware, this process transcends the settler, although at times Sartre stakes his whole analysis on him. In reality it is France, the French state's willingness to do the settler's bidding that is at issue. The power of the settlers to influence the state was not as absolute as commonly asserted. The state acquiesced to their demands, tolerating the use of torture *in* France. Sartre rightly explains that the French state *created* the colonist with economic largesse and political privileges, and in so doing it also created the native Algerian, one living at the expense of the other. This means that the state was instrumental in keeping native Algerians in a subjugated status.

Sartre invoked the colonist's constant fear and dread that universal rights (as theoretically guaranteed by the state) might be applied to natives. Although he availed himself of liberalism in France, the colonist "hated the—at least formal—universalism of metropolitan institutions precisely because they apply to everyone and Algerians could claim them." Consequently, "he leads a double and contradictory existence: He has a "motherland," France; he also has his "country," Algeria. In Alge-

ria he represents France, and demands to deal only with her. But his economic interests lead him to oppose the political institutions of his motherland."[6] The rights and privileges that the colonist enjoyed underscored
the positive consequences for the colonist of the dual status of Algeria as
an integral part of France, yet a colony.

However, this analysis does not go far enough to explain why the state
was complicit with the colonist in allowing a legal double standard to take
place in Algeria where the colonist had more than the rights he enjoyed
in France, since he also had the right to oppose the extension of full citizenship to native Algerians. The colonist's economic situation determined
his political attitude toward natives, and the political economy of colonialism required political inequality. Should the state implement its role
as a universalistic institution extending equal rights to all citizens regardless of race or religion, the colonial system would wither away, and Algeria would really be France. In this sense, torture is not just a "vain fury,"
or a disease such as "chicken pox"[7] as Sartre put it. The medical analogy
stresses the undetermined yet determining character of the practice, thus
undermining Sartre's contribution to the analysis of torture as being situ-
ated in a tangible, material system. The analogy may help to explain how
torture takes on a life of it own and proliferates, but it does not account
for its willed character.

Sartre's conception of colonialism as a *system,* that is to say, a structured configuration of hierarchical power and social relations that reproduces itself over time, holds the key to understanding the politically necessary use of torture. It is because colonialism is a *system* that coercion,
punishment, and degradation are socially necessary to reproduce not only
the identity and self-worth of the colonist, but also the system itself. Nevertheless, Sartre acknowledges the *political* nature of torture that makes
its use by the *state* necessary. He points out that "embarrassed by their
own power, the 'forces of order' [the army] can oppose nothing to the
guerillas except searches and operations of reprisals; they fight terrorism
with terror. Something is hidden everywhere and by all: people must be
made to talk."[8] Indeed, torture is an instrument of terror willingly chosen by the state, which could have devised other means to quell the war.
Torture becomes self-propelling only after it has been instituted as a tool
of government. When it is routinized, it becomes self-determined, free
floating, and escaping any control.

Yet Sartre sidesteps the organized character of torture and its role in the
militarization of the colonial state. The colonial *system* makes torture *necessary*, but it is the militarized colonial state that provides the power and
means to translate a structural necessity into a concrete reality. By and
large, torture in Algeria transcended the bounds of the relationship be-

tween French settler and native Algerian. It was tied to the role the French Empire played in the constitution of the identity of the Frenchman serving in the army.

Sartre and Fanon: Torture as a Category of Violence

In *The Wretched of the Earth*, Fanon transformed the concept of force, which the military and colonists alike had asserted was necessary to subdue the "nature" of Algerians, into a source of psychological and physical liberation when used against colonial domination. Like Sartre, Fanon understood torture to be a feature of the colonial situation. He examined the psychoanalytic source of violence during a war of decolonization, arguing that the exercise of unrestrained force in the European conquests of foreign lands created a psychological syndrome that thrived during colonial rule. From this perspective, the use of physical force was only one aspect of the colonial venture. Expropriations, unemployment, educational policies that denigrated and dismissed local cultures and history, police brutality, and rampant poverty were all manifestations of colonial force. Thus, violence, an outcome of force, suffuses life in the colonies. Colonized people know violence intimately: They are born into it, grow up with it, and are surrounded by it. Although Fanon did not specifically distinguish between symbolic violence and brute force, he clearly meant that an Algerian who was not taught his mother tongue in school was as much the product of violence as a man/woman who was brutalized in a police station. However, violence is determined and determining in turn. It recreates itself. The fear that the colonized man feels before the colonizer's physical force prevents him from expressing his anger at being considered a *sous-homme*, having his dignity trampled, or being dispossessed. He is filled with diffuse anger. At first he turns his anger against his own people as exemplified by the daily acts of violence committed for apparently anodyne reasons.[9]

When he becomes politically aware of the significance of his subjugation, the colonized man realizes that his condition is not naturally ordained but, rather, the product of colonial power relations. He experiences increasing dissatisfaction with his circumstance and yearns to regain his humanity. Fanon rightly viewed the colonial situation as total: It embraces psychological, emotional, social, political, and economic conditions. Even when life improves for some natives, they still do not enjoy full political rights, and relative deprivation sets in, as life for the settler is much richer in comparison. After playing by the rules to bring about change, the colonized man realizes he cannot transform the colonial system peacefully. He must overturn it. Soon he stakes his life on regaining his dignity, on living like a *man*. He unleashes the violence built into him by the colonial system against the colonizer. This momentous act has a cathartic effect: In killing his oppressor, the colonized man frees himself of the fear that had been kneaded into him. By the same token, he reclaims his humanity, denied by the colonizer's ideology; he is born anew. Thus, violence, the "link in the chain of colonialism," also helps to break the chain.[10]

Admittedly, long-suffered repression brings emotional relief when it is released. Raising a hand against a long feared colonist may also be emotionally exhilarating. However, Fanon's conception of colonial violence and counterviolence leaves a number of questions unanswered. It is true that all peaceful means of bringing about change in the lives of Algerians had failed. War was an inevitable outcome of a rigid colonial system unwilling to reform itself. But does war against a colonist necessarily bring about the birth of a new human being? Does violence against a colonist truly cleanse the colonized man or woman of the entire complex psychological trauma built into him/her? Fanon was aware that anticolonial violence was a necessary but not sufficient step toward psychological decolonization. However, by endowing such violence with a cathartic effect that implicitly sustained the anticolonial war, he imbued it with an overdetermining significance.

A distinction needs to be made between the temporary psychological release that may be achieved through violence, and its long term transformative impact. Killing by itself does not bring about the justice one kills for. The psychology of the colonial situation was far too complex to be undone by simply experiencing the cathartic thrill of killing individual owners of farmland that once belonged to Algerians or policemen who routinely abused their Algerian victims. To argue that the act of killing a colonist is transformative in a psychologically positive manner is a claim that has not been and cannot be verified. It is a thin line that Fanon was treading as he unwittingly skirted the issue that nationalism in the colonies was a pathological condition. Indeed, if colonial violence shaped the psychology of the colonized, then their actions were dictated by psychological-emotional needs, instead of politics.

It is Sartre who clearly brings out the pathological character of the colonial situation inherent in Fanon's analysis. Using examples provided by Fanon, Sartre points to the existence of a number of local customs as strategies of accommodation to, or escape from, the demeaned life of the colonial subject. He notes the fractured psyche of the African who "dances all night, and at dawn struggles through the crowd to hear mass. . . . Being a native is a neurosis, introduced and maintained by the colonist in the colonized people *with their consent.*[11] The native in the colonies is in effect "possessed" by Western culture in the same way that he, at times, believes himself possessed by spirits. Colonial alienation thrives on and supports "religious alienation." A different culture was forced onto the colonized man's, which it sundered. In the resulting "fissure," "colonial aggression enters as terror in the colonized people. . . . They are stuck between the guns we point at them, and their own impulses, and inchoate desires to murder us, welling from the bottom of their hearts. . . . At the height of their powerlessness, murderous madness inhabits their collective unconscious." Colonized men are "thirsty for blood," the colonists' blood. Clearly this interpretation is a departure from Fanon's view. Sartre shifts the analysis from the purely psychoanalytic task of understanding the meaning for a colonized man of raising his hand against his colonizer, to an interpretation of the psychology of colonized people as being abnormal. From Sartre's perspective, colonized people are potential murderers who must be forgiven because their mental condition was caused by the colonists. Unwittingly, Sartre gives credence to the pseudoscientific and racially prejudiced literature (which he had denounced) that defined North Africans in France as born criminals. By claiming that the desire to kill the colonist was not only a dream but an organic condition albeit born of socioeconomic and political circumstances, Sartre deprives the nationalist movement of its true political character. This is at odds with his emphasis on the political dimension of colonialism as expressed in the phrase "colonialism is a system."[12]

In his preface to Fanon's *The Wretched of the Earth*, Sartre went further than Fanon in declaring all colonial societies pathological. It is true that in his previous writing he had also diagnosed France as "very ill, feverish to the point of prostration, obsessed with old dreams of glory, and making out her shame."[13] The pathology thesis is not without merit. Local customs in the colonies had ossified; native languages were marginalized and devalued by the preeminence of the colonizers' tongue; perceptions of self were affected by a total domination. In this context, the meaning of cultural rituals shifts: Colonized people used them as channels for the politically induced anger they experienced. These practices had a dual significance. On the one hand, they provided the colonized people with an emotional outlet for pent-up anger; on the other hand, they confirmed the colonists in their dismissal of natives as "primitive." From acting out anger, or channeling it in rituals (ranging from dance to magic, and pilgrimage to saints' mausoleums), to taking up arms is a long psychological journey that neither Sartre, nor Fanon truly unravel.

The transformation that must take place from a condition of angry subjection to taking up arms, not to commit homicide, but to wage a war for the recovery of dignity, requires elucidation. Barring this, revolutionary terrorism is turned into a (psycho)pathology akin to serial murder. The act of killing a colonist cleanses the colonized man of the "Western cul-

ture" of which he is "possessed" only if the colonized man perceives dimly
or clearly that "Western culture" not the colonial police and political apparatus dominated him. In the wake of Fanon's analysis, Sartre abstracted
the psychological component of a complex empirical situation and recast
it as a generalized pathological condition located in the unconscious. Such
a move undermines the conscious will to freedom and responsible political action. Indeed, how is political action to be carried out if its agent is
not aware of his/her motives? Conscious action is consequently diminished. The Algerian War and torture are reduced to the lust for blood on
both the colonist's and the native's sides.

In fact the war, as the ultimate expression of violence, started after a
long period of psychological maturation. A movement of cultural regen-
eration had been under way since the 1920s, extolling the virtues of pris-
tine Islamic culture and condemning precisely the ritualistic practices that
had thrived under the benevolent eye of colonial administrators. The
'Ulama movement, spearheaded by Ibn Badis, sought to give Algerians renewed pride in their culture while at the same time reviving the memory
of a precolonial past.[14] Furthermore, nationalists weighed their options
before choosing the path of war. They chose to strike when they felt the
time was ripe, and selected their targets according to their strategic plans.
Striking the colonial system transcended the cathartic value of killing one
colonist. Also, Fanon's conception and Sartre's explication do not help to
explain how it was that a number of captured guerillas who should have
felt psychologically free of the *colonist in them* were "turned" and joined
the French army in hunting down, capturing, and torturing their former
comrades.

A second distinction should be made between the use of violence for
political aims, and its cathartic function. The FLN, or the Mau-Mau in
Kenya, consciously and deliberately chose to take up arms against their
colonizers. Yet, engaging in the act of killing a colonist was not always
welcomed by men who sought to join the FLN. In fact, many men could
not join the urban guerilla because at the last minute they could not fulfill the FLN requirement of proving their mettle by killing a Frenchman.
The film the *Battle of Algiers* depicts Ali-la-Pointe, an unemployed young
man, eager to join the underground, pointing a gun at a French policeman that would not fire. Apparently, this was another test of his resolve:
run the risk of being caught while committing a violent act against a colonial policeman. In urban guerilla warfare killing another man is a political requirement. Such acts are seldom carried out according to the whims
of one man. Admittedly, the ordered act of violence may have had the unintended benefit of making the perpetrator feel good about somehow
avenging ancestral wrongs done to him and his countrymen. This is a sec-
ondary (albeit important) function of violence in a colonial situation, the

social consequences of which can only be determined empirically. Colonial wars, like other wars, are fought against enemies. Killing one's enemy may indeed bring satisfaction for a job well done. And so might torture.

At an abstract level, Fanon was right. He drew attention to the psychologically loaded nature of the colonial situation. He identified the Manichaean context of this situation and sought to work out its psychological ramifications. He noted the mimetic self developed in the colonized man who desires to survive as a pale copy of the colonizer. Being like a Frenchman, speaking his language, dressing like him, availing himself of his (theoretically humanistic) ideas rarely made the colonized man the equal of his colonizer. But the colonizer had promised him that it would. All the symbolic violence that the native may have wrought upon himself in this drawn-out mimetic process was to no avail. In the end, he was led to denounce and (temporarily) renounce the cultural baggage he had borrowed. Sartre adequately explained this process: "A 'French-speaking' *ex-native* [emphasis added] bends this language to new exigencies, and uses it to address only the colonized people."[15] But the question still remains whether Fanon's conception of the redemptive quality of violence applies to all those engaged in the struggle for decolonization, or to only some of them.

The Algerian War was a peasant war. It was the peasantry that bore the brunt of the French army's operations and that was the least culturally affected by the colonial system. Few peasants spoke or understood French. Culturally, they were outside of French colonial society; economically they were at the center of it, having lost their land and working as cheap seasonal laborers for the settlers. The dire circumstances under which the majority of them lived, and the memory of property taken away from previous generations, were constant reminders of their colonial status. Migrations to the city aggravated peasants' sense of social disorientation and alienation. Nevertheless, they surely understood that killing a settler did not bring back their property and dignity. For them, the violence of decolonization was part of a larger struggle with an unknown outcome. Unlike peasants, urban Algerians were less anchored in stark oppression although they too experienced powerlessness, and suffered from unemployment.

The young peasants constituted the rank and file of the nationalist movement. More important, neither peasants nor urban guerillas had received an idealist philosophical education such that they would engage in acts of violence for immediate psychological gain as, for example, nihilists did at the end of the nineteenth century. In Algeria, practice preceded theory. The existence of Lycée graduates among FLN militants and in the ALN did not necessarily give the war a philosophy, as happened in the Bolshevik and Chinese revolutions. This is not to say that the Algerian War had no ideals. To the contrary, it was inspiring because it responded concretely, not ideologically, to genuine oppression and historical injustice, which means that the interpretation of the psychological function of violence that Fanon proposed was grounded in a philosophical tradition lacking among the guerillas. It is not that the decolonization process had to be carried out or led by Ph.Ds in philosophy but that a Hegelian interpretation of the psychological dynamics of guerilla warfare must at the least assume that there be some philosophical-theoretical understanding by the guerilla of his situation. Barring this, it is just we, intellectuals, imparting our meaning to concrete reality—an act that might be confounding, instead of enlightening. Conversely, the colonists did not evince any theoretical understanding of the colonial situation either, although they found justification for their stereotypical views of the natives in colonial treatises and historical accounts of the Empire. Consequently, it is difficult to determine which groups among the Algerians were more likely to experience individual attacks against colonists as transformative of their being.

Peasant and urban people fought for a better life and for rights. This much Fanon demonstrates masterfully. The psychological dynamic proposed by Fanon as an explanation for the violence unleashed in wars of decolonization is enticing. It points to the accumulation of acts of physical and symbolic violence perpetrated by the colonial system on colonial subjects, their impact on the psyche of the colonized, and their inevitable outcome: liberty or life. Nevertheless, in order for Fanon's interpretation to escape facile generalization, it must be tested against the real-life conditions that existed, at the time, for the combatants, peasants as well as city dwellers. Fanon was right in foregrounding the psychic constitution of the colonial subject. But in theorizing the process of decolonization, he may have overlooked the complex ways in which the social system of colonialism affects the subjects it inscribes. For the violence that embeds the colonial subjects to be transcended, it cannot simply exhaust itself in itself through the act of killing a colonist or his representative. It cannot reproduce itself with each additional killing as a mechanical response of the colonized to the colonial system of domination.

It is not possible to argue that Fanon pointed to an irrational response to colonial inequities, since he staked his analysis on the birth (or rebirth) of a new man out of the colonial-psychological morass. In Hegelian terms, to follow Fanon's and Sartre's analytical model, violence needs to be sublated. The sublation proposed by Fanon, in the form of the birth of a new self, a new man, is as problematic as it is fetching. The negation of the colonizer's violence by the colonized man's violence produced additional violence that may have been *necessary* in the sense of being an adaptive response to structural violence. It was, however, premature for Fanon to make the leap from physical violence to psychological cathartic well-being. The birth of the new man was to take place in the context of the transcendence of violence by violence. Without that birth, escalating violence would be meaningless; it would be chaos. The psychoanalytic understanding of violence in the context of decolonization has its limitations. For one thing, decolonization requires a collective, not individual, commitment to a struggle so risky that torture and death are the most certain outcomes. Violence in the Algerian case was in reality justified *politically*.

Sartre is often criticized for having accepted, and thus legitimized, Fanon's interpretation of violence. In reality, he did not think that Fanon's book was a violence manifesto, but understood it to be a wake-up call for Europe to open its eyes to changes that had taken place in the *minds* of its colonial subjects. He reminds his readers that Fanon is no "fascist Sorel," but "the first since Engels to *shed light* on the midwife of History [emphasis added]." According to Sartre, Fanon should be read by Europeans only because he deconstructs for them "the mechanisms of our alienation. Use it to discover your truths as objects [of study]." Clearly, Sartre did not entirely agree with Fanon's views, though he found them justified. He reminds readers that Fanon presented an "interpretation" of the colonial situation. He was also aware that reading Fanon was beneficial to a European scholar. After all, European writers are wont to say that Europe is "finished" but usually add "unless" something is done according to their view of things. He, Sartre, read Fanon's book as "the book of an enemy which I will turn into an instrument for curing Europe."[16] Sartre was affected by Fanon's book in a way that is both intriguing and insightful. He argues that the book was intended for colonized people, not Europeans; it deconstructs Europeans' mind and actions in the colonies, thereby objectifying them. He admits having learned about himself as a European (not a Frenchman only). He hails Fanon for turning Europeans, who traditionally studied non-Europeans, into subjects of his knowledge for the colonized people's benefit. Implicitly, and one wonders why Sartre did not make the fact explicit, Fanon, a colonized man, empowered himself, claimed for himself the right to analyze and know Europeans qua colonizers and to share his knowledge with people like himself.

There is a wistful tone in Sartre's insistence that Fanon not only exposed the nature of violence in the colonial situation, but also brutally revealed the hollowness of European humanism, and the blindness of complacent liberalism. He exclaims:

> First and foremost, we have to confront an unexpected spectacle: the striptease of our humanism. There it is, all bare and unsightly; it was but an ide-

ology of lies, a tantalizing justification of plunder. . . . There is nothing more potent for us than racist humanism since the European could not experience his humanity without manufacturing slaves and monsters. As long as there were natives, this charade was not exposed. We had found in the human species the grounds for postulating an abstract universalism suited for covering up more mundane practices.

Decolonization means colonial violence turned against the perpetrators of the humanist imposture. He wonders, "Whatever happened? It is that, simply put: We were the subjects of History and now we are its objects." This odd response reveals an admission that he too fell prey to the notion that history (which he capitalizes) could only be made by Europeans. In this sense, Fanon's book helped Sartre confront himself as a European/Frenchman. The colonized man, therefore, liberated the scholar belonging to the colonizer country from himself. However, I am bewildered by Sartre's unexamined assertion of his double identity as Frenchman and European, one specific, the other generic. Nevertheless, as Sartre put it, "The colonized man reconstructs himself, but we ultras, colonists and 'metropolitans' [French from France] we deconstruct ourselves."[17]

The completion of the dialectic of colonialism requires that the "people of Europe be decolonized. This means that the colonist in each one of us be excised in a bloody operation." Will Europe be cured, asks Sartre? He answers affirmatively, pointing to the healing power of violence which he compares to Achilles' lance.[18] Evidently, Sartre did not mean, as some commentators have argued, that he invited violence against all Europeans and Frenchmen on account of their tacit complicity with abusive colonial rule. Rather, he felt that the violent liberation of colonized people from the dehumanization pressed onto them by the colonial social system was also the liberation of the Europeans in Europe. And, as the logic of the argument goes, this was only justice, since the violence unleashed in the process of decolonization was European-made, returning to those who created it. Just as violence changes the "false native" into a man, it must also change the European qua colonist or qua spectator of abuse into a man who partakes in the humanity of the former "native." Sartre takes Fanon's view to its formal-logical conclusion. Fanon, the "native" in the process of becoming a man is met by the deconstructed European, French humanist-existentialist, who feels guilt by association for the colonial crimes, including torture, committed in his name. The European recaptures his humanity as a decentered Frenchman, just as the native recaptures his humanity by recomposing himself out of the ashes of his formerly colonized self. The liberation of the colonized man from colonialism as a system is incomplete without the parallel liberation of the colonizer from the system he created. Herein lies Sartre's contribution to the analysis of decolonization.

Intersubjectivity and Colonial War

Sartre's analysis (just like Fanon's) poses the philosophical problem of intersubjectivity at the heart of the colonial situation. The colonist denies the humanity of the Algerian and stakes his own life on the denial. But, he also cannot but acknowledge that his denial is born out of the power conferred on him by conquest. He constantly refers to his conquering generals and the "humanizing," "civilizing," "pacifying" mission they allegedly accomplished in the colony. Whatever he takes away from the Algerian appears legitimate as a spoil of war. No matter how much or how well the Algerian works for the colonist, his labor is devalued, and unvalued. The Hegelian metaphor that informed Sartre's analysis illustrated a conception of intersubjectivity as mediated by labor. It is through labor, according to Hegel, that the humanity of the slave imposes itself on the master; it is through labor that the master realizes the limitation of his consciousness as a master and embraces his shared humanity with his former slave. Both are free of each other as subject and object, face each other as equal subjects, and commune in their shared subjectivity. In the colonial situation as analyzed by Sartre, violence appears as the functional equivalent of labor. But this substitution of violence for labor does not quite work. The colonist as the iconic figure of the colonial system does not acknowledge the humanity of the man (or woman) he transformed into a "native." The colonist institutionalized the "native's" dehumanization before the war and degraded him further during the war through torture and other means of coercion.

If violence, turned back against the colonist, has a liberating effect on the colonized man or woman, it only calls for surplus repression from the colonist. It is difficult to see how the armed confrontation between a man seeking freedom and sovereignty, and one historically bent upon denying him those values could liberate both. The crescendo of abjection reached its climax with the transformation of the combatant into a torturer. Hence a twist in Sartre's dialectical conception of violence in the colonial situation. Admittedly the renewed violence of the colonist only delays the resolution of the philosophically conceived dialectical relationship between colonizer and colonized. Nevertheless, war transcends the bounds of a relationship between two abstract and opposed individuals. It unleashes violence on all fronts and at all levels, crystallizes perceptions of self and others, but also confuses minds and destroys solidarities. One drafted "metropolitan" soldier may gingerly join in torture sessions; another soldier may question his role at the sight of the abuse of prisoners. Conversely, a nationalist may get cold feet when the time comes to engage in urban guerilla warfare, as did the man who tipped off the director of general security, Jean Vaujour, on the eve of November 1, 1954.

Would this be proof that Sartre and Fanon were right to locate the liberation of the colonized person in the violence spawned by the severe social inequalities inherent in the colonial system? In reality, the psychoanalytic interpretation of the cathartic effect of violence in the war of decolonization connotes an individual, rather than a collective condition. More important, it reveals a lack of intersubjectivity. According to both Sartre and Fanon, the colonist convinced himself of the separate, primitive, even bestial nature of the native Algerian. When the latter took up arms to regain his humanity, the colonist perceived this as confirmation of his conception of the native's bestial nature. For the redemptive value of violence to operate for the benefit of *both* colonizer and colonized, it must be grounded in a notion of intersubjectivity shared by the protagonists. Sartre understood very clearly that intersubjectivity is mediated by economic and political factors when he argued that the Frenchman should, ideally, experience *in himself* what it means to be a "native," and that this could only happen if "our soil were occupied by the formerly colonized people and we suffered the pangs of hunger." Barring the colonization of France by Algeria, which was unlikely, for a Frenchman to overcome the colonist in himself, he must demystify colonialism and distinguish the Empire from France, instead of saving the Empire at the expense of "our liberties, rights, democracy and justice."[19] By understanding what the denial of the very democratic values that he holds dear would mean to him, the Frenchman would empathize with the colonized person. In other words, it is as a political being that the Frenchman can understand the plight of the colonized man. But it is only intersubjectivity (not political empathy) that would make the Hegelian metaphor useful in understanding the resolution of the crisis of consciousness created by the original act of colonization. Short of this, Sartre's laudable goal to seek the liberation of the colonist from his own prejudices is vitiated. In this sense, Fanon's view is theoretically more appropriate: He understood that the immediate task for the colonized man was to deliver himself of the colonists' psychic grip on him. Fanon was not concerned with the transformation of the colonist's consciousness. He had given up on it, a fact Sartre knew. For intersubjectitivy in the colonial situation to avail, psychoanalysis was required of both colonizer and colonized as a method of elucidating the induced colonial subject in the colonist and in the "native." But independence from colonial rule could not be fought on a psychiatrist's couch. Or could it?

Sartre saw the impossibility of shifting from the individual to the social levels of analysis in addressing the transformative effect of violence. He found in the social unconscious a useful category to link one level to the other and to explain recourse to violence as *socially* liberating. There is a lot to be said about the social unconscious of the colonized people (as well as the colonists). But the use of this concept often leads to a facile generalization about the impact of the colonial system on the actions of Algerians during the war. Violence may, under historically specific conditions, simply entail more violence for both colonized and colonizer, with no *necessary* cathartic effect. The idealist metaphor cannot be mistaken for concrete reality, just as interpretation should not force reality into a conceptual framework that does it violence. This does not mean that Sartre's desire to take the logic of violence in the process of decolonization to its ultimate conclusion was misplaced. In fact, Sartre's contribution is inestimable. From his perspective, Henri Alleg was the best illustration of the decentered "European"/Frenchman who *experienced* what it meant to be a (or like a) native in the hands of Frenchmen defending the colonial system. Nevertheless, considering that violence was organized on both sides, its cathartic effect was overshadowed by questions of strategy and opportunity. Commitment to independence from colonial rule may not require giving any redeeming value to violence. But it does require political conviction and consciousness. Struggling for freedom can be liberating whether this involves violence or not. Putting up with the hardships of a life in and out of mountain caves, with ambushes, arrest, and torture as its main fare could be rewarding to the nationalist who decided to stake his life for the freedom of his country. What is remarkable is Fanon's as well as Sartre's determination to justify or explain away violence in the colonial situation. Why was it necessary to make sense of violence in psychoanalytic terms? Did Fanon and Sartre imply that there would have been no war had the colonists treated the colonized people better? If so, their conception of colonialism as a fundamentally flawed system, quite incapable of reforming itself would no longer be valid. To what extent does the strenuous dialectical interpretation of violence detract from the importance of the cause (social justice and freedom) for which the war of decolonization was fought?

The decision by General De Gaulle to end the war was a *recognition* of the FLN as the legitimate representative of Algerians. In this sense, violent struggle brought about its desired goal. Guerilla combatants prevailed over the colonizing power to treat them as full-fledged negotiators. But was this recognition an expression of a transformed consciousness on *both* sides? The French military claimed—not without reason—that it had won the war. Did violence give birth to a new man, free not only physically, but also emotionally of all forms of induced colonial subjectivizations? Did violence help the Pieds-Noirs and other Frenchmen understand the dehumanizing foundations of the colonial system they supported?

Fanon wrote as a colonized man from Martinique, partaking in the decolonization of Algeria, another French colony. To reiterate, his aim was to explain that struggles for decolonization are *necessarily* violent, and that such violence is not simply destructive, it is also creative and redeeming: It brings about the dignity and humanity of the colonized man. It is inaccurate to accuse Fanon of glorifying violence, although at times he merges the descriptive and the normative. His was a theory of "revolutionary terrorism" used in movements of national liberation.[20] By locating violence in psychoanalytic dynamics, he risked endowing it with a supplemental meaning that he did not fully account for. Excising the colonial subject out of one's self was an enterprise that required more than the physical removal of the colonist. Fanon's merit was to acknowledge the seriousness of the colonial subjectivity kneaded into the colonized person. Sartre's merit was to understand that the colonist as well as those implicated in the colonial system, directly and indirectly, are molded out of the same mystifications as the colonized. They, too, are in need of liberation. Whether violence would do the trick was another story.

If there is an application of Fanon's conception of the meaning of colonial violence, taken as a metaphor (in the sense that Hegel's *Lordship and Bondage* was a metaphor), it is in the torture chamber. Here the confrontation between the colonial *system* as embodied in the torturer (either a Frenchman from France or a Pied-Noir) and the colonized person acquires its full psychological, historical, and cultural significance.

Albert Camus: Between Mother and "Arabs"

Albert Camus, the Pied-Noir intellectual, cuts a "heroic" figure because he condemned the violence of both sides in the Algerian War, the French and the Algerian. Unlike Sartre, he was born in Algeria to a working-class family—a Spanish mother and an Alsatian father who was killed during World War I, while Camus was still an infant. However, unlike Fanon, who rejected the colonial system after observing the psychological damage it wrought on the colonizer and colonized, Camus had an emotional commitment to the Pied-Noir community that clouded his understanding of the significance of the colonial problem for the colonized. His class position did not help him grasp the meaning for Algerians of the structural inequities of colonial rule although he had in 1939, when a journalist, documented dire poverty in Kabyle villages. Growing up in relative poverty for a Pied-Noir was not the same as being colonized. Camus belonged to a stratified colonial society in which the working class sought to distance itself from the society of natives, which it frequently despised. It is interesting to note that it was Fanon, a non-European and native of the colony of Martinique, who was eager to understand the psychological springs of violence, whereas Camus, a European born in a colony, confined himself to rhetorical condemnations of violence on both sides. However, since Camus defended the right of France to remain in Algeria, his condemnations were self-serving. Denouncing violence is one thing, upholding the side of the colonists who benefited from its social, legal, and political institutions is another. Camus exhorted all sides to coexist peacefully, a hollow and pious wish since he failed to comprehend two important factors. On the one hand, blind military repression generally supported by the colonists had gone too far, and affected millions of Algerians and colonists, leaving little hope that either side to the conflict would contemplate life together. On the other hand, coexistence would have required a complete transformation of relations between colonizer and colonized mediated by legal, political, and economic equality. Judging by the power imbalance between colonists and Algerians, and the influence that wealthy land holding settlers had on French colonial politics, the prospects of such transformation were slim. Nevertheless, Camus did not militate concretely for the transformation, confining himself instead to subsuming violence in the Algerian context under generic violence, which from his perspective encompassed World War II and Stalinism. Neglected was the issue of freedom for Algerians under the strictures of colonial rule.

Yet, Camus's view of violence was at times right on the mark. He noted the contagious character of violence—which prompts the system that seeks to put an end to it to use it with a vengeance. He did not however categorically reject the use of violence, for he was committed to using it to fight fascism. His position was similar to that of contemporary moral philosophers who, claiming realism as their motivation, condone the use of torture in circumstances they define as exceptional. In his fourth letter to a German friend, Camus underscores the necessity of violence for survival: "We were obligated to imitate you in order for us to avoid death." He justified his attitude as a response to the "injustice" that his friend represented. But what strikes me as an oddity for a writer-philosopher is his uncompromisingly violent attitude toward his "friend," mitigated by an ostensibly magnanimous absence of hatred: "I can tell you that at the very point when we will destroy you pitilessly, we shall nevertheless harbor no hatred against you."[21]

Yet, the philosophy of the absurd, which theoretically grounded Camus's conception of the world, would normally have dictated that he display a disengaged and noncommittal stance toward violence. But Camus bends the absurd and turns it into a "rule of action" that "renders murder at least indifferent, and thus possible." He therefore feels entitled to both uphold and condemn violence. It is this selective political commitment, this picking up and dropping of the philosophical flag of the absurd that vitiates Camus's view of terror and terrorism within the Algerian context. In his philosophical treatise *L'Homme Révolté* (*The Rebel*) he develops a Eurocentric notion of revolt and revolution that extols them as purely European occurrences. As such, they are self-referential, requiring no discussion of forms of revolt outside of the European world. He knits revolution, justice, and freedom into a circular dilemma in which he locks the "rebel," all the while letting the sociopolitical and economic framework within which revolt and revolution occur to fade out of the analysis. He locates a "Western" form of revolt and revolution in the secularization process, which results in the transformation of (European) man into a purportedly divine figure, and the concomitant desacralization of God. Although he does not approve of the terror that accompanies revolution, he nevertheless thinks of "Western" forms of rebellion (whether metaphysical, historical, or artistic) as consecrating the superiority of the "West" over the non-West. It remains unclear why the divinization of "man" did not prevent colonial ventures from taking place.

It is precisely the relegation of colonialism to an inconsequential historical happenstance that deprives Camus—a man born into a colony, and a witness to its excesses—of the philosophical power and legitimacy to speak for one side or the other of the Algerian War equation. Yet, his conception of state terrorism was applicable to the Algerian War, specifically his analysis of the logic of empire and techniques of propaganda. To wit: "Empire presupposes negation and certainty: Certainty born of the infinite plasticity of man, and negation of human nature. Propaganda techniques help to measure such plasticity, and strive to match thoughts with conditioned reflexes."[22] But Camus's political critique of Marxist thought and of Soviet Russia, obscures the intrinsic contradictions of his conceptions of violence.

His attitude toward the Algerian War has often been hailed as reflecting a conflicted conscience, as well as a courage for having rejected the idea of an Algeria free of France. In reality he did not have to make a choice. He acted as a Pied-Noir intellectual, not a humanist intellectual who understood the logic of the colonial system of domination. He was emotionally committed to colonial Algeria albeit willing to share it with native Algerians. He often uncritically repeated the arguments made by the military to justify repressive methods, such as his invocation of a Cairo conspiracy to destabilize Algeria, the alleged threat of Pan-Islamism and Pan-Arabism. He posited the primacy of the "West" over the "East," in which he found a comforting sense of superiority. He routinely referred to Algerians using the generic "Arabs," or "Arab militants," and to himself as a Frenchman. He was willing to recognize "Arab personhood" but only as mediated by "French personhood." He evinced sensitivity to his identity as a Frenchman, pointing out that France could not be accused of racism because of the abusive actions committed by what he claimed to be a few soldiers. He insisted that clearing France's name was a precondition for the recognition of an "Arab personhood." It is important to note that the vocabulary Camus used for identifying Algerians was common currency among Pieds-Noirs. What is at issue is not that Camus was opposed to Algeria's independence, but that he failed to grasp the complexity of the colonial situation, the fundamental injustice of colonial rule, *and* his implication in it. His reflexes were those of a partisan who used the same arguments as civil authorities in his calls for peace and co-existence. In an apparently evenhanded gesture, he denounced terror on both sides of the war, but managed to justify repression by equalizing *state* terrorism with that of the FLN.[23] He was unwilling, or unable to acknowledge the imbalance of power between the military and the FLN, just as he was unwilling to question the validity of colonial rule. However, more than many of his fellow Pieds-Noirs, he was willing and able to acknowledge the brutality of military repressive methods, but reluctant to locate them in an unjust and long history of structural abuse. I find no heroism in his attitude, only a justification of France's continued presence in Algeria. I find no empathic understanding of the colonized Algerian population, but an abstract and politically motivated attachment to imperial France.

Camus' doubts about terrorism would have gained considerable weight had he rejected violence. But opting not to do so, he logically had to accept the violence of the FLN, within the colonial context, since "revolt is profoundly positive because it reveals there is always something in man that is worth struggling for." But, I am not sure that Camus saw the Algerians' struggle for their freedom as a revolt or a revolution, having defined both as moments in "Western thought."[24] Although he appeared to be a figure tormented by his allegiance to France and committed to the colonial order, he was unable to rise above either. Nevertheless, he condemned torture, although at times he seemed to condone repressive methods if the alternative meant that France would leave Algeria.[25] The romanticism with which his attitude toward Algeria is frequently imbued obscures the essentially simple idea that he had *chosen* to be on the side of colonial Algeria, notwithstanding his own admission that "man does not choose."[26] During a debate organized as part of the ceremony for the Nobel Prize he received on December 14, 1957, he told an Algerian student who questioned his silence regarding the atrocities of the Algerian War, "I believe in justice, but I will defend my mother before justice."[27]

If it is important to be "neither victim, nor executioner,"[28] it is dubious to wish to salvage the system that nurtured both individuals.

In sum, Sartre sheds light on the ideological underpinnings of the political economy of French colonialism. Grounded in a tradition of critical philosophy and existential humanism, he was able to see that torture was *required* by the political economy of colonialism, which supported colonists' power over the colonized. From his perspective, the act of colonization created a philosophically untenable situation of psychological degradation in which the humanity of the colonized was inevitably denied and repressed. Sartre avoids the means-ends explanation of torture by pointing instead to the human bond that ties colonizer and colonized, torturer and tortured, advocate of torture and the indifferent. When a person is tortured, any other person anywhere in the world is threatened by this, and degraded by it. Fanon's psychoanalytic explanation of the violence inherent in decolonization wars sheds light on the intensity of the violence, but remains questionable. It locates movements of national liberation's impetus for action in the psychological condition of the colonized people, assumed to be pathological. However, Fanon captures the social-psychological climate that prevailed during the Algerian War. Like Sartre, he points to the inevitability of violence—and this means torture— in the structural context of the colonial system of rule. By comparison, Camus's understanding of the war did not differ significantly from that of a post–May 13, 1958, colonist. Camus nevertheless sheds light on the philosophical justification of colonial consciousness, unable to reflect upon itself in a decentered manner, or to perceive itself as but a moment in the larger historical canvas in which might does not make right. However, his thought does shed light on the complexity of the issue of torture, as many of Camus's views resonate with the precepts of revolutionary-war theory.

PART IV
REFLECTIONS ON TORTURE

Chapter 10

MORALIZING TORTURE

> Nothing will ever justify torture because
> it assaults the human condition.
> —Esméralda, *Un été en enfer*

IN HELPING THE MILITARY justify the systematic use of torture, the Christian-right moralists made use of the vocabulary of evil, retribution, and redemption. Although their views were wrong, they made sense when read as part of the medieval and colonial legacy of the Church. By contrast, contemporary secular intellectuals or moral philosophers writing in defense of torture lack a compelling intellectual foundation on which to build a case for the practice. They resort instead to arguments adopted by the state, especially the justification of means by ends, and the exceptionality of situations that purportedly make the use of torture necessary. Uncritically espousing the state's logic and alibis they lend their authoritative support to policies that destroy civil rights at home and contribute to chaos abroad. Yet, philosophical critiques of the "ends justify the means" formula (such as Hegel's or Kierkegaard's) are seldom engaged by the most noteworthy among contemporary moral philosophers and apologists, such as Michael Walzer, Jean Bethke Elshtain, and Michael Ignatieff. Reviewing these critiques helps shed light on the structure of the arguments made by the proponents of torture, and clarifies the role they implicitly assign torture in imperial politics, such as those pursued in Iraq.

Dilemmas So-Called or the Torture of Torture

Informed by a utilitarian perspective that seeks to maximize gains and minimize losses, the formula "the ends justify the means" considers torture an efficient means to achieve ends deemed morally worthy. Its variant, to which I will refer as the apologetic perspective, condones the use of torture as one of the options a politician might have to choose in a situation of crisis. This perspective has roots in the premise that politicians are not necessarily moral people; "they are often killers."[1] Of course, some decent men do at times enter politics. And when they do, they sometimes face "moral dilemmas" that they resolve by ordering actions that dirty their hands. An example of such a politician, according to Michael Walzer, is a man who wants to put an end to colonial domination and start a new era of peace. However, as he is about to embark on his (worthy) decolonization initiative, he is faced with deciding whether to order the torture of a captured "rebel . . . who probably knows the location of a number of hidden bombs."[2] He makes the decision to torture. Thereafter, the decent but morally dirtied politician will reap guilt as punishment for his (supposedly necessary) deed. Since Walzer makes several references to Sartre and Camus, I conclude that he had Algeria in mind. However, my research did not find a prime minister who was genuinely eager to solve the problem of decolonization in Algeria, and felt compelled, instead, to order torture against "rebels." Guy Mollet knew of torture but lied about it to the public before finally acknowledging that it might have happened—for good reasons.[3] Robert Lacoste, during his tenure as resident minister in Algeria, condoned and covered up torture and other atrocities. He did not evince any moral conflict, nor did Generals Aussaresses or Massu. Furthermore, the terror unleashed by the OAS, aided by the police, elicited no "dilemma" for the colonial government, as it was allowed to proceed until 1962.[4] This raises the issue of the selectivity of the moral philosopher's opposition to terror: It is justified if the state engages in it; it is condemned if extra-state actors use it. But terror is terror no matters who wields it; its consequences are the same for each defenseless individual.

Admittedly, reference to a mythical politician simply illustrates a hypothetical situation that explains how a politician might dirty his hands. But this method of reasoning reflects a major problem plaguing the apologetic perspective: It thrives on hypothetical situations, which, in this case at least, are simplifications of what actually occurs in real life. And because they are simplifications, these hypothetical situations rest on the selection of one or two features (a "rebel" and "bombs") from an intricate political reality requiring serious analysis in order to shed light on the decision to use torture. This reductive approach helps to turn the instrumental use of torture into a crise de conscience.

Three aspects of this view deserve close scrutiny: First, the assertion that a moral dilemma precedes the decision to torture deemphasizes the deliberateness of the order to torture and makes it seem a last resort reluctantly adopted. Prime actors in the establishment of torture as a war weapon during the Algerian War hardly concerned themselves with its ethics. Placed in contiguity with the "moral" side of the "dilemma" and presented as the solution (or consumption) of the "moral" dilemma, torture is infused with a moral content that it does not have. If torture, the willful infliction of pain and often death by the state, is moral, on what grounds is an act of terror that functions in the same manner considered amoral when committed by others?

Hegel's thoughts on the "ends justify the means" formula provide insights into the question. Placed under the rubric "Good and Conscience," in the *Philosophy of Right*, Hegel's discussion of morality seeks to unravel the relationship between will, conscience, good, and evil.[5] From his perspective, the moral act includes three aspects: (a) the right to act as embedded in the purpose of my action, which represents my (subjective) will; (b) my intention to act, which constitutes the "inner content" of my action as aiming for the general good, and a particular character of being good for my welfare; (c) correlatively, the content of my will, which embodies my awareness that the good as universal represents my conscience. My conscience encapsulates the subjective incarnation of the universal, of the good as universal. That this subjective character of my conscience might go astray and get disconnected from the universal, and even set *itself* up as a universal of sorts, is a problem that, according to Hegel, explains perversions of the will such as fraud, hypocrisy, and evil. From Hegel's vantage point, the good is universal, and the will aims at the good. To justify an act that is wrong by the intention behind it is to isolate one aspect of the action and turn it into its essence. This has a consequence for how one judges a wrong act. As Hegel put it:

> In a living thing, the single part is there in its immediacy not as a mere part, but as an organ in which the universal is really present as the universal; hence in murder, it is not a piece of flesh, as something isolated, which is injured, but life itself which is injured in that piece of flesh.

Similarly, the tortured person is not just an isolated suspect body subjected to injury; it is the tortured body of a man or a woman, a sentient being deprived of subjectivity, of will. It could be that of any man, or any woman anywhere. It could also be the body of the torturer. If the subject is "the series of his actions," and his actions are wrong, there is no salvaging them by arguing that they were motivated by his good intentions. And this is so for at least two reasons. First, the process of salvaging leads to a pseudoheroic attitude that thrives on what Hegel refers to as the command: "Do with abhorrence what duty enjoins."[6] This is a morality that justifies decisions that allow practices such as torture to be an inevitable, although despicable, part of wielding power, and thus requiring a degree of "fortitude." Second, it obscures the notion of responsibility and accountability by defining the notion of duty restrictively. Duty to the

French nation, for example, not only excluded Algerians from the nation, but also meant violating the very foundations of duty: respect for law, the law that is there to deal with offenders.

For Hegel, the formula "the ends justify the means" is one moment in a series of perversions of the good into evil, of which bad conscience, hypocrisy, "probabilism," and the notion that willing good makes good are the most notable. Probabilism is close to the means-ends logic insofar as it upholds an action as good provided that a reason is found for it. It does not matter where the reason, or principle, can be found. Father Delarue and adherents of Cité Catholique found in religion reasons for torture, while the experts in psychological action found them in the Algerians' alleged "primitive" psychological makeup. Similarly, Walzer finds overwhelming reason in the ticking-bomb scenario. From Hegel's perspective, these perversions are also "stages of subjectivism," by which he understood the diremption (or splitting up) of the subjectivity of the will from its universal purpose. In probabilism, the need to find an "objective" reason for a wrong action betrays a veiled understanding that some standard outside of the subjective will of the agent of action is needed. But in a world of competing reasons, there is no way of determining which one is the best. Consequently,

> caprice and self-will are made into the arbiters of good and evil, and the result is that ethics as well as religious feelings are undermined. But the fact that it is private subjectivity to which the decision falls is one which Probabilism does not openly avow as its principle; on the contrary . . . it gives out that it is some reason or other which is decisive, and Probabilism is to that extent a form of hypocrisy.

Unlike probabilism, however, which seeks an external reason, the "means-ends" formula is tautological. Hegel argues that "the means is nothing in itself but is for the sake of something else, and therein, i.e., in the end, has its purpose and worth—provided of course it be truly a means."[7]

Appeal to the formula ("the ends justify the means") means that to do the wrong thing, to commit a crime is not only permissible, but even a duty. The logic of the formula can also be turned against its proponents. If my welfare and that of my family is an end that justifies wrongdoing, so it too "must be subordinated to some higher ends, and so reduced to means of their attainment." In other words, ends and means are reversible, and what was means can become an end. And thus, "the absolute and valid determinate character assigned good and evil, right and wrong, is entirely swept away, and the determination of them is ascribed to the individual's feeling, imagination and caprice." The end that justifies the criminality of the crime committed for it is "simply objective opinion about what is good and better."[8] Consequently, the means-ends formula is arbitrary and cannot be justified morally since it is its own standard. Like probabilism, it has a multiplicity of means to choose from, and only subjective (read separated from the universal good) standards by which to determine which means are the most suited to their ends. Furthermore, the ends themselves are "subjective." More concretely, was keeping Algeria French the best end, and was it best served by torture and terror as its means? Is torture the best way to fight "terror"? Or, was invading Iraq the best way to achieve stability in the Middle East?

A detail stands out in Hegel's deconstruction of the means-ends formula: Its proponents are *aware* of the immorality of their actions. The "consciousness" of the tenth commandment, Thou shalt not kill, "floats before [their] minds."[9] This floating signifier of a morality higher than the one they established subjectively accounts for the lengths to which proponents of torture go to explain away the practice as mere discomfort. However, objectionable as the means-ends formula is when it justifies willed pain, death, and destruction, it is expected from military men when given the power to administer a community. It is less so when adopted by intellectuals who seek to present it as a normal method of fighting terrorism. Then the formula has a blinding power on the mind. It prevents it from seeing alternatives. Instead, it compels the mind to dig into history and philosophy for an ever increasing number of instances of normalization of terror. This is the situation that Hegel identified as a perversion of evil into good.

To return to Walzer's conception of the assumed morality of torture: Its second problematic aspect resides in the undefined nature of what constitutes the "moral." Is the moral situational and conjunctural, or is it universal? Does the practice of torture require an elastic conception of morality to justify it? That a "rebel" might know the locations of bombs, is not sufficient to resolve the politicians' assumed moral dilemma. What if the prisoner does not know? Apparently, the politician cannot take the risk of letting a man go pain-free when he might possess needed information. In other words, torture is ordered not because of a strong presumption of guilt, but because of a presumption of *knowledge* of information. Knowledge, however, can be defined in very broad terms and include having seen but failing to report someone whose looks are unfamiliar.

The actual Algerian situation to which Walzer implicitly refers contradicts his scenario altogether. General Massu's actions in Algiers in 1957 included the systematic torture of men, women, and children, in their homes, by day and night, not to discover the location of bombs but to break an eight-day strike called by the FLN and to dismantle the FLN Zone Autonome. The terror he unleashed on a defenseless civilian population followed rather than preceded exploding bombs in cafés. In this sense torture did not truly help to prevent the explosion of bombs. The efficiency of Massu's methods was such that it alienated the native population in Algiers, and raised the stature of the FLN.

The probabilistic assumption of the knowledge possessed by a captured "rebel" is tautological and rests on the strategic (not moral) opinion of the politician. The "rebel" would have been tortured anyway, because he was a "rebel." Furthermore, Walzer's scenario is constructed in a way that foregrounds the impact of torture on the man who orders it. It has no room for the effect of torture, or its meaning for the man who is tortured and might be innocent. Consequently, the scenario is predicated on the humanity of the man ordering torture, but denies, by omission, that of the man being tortured. Yet, a more universalistic conception of the moral would include both men, the tortured *as well as* the torturer.

The politician will allegedly experience guilt for having ordered the torture of the "rebel." The assumption of guilt as punishment of the agent of torture is equally fraught with problems. In a war of decolonization (the chosen hypothetical situation), guilt is superfluous. Maillard de la Morandais, the seminarian, did not report feeling any guilt for having remanded a "suspect" to a torturer, and watching him being tortured. The "moral dilemma" scenario attempts to equate the unmentioned physical pain of the tortured "rebel" with the psychological discomfort of the torturer. Perhaps this is what is meant by the "moral" in "moral dilemma." I am moral because I know that torture hurts. But because I am a politician, I want to save (hypothetical) lives by ordering a man tortured even though I do not know whether he has the information I need to save these lives.

The apologetic approach thrives not only on an extreme simplification of concrete situations, but also on their distortion. Furthermore, by evoking a concrete case, decolonization, the scenario seeks to convey the realness of the situation, which gives the "moral dilemma" a dramatic appearance. But the reality of the case is fictionalized to serve a legitimating function. This mental operation short-circuits the historicity and facticity of torture, but since it needs to close the circle of plausibility, it is compelled to find additional supportive arguments by borrowing from genuine fiction. Thus characters from Sartre's play *Les Mains Sales* (*Dirty Hands*), and Camus's *Les Justes*, are harnessed in the task of building a moral case for the inevitability of torture. He who shrinks away from torturing is not fit to lead; a good politician is aware of the "paradox" of power that helps a politician inflict harm in order to bring about good. The scenario, just like the formula (of means and ends) that grounds it, falls short of questioning the means as well as the ends of torture. It fails to examine the morality of the "moral dilemma," just as it fails to provide a compelling argument for torture, except as a necessary evil for which the tough politician must be admired. The ends pale in importance before the means.

Where Hegel saw perversion of good into "evil," the apologetic perspective sees a "paradox." Yet, it is not the "paradox" (if there is one) that ought to be unraveled, but the very notion that the perversion would be termed a paradox. The self-centeredness of the apologetic perspective impedes any self-reflexivity: It hides its justificatory function from itself. It abstracts from fiction and the real-world features calculated to overpower objections. These are dismissed as stemming from a lack of understanding of the unhappy bind in which the politician, schooled in Machiavellian or Weberian thought, is assumed to find himself. The stalwart politician will have to reluctantly dirty his hands. I am reminded of two meanings of the word "justification." The *American Heritage College Dictionary* defines it as: to "declare free of blame." The French dictionary *Littré* adds a more explicit theological meaning, "to restore a sinner to a state of grace." Torture moralists do both, but for the person who orders torture: the politician.

This justification of torture denotes a form of moral realism[10] that takes it for granted that all politicians (and I wonder where this leaves all the military officers who engaged in torture with and without the approval of politicians) are aware or exhibit understanding of moral principles. It is noteworthy that this perspective leaves no room for a discussion of conscience. And it also speaks in the name of all readers by assuming that we somehow share in a common understanding of morality as a formal set of rules exemplified in a "moral code" that can (and allegedly should) be infringed occasionally. What if the "moral" code used by the politician is a mere instrument that helps to define others as essentially "evil" because of their ethnicity or culture? In this context, reference to the "rebel" in the scenario is troubling: It loads the deck against the prisoner. Perhaps, to be compelling, the scenario ought to have presented the complex political situation in which the politician decided that torture was the *best* means to achieving his ends.

The constant shifting of the grounds of the argument, from the hypothetical decolonization situation to the character of abstract politicians and plainly fictitious characters, deprives it of a compelling plausibility, except at a superficial level. Indeed, if one stays with the decolonization example, one is dealing with total war in which moral dilemmas are few and far between. The issue is well phrased by Hegel in his remark: "Executioners and soldiers have not merely the right, but the duty to kill men, though there it has been precisely laid down what kind of men and what circumstances make the killing permissible and obligatory."[11] In grounding his analysis in the hypothetical case of colonialism, Walzer's defense of torture is indistinguishable from a defense of colonialism.

A final, and perhaps not so minor detail: An inversion of meaning occurs at the end of the "ends justify the means" scenario. It is "us" who will need to "dirty our hands" in order to make the politician-prince who "lies, manipulates, and kills" (no longer tortures) pay the price for his misdeeds. As befits an argument that proceeds along a process of infinite regress, "we" will be punished for it too, and this will start the process anew, as we will dirty our hands, causing others to punish us who will also dirty their hands in the process. This distant and distorted echo of Sartre's existentialist conception of humanism dissolves a glimmer of accountability into an exacerbated relativism. This moral *geste raté* ostensibly claims inspiration from the Catholic notion of sin as culpability and the resulting expectation of punishment.[12] But, this pessimistic relativism is grounded in Camus's conception of terror,[13] which although problematic, is presented as normative. Against this view, I must reiterate that the Church was strategically silent on torture in Algeria, as shown in chapter 8. Father Delarue, who condoned torture, was not condemned by the Church for his views. It must be remembered that activists in the Cité Catholique had no moral qualms about torture or psychological action; they found both palatable.

Henry Schue points to the artificiality of the realist scenario: "But there is a saying in jurisprudence that hard cases make bad law, and there might well be one in philosophy that artificial cases make bad ethics."[14] Finally, "dirty hands" works well as the title of a play, but in moral defense of torture, it displaces the focus of the amorality of torture from conscience to body, a method that is the reverse of torture, which proceeds from the body to the mind. All discussions about "dirty hands" reduce a highly complex phenomenon to a quasi-religious morality based on dirt, pollution, which implicitly can be washed off. The state, in the name of which the politician orders torture, is lost sight of; torture becomes a man-to-man issue, not one of institutional power over the individual.

Unlike Walzer, Kierkegaard examines a genuine moral dilemma in his analysis of the "teleological suspension of the ethical." He poses a crucial question: "Is there a teleological suspension of the ethical?" Like Hegel, he posits the universality of the ethical and problematizes the relationship between the singular and the universal. "Where the singular individual asserts himself in his singularity before the universal, he sins." If I were to bypass the religious concept of "sin" and think of it as transgression of social morality, which Kierkegaard equates with the ethical, I would conclude that a person who might not have information should not be tortured. It might be argued that Kierkegaard is not the right philosopher to invoke under the circumstances because he also wrote: "and only by acknowledging this sin, can he [Abraham] be reconciled with the universal." Wouldn't this mean that the commission of a bad deed is absolved through confession? Maybe so, but Kierkegaard's point was that Abraham realized he was in a situation of "spiritual trial," a realization brought about by the absurdity of his having to sacrifice his son to please his God. And he did not sacrifice his son. The "moral dilemma" discussed earlier that results in "dirty hands" may have been inspired by this religious myth, but it falls short of capturing the full force of the ethical question it raises. A suspect is not a son, and saving hypothetical lives is different from pleasing a God. Abraham was willing to sacrifice his son for his faith; to please his God he was willing and ready to play God with his son. And this deprives him of any redeeming feature. He is "appalling."[15] Just like the officer who orders a person tortured out of duty is not heroic, Abraham, in Kierkegaard's view, lacks the qualities of a tragic hero. Abraham's relation to the absolute is unmediated. He stands alone, identifying with the godliness of God before God, and acts as if he were God. So did the military officer who used torture routinely. The torturer might argue that he did it for reasons of state, but this would be disingenuous given that he was already using powerful military means to satisfy reasons of state. The additional "sacrifice" of men, women, and children fell outside of the realm of the ethical.

Casuistry and Torture

Another variant of the "ends justify means" formula underscores the reification of torture as a set of methods that can be ranked on a scale measuring the degree of pain each inflicts on the prisoner. Thus Jean Bethke Elshtain claims to have found an alternative to the quandary posed by torture. She is neither entirely for it, nor against it. She advocates a mild or "light" torture as described by Mark Bowden, the author of the "Dark Art of Interrogation."[16] And these include "exposure to heat and cold, the use of drugs to cause confusion, rough treatment (slapping, shoving or shaking), forcing a prisoner to stand for days at a time,"[17] and so on. Each of these methods causes severe, and often irreversible, harm to the body and the mind of prisoners. Shaking has caused cerebral hemorrhage; slapping, an apparently banal form of punishment, damages hearing when done by powerful torturers using the victim as a slapping bag; forcing victims to stand spread-eagle against a wall with their feet away from the wall so that their body weight is carried by their hands for several days with no possibility of a break caused Irish prisoners to lose the use of their hands to write or hold a cup. They also had to urinate and defecate on themselves through the duration of their ordeal.[18] In real life, in the torture chamber, none of these methods is used alone. Irish prisoners were deprived of sleep for six consecutive days, in addition to being spread-eagle against a wall and ceaselessly bombarded by thundering noise for hours on end. Elshtain is less appalled by these methods than by tales of needles forced under nails, pulled nails, or electricity attached to a person's genitals. Torture is not reducible to a slap, or a kick, or an insult as Elshtain argues, it is all of these *and* more. Torture is also inseparable from the intent to harm (for a purpose, of course); it represents the defenselessness and the reduction of a human being to a thing acted upon at will.

Elshtain's defense of torture rests on a number of mystifications: To begin with, it divorces torture from the holistic character of the pain it inflicts. It assumes not only that torture methods function independently of one another but also that they result in sensations the intensity of which can be distinguished by the moral philosopher who has not endured them. In comparison, General Massu had subjected himself to torture albeit not in the manner that his victims had been, or for the same length of time.[19] The suggestion is not that Elshtain undergo torture, but that she comprehend the implications of her solution on real, concrete, sentient beings. Elshtain's advocacy of "light" torture inexplicably places faith in the torturer, assumed to be a professional of pain, who will carefully calibrate suffering in accordance with a semantic distinction between "light" and severe.

Secondly, Elshtain omits a discussion of the relationship between language and the pain of torture without which her acceptance of torture "light" is meaningless. While all pain is hurtful, torture pain is even more so because of its deliberate relentlessness, and its political purpose. Its authorization by the state gives torture pain an additional force, as its practitioners feel justified, if not entitled, to carrying it out with the intensity that suits their cultural or political identity claims. The pain endured by the victim is often inexpressible in language, causing the victim to remain irremediably alone after her ordeal ends. It is sobering to note that forty-seven years after her torture at the hands of paratroopers for two and a half months, Louisette Ighilahriz is still unable to fight back tears when she discusses the subject. Her trauma also caused her to abort her first pregnancy after her marriage, thinking she might be carrying a little Bigeard or Massu.[20] Esméralda writes, "Sometimes I am seized by sudden panics, and paralyzed by terrible anxieties. At least I know where they come from. I will die with them."[21] Neither Ighilahriz nor Esméralda can pinpoint which method of torture was more or less traumatic. Torture is holistic in its effects; it is "hell."[22] The depth of the emotional trauma that it causes cannot be conveyed in a language that unburdens the victim. Trauma is present in all facets of torture; it is impossible to ignore it. Making a determination about what method of torture is bearable is but a gratuitous exercise in cruelty masquerading as realism.

Finally, Elshtain's view fails to critically examine the relationship between torture as a means, and the ends it is assumed to serve. These significant silences and gaps in her arguments are grounded in her expressed fear of the "enemy," the "terrorists," "radical Islamism," "violent marauders"—categories that strike by their lack of precision. A moralist's middle-class sense of certainty and trust in law may be shattered by acts of terror, but defending the willful infliction of pain and suffering requires that the moralist rises above personal anger. Having counterposed the secular values of "Americanism" to a "crisis"-ridden Islam,[23] Elshtain finds justification for her tolerance of torture, not in an ecumenical or secular morality, but in a "Christian moral thinking and the tradition of casuistry that arose from it." Within this tradition the stateswoman who orders torture "can stand before God as a guilty person and seek forgiveness."[24] However, if we must enter the religious domain, there is good and bad casuistry. Good casuistry is

> deeply informed by the spirit of the law, and knows how to resolve all cases in light of this spirit. Bad casuistry concerns itself only with *the letter of formulas* [such as ends justify means], and making its way through a maze of texts, gets bogged down in subtleties, or worse still, excuses and tricks at the expense of sincerity, in order to disguise bad faith as duty.[25]

Elshtain's argument, like Walzer's, is predicated on a hypothetical scenario of a city school in which a bomb has been planted and a "terrorist" is taken into custody. Its plausibility is secured by merging reality with genuine fiction. Elshtain uses the film *Marathon Man* as an example of torture techniques used by terrormongers. Laurence Olivier tried pulling out Dustin Hoffman's nails and drilling Dustin's teeth. Thus the depiction of torture in a film serves as the grounds on which Elshtain distinguishes between "light" and severe torture. The moral disarray underlying this attitude is best expressed in her evaluation of various methods of punishment to determine whether they rise to the level of torture. Elshtain rejects the human-rights paradigm because of its allegedly excessive moralization of abuse, which she likens to a "sort of deontology run amok."[26] Whatever the merits of this assessment, Elshtain's suggestion is equally extreme as it trivializes torture through categorizing it as "light" and severe. Unlike Walzer, Elshtain seeks no moral justification for torture other than self-defense. It is to save her own children in the hypothetical scenario that she seeks the torture of the man whom she is *almost* sure knows the whereabouts of the bomb. Stemming from a reflexive response to assuaging fear, this approach forecloses the search for alternatives to torture. The person who orders (or commits) torture finds solace in confession and God's forgiveness. Divine forgiveness does away with accountability in the here and now.

What is troubling about Elshtain's perspective is its easy justification of physical pain, and its rejection of our modern sensitivities to expanding, rather than restricting, the space in which the body and the mind are shielded from intentional harm (even that caused by verbal insult), which the author dismisses as inconsequential. In this sense, advocates or apologists for torture wish to roll back the clock, and return to a premodern conception of the body, self, and state coercion. They fail to question the *right* of the state to torture its and others' citizens. The choice made by Walzer and Elshtain to ground their defense of torture in fictional scenarios functions as a ploy that evades a discussion of the significance of torture for understanding the nature of the avowedly democratic state. Realism *oblige*. If the state arrogates the right to torture, the individual has a duty to not only question this but to oppose it. Challenging the state on the right to torture is essential lest the legal system permit the military, as it does in Israel, to engage in this practice when it deems it "necessary."[27]

Exceptionalism and Torture

A more elaborate conception of torture as a requirement for ensuring security is formulated by Michael Ignatieff, the former director of Harvard University Carr Center for Human Rights Policy. Ignatieff opposes torture on moral grounds, but condones it for political realist reasons. He rightly condemns it as a violation of "human dignity," a "core value" that should not be compromised by the "war on terror."[28] Nevertheless, he favors its use as well as the suspension of the civil liberties that are part of core democratic values because of the "emergency" situation allegedly created by "terrorism." The asserted existence of a state of emergency enables Ignatieff to adopt a formal heroic stance approximating Walzer's dilemma-plagued fictitious politician, but deprives him of moral arguments for condoning the use of torture.

A state of emergency is a state of *exception* in which the legal system "suspends itself." The significance of such an occurrence dictates that questions be raised about who decides that an emergency exists, what the sociopolitical conditions are under which an emergency is decided, and who benefits from constructing a situation as an emergency. What if a state of emergency-exception leads to "juristic chaos"[29] or an anarchy far greater than what it is meant to remedy? What if state of emergency functions as a myth that enables a willed subversion of "democracy" or becomes a method of government.[30] To what extent do antidemocratic means tolerated in the name of democracy result in the very destruction of the democracy they ostensibly seek to preserve? In reality it is unclear how "democracy" is threatened by acts of terror, unless the state frames such acts as challenges to its own policies, which it deems unquestionable.

In other words, the conflation of the defense of torture with the defense of democracy is ideological, as torture is a means to corrupt and distort the meaning and practice of democracy. The conflation denotes a conception of democracy as a transitory form of government teetering on the edge of acceptable totalitarianism.

Since the "emergency" factor alone lacks a compelling moral dimension in which to ground a rehabilitation of torture, Ignatieff resorts to justifying the practice by submerging it in a defense of state terrorism. Arguing against the "moral perfectionist stance," which he considers "unrealistic," too facile to make and too difficult to implement, he indulges in a casuistry of his own, asking "what is the line between interrogation and torture, between targeted killing and unlawful assassination, between pre-emption and aggression?" This exercise in nominalism helps the author to not only distinguish between "permissible" and "impermissible" torture, but also to advocate expedient, if not summary, justice: "If the targeted killing of a terrorist proves necessary, it can be constrained by strict rules of engagement and subjected to legislative oversight." This view dispenses with a definition of terrorism and opens the door to killing men who fit a predetermined "terrorist" profile regardless of guilt or innocence. Thus, Ignatieff deplores but finds justified the unlawful arrests of five thousand "males of Muslim or Arab origin."[31]

Seeking to give this crude realism a moral cover, Ignatieff invokes the "lesser evil" argument that Father Delarue made notorious in Algeria. This helps him resolve the paradox of arguing against torture while advocating the conditions of its possibility. Eschewing an evaluation of the morality of fighting terror with terror, Ignatieff explains that he, a secular man and not a priest, uses "the word evil instead of harm" to indicate that there is always a "moral risk" in maintaining a functioning democracy. Nevertheless, the concept of evil connotes a symbolic imagery that deemphasizes the responsibility of the state and conjures up demonic figures as the enemy. In the end, a concept embedded in religious thought is substituted for an analysis of "terrorism," an essentially political act. Ignatieff uses the "lesser evil" defense as self-explanatory and needing no moral discussion. Unlike Morandais and Father Peninou who addressed and defined different types of morality, Ignatieff confines himself to describing "a lesser evil morality" in terms of its functions. It is "designed for the skeptics. . . . This is an ethics of prudence rather than first principle, one that assesses what to do in an emergency with a conservative bias against infringements of established standards of due process, equal protection, and basic dignity." However, regardless of its lofty functions, this "ethic" is in reality a justification of the very infringements it denounces since it legitimizes targeted killing and torture. The fact that the author is fully cognizant of the abuses that might result from such infringements pales before the imperative of the lesser evil, which from his perspective rests on a balancing act between necessity and emergency, evil and terror, security and liberty.[32] Yet, "prudence" can just as easily be turned against torture's advocates. The "virtue of prudence" may serve as a constraint on the use of political power as a technique of control applied to people perceived as things.[33] For whom is it "prudent" to subject "suspects" to torture? How prudent is it to make torture an acceptable method of interrogation at home and abroad with little regard to its consequences? How efficient is torture in fostering security? There is nothing ethical about the state violating fundamental democratic rights, and flouting the international conventions to which it is a signatory. And there is nothing admirable about advocating a "lesser evil" while allowing that evil still rules.

Ignatieff's justifications of coercion and state terror are striking because of their one-sidedness, and because they fail to draw attention to the universal character of moral acts. They wrap themselves instead in a moral discourse devoid of moral content. His discursive invocation of the moral factor appears to be more ritualistic than substantive: It is a residue of an intellectual tradition seeking to maintain a moral façade in discussions of the infliction of pain and suffering on others that has already been rendered moot by an unbridled realism finding added force in a climate of fear. The "lesser-evil morality" anoints controlled terror (which thrives on torture) while protecting itself from the charge of defending torture. The "lesser-evil morality" is neither religiously compelling, nor ethically convincing. Politically, it rests on an unwarranted belief in liberal democratic systems correcting themselves even as they engage in unliberal acts. Such unbound faith is eerily similar to that expressed by French civil and military authorities as it describes the same situation: "The fact that liberal democratic leaders may order surreptitious killing of terrorists, may withhold information from others, may order the suspension of civil liberties need not mean that 'anything goes.'"[34] What else is left "to go"?

Ignatieff like Walzer and Elshtain, represents the professional intellectual who lends the cover of his ideational expertise to the politician qua torturer; one defends democracy with torture, the others defends fictitious lives assumed to be in danger with real torture. In defending torture, authors writing about others or in the name of others can make no claim to understanding otherness; they have forfeited their right to write about others.[35] They act as theoreticians of the practical use of torture: Finding torture permissible is the first step toward normalizing and routinizing the practice at home and abroad.

What is at issue is not the rarity of the ticking-bomb scenario that informs defenses of torture, but these authors' reflexive, conditioned response to a situation of political challenge. Torture seems a swift and efficient method for getting results. This view obviates the need to consider other methods of not only preventing "emergency" situations of the kind described by the ticking-bomb scenario from occurring, or for meeting them when they do occur. It does not address the development of technologies to enhance security, promote a nonadventurist foreign policy, or creatively deal with sources of strife. Furthermore, this defense of torture asserts the inevitability of a ticking-bomb situation no matter what measures are taken to prevent it. Dogmatism and fatalism of this kind are uncharacteristic in a highly technological society, and they thrive on an abstract magnification of an impending catastrophe that imparts a degree of permanence to the "war on terror." Torture thus becomes a favored and necessary war weapon.

The charge of moralism often made by torture's apologists against their opponents obscures the fact that the ticking-bomb scenario grounds security-defense in the body of a suspect, which may or may not break. Torture often triggers resistance. And in a true believer, it meets with a commitment to die rather than talk. In other words, there are limits to what torture can accomplish, even, and perhaps especially, in such situations of dramatic emergency as those outlined by hypothetical cases. In this sense, torture's limitation is inseparable from its own structure. Seldom discussed by the proponents of the means-ends formula, torture's inherent limitation widens the circle of its potential victims by making their relatives torturable. Historical evidence indicates that the torture slope is slippery, and its "morality" as dubious as the certainty of the hypothetical scenario.

Similarly, the rhetorical games that frame calls to legalize torture surprise by their disingenuous moral concern for limiting the occurrence of torture by requiring "torture warrants."[36] The history of torture reveals that when torture becomes judicial (and this means legal) it also becomes routinized.[37] Torture is different from smoking marijuana, or becoming involved in espionage. It is also not a commodity. Laws permitting torture demonstrate an understanding of the radical aspect of torture's power that does not permit its selective use. It belongs to a different order of things; it thrives in an amoral universe that cannot be "authorized" without undermining society as a moral community in the Durkheimian sense of the word. If sanctioned academically and politically, exploratory torture—which is what torture is when it is inflicted on a person *suspected* of knowing useful information—will degrade the juridical process by subjecting all suspects, political and criminal, to torture on the grounds of "emergency."

The "utilitarian" view of torture under which the "dirty hands" discussion is subsumed—as well as the national-security justification upheld by the U.S. Department of Defense—is often contrasted with the "absolutist" view. This approach states that torture is unacceptable, and should not be practiced under any circumstance. Finding its inspiration in Kantian philosophy, it categorically rejects the use of the person as a means to an end. Its uncompromising stance is informed by an awareness of the morally distorting effects of torture, a humanistic view of the instrumental uses of pain, and a sacral vision of the body and mind. Although it takes courage to transcend the fear, anger, hatred, and revenge that lurk behind the compulsion to torture, this view seems to its critics soft and out of touch with the real world. Yet, advocacy of torture is not heroic; it is the easiest, if not the laziest, path to follow, as it is informed by a situational morality framed either as tragically necessary in a purportedly dilemma-plagued political world, or by a conviction that it is the only response to violence committed by others. Either way, the infliction of pain becomes a remedy to be prescribed in accordance with a medieval understanding of the relationship between body and politics. The moral philosopher begins to speak the language of the torturer, virtually becoming his aid and counselor. The medical doctor who has used his knowledge of the human body in service of the torturer is now assisted by the moral philosopher who finds torture justified. The defense of torture appeals to the weary primarily because of its oversimplification of reality and its foreboding depiction of a brutal state of nature requiring swift and merciless action.

In the end, torture cannot be separated from the state's (geo)political ambitions. French military strategists stated their goal of saving their nation's empire unambiguously. Although they often hit and run, the apologists of torture discussed in this chapter also defend old and new empires. They frame the state's right to use torture as a realistic response to a "dangerous" world. Walzer finds a universal application of the use of torture in the hypothesized colonial situation. Elshtain approves the establishment of a "new imperialism," as advocated by Ignatieff and others: "Sometimes, the most effective new frameworks are old ones resituated in a new reality."[38] Nostalgia for the romanticized orderliness of the old empire is thus inscribed in the rehabilitation of torture as a weapon for defending a new empire. The line between democracy, a major justification of torture, and empire blurs. Torture becomes a weapon with which to defend imperial politics. Thus, torture establishes continuity between France in Algeria, and the United States in the world. Torture is a cornerstone of the structure of power and geopolitics.

Chapter 11

REPETITIONS: FROM ALGIERS

TO BAGHDAD

THE SYSTEMATIC USE OF torture during the Algerian War did not help win the war. The claim often made by advocates of torture that it saves lives cannot be verified, since torture was not used in Algeria for this purpose but to obtain any piece of information that had a bearing on the war. Clearly torture had a corrupting effect on its practitioners, a demoralizing impact on soldiers with a conscience, and caused lasting trauma in its victims. Torture was not about saving lives. So, why use so destructive a method? The Algerian case provides a multifaceted answer centering on the preeminent role the state plays in the use, routinization, and justification of torture. In situations of political crisis, genuine or imagined, the avowedly democratic state reaches deep into its reserve of pure power, breaking loose from the usual restraints on its capacity to eliminate resistance through the infliction of physical pain. This renders the question just posed redundant and makes its formulation in a negative form more appropriate: Why not use torture? The Algerian case reveals that the democratic state is in constant danger of allowing its predemocratic core to emerge and engage in violations of laws guaranteeing civil liberties, the sanctity of the person, and due process. It also reveals the fragility of the democratic state when it operates as a colonial institution and finds itself defending the privileges of colonists over and against the rights of its native citizens qua subjects. More important, the Algerian case documents the far-reaching consequences of a state's capacity to believe in its own ideology of freedom and promotion of the individual while using measures, including torture, that deny both.

State terrorism is the outcome of the willingness of the democratic state in crisis to resort to a predemocratic mode of functioning in a process marked by militarization upheld through law. In Algeria, the colonial state moved into a totalitarian stage incrementally over a period of eleven months. The government first declared a state of emergency, then gave its colonial authorities special powers, and subsequently surrendered police and judicial powers to the military. It suspended local elected officials because of their political views, and censored the press, radio, and television. In its descent into militarization, the state violated the emergency law by allowing the establishment of internment camps. The surrender of police and administrative powers to the military was a crucial step in establishing torture as a central component of the war: It enabled the military to acquire political powers as demanded by *guerre révolutionnaire* theory and doctrine. Once in control, the military implemented its anti-subversive strategy of fighting terror with terror, using torture as a war weapon. The military placed torture at the core of a matrix of terror techniques that included summary executions, exposure of killed combatants, reprisals, and forced displacements of rural people resettled under conditions of de facto captivity. If torture was a war weapon, and techniques of terror its necessary adjuncts, the population was its terrain. Conquering, or reconquering the population-friend-enemy gave a younger generation of colonels and captains the opportunity to implement various modalities of "pacification" as they saw fit. The surrender of police and administrative powers to the military unleashed its own contradictions as the army sought to do away with the tattered remnants of control that a few civil authorities sought to maintain locally without much hope of success, to resist the escalating power of the military.

The first act of militarization—declaration of emergency—was not motivated by the weakness of the state to ensure security, as colonial officials asserted. Fear of the native population, barely ten years after it had expressed its demand for change (in May 1945), and anxiety before a crumbling empire loomed large in that decision. From the beginning, a highly political issue was defined in military terms, thus causing a cascade of decisions, extreme in their nature, that could only lead to the normalization of torture and other atrocities.

In this context the structure of torture mirrored the psychological frame of mind of the generals prosecuting the war. These were men in the throes of an identity crisis aggravated by their defeat in Vietnam at Dien Bien Phu, members of an institution that had been struggling with its eroded status in society since 1940, if not 1870. Algeria was the test of their redemption as soldiers and as Frenchmen imbued with a mission to save the nation from a democratic system perceived as corrupt, dysfunctional, and lacking the will to fight. In more than one way, the war was for the generals and the contingent they sought to influence, a process of identity reshaping and reconstructing. For the Algerian combatants as well as much of the population, the war was a process of crystallization of political identity mediated by a shared experience of repression. It is in the torture situation that the dynamics of identity, memory, and history played themselves out. The structure of torture was embedded in an anxiety-ridden sense of the superiority of French qua Christian culture deemed in danger of subversion by a native qua Muslim will to freedom. A remarkable feature of the structure of torture in a colonial setting is its blindness and imperviousness to the existential reality of colonialism for the tortured. The practice of systematic torture thrives on an amnesiac attitude regarding the inequities of a socioeconomic and political system that causes groups to "rebel" in the first place. This amnesia gives torture its arbitrary character just as it adds another layer of powerlessness to the tortured since they cannot argue their case, but can only speak the language sought by the torturer: that of betrayal. In the Algerian War, the structure of torture was also embedded in a double historical revenge, against military defeat at the hands of other colonized people, and against a failed Frenchification of Algerians that needed to be reconfigured. Hence torture was a prerequisite for psychological "reconditioning"; it was an essential component of psychological action targeting native suspects and combatants.

Theories of crowd behavior and mass manipulation by fascist movements provided the conceptual tools necessary to use torture as a preliminary step toward fashioning "new" colonial subjects in a new Algeria free of the FLN. Just as the war opened up prospects of a "revolution" to be carried out by the military, brainwashing appeared as an efficient method for creating a new Algerian political elite conditioned to sustain the continued existence of the Empire. Within this framework, torture was not about torture: It was about a constellation of practices designed to resocialize Algerians. It was a method for screening individuals picked up at frequent roundups. Torture helped to further select among detainees in the various internment camps subjects appropriate for brainwashing, and to differentiate friends from enemies. In this sense, torture was a test of commitment to France, and a reinscription of native Algerians into the French view of the Empire. Torture was meant to rebuild the native "suspect" or combatant from the ground up in a psychological action based on sex, masculinity and femininity—through stripping, electricity *séances*, and searching women's genitals. Thus, "turning" a frightened youth into a Harki, a former combatant into a torturer of his comrades, or an "intellectual" into an active promoter of colonial rule, transformed the war into a mission of social engineering.

The Algerian case highlights the power of ideas when drawn to their extreme logical conclusions. Torture and terror emerged as tactical imperatives in a theory-driven doctrine of total war. The "pacification" of the population was a euphemism for a policy of destruction of the social fabric in a laboratory-like experiment that created a society held together by fear, constant observation, control, and obedience. That the army implemented this strategy underscores the extent to which the desires of a few generals outstripped military realism. It also points to the crystallization, in the minds of the generals, of the idea of Empire at the very time when they understood it was collapsing. The twilight of empire helped to draw out in dazzling clarity the narcissistic and ideological cultural core of colonial rule. Algeria provides the best example of the failure of extreme methods of combat and control when they do not take into consideration the causes for which people take up arms.

Yet, the military tactical-torture imperative has not served as a fruitful lesson from which other states could learn, including Algeria itself. After the war, the Algerian independent state tolerated torture in violation of its first constitution, which prohibited the practice. Other countries, including Egypt, Jordan, Morocco, and Indonesia, participate in "rendering" or performing torture on prisoners sent to them by the United States in *its* war on "terror." However, Algeria's entanglement with torture acquires greater significance because Algerians had experienced torture directly. In an uncanny repetition of history, Algeria found itself in a situation remarkably similar to that of colonial France. It was faced in 1992–2002 with an Islamist-inspired guerilla movement that questioned the legitimacy of the government, which it likened to its colonial predecessor. The postindependence state was faced with the conundrum of managing Islam when Islam was used by an opposition movement as its ideological legitimation. Roles were suddenly reversed: Algerian leaders, whose religion was Islam, confronted an Islamist opposition. Ironically, the government responded in a fashion made familiar in this book: It ignored the root causes of the Islamist opposition and chose to deal with the political challenge in military terms. The gravity of the problem the Algerian government faced cannot be minimized: A civil war was in the making. Nevertheless, the state designed a countersubversive strategy that included a declaration of a state of emergency, and operations against "terrorist bands," house searches, and torture.

However, the perceived threat to political stability was entirely the result of the government's own actions. The political success of the Front of Islamic Salvation (FIS) during the 1991 parliamentary elections meant a loss of power for the FLN, the only party from 1962 to 1989. The cancellation of the second round of elections, which would have ensured the victory of the FIS, was framed in terms reminiscent of the French military perception of Islam as the victory of backwardness over progress, dictatorship over democracy. There are many aspects of the FIS social agenda that justified criticism, especially its conception of the role of women in society. However, in a move that denoted a cultural phobia of Islam akin to that of *guerre révolutionnaire* advocates of yesteryear, the government equated various modalities of observance of Islam with terrorism. By definition a "terrorist" was an "Islamist," just as during the war a "Muslim" Algerian was a potential "terrorist," a *fellagha*. Historical symmetry and repetition gave the repressive measures taken by the Algerian government a loaded symbolic meaning. The hounded "Muslim" of yesteryear was now in a position to hound the Islamist.

Was torture used systematically on members of the outlawed FIS, and the various factions that split off from it? There is evidence that it was, as the government obliquely acknowledged it. Torture had already existed prior to the FIS advent, as a former FLN activist, Dr. Ahmed Taleb-Ibrahimi, narrates in his memoirs. He was arrested by the military secret police in July 1964 on a charge of belonging to a newly formed opposition group, and received the same water and electricity treatment others had at the hands of French torturers two years earlier.[1] And just as had happened during the war, torture was accompanied by internment camps. Jacques Vergès, retained as counsel by a leading member of the FIS and his son, noted that as of 1992 there were three thousand people detained in camps in crowded and unsanitary conditions. He saw unmistakable signs of torture on detainees leaving military internment camps: "The same expressionless look in their eyes, the puffed face, and the trembling hands of those who came back from hell." Vergès also noted the appointment of special courts whose magistrates remained anonymous as a further indication that due process no longer availed in the war against Islamist opposition.[2] Clearly anonymity was meant to protect judges from retaliation. But given a general climate of repression in which the military had the upper hand, the very creation of special courts compounded the ferocity of this second Algerian war without a name. An Islamist belonging to the Mouvement Islamique Armé (MIA), which preceded the FIS, wrote briefly about his detention in the Berrouaghia prison, notorious during the Algerian War, but now used by the independent state. The man, Ali Merah, had initially surrendered and started working with the state's security forces. He made no charge of torture. However, he described the sympathy that detainees accused of Islamist views enjoyed from the staff of the prisons, at least in the early 1980s. But when he was transferred in the 1990s to the no less notorious Lambèse internment camp, circumstances had changed. He described a particularly crowded and unsanitary camp in which political prisoners shared small cells with common criminals, and age groups were also mixed together.[3] He reports that wardens blamed the abysmal conditions under which prisoners lived on an overzealous justice system that convicted individuals with no concern for the capacity of penitentiary institutions to accommodate them. It is hardly necessary to point out the similarity with the French military tribunals that caused the CTTs and Centres d'Hébergement to overflow with detainees.

Just like its colonial predecessor, the Algerian government refused to call the conflict with Islamists a war. Furthermore, the frequent death sentences and executions carried out in a climate of terror took on the appearance of retaliations against Islamists rather than the result of a nonpartisan justice system.[4] A study of the excesses of the military as well as the Islamist movement is beyond the scope of this book. My purpose is to underscore the repetition of the history of torture in Algeria: different cast of characters, similar situations, similar response. The military called the shots, the justice system caved in, politicians generally looked the other way. Reasons of state were invoked to fight mercilessly a merciless war. The colonial method was replicated in a gesture that reinstalled the past into the present. Vergès encountered among his friends from the 1950s, now highly placed in the government structure, the same reticence as among French magistrates, when he defended Algerian victims of torture.

The event that most spectacularly dramatized the logic of repression against Islamists took place in a courtroom in July 2002 at a defamation trial brought by a retired Algerian general, Khaled Nezzar, a key figure in the repressive campaign to fight the FIS against a deserter, Habib Souaïdia, who had accused him on the French television channel La Cinquième, of torture and massacre of the civilian population. Before the same court, nine Algerians had lodged charges of torture against General Nezzar. The trial became an opportunity for the army, in the person of General Nezzar, to defend its repressive methods before a French court, which a few years earlier, in 1961, had tried its own unruly generals Zeller, Salan, and Challe.[5] Witnesses for the general included a former primer minister, Ahmed Ghozali, who spearheaded the move to abort the electoral process in 1992. The arguments used to defend this decision and the repression that ensued were strikingly similar to those made by the French generals less than forty years earlier. General Nezzar explained that had the FIS been allowed to ascend to power, the country would have experienced a "deadly retrogression." He explained that he and his comrades had faced a "dilemma": cancel the elections and essentially start a civil war, or abide by democratic rules. No elections, he stated, "even if apparently clean," could legitimate an FIS victory. In support of the general, Ghozali explained that a FIS victory would have meant "abandoning Algeria." The notion of abandonment layers the comment with a condensed historical meaning as it keys postindependence Algeria into a colonial discourse of recent memory while surreptitiously hailing Algeria as still French. Ghozzali further defended the creation of internment camps, confinements, and so on as legal measures grounded in the constitution. He noted that all the accusations made against the army were fomented by Islamists and were calculated to obscure the fact that "Islamism is the most totalitarian ideology of the century." Whether this was true or false is not the point: The FIS, in the minds of the Algerian generals and hard-line politicians, played the same role as the FLN had for the French generals; the arguments were the same. As if to blunt this uncomfortable similarity, the former prime minister, with a secular lifestyle, reminded a packed courtroom that he was a practicing Muslim. Also, in a manner that had become familiar during the Algeria War, both the general and the former prime minister acknowledged that though there might have been excesses, the struggle was just and thus the end justified the means.

The similarities between the French colonial army and the Algerian did not end with arguments used to justify atrocities. It also extended to strategy: fighting the Islamist guerilla with their own weapons by creating counterguerilla groups posing as Islamists.[6] The revelation of this strategy in a French court by a witness, a former captain at the Direction of Intelligence and Security, was defended by the general as a standard method of infiltration of the enemy used by other armies in the world. The point is not that the Algerian army is a colonial army, but that repressive methods that include torture, expedient justice, and summary executions are consistently justified by recourse to reasons of state. Ironically the same historical agents who suffered from French repression exercised their own. However, what stands out as the most significant factor in this replication of history is the symbolism of Islam. General Nezzar and the former prime minister stood before a French court to denounce Islam as a carrier of a "totalitarian ideology" that had to be fought by all means necessary. They knew their plea would receive sympathy, but their methods harked back to a recent French past. But perhaps aware of this inverted colonial/postcolonial drama, the court concluded that the general had not been defamed. Missing from this reenactment of history was a general who, in the manner of Bolladière, broke ranks with his comrades and stood for respect of the rules of engagement, as well as the inviolability of the dignity of the person, even that of an Islamist.

Does this mean that torture is inevitable and that the atrocities committed by the French military are excusable? It means that torture, just like the atrocities that come along with it, is a clear and present danger. It cannot be authorized for exceptional use. It cannot be tolerated. It must be abolished in no uncertain terms. The right to silence should be uninfringeable, thereby supporting the right to freedom from torture. If freedom of speech is guaranteed, the right not to speak should also be.

Repetition Redoubled

The relevance of the Algerian War to the United States invasion of Iraq and its management of the ensuing war is compelling. This is so because wars of occupation share one thing: They seek to disguise material and strategic interests as either a "civilizing" or a democracy-disseminating mission. The initial justification for the U.S. invasion, the search for non-existent weapons of mass destruction, was made palatable to the public by a conjoining of the 9/11 attacks and Saddam Hussein's political record. But soon the leap was made from removing him, to remaking the political map of the Arab Middle East by transforming Iraq into a beacon of democracy and reforms. Perhaps there was no leap at all. The very fact of the invasion implied occupation, and occupation implied putting in place a new regime. The tortures inflicted on Iraqi men and women picked up in roundups were a replay of the *rafles* that the French military engaged in routinely. The uncoupling of torture from its customary justification, the search for intelligence, reached a paroxysm of abuse in the torture of some men simply because their names were the same or similar to their former president's. Most were suspects because of their nationality. One man was tortured for having reported suspicious activity around a car be-cause he feared an explosion. As an Iraqi, he was not only a suspect, but also deemed incapable of concern for life, and security.

The Iraq War atrocities need not be revisited, but the logic of occupa-tion deserves analysis. The war fought in Iraq was not declared: Iraq was treated as land that invited invasion and occupation, just as Algeria ap-peared to France in 1830. There is a difference of degree, however. Be-nighted history has it that Algeria was invaded to expunge the affront made to a French ambassador who had been hit with a fan by an irate dey of Algiers when France refused to pay her overdue debt. Weapons of mass destruction are admittedly a more compelling reason to invade than dero-gation from the rules of protocol. Yet, fan and weapons were used as pre-texts, excuses for invasion and occupation. Admittedly, France colonized Algeria for 124 years, and for all intents and purposes reoccupied it with nearly 500,000 troops for another 8. It would be rash to suggest that the United States would like to follow suit in Iraq. However, occupation is oc-cupation. It means more soldiers in a foreign land, spiraling violence, in-creasing alienation of civilians and soldiers alike, and a lasting trauma for helpless individuals caught in the storm.

It is the ease with which torture has been practiced in violation of ex-isting laws that ties the French experience in Algeria to that of the United States in Iraq and Afghanistan. Torture had been used in Afghanistan by the U.S. military, but hardly reported. It was the leaking to the press of the famed pictures of tortured Iraqi prisoners that revealed the extent to which torture was also inflicted in Afghanistan and Guantanamo Bay. Whereas in France news of torture entered the public domain primarily as a heinous method that soiled the image of the nation, torture aroused less public ire in the United States, especially among intellectuals, and sparked *more* discussions about its advisability and efficiency. While French authorities sought to distance themselves from the practice, their American counterparts mobilized legal experts to redefine torture in such a way as to make it "legal." It is this general acceptance of torture as a lesser evil in relation to the greatest evil of terrorism that distinguishes the French from the American public response.

That the U.S. military would engage in torture, just like its French counterpart, is less remarkable than the U.S. administration's search for a means of legalizing torture by redefining the nature of pain. The intrusion of the state into the management of body torment is the most telling sign of torture's appeal to a state in crisis. French civil authorities covered up systematic torture; the United States claimed it and found intellectuals to build its arsenal of justifications for engaging in it. The ease with which the government was able to set the tone for an acceptance of torture may be attributable to the 9/11 attacks. However, in spite of the trauma these understandably caused in the national psyche, they are not central to explaining the emergence of the acceptability of torture. Indeed, the routine torture of Iraqis, who had little to do with the attacks, invalidates such an explanation. The U.S. government, like its French colonial counterpart, reflexively dipped into its source of pure power, thus relinking with predemocratic political formations for reasons of state. Although security concerns were real, reflexive recourse to torture was not as compelling as it was made to appear. It is ironic that instead of finding alternative methods for managing these concerns, effort was spent determining what degree of pain rises to the level of torture. This retreat into the tormented body in an age of sensitivity to human rights speaks of a lag between the rhetoric of rights and the unbridled power of the state.

Noteworthy is the process that led to legitimizing the use of torture. Like the French military theorists of *guerre révolutionnaire*, the Pentagon defined "terrorism" as a "new kind of war." Paraphrasing the Pentagon, While House legal counsel Alberto R. Gonzales noted that the new war "is not the traditional clash between nations adhering to the laws of war." In preparing to impeach the foundations of the 1949 Geneva Convention on the Treatment of Prisoners of War, he argued that the formulation of the Convention was informed by conventional wars, not the new war. Yet, the Vietnam War, which French officers had defined as a revolutionary war, and therefore a "new" war, predated the Geneva convention. Nevertheless, Gonzales's argument sought to ground the legitimacy of torture in the specific character of the new war. As he put it:

> The nature of the new war places a high premium on new factors, such as the ability to *quickly obtain information* [emphasis added] from captured

terrorists and their sponsors in order to avoid further atrocities against American civilians, and the need to try terrorists for war crimes such as wantonly killing civilians.

Hence the search for information was coupled with the desire to try "terrorists" for *war* crimes as the preponderant reasons for not treating men accused of terrorism as prisoners of war. The new war, in the estimation of Gonzalez, was a "new paradigm [that] renders obsolete the Geneva Convention."[7] Gonzalez poked unnecessary fun at the Convention calling "quaint" its provision to accord amenities to prisoners of war, such as "commissary privileges, athletic uniforms," and so on. His consolidation of a list of recommendations that the Geneva convention had addressed in separate articles betrays the intention behind his prejudiced reading. In reality, the Geneva convention's call to treat prisoners humanely simply stated that

> While respecting the individual preferences of every prisoner, the Detaining Power shall encourage the practice of intellectual, educational, and recreational pursuits, sports and games amongst prisoners, and shall take the measures necessary to ensure their exercise thereof by providing them with adequate premises and necessary equipment.[8]

Without a definition of terrorism, and who is considered a terrorist, it is difficult to logically argue in favor of torture, if such an argument should be made at all.

Gonzalez also shifted the focus from what constitutes war, to the nature of the state the Taliban came from. He deemed it a "failed state" for a number of reasons, the most significant being that "it was not capable of fulfilling its obligations (e.g. was in widespread breach of its international obligations)." This definition of the Afghan state was meant to indicate, as the attorney general, John Ashcroft, pointed out, that Afghanistan was not a signatory to the Geneva convention during the "relevant time of combat,"[9] meaning when U.S. troops moved into Afghanistan. In other words, the Geneva convention was rendered obsolete on two grounds, the nature of the Afghan state, and the nature of the "new war." The right to torture—for this was a search for a legal endorsement of torture—was thus predicated on failed statehood and the construction of international terrorism as a "new war." Where the French officers sought to logically construct a doctrine that made recourse to torture inevitable, Gonzales used a regressive method that enabled him to start with torture and work his way back to the Geneva convention. However, the general structure of justification is the same. Gonzales's arguments were based on an unquestioned premise that "terrorism" is war. The legal gymnastics that ensued became a mere exercise in justifying torture independent of whether there was a war against the United States, or terrorism was a "new war." This method helped Gonzales set a precedent for the future. Perhaps Iraq was already in the back of his mind. Consequently, the treatment of Iraqi prisoners could not have been otherwise. One would have expected a new discussion about why the Iraq War did not rise to the status of a war. But this did not happen, and was not meant to happen because it might have resulted in a revalidation of the Geneva convention.

The discussion of the presumed obsolescence of the Geneva convention was motivated by a preoccupation with suits that might be brought against the United States under the 1996 War Crimes Act. As Gonzales explained, a war crime "is defined to include any grave breach of GPW or any violation of common Article 3 (outrages against personal dignity"). He further argued that since the War Crimes Act also applies ("if the GPW applies") to individuals who may not be POWs, and "punishment for violations of Section 2441 include the death penalty," exempting the Taliban from POW status would make Section 2441 inapplicable. In a move that paved the way to a redefinition of torture, he noted the "undefined language" of the GPW—such as "outrages upon personal dignity," or "inhuman treatment"—as one more reason to invalidate the Convention. This language is, as Gonzales suspected, the language of torture. The decision to disable the Geneva Convention on the Treatment of Prisoners of War in order to open the way to systematic torture was so emphatic that objections raising the likelihood that the same might be done to U.S. prisoners were quickly dismissed as Gonzales also stated that "even if the GPW is not applicable, we can still bring war crimes charges against anyone who mistreats U.S. personnel." Clearly might makes international right. To the equally important objection that torture (not named as such) might corrupt military culture, Gonzales absurdly replied that "our military remain bound to apply the principles of GPW because that is what you [the president] have directed them to do."[10]

Once the legal framework for torture was set, the next step was to redefine torture proper so that it would not fall under existing domestic international laws that prohibited its use and could incur trial of U.S. agents in the International Criminal Court. John C. Yoo, deputy assistant attorney general, reviewed the texts governing the prohibition of torture in 18U.S.C. §2340–2340A as well as the Torture Convention to which the United States is a signatory. Yoo noted that 18U.S.C. §2340A made it a criminal offense for a person to commit torture outside the United States "under the color of law specifically intended to inflict severe physical or mental pain or suffering (other than pain or suffering incidental to lawful sanctions) upon another person within his custody or physical control."

Section 2340 specifically clarifies the meaning of "severe mental pain and suffering" as the

> prolonged mental harm caused by or resulting from (a) the intentional infliction or threatened infliction of severe physical pain or suffering; (b) the administration or application of, or threatened administration of mind-altering substances or other procedures calculated to disrupt profoundly the senses or the personality; (c) the threat of imminent death; or (d) the threat that another person will imminently be subjected to death, severe physical pain or suffering, or the administration or application of mind-altering substances or other procedures calculated to disrupt profoundly the senses and personality.

Yoo's opinion reduced this comprehensive definition to its introductory phrase "prolonged mental harm." In reviewing the Torture Convention, Yoo stressed that the first Bush administration had ratified it with a reservation that it understood the Convention in terms of Section 2340 of 18 U.S.C., stressing "intent" in the infliction of severe mental and physical pain. He further noted that the United States did not accept the jurisdiction of the International Court of Justice, thereby thwarting any litigation stemming from torture that might be committed in the name of the United States. Similarly, Yoo felt that the "interrogation" of Al Qaeda operatives could be neither investigated nor prosecuted by the International Criminal Court, not only because the United States had not recognized the Court, but also because under the Rome Statute, to fall under the "crimes against humanity" category, a crime must be part of a broader and "systematic" attack against a civilian population. The Rome Statute also makes prosecution of a person for torture by the ICC contingent upon the victim's protection by the Geneva convention.

After a review of a number of cases of torture (with detailed descriptions of its methods), and examining their treatment by various U.S. courts, the European Court of Human Rights, and the Israeli Supreme Court, Gonzales formulated a legal defense against the prosecution of the United States for a violation of its own prohibition against torture as contained in Section 2340A, based on the "lesser of two evils" formula similar to Father Delarue's. Thus necessity and self-defense constituted grounds for legitimizing the use of torture. The casuistry implied in this act is less remarkable than the rewriting of the law drawn by the very state, the United States, that passed it. This regressive undoing of laws protecting the individual from intentional physical and mental pain by designing loopholes invalidating their application is the most telling example of the incremental steps a militarized state undertakes in its gradual evolution toward totalitarianism. Gonzales found that "torture as defined and proscribed by Sections 2340–2340A covers only extreme acts. Severe pain is generally of the kind difficult for the victim to endure. Where the pain is physical it must be of an intensity akin to that which accompanies serious physical injury such as death or organ failure."[11]

This custom-made definition of what constitutes torture raises the threshold of pain to the point when the victim cannot talk because she is dead or near dead. It is not supported by the experiences victims have had with torture. It also defines torture by its end point, instead of by the process through which the infliction of pain leads to the body's breaking point. Defining the body's breaking point as reflecting "severe" pain rests on a purely subjective definition of severity. Electrical shock to a man's genitals that causes castration is "severe" for the victim. Electric shock also kills its victims, as was the case in Algeria.[17] Once torture is reduced to a semantic game of euphemisms as happened in Algeria, it has already been accepted and is well on its way to becoming routinized. Gonzales points out that "because the acts of inflicting torture are extreme, there is significant range of acts that though they might constitute cruel, inhuman, or degrading treatment or punishment fail to rise to the level of torture." This bold assertion of an unbound political will decides in advance how the *victim* of torture *should* experience the intentional pain she will be subjected to.

I think it inappropriate as well as unproductive to engage in a discussion of what pain is or is not, but will draw attention instead to this legalization of torture. Torture is redefined in such a way as to invite its use with impunity. I will also draw attention to the invocation of "cruel, inhuman, and degrading treatment" as not constituting torture. This begs the question of what torture is. Acts fitting this description are dealt with everyday in American courts and punished in one way or another. What would be the justice in punishing them in civil and penal courts, but making them legal for the military for reasons of presumed necessity, and self-defense? Equally problematic is Gonzales's contention that only narrowly defined "severe" pain results in "lasting psychological harm, such as seen in mental disorders like posttraumatic stress disorder."[13] This is an empirical issue that could not be stated in such categorical terms without citing evidence to the contrary. As mentioned earlier in this book, Fanon, the psychiatrist, had identified a series of mental disorders caused by each method of torture used by the French military in the 1950s. Torture *is* physically and mentally scarring because it is always severe to the mind and the body. At any rate, Gonzales set the legal stage for the Abu Ghraib tortures, as well as those unfolding in other prisons and detention centers throughout Iraq.

However, as in colonial France, the legitimation of torture does not occur in a vacuum. It is usually accompanied by a restriction on civil liberties. The Patriot Act passed on October 24, 2001, curtailed civil liberties in order to "deter and punish terrorist acts in the United States and around the world, to enhance law enforcement investigatory tools, and for other purposes." Security concerns are naturally legitimate, but pursuing them at the expense of rolling back laws that protect the citizen from the (pure) power of the state results in surrendering to the state the means by which to control it. The French colonial state started this process with a declaration of a state of emergency and chose anticommunism as its ideological ploy. The United States followed a different path, seeking to rewrite international conventions to justify torture by claiming to spread democracy and culture change in the Middle East, goals assumed to be thwarted by terrorist acts.

A thorough treatment of torture since 9/11 is beyond the scope of this book. I merely wish to point to the continuity across time and political cultures in recourse to, and justification of torture. As shown in colonial France and contemporary America, in situations of crisis, democratic restraints on the power of the state are easily removed. Torture inevitably emerges as the most efficient method of obtaining information in spite of evidence to the contrary. There are at least three reasons for this near-automatic recourse to torture. Torture satisfies an impulsive need for immediate punishment or revenge on categories of people deemed dangerous, inferior, or different in one way or another. In addition, it contributes to a sense of accomplishment after it has been carried out, even though it may not have resulted in any tangible information. Finally, because it targets the body—the locus of vulnerability—torture brings about a sense of its appropriateness regardless of the nature of the supposed crime. But these are the reasons that laws prohibiting torture came about—to emphasize the inviolability of the body and mind of a captive. The return to torture also reveals the fragility of the moral principles that underpin the defense and protection of individual rights. If individual qua human rights are violated as soon as a crisis occurs or is engineered, it means that the (democratic) state had merely tolerated these rights and not accepted them as inviolate. And despite the differences in time and circumstances, such violations also place the U.S. military strategists in the same position as the French military theorists who advocated adopting the methods of the guerillas to fight "subversion." Sanctions taken against subalterns accused of torture, as happened in the aftermath of Abu Ghraib, may be good for publicity purposes and for reassuring the public of U.S. accountability. However, such sanctions also underscore the obfuscation that has occurred at the highest levels of government, as the Geneva convention against torture has been redefined. As in Algeria, the suspension of civil liberties at home paved the way for torture at home and abroad and made its use inevitable.

It is the accepted inevitability of torture that accounts for politicians' desire to insist on oversight. In the aftermath of the public exposure of the tortures at Abu Ghraib, the need to scrutinize the Administration's treatment of detainees resulted in the Defense Department issuing a new Field Manual on Human Intelligence (HUMINT) Operations that established the Geneva Convention on the Treatment of Prisoners of War, especially Article 3, prohibiting torture, as one of the constraints on the "principles and techniques of intelligence operations."[14] The use of the word "operations," normally associated with military action, connotes the mindset of the framers of the intelligence manual. Intelligence-gathering is seen as warfare in its own right, and as such it requires methods that demand the use of force. Indeed, the other "constraint" on intelligence operations is the Detainee Act of 2005, which (in Section 1004) protects interrogators from legal action brought against them by potential victims of their techniques.[15] Noteworthy are the concrete examples of interrogation techniques that the manual provides: They are drawn from the wars in Iraq or Afghanistan, an intimation that the manual focuses on the "new" wars of invasion and remapping of the Middle East. The inclusion of Article 3 of the GPW as an appendix to the manual may be a step in the right direction. However, the release of the manual occurred simultaneously with debates and negotiations in Congress on the White House call for the creation of military tribunals as well as a redefinition of the GPW, which raises the issue of the permissibility of charges against detainees that stem from the torture of third parties. In other words, the manual does not put an end to the debate over the permissibility of torture. It partially allays fears of a lack of transparency in the conduct of intelligence warfare. In spite of some of the senators' good intentions, the apparent fierceness of the Congressional debate in mid- to late September 2006 turned into a linguistic joust. As Stephen J. Hadley, the national security advisor put it, "The goal was whether we could find language mutually agreed between the Senate and the White House that would achieve those objectives [to meet our international obligations]."[16] The agreement centers on a number of definitions of the constitutive terms that define torture as the infliction of "severe physical or mental pain or suffering for the purpose of obtaining information or a confession." Discussions focused on the difference between "severe" and "extreme," as opposed to "serious"; "prolonged" as opposed to "nontransitory" pain.

To make it clear that nothing fundamental had changed in the perspective of the Administration, Mr. Bush pointed out, "The agreement clears the way to do what the American people expect us to do: to capture terrorists, to detain terrorists, to question terrorists, and then to try them."[17] This realist assessment sidesteps the issue of the manner in which guilt is established that is crucial to the use of torture, and was central to the Congressional debates, at least formally. In a sense, the Congressional debates represented a public acceptance of the principle of torture as a technique of intelligence-gathering, as they sought to merely limit its scope or intensity, which *in practice* is next to impossible. In the torture chamber, the battle of wills for the release of intelligence (no matter how this is defined) causes a contested GPW to easily fade away. What constitutes torture, the question addressed by Gonzales, remained open. The president retained the right to define interrogation techniques (used by the CIA) by executive order although he is required to publish the order in the public record. Accountability for torture in a climate of fear of "terrorism," and election politics centering on who is "soft" on security, is as elusive as its unambiguous prohibition.

To return to the treatment of detainees at Abu Ghraib in Baghdad: The sexual torture techniques struck the American public as crude, but in the minds of many there was doubt that they were torture and not mere distasteful maltreatment.[18] Yet, torture *is* sexual in nature. Chapters 5 and 6 described torturers' reenactments of sexual fantasies, and the castration of their male victims. Toying with a person's sexual identity, violating her most private domain by compelling her to act out the pornographic desires of the torturer *is* physical and mental torture. Iraqi victims were placed in awkward and stress-producing positions for hours, *played* with as they were derided, taunted, and photographed for future entertainment. The eye of the camera was meant to permanently fix and transfix the victim's degradation, haunting her with exposure forever, rendering her shame indelible. This method perniciously breaks the will of the victim and, by making her do or die, turns her into a traitor not to comrades—since these men and women were picked up at random, and thus were not members of an organized armed group—but to herself. Enforced sexual acts with or without an audience of soldiers are violations even if they fall short of actual rape, although instances of both rape and sodomy were documented at Abu Ghraib. They partake in the same order of things: breaking of the will; physical and psychological humiliation and degradation; and reduction of the human person to a thing. The most striking act of deprivation of the will was exemplified by the treatment of the human person as a dog, with all the paraphernalia, including a leash and an owner. This too is part of sexual torture, layered with additional gender symbolism. The female soldier Lindie England, who had earlier engaged in sexual play with a group of soldiers (also in front of a camera), now had control over male prisoners whom she walked on a leash as men-dogs while cheerily pointing to their genitals. Abysmal as they were, the pictures of torture at Abu Ghraib depict the core of torture: absolute domination of the victim whose body and mind become a surface on which to imprint the torturers' fancy. The Abu Ghraib scenes also illustrate the arbitrariness of torture: None of the victims had information to give to make their torture worthwhile.[19] And the torturers were not looking for any specific information in the postinvasion chaos. The technical requirement of "softening up" prisoners was fleetingly evoked by some of them as a lame justification for their acts. Being in a foreign land as citizens of a powerful nation during a war of occupation meant being in a situation of absolute power. French conscripts and paratroopers on operations in the Algerian hinterland expressed a dizzying feeling of immense power that led to similar abuse.

In reality, sexual torture was part of a larger configuration, as it usually is, which included "breaking chemical lights and pouring the phosphoric liquid on detainees," as well as having a police guard stitch the wounds inflicted on a detainee. Whatever the nature of the torture carried out at Abu Ghraib, it is the power behind it that makes it stand out as an assault on the humanity of us all. Fear and anxiety before an enemy whose goals are not entirely clear have clouded the army's thinking about the implications for a superpower endowed with enormous technical capacity to engage in the oldest, most discredited, and patently inefficient method of information-gathering. The propensity to retreat into torture as the most tried method of getting information reveals the archaic nature at the core of the democratic state. Unless this core is identified, and extirpated, torture will recur again and again under the sponsorship of the state. No one is safe from it, not even its apologists. The "war on terror" has become a war of terror. Just like the French officers who decided to turn the army into guerilla bands to "counter" the FLN guerillas operating day and night, the U.S. military feels free to arrest, detain, interrogate, and torture anyone it deems suspect anywhere in the world. The circle of torture is drawn wide; it links Algiers and Baghdad through Washington, D.C., and her satellite cities and states around the globe.

NOTES

INTRODUCTION

1. Louisette Ighilahriz, *Algérienne*. Narrated by Anne Nivat (Paris: Fayard/Calmann Lévy, 2001).

2. Général Aussaresses, *Services Spéciaux. Algérie 1955–1957* (Perrin, 2001). The book appeared in English translation as *Battle of the Casbah: Terrorism and Counter-Terrorism in Algeria, 1955–1957* (New York: Enigma Books, 2002).

3. Such sentiment appears in one form or another in Bernard W. Sigg, *Le silence et la honte. Névroses de la guerre d'Algérie* (Paris: Messidor /Editions Sociales, 1989), as well as in interviews in Claire Mauss-Copeaux, *Les appelés en Algérie: La parole confisquée* (Paris: Hachette Littéraire, 1998), among others.

4. As of January 20, 2005, the service was renamed Service Historique de la Défense, and incorporates documents from land, navy and air forces.

5. See, for example, Raphaëlle Branche and Sylvie Thénault, eds., "La Guerre d'Algérie," *Documentation Française*, Collection Documentation Photographique, no. 8022, August 2001. See also the review *Quasimodo*, which reproduces war art, but often illustrates articles with war pictures, as in Sidi Mohammed Barakat, "Corps et Etat. Nouvelles Notes sur le 17 October 1961," no. 9 (Spring 2005): 153–162. There is a parallel trend expressing colonial nostalgia that reproduces pictures of cities and people taken during the colonial era, both in Algeria and France. See among others, *Les trois dames de la Kasbah de Pierre Loti*. Photographs from the Collection of Messikh (Alger: Editions Rais). The book illustrates Loti's short story with nineteenth-century colonial pictures; Gustave le Truc, *Paysages d'Algérie, economie et traditions, 1900–1930. Collection mémoire en images* (Saint-Cyr-sur-Loire: Alan Sutton, 2000).

6. See Sylvie Thénault, *Histoire de la guerre d'indépendance algérienne* (Paris: Flammarion, 2005). The point is not whether the author is right or wrong, but that she decided what the war should be called without a thorough discussion of why she rejected the term "revolution," or what her implication as a historian from a former colonial power is in the choice of a new label. The new name for the Algerian War and for nationalists has been quickly adopted by others. For example, Marie-Monique Robin, *Escadrons de la mort: L'école française* (Paris: La Découverte, 2004). It was not until June 10, 1999, that the French government acknowledged that the Algerian War was indeed a war, and not an operation to "restore order." See Benyoucef Benkhedda, *Alger, capitale de la résistance, 1956–1957* (Alger: Editions Horma, 2002), 42.

7. Alan Riding, "French Algerians' Tomorrow," *International Herald Tribune*, April 14, 2005. See also Associated Press, "France Orders Positive Spin on Colonialism," October 21, 2005; Claude Liauzu and Gilles Manceron, eds., *La coloni-*

sation, la loi et l'histoire (Paris: Editions Syllespe, 2006). Article 4, paragraph 2, the controversial part of the law (No. 2005–158 of February 23, 2005), was ultimately repealed on February 15, 2006, by decree No. 2006–160, under pressure from French historians and intellectuals, as well as diplomatic protests and demonstrations in the overseas territories of Guadeloupe and Martinique. In retaliation, Algeria postponed the signing of a friendship treaty with France.

8. Article 13 of the February 23, 2005, law was maintained.

9. The General Secretariat for Administration at the Ministry of Defense includes among its subdivisions a Direction de la Mémoire du Patrimoine et des Archives. One of its functions is to examine requests for releasing restricted materials.

10. One can argue that the issue is not whether colonial rule benefited the colonized, but that its benefits were not greater, more equally distributed, *and* commensurate with the benefits that accrued to the various classes of colonists for the duration of the colonial ventures. Clearly this is a complex issue that must question what constitutes a benefit and at what price. Various trends in revisionist histories of empire include Niall Ferguson, *Empire: The Rise and Demise of the British World Order and the Lessons for Global Power* (New York: Basic Books, 2002); Linda Colley, *Captives: Britain, Empire, and the World, 1600–1850* (New York: Anchor Books, 2005); Michael Hardt and Antonio Negri, *Empire* (Cambridge: Harvard University Press, 2000). See also the problematic use of the phrase "colonial humanism" by Gary Wilder, *The French Imperial Nation-State: Negritude and Colonial Humanism between the Two World Wars* (Chicago: University of Chicago Press, 2005), 23.

11. In Kenya under British rule, interrogation and torture were called "screening." See Caroline Elkins, *The British Gulag: The Brutal End of Empire in Britain* (London: Jonathan Cape, 2005).

12. For an analysis of torture (as violence) and state power, see Allen Feldman, *Formations of Violence: The Narrative of the Body and Political Terror in Northern Ireland* (Chicago: University of Chicago Press, 1991). Blending a phenomenology of political resistance with perceptions of suffering, Feldman argues that torture is not a mere disciplinary response of a state challenged in its legitimacy, but the means through which the state embeds itself in the body of the political recalcitrant. See also Feldman, "On Cultural Anesthesia," in Nadia Seremetakis, *The Senses Still* (Chicago: University of Chicago Press, 1994).

13. Marie-Monique Robin, *Escadrons de la Mort.*

14. Olivier Le Cour Grandmaison, *Coloniser, exterminer. Sur la guerre et l'état colonial* (Paris: Arthème Fayard, 2005), 152–56.

15. Grandmaison points out that whipping in police stations was prohibited in 1930 by the governor general on the occasion of the celebration of the one hundredth anniversary of the fall of Algiers. Ibid., 154.

16. Jean Vaujour, *De la révolte à la révolution* (Paris: Albin Michel, 1985), 48. The expression is borrowed from historian Charles-André Julien.

17. Le Genre Humain. *Juger en Algérie 1944–1962* (Paris: Editions du Seuil, 1997), 165–78. This law also instituted the teaching of Arabic in all grades in schools—a remarkable achievement. However, women's right to vote was subjected to "conditions" to be specified at a later date. More important, the law per-

mitted Algerians who had served in the military and the civil service (there were very few of these), or held French diplomas to be eligible for inclusion in the first electoral college, reserved for the colonists. Finally, the law upheld the legal distinction between people with "French civil status," and those with "local status," meaning those who "did not expressly renounce their personal status" (Title IV, Art. 3). Personal status referred to accepting the application of Islamic law in matters of marriage, divorce, and inheritance.

18. I use this concept for convenience, despite my misgivings. Decolonization connotes the overthrow of the colonial order because of its inequities, and without a clear vision of the political system that would replace it; nationalism denotes the will to create a nation-state for its own sake, regardless of its political orientation.

19. It was not uncommon to transfer prisoners from Algeria to French jails in France. For example, Louisette Ighilahriz was transferred from Barberousse jail in Algiers to several prisons in France, including Corsica. For Algerian students tortured in Paris, see Boumaza, Bachir et al. *La Gangrène* (Alger: Rahma, 1992). The FLN had an organization in France. Its members were on occasion arrested. See Ali Haroun, *La 7ième wilaya. La guerre du FLN en France 1954–1962* (Paris: Editions du Seuil, 1986).

20. See Jean-Luc Einaudi, *La bataille de Paris* (Paris: Plon, 1991).

21. Elaine Scarry, *The Body in Pain* (New York: Oxford University Press, 1985). According to Scarry, without "civilization," torture would be inconceivable: Animals do not torture one another. At the point of undergoing pain with objects-products of civilization's generalized labor, the victim's own location in civilization is sundered, destabilized. Taken to its logical conclusion, the civilization matrix identified by Scarry reaches beyond the individual act of torture committed against one person to embrace a larger human collectivity. It implies an existential humanism that questions the complicity of all participants in the matrix. If torture is informed by civilization, and since we all partake in the production of civilization, we are all torturers and tortured as well. However, Scarry's original, yet abstract, conception of the deep structure of torture skirts a formalism for lack of historically embedded concrete situations where "civilization" looms as an unavoidable factor, directly, between peoples deemed to belong to different "civilizations." Algeria in the mid-1950s provides such a situation.

22. Historians of torture have generally confined themselves to tracing its genesis as they seek to identify the patterns of its entanglements in law and political power. Legal scholars seek to distinguish shades of pain to locate the legal terrain of torture. See John H. Langbein, "Torture and the Law of Proof," in Sanford Levinson, ed., *Torture: A Collection* (Oxford: Oxford University Press, 2004).

23. Marcel Mauss's conception of the "total social phenomenon" fits the torture situation. See *The Gift* (New York: Norton, 1967).

24. Elaine Scarry, 28–29. Scarry adequately suggests that torture is not about information.

25. Alain Maillard de la Morandais, *L' honneur est sauf* (Paris: Seuil, 1990), 336–37.

26. The view expressed by Michel Foucault that the modern state found better

methods of disciplining its citizens than torture, which he defines as a "technique of pain," is singularly shortsighted. It assumes that these new methods have a self-sustaining socializing function but fails to consider that the modern state can purposely sponsor *torture* and use it as an instrument of behavior modification. Ironically, Foucault lumps together the colonized and "madmen, children at home and in schools," as the subjects of "supervision" not punishment as he defines torture. See *Discipline and Punish: The Birth of the Prison*, trans. Alan Sheridan (New York: Vintage Books, 1995), 3–33.

27. It is symptomatic that the only contributor to an anthology on torture who categorically opposed the use of this practice was its survivor. See Ariel Dorfman, "The Tyranny of Torture: Is Torture Inevitable in Our Century and Beyond?" in Stanford Levinson, ed., *Torture*, 3–18.

28. Arno Mayer, *The Furies: Violence and Terror in the French and Russian Revolutions* (Princeton University Press, 2000), 108. See also Victor Pierre, *La terreur sous le directoire* (Paris: Retaux-Bray, 1887).

29. Quoted in Victor Pierre, v.

30. Edgar Quinet, quoted in Arno Mayer, *The Furies*, 106.

31. Hannah Arendt, *On Violence* (New York: Viking, 1971), 95. Arendt was aware that "hypocrisy" was not a sufficient cause of terror. See also Arno Mayer, 112–13.

32. Maurice Merleau-Ponty, *Humanism and Terror* (Boston: Beacon Press, 1969), 180. The original text was published in 1947.

33. Michael T. Kaufman "What Does the Pentagon See in the 'Battle of Algiers'?" *New York Times*, September 7, 2003. See also Stephen Hunter, "The Pentagon Lessons from Reel Life," *Washington Post*, October 31, 2003. The book Mr. Bush referred to was Alistair Horne's *A Savage War of Peace: Algeria, 1954–1962*, rev. ed. (New York: Penguin Books, 1987).

34. Maureen Dowd, "Aux Barricades!" *New York Times*, January 17, 2007.

CHAPTER 1
REVOLUTIONARY-WAR THEORY

1. See SHAT, 1H2537D1, Battalion Chief Desgratoulet's Note de Service, "Action militaire et politique à mener dans le quartier de Warnier, no. 153/OR, May 30, 1957.

2. Roger Trinquier, a revolutionary-war theorist and expert in psychological warfare, felt that "The use of terrorism as a war weapon necessarily calls for the use of its antidote, torture." *Guerre, subversion, révolution* (Paris: Robert Laffont, 1968), 70.

3. Pierre Mesmer, interview by Marie-Monique Robin, *Les escadrons de la mort*, 174.

4. Quoted in Peter Paret, *French Revolutionary Warfare from Indochina to Algeria* (New York: Frederick A. Praeger, 1964), 30.

5. Raoul Girardet, *Le nationalisme français* (Paris: Armand Colin, 1966), 14.

6. Ibid., 25. In addition to death and decadence, themes explored by *national-*

isme intégral included an exaltation of the military as the repository of patriotism, as well as a quasi-mystical notion of Frenchness. Maurice Barrès, a leading advocate of Action Française alongside Maurras, bemoaned the "humbling of France" and thought of the French nation as "disappearing." He wondered whether he and his contemporaries were not going to be "the last of the French people [p. 17]." "Decadence" would later appear in the title of a book written by one of the officers who fought to keep Algeria French, Antoine Argoud, *Décadence, l'imposture et la tragédie* (Paris: Arthème Fayard, 1974). Death, blood, and decadence were also central to National Socialism. See Ernst Jünger's diary, *Storm of Steel* (London: Penguin Books, 2004).

7. Quoted in Eugen Weber, *Action Française: Royalism and Reaction in XXth Century France* (Stanford: Stanford University Press, 1962), 13. Intellectuals who acknowledged the influence of Maurras's ideas included André Malraux, Georges Bernanos, Henry de Montherlant, Philippe Ariès, and François Mauriac (p. 13). Among politicians were François Mitterrand; and Georges Bidault, founder of the Party of Mouvement Républicain Populaire and leader of the French underground terrorist organization in Algeria, *Organisation de l'Armée Secrète*, 516. Weber attributes the widespread influence of Action Française to the appeal of Maurras's and Barrès's nationalist ideas, as well as the longevity of the movement, which spanned World Wars I and II. It was also due to the two-pronged strategy of the movement to reach a wide audience: political training and advocacy, combined with intellectual debates and literary production.

8. Eugen Weber, *Ibid., 17. Weber dates the origin of Action Française* from the publication of "Apologia for Colonel Henry," which Charles Maurras wrote in defense of the officer who had wrongly accused Alfred Dreyfus of treason, and forged the letter that helped to convict him.

9. Quoted in Jean Vaujour, *De la révolte à la révolution*, 293.

10. John Stewart Ambler, *The French Army in Politics 1945–1962* (Ohio: Ohio State University Press, 1966), 308.

11. See Colonel Charles Lacheroy, *De Saint-Cyr à l'action psychologique. Mémoires d'un siècle* (Charles Lavauzelle, 2003), 19, 68–69.

12. Peter Paret, *French Revolutionary Warfare*, 7. Paret identifies Hogard and Souyris as having served in Indochina as "platoon leaders or intelligence, civil affairs, or propaganda officers."

13. Marie-Monique Robin, *Escadrons de la mort*, 168–69.

14. Colonel Charles Lacheroy, *De Saint-Cyr à l'action psychologique*, 68.

15. See Marie-Monique Robin, *Escadrons de la mort*, 168–69, part II; João Roberto Martins Filho, "The Education of the Brazilian Golpista: Military Culture, French Influence and the 1964 Coup," unpublished paper (Universidad Federal de São Carlos); Michael McClintock, *Instruments of Statecraft. U.S. Guerilla Warfare, Counter-Insurgency, and Counter-Terrorism, 1940–1990* (New York: Pantheon Books, 1992).

16. Articles in the two major military journals, *Revue De Défense Nationale* and *Revue Militaire D'Information*, strike by their clarity, systematic logic, and didactic quality.

17. The demise of the Vichy government at the end of World War II also sig-

naled the end of Action Française as an organized movement: Charles Maurras was arrested and tried for his active support of Marshall Pétain.

18. Trinquier, *Guerre, révolution, subversion*, 9.

19. Peter Paret, *French Revolutionary Warfare*, 9.

20. Bourgès-Maunoury, "L'armée de demain," *Revue Militaire d'Information*, 272 (June 10, 1956): 5.

21. Trinquier, *Guerre, révolution, subversion*, 34.

22. Hogard, "L'armée française devant la guerre révolutionnaire,"*Revue de Défense Nationale* (January 1957): 78.

23. Trinquier, *Guerre, révolution, subversion*, 1.

24. I am grateful to Professor Peter Paret for pointing this out to me.

25. Yet, theorists were aware of the problem of colonial inequities. One of them, Trinquier, noted the imbalance between an economically prosperous world, and one, like Algeria, that "barely emerges from miserably poor and primitive living conditions," which created "a permanent war climate." See *Guerre, révolution, subersion*, 20.

26. Capitaine Souyris, "Les conditions de la parade et de la riposte à la guerre révolutionnaire," *Revue Militaire d'Information* 281 (February–March, 1957): 97.

27. Pan-Islamism/Pan-Arabism was added to communism as threats to the maintenance of the colonial empire in an attempt to adjust the theory to local conditions. See Trinquier, *Guerre, révolution, subversion*, chapter 12.

28. Souyris, "Les conditions de la parade," 97. Hogard shared this opinion, calling the error one of a confusion of the cause of the war with the means with which to fight it. See J. Hogard, "Guerre révolutionnaire et pacification," *Revue Militaire d'Information* 280 (January 1957): 13.

29. Hogard, "Guerre révolutionnaire et pacification," 14.

30. I am using this concept somewhat loosely. Paret uses the more adequate concept of "anticolonial" war.

31. Hogard, "Guerre révolutionnaire ou révolution dans l'art de la guerre," *Revue de Défense Nationale* (December 1956): 1498. There was some disagreement as to whether revolutionary war was an entirely new kind of war, or simply the continuation of "classic" war but on a limited scale. The disagreement was generally resolved by arguing that revolutionary war can be subsumed under classic war in its most general features.

32. Hogard, "L'armée française devant la guerre," 78.

33. Hogard refers to the French Revolution twice in his article "Guerre révolutionnaire ou révolution," 1498, 1502.

34. Capitaine H. Martin, "Guérilla, guerre en surface, guerre révolutionnaire," *Revue Militaire d'Information* 286 (August 1957): 17.

35. Lieutenant-Colonel Le Mire, "Quelques enseignements pratiques de la guerre de Corée," *Revue Militaire d'Information* 241 (November 10, 1954): 16.

36. Capitaine H. Martin, "Guérilla, guerre en surface," 9.

37. Ibid., 11, 9.

38. Souyris, "Réalité et aspects de la 'guerre psychologique,'" *Revue Militaire d'Information* 302 (February 1959): 8.

39. Souyris, "Les conditions de la parade," 95.

40. SHAT, 3K28. Audiotape of an interview carried out on December 8, 1997. Massu laughed when asked whether he believed in a communist threat to Algeria. He also admitted that he and other hard-line officers had planned to throw key parliamentarians into the Seine River "to scare them."

41. H. de la Bastide, "Regards sur l'Islam, *Revue Militaire d'Information* 277 (October 1956): 15–16. Bastide deduced Islam's compatibility with communism from the presence of graduates of Al Azhar University, the foremost religious institution in Cairo, among communists in Egypt. More scholalry studies of Islam also appeared in military journals, but do not seem to have had the same effect on strategists as those that supported their views. See, among others, Marcel Colombe, "L'Islam d'hier et d'aujourd'hui," *Revue Militaire d'Information* 273 (June 1956): 20–43; 275 (August 1956): 58–71.

42. Pierre Chateauvieux, "L'islamisme et le bouddhisme," *Revue Militaire d'Information* 277 (October 1956): 18. The author compared Islam to Buddhism, which he claimed, in spite of its peace-loving character, had been used by China to bolster its policies in Mongolia and Tibet. He concluded that Islam too can accommodate communism, especially where it has been "degraded to the point of becoming a mere communal cult" in dire need of reform. Hence, communism finds an opportunity to play a corrective role. See p. 22.

43. Colonel Villiers de L'Isle-Adam, "Bourguibisme et matérialisme dialectique," *Revue Militaire d'Information* 305 (May 1959): 52.

44. Hogard, "L'armée française devant la guerre révolutionnaire," 77, 78. Mohaou-Hammou Zayane was a Moroccan military figure who opposed France's incursions into Morocco, defeating French troops at the Elhri battle in 1914 before his country became a protectorate. Samory Touré was also an anticolonial leader from southeastern Guinea, who fought French colonial troops in the late nineteenth century to protect the Wassoulou empire he had established in West Africa before being defeated.

45. Hogard, "Guerre révolutionnaire ou révolution," 1504.

46. Ibid.

47. Souyris identified a "preinsurrectional period" or gestation period that essentially overlaps with Hogard's phase one. See "Les conditions de la parade," 99.

48. Hogard, "Guerre révolutionnaire ou révolution," 1504.

49. Souyris, "Les conditions de la parade," 94.

50. Martin also shared this opinion. He felt that overconfidence in one's firepower goes hand in hand with mounting several operations aimlessly, thinking that each might be decisive. See "Guérilla, guerre en surface," 15.

51. Souyris, "Les conditions de la parade," 98.

52. Martin, "Guérilla, guerre en surface," 17.

53. Trinquier, *Guerre, subversion, revolution*, 1. Although a discussion of Clausewtiz's views on war is beyond the scope of this book, this definition is not fundamentally different from Clausewitz's second definition of war: "an act of violence intended to compel our enemy to do our will." Carl von Clausewitz, *On War*, edited and translated by Michael Howard and Peter Paret (Princeton, NJ: Princeton University Press, 1984), 75.

54. Trinquier, *Guerre, subversion, révolution*, 12, 18.

55. Martin, "Guerilla, guerre en surface," 13, 17.

56. For a detailed discussion of the counterrevolutionary doctrine, see Peter Paret, *Revolutionary Warfare*, chapters 3–4.

57. General Jacques Faure, division general for Algiers' army corps, calculated that for the city of Tizi Ouzou, the capital of the mountainous area of Grande Kabylie, the troop-population ratio was 1/48 for a troop-area ratio of 6 per km². For the small town of Tigzirt the ratios were 1/15 and 2.5, which means that there were relatively more troops in small villages than in larger cities in the region. SHAT 1H3434D1 "Rapport troupe-population. Rapport troupe-superficie." No 145/3/ZEA/S.

58. SHAT, 1H3434D1, Directive No. 478/CAA/3/OPE sent for dissemination on March 6, 1959, by Division General Jacques Faure commanding Zone East Algiers region, and the 27th Alpine Infantry Division.

59. This was an imitation of the Viet Minh "parallel hierarchies" that the theorists had described at length.

60. SHAT, 1H2524, 4. In French, the slogan was "S'imposer. Organiser. Engager." The verb *s'imposer* literally means "to impose one's self on others, or to impress/dominate others with one's power."

61. SHAT, 1H2524, 5.

62. SHAT, 1H3434D1, *La Technique Militaire*, No. 1398/CAA/3/OPE, May 19, 1959, 5–6. Annex No. 2 to directive générale sur la guerre subversive, No. 478/CAA/3/OPE of February 24, 1959. Tactical mobility calls for "intensive physical training" of the troops to increase their endurance and speed when they go out on operations by day and night. For Massu "the cell" may be as small as "a tank and a jeep," p. 6.

63. Ibid., Annex No. 2, p. 4.

64. Martin, "Guérilla, guerre en surface," 15.

65. Hogard, "L'armée française devant la guerre," 79.

66. Paret, *Revolutionary Warfare*, 30.

67. General Allard, quoted in ibid. Allard was one of the generals who oversaw the war in Algeria.

68. Paret, *Revolutionary Warfare*, 31.

69. General Allard felt that "pure military action, which is of first importance in conventional war, takes a back seat to psychological action." In reality military action was *supplemented* with other social-psychological and political methods. Paret, ibid., 30.

70. Hogard, "L'armée française devant la guerre," 81, 82, 79.

71. Martin, "Guérilla, guerre en surface," 13.

72. R. Labelle-Rojoux, "Face aux impératifs de la technique faut-il repenser l'éducation classique?" *Revue Militaire D'Information* 234 (May 25, 1954): 27. Interest in psychology as a discipline, a method of "pacification," as well as conditioning of the troops was paramount among the military in the 1950s and 1960s. An assessment of the education received by young men before they entered the army revealed that they were deficient in scientific and technical training, which included psychology. Experts argued that the inclusion of the "new psychology,"

or "applied psychology," in military curricula was necessary for at least two reasons: the draft democratized the composition of the troops, and thus presented the army with problems of social integration different from those of the professional armies of old; the incipient rearrangement of the structure of the French Empire into a federation of states (the "Union Française") under the aegis of France was felt to require new technologies of control to keep disparate countries and cultures in the fold. Being on the cutting edge of this type of technology was also seen as a mark of "the enduring supremacy of Europeans over the entire planet," over "Muslim and Oriental cultures" that "favored theology and poetry." Ibid., 27.

73. See Gustave Le Bon, *Psychologie des foules* (Paris: Félix Alcan, 1895).

74. See Serge Chakotin, *The Rape of the Masses* (London: George Routledge and Sons, 1940).

75. Simplet, "Guerre révolutionnaire ou guerre psychologique ou guerre 'tout court'?" *Revue Militaire d'Information* 309 (October 1959): 97–102.

76. Ximénès, "Guerre révolutionnaire en Algérie," *Revue Militaire d'Information* 297 (August–September 1958): 27–40. Ximénés had previoulsy published articles in support of *guerre révolutionnaire* theory. See his "Essai sur la guerre révolutionnaire," *Revue Militaire d'Information* 281 (February–March 1957): 9–22.

77. Simplet, "Guerre révolutionnaire ou guerre psychologique," 100. He poked fun at psychological action in these words: "March forward for brainwashing! March forward loud-speakers companies! March forward and kick up a war!"

78. Ximénès, "Guerre révolutionnaire en Algérie," 28. In theory, a revolutionary war is caused by "a state of sociological imbalance"; a "disconnection of the population from established authority"; the existence of an active minority incited or encouraged by a foreign power; "a will to fight reaching the breaking point."

79. Ibid., 29.

80. Ximénès calculated that 5.8 million lived off agriculture. Their per capita income was less than 20,000 francs.

81. Cherrière, "Les débuts de l'insurrection algérienne (Novembre 1954–Juin 1955), *Revue de Défense Nationale* (December 1956): 1459.

82. M. Garrigou-Lagrange, "Intégrisme et national-catholicisme," *Esprit* (November 1959): 515.

83. John Shy and Thomas W. Collier, "Revolutionary War," in Peter Paret ed., *Makers of Modern Strategy from Machiavelli to the Nuclear Age* (Princeton, NJ: Princeton University Press, 1986), 819, 844.

CHAPTER 2
MILITARIZATION OF THE COLONIAL STATE

1. SHAT, 1H3434/1. "Directive" No. 478/CAA/3/OPE, 1959, 9.

2. Ibid., 145–47.

3. Among his contemporaries, Vaujour is unique in apologizing for using terms such as "rebels," "*fellagha*," and "terrorists." See *De la révolte à la révolution*, 15. Regretting the ascent of the military to politics, he claims that after the No-

vember 1 attacks, he insisted on civil authorities' control over the military, should the army be brought in.

4. A march organized to celebrate the surrender of German forces to the Allies was the occasion for nationalists to call for political autonomy. Riots and deadly assaults against a number of Pieds-Noirs ensued, which the colonial government crushed with fighter bombers, and particularly severe retaliatory measures resulting in a large number of victims. Algerians estimate these at 45,000 dead.

5. Vaujour recalls that Henri Borgeaud told him point blank that he would oppose his appointment as directour of Sûreté Générale because he was not sure he would be willing to get "his hands wet," by which he meant be as tough with natives as was needed "since the events of May 8, 1945, in Sétif and Guelma." Ibid., 27. Nevertheless, Vaujour was appointed.

6. Ibid., 217. The state's appeal to the military must also be understood in light of the paradox of the special political status of colonial Algeria in the French Empire as a series of three departments across the Mediterranean. Thus, Jean Vaujour could claim that the war of decolonization was a "civil war" that had to be dealt with accordingly. Ibid., 15. In this view Algeria appeared as a twentieth-century version of the Vendée with nationalists cast in the role of Royalists, and the state representing the Republicans. See Paret, *French Revolutionary Warfare*, 43. Vaujour's reference to nationalists as "separatists" illustrates this domestication of the war, which helped to erase the legitimacy of challenge to Algeria's colonial status. See 47, 111, 413.

7. A measure of this perception lag can be gauged by General de Gaulle's opening his address to the colonial population in 1958 with the famous words "I understand you!" ("Je vous ai compris!").

8. That France resisted alarmist calls from Algiers was understandable. Since the nineteenth century there had been a tug of war between colonists who often made unrealistic demands on the French government, and the military, which initially sought to stabilize the administration of the colony. See Mostéfa Lacheraf, "Constantes politiques et militaires dans les guerres coloniales d'Algérie (1830–1960)," *Les Temps Modernes*, 177 (December 1960–January 1961): 726–800.

9. Vaujour, *De la révolte à la revolution*, 336–39.

10. Michel Hardy, Hervé Lemoine, and Thierry Sarmant, eds., *Pouvoir politique et autorité militaire en Algérie. Hommes, textes, institutions, 1945–1962* (Paris: Service Historique de l'Armée de Terre. L'Harmattan, 2002), 150. In fact Title I of this law first defined the conditions under which a state of emergency could be instituted "in part or all of the territory of metropolitan France, Algeria and overseas departments either in case of an imminent danger resulting from serious acts against public order, or in case of occurrences, which by their nature or gravity take on the character of public calamities." Title II declared the state of emergency in Algeria. See 147–51.

11. Ibid., 149, 150.

12. Ibid., 152.

13. Ibid., 153, 157, 159–60, 161.

14. Vaujour, *De la révolte à la révolution*, 355, 354, 355.

15. This was done in the Constantine region where General Gaston Parlange

was appointed prefect of the city and civil-military commandant of the Aurès-Nementchas area where the war had started.

16. Hardy, *Pouvoir politique*, 51–52.

17. SHAT, 1H3196D1. *Rapport sur la campagne d'Algérie*, No. 1952/DO/3/OPE.S, November 19, 1956, 3. This was a report from the region of Oran. It blamed the lack of coordination on "the omniscience that certain civilian authorities evince, and their reluctance to discuss the efficiency of the army preferring instead to focus on its difficulties."

18. Hardy, *Pouvoir politique et autorité militaire*, 53. The Mangin Report quoted by Hardy also recommended that all civilians under military authority be discharged and sent back to the government.

19. SHAT, 1H3196D1, *Annexe au rapport sur la campagne d'Algérie*, No. 2203/4oDIM/3–0-S, November 12, 1956, 3.

20. Adapted from SHAT, 1H2403D1, *Exposé sur le rôle du 6ème bureau et sur l'organisation civile et militaire avant et après le 13 Mai 1958*, No. 638/RM.10/6.SC. 2. "Mixed" refers to civil-military command.

21. SHAT, 1H3196D1, *Rapport du Colonel de Peyrelongue commandant le 5ème Groupe de Chasseurs à Pied*, No. 1643/5OG.C.P./3/ S. 2.

22. SHAT, 1H3196D1, *Annexe au rapport sur la campagne d'Algére*, No. 2203/4.DIM/3-O-S, November 12, 1956, 2.

23. See Paret, *French Revolutionary Warfare*, 46–52.

24. SHAT, 1H3196D1, *Annexe au rapport sur la Campagne d'Algérie*, No. 2203/4oDIM/3–0-S, November 12, 1956, 2, 3.

25. SHAT, 1H3196D1, *Rapport sur la campagne d'Algérie*, No. 1033/4o DIM/TRANS/S, November 8, 1956, 2.

26. SHAT, 1H2556D1, *Directive no. 2 sur l'action politique et sociale à mener par les chefs des SAS*, No. 39/CAB/CIV, June 10, 1958.

27. See Paret, *French Revolutionary Warfare*, and Alf Andrew Heggoy, *Insurgency and Counterinsurgency in Algeria* (Bloomington: Indiana, 1972).

28. SHAT, 1H2556D1, *Directives au sujet des officiers des affaires algériennes*, No. 132/K/Pol, March 1, 1956. See also *Mémento administratif à l'usage de MM. les officiers des Affaires Algériennes chefs de SAS*, January 1957.

29. This was apparently the case of Jean Pouget, head of the SAS at Bordj de l'Agha. See, Alexander Zervoudakis, "A Case of Successful Pacification: The 584th Bataillon du Train à Bordj de l'Agha," *Journal of Strategic Studies*, Special Issue, 25, No. 2 (2002): 54–64.

30. Paret, *French Revolutionary Warfare*, 50.

31. Hardy, *Pouvoir politique*, 54.

32. For one succinct example of material needs, see *Rapport du Colonel de Peyrelongue*, 1. See also a similar report in 1H3196D1 from the 31st Groupe de Chasseurs à Pied, No. 1265/31/S, assumed date: November 9, 1956, 2. See also Report No. 209/20o BCP/3 Bs, November 15, 1956, 2–3.

33. Adapted from SHAT, 1H2403D1, 4.

34. Jean-Pierre Vittori, *On a torturé en Algérie. Témoignages recueillis par Jean-Pierre Vittori* (Paris: Editions Ramsay, 2000).

35. SHAT, 1H1261D4, *Instruction sur la lutte contre la rébellion et le terrorisme*, No. 339/S/EM.10.JM.DG., April 30, 1957, 3.

36. SHAT, 1H1261D4, *Instruction personnelle et secrète*, No. 3, June 11, 1957, 2.

37. Raphaëlle Branche, *La torture et l'armée*, 195, 196. Branche argues that the RAP represented "the revenge of the military over civil authority."

38. Vittori, *On a torturé en Algérie*, 42.

39. Pierre Vidal-Naquet, *Les crimes de l'armée française. Algérie 1954–1962* (Paris: Editions La Découverte, 2001), 115, 258.

40. Branche, *La torture et l'armée*, 199.

41. Vittori, *On a torturé en Algérie*, 42.

42. Branche, *La torture et l'Armée*, 199, 200, 203, 199, 262, 256, 204.

43. Vidal-Naquet, *Les crimes de l'Armée*, 88.

44. SHAT, 1H2581D1, *Mémento à l'usage des petites unités concernant certains aspects de la recherche et de la capture des hors-la-Loi*, May 1957, 4. However, the text also advises the military to give the gendarmerie or the police all the time they needed to take custody of the individual. This meant that the army could use the time to interrogate the suspect.

45. *Mémento*, 11.

46. This practice partially accounts for the disappearance of "suspects" without a trace.

47. SHAT, 1H2581D1, *Attitudes à observer à l'égard des rebelles pris les armes à la main*. November 24, 1957.

48. SHAT, 1H1493, *Attributions du Colonel Adjoint en ce qui concerne les internés*, No. 1020/R.T./C.A.A./2S, May 11, 1960, 85. General Vezinet, commandant of the territorial region and Algiers army corps, explained that one month was devoted to the "exploitation" of detainees by intelligence officers, and two for their reeducation.

49. Ibid., 86.

50. 1H1493, *Visite des lieux de détention ou d' interrogatoire de suspects*, No. 83/I.G.C.I., May 12, 1960. See also note No. 1509/RT/CAC/3/P.H., April 25, 1960, and General Salan's note No. 431/RM./10/6.S/C, May 1, 1958, 1. A report by the International Red Cross Committee (CICR) identified the existence of "Passage Centers." SHAT, 1H1493, Mission du Comité de la Croix Rouge en Algérie, No. 2056/CSFA/EMI/MA, November 12, 1961.

51. Salan, 1H1493, 3.

52. Pierre Vidal-Naquet, *Les crimes de l'Armée*, 84, 87, 90, 84.

53. 1H2581D1. *Fiche. Rebelles faits prisonniers les armes à la main. Camps d'internés militaires*," March 10, 1958.

54. Vidal-Naquet, *Les crimes de l'armée*, 85.

55. The Report of the Commission issued in December 1957 documents specific cases of torture and other acts of "violence." See *Le Monde*, December 14, 1957, 8. See also SHAT, 1H1493, January 13, 1962. There had been two previous reports, one by the inspector of security, Wuillaume, the other by the director general of security, Mairey, who in 1955 had noted that methods used by the police and gendarmerie had been compared to those of the Gestapo.

56. See SHAT, 1H1493, Letter No. 4.158/CM, July 9, 1960, and letter marked A508. See also DGA, Cabinet militaire, No. 539/CM 1H1793, February 7, 1962; see also SHAT, 1H1493. Letter No. 4.158/CM, July 9, 1960.

57. Ibid.

58. General Le Corbeiller, Inspections Report, 1H1493, February 24, 1962, 2. Le Corbeiller reported that detainees in Camp "S" where PAM were kept under orders of the commanding general of the Algiers army corps "did not look as deliberate in their deportment as those in the other camp. One finds in their eyes the meanness and hatred that had been already detected at the CMI of Hammam Bou Hadjar."

59. See SHAT, 1H1493. *Rapport de visite du secteur d'Akbou,* No. 33/I.G.C.I., March 15, 1960, March 23, 1960, 2. The inspector also reported "the search for a certain efficiency through physical pressure" that led the CTT to use interpreters to assist in the torture of detainees.

60. SHAT, 1H1493, Letter No. 422/CICDA, *Garde des centres de détention administrative,* February 20, 1962. In general, guards were supposed to be recruited among the gendarmerie, but the army used its own personnel. Forced labor was seen as a "form of psychological action." SHAT, 1H1493, *Rapport d'inspection du secteur de Sidi-Bel-Abbès,* March 31, 1960, April 11, 1960, No. 47/I.G.C.I., 3.

61. The Commission for the Safeguard of Individual Rights and Liberties had already flagged the particularly inhumane treatment of those on death row who "are piled up three to a cell, waiting anxiously for a decision on their fate." *Le Monde,* December 14, 1957, 9. The total number of people registered as detained in the various camps reached 32,160 in November 1961, of whom 197 were French, an increase from 21,000 the year before. See SHAT, 1H1493, "Etat Statistique," No. 4556/CM.

62. SHAT, 1H1493, *Encombrement des CTT,* November 1961, 1–2. See also 1H100D/1, "Note annexe No. II" to Letter No. 125/IGCI, November 1961, 1; Etat statistique à la date du 30 Novembre 1961, No. 4556/CM.

63. SHAT, 1H1493, *Attributions du Colonel Adjoint en ce qui concerne les internés,* May 11, 1960, No. 1020/R.T./C.A.A./2.S.

64. SHAT, 1H1493, *Libération des internés des CMI,* No. 284/I.C.I., October 12, 1961.

65. SHAT, 1H1493, *Situation des établissments pénitentiaires d' Algérie. Application des mesures de clémence,* December 11, 1961, 2.

66. SHAT, 1H1493, *Solutions au problème du surpeuplement des établissements pénitentiaires,* no number, 1961. Civil penitentiary officials started to refuse new prisoners. This caused the military to hold those convicted in CTT, in violation of the law. See SHAT, 1H1493, "Encombrement des CTT," no number, 1.

67. SHAT, 1H1493, *Sécurité intérieure des centres pénitentiaires et d'hébergement,* No. 0504/CSFA/EMI/MA, February 17, 1962. In addition, overcrowding caused prisoners to take matters into their own hands and to seek relief wherever they could.

68. SHAT, 1H1100D1, *Note annexe No. II* to Letter No. 125/IGCI, March 8, 1960, 3.

69. General Le Corbeiller, SHAT, 1H1493, 3. At the CTT of Boghari, Le Corbeiller warned that keeping 728 PAM in a relatively small space, guarded by ninety young conscripts could constitute a danger should they organize mass demonstrations.

70. See SHAT, 1H1097D1. *Instruction générale sur le service des avocats généraux et procureurs militaires*, No. 298/EMI/PGM, June 2, 1961, 6.

71. 1H2581D1.

72. See Sylvie Thénault, *Une drôle de justice. Les magistrats dans la guerre d'Algérie* (Paris: La Découverte, 2001), especially chapter 1. See also *Le Genre Humain, Juger en Algérie* (Paris: Editions du Seuil, September 1997), especially "Testimonials," 121–58.

73. See footnote 50.

74. SHAT, 1H1097D1. Letter No. 14214, May 7, 1960, 2–3.

75. SHAT, 1H1097D1. Letter from Paul Delouvrier, head of the government in Algeria, summarizing a letter by Prime Minister Michel Debré, No. 722/AP, May 20, 1960, 1. The February 20 decree ostensibly returned to civil authorities the bulk of the judicial functions that had been given to the military, "within limits."

76. SHAT, 1H1097D1. Letter No. 722/AP, May 20, 1960, 2.

77. For example, the prosecutor was subordinated to the intelligence officer in charge of operational investigation in the sector and sternly warned against "compromising the operational exploitation [of suspects] for the sake of accelerating by a few days the appearance of a delinquent before the judge." Not only would such an officer "singularly be lacking in intelligence," but because of him "a cache stuffed with explosives will not be discovered, and will continue to supply attacks in the next city; an armed group will disperse when it could have been annihilated. The magistrate's error will generally result in a heavy deficit." Instruction No. 298, 6.

78. SHAT, 1H1097D1. Letter No. 003.094 MA/CC, January 30, 1962, 1. Mesmer's move was motivated by his concern for "the overcrowding of penitentiary establishments as well as the material conditions of detention."

79. SHAT, 1H1097D1. Letter No. 003.094 MA/CC, January 30, 1962, 2 (emphasis in text).

80. Of significance is also the political context within which Mesmer's decision was made. The rebellious generals' putsch had already taken place, the OAS had stopped its activities, and public opinion in France was in a state of uproar. However, Mesmer's decision must be read against the background of an *instruction générale* issued by the chief command of forces in Algeria on June 12, 1961. This comprehensive 74-page document divided into ten chapters covers all phases and characteristics of judicial procedure. It makes it very clear that even though military prosecutors are civil magistrates recalled to serve in the army, they are "part and parcel of the army." Nevertheless, they "must understand that they are also officers subjected to the chain of command. They would be making a grave mistake if they considered themselves members of some parallel hierarchy, placed alongside the army for the purpose of observing and controlling its activity." SHAT, 1H1097/1, *Instruction sur le service des avocats généraux et pocureurs militaires*, 4–9.

81. Ibid., 4–9.

82. For a matter-of-fact account of how terror was carried out, see Général Aussaresses, *Services spéciaux*, 151–59.

83. Captain Amphyoxus, "La guerre en Algérie: Regards de l'autre côté,"

Revue de Défense Nationale (January 1959): 90–91. Seeking to be fair, the author suggested paying the blood price (*dya*) whenever the army killed an Algerian by mistake. Amphyoxus argued that the nineteenth-century Bureaux Arabes had an intimate understanding of natives' psychology, and thus ought to be taken as guides for the proper attitude to adopt before the population in the 1950s. The idea of death as an anthropological factor through which to understand natives was also developed by Jean Servier, "La pensée religieuse en Algérie," *Revue Militaire d'Information*, no. 277(October 1956): 36. By renaming the cult of saints, cult of the dead, Servier turned Islam in North Africa into a different belief system, which glorified death. By implication, death during the war was at once trivialized and transformed into an outcome that was expected and welcomed by its Algerian victims.

84. Vidal-Naquet, *Les crimes de l'armée*, 72.

85. Branche, *La torture et l'armée*, 284, 285.

86. Jean-Charles Jauffret, *Soldats en Algérie 1954–1982* (Paris: Editions Autrement, 2000), 265. The embalming was done by the 6th RPIMA, or Regiment of Marine Parachute Infantry.

87. Ibid., 78–79.

88. When General Boyer-Vidal, inspector general of internment centers asked general Gouraud, commandant of the Constantine region to supply him with a list of detention locations, he received a flat rejection on the grounds that since units use mobile centers on their frequent operations, any accounting would be inaccurate. See SHAT, 1H1493, Note No. 1509/RT/CAC/3/P.H., April 25, 1960.

89. Vidal-Naquet, *Les crimes de l'armée*, 67, 25. The same soldier recounts other incidents where chickens were killed and taken by his comrades. See p. 29.

90. Claire Mauss-Copeaux, *Appelés en Algérie* (Paris: Hachette Littératures, 1998), 154, 152, 150.

91. Général Bigeard with Patrice de Méritens, *Paroles d'Indochine* (Editions du Rocher, 2004), 96–97.

92. Vittori, *On a torturé en Algérie*, 63.

93. Diaries and confessions made by former soldiers are filled with accounts of wanton destruction, executions, and at times sadistic acts (other than torture) committed against the rural population.

94. Fanon, *The Wretched of the Earth*, trans. Constance Farrington (New York: Grove Press, 1963), 259–60.

95. Vidal-Naquet, *Les crimes de l'armée*, 25.

96. Michel Cornaton, *Les camps de regroupement et la guerre d'Algérie* (Paris: L'Harmattan, 1967), 123. Although carried out before the military archives were opened to the public (in 1993), Cornaton's analysis and estimates have held up. See Keith Sutton, "Army Administration Tensions over Algeria's Centres de Regroupement, 1954–1962," *British Journal of Middle Eastern Studies* 26, No. 2 (Nov., 1999), 243–70. Neither author mentions the epoch-making Rocard's report.

97. Cornaton, *Les camps de regroupement*, 123.

98. Michel Rocard, *Rapport sur les camps de regroupement* (Paris: Mille et Une Nuits, 2003), 134–135. CIMADE was initially an umbrella organization of protestant youth groups, formed to provide support to evacuees from Alsace-Lorraine during World War II. It has since become an ecumenical organization helping displaced people, refugees as well as asylum seekers.

99. Ibid., 126. Where a resettlement was located near a city, it was possible to drive an infant to the nearest hospital to receive care.

100. Rocard pointed out that in 1954, there was one doctor for 5,137 people in Algeria as compared with one for every 1,091 in France. See footnotes 87, 90.

101. Cornaton, *Les camps de regroupement*, 196.

102. Ibid., chapter 6, 103–18, Rocard, 124–26.

103. Quoted in Cornaton, *Les camps de regroupement*, 105, 132, footnote 1.

104. Keith Sutton's uncritically accepted the view expressed by hard-line generals such as Le Mire that the resettlement policy was a "success." Sutton uses "pacification" normatively, and adopts the language of the military in referring to the Algerian combatants as the "rebels." See "Army Administration Tensions," 246, 260–67. Equally problematic is Heggoy's essentially benevolent conception of the SAS, which must be questioned.

CHAPTER 3
PSYCHOLOGICAL ACTION

1. See his memoirs, *De Saint-Cyr à l'action psychologique*.

2. SHAT, 1H2403D1, "Instruction provisoire sur l'emploi de l'arme psychologique," July 29, 1957, 13.

3. Ibid., 29. See also SHAT, 1H2403D1, *Recherche et exploitation du renseignement psychologique*, No. 687/MI/5/ETU, May 20, 1959.

4. SHAT, 1H2524, "La guerre psychologique. Conférence no. 3," Centre d'Instruction Pacification et Contre-Guérilla, 1, 5, 6. Interest in Goebbels rested on his conception of the "7% Law" or the minority of people who resist totalitarian rule, and for whom "concentration camps are made," 1. Ostensibly such references, several of which were drawn from Chakotin's book, were meant to help strategists understand how "totalitarianism" functioned. However, they were discussed for use in Algeria, a different milieu from Russia or Nazi Germany. Page 4 of Conférence (e.g. lecture) no. 3 reproduces a graph that appears on p. 100 of Chakotin's book.

5. SHAT, 1H2524, "La guerre psychologique." Conférence no. 2, Centre d'Instruction Pacification Contre-Guérilla, 4–9.

6. SHAT, 1H2524, "La guerre psychologique. Conférence no. 3, Centre d'Instruction Pacification Contre-Guérilla, 2. Although they noted the role played by the unconscious in the "American School," the military strategists' conception of their enemy's unconscious was inevitably mechanistic since they felt compelled to assume the existence of culture-bound psychic configurations divorced from the colonial nature of the political milieu that shaped them.

7. See, among others, Jackie Clarke, "Engineering a New Order in the 1930s: The Case of Jean Coutrot," *French Historical Studies* 24, no. 1 (Winter 2001):

63–86. Coutrot's Centre d'Etudes des Problèmes Sociaux discussed the psychobiological conditions under which a "new man" would be brought about. The center was patronized by eugenicist Alex Carrel, although Clarke argues that his ideas concerning "biological elites" were not shared by Coutrot and his associates, 73–74.

8. Serge Chakotin, *The Rape of the Masses* (London: George Routledge and Sons, 1940). See also Gustave Le Bon, *Psychologie des foules* (Paris: Félix Alcan, 1895).

9. For an analysis of the concept of "masses" in political-philosophical thought, especially as discussed by Spinoza, see Etienne Balibar, *Masses, Classes, Ideas* (New York: Routledge, 1994), chapter 1.

10. Serge Chakotin, *The Rape of the Masses*, 89.

11. Gustave Le Bon, *Psychologie des foules*, 24, 67, 102–3.

12. Ibid., *The Psychology of Revolution* (New York: Putnam and Sons, 1913), 24, 26.

13. Ibid., 75, 76.

14. Hilde Hardeman, *Coming to Terms with the Soviet Regime* (Dekalb: Northern Illinois University Press, 1994), 78, 161.

15. Chakotin, *The Rape of the Masses*, 18–20, xv.

16. Chakotin was critical of Le Bon for exaggerating the role of crowds in public life, failing to distinguish between a crowd and a mass of people, and not appreciating the aims of the "revolt of the masses against a psychical oppression that has become intolerable," p. 36. Nevertheless, he too did not escape behaviorist reductionism.

17. Chakotin, *The Rape of the Masses*, 13.

18. Captain A. Souyris, "Les conditions de la parade et de la riposte à la guerre révolutionnaire," *Revue Militaire d'Information* 281 (February–March 1957): 102, 109.

19. CAOM, SAS/Doc/5, *Mémento de l'officier d'action psychologique en Algérie*, Annex III, 1.

20. H. G. Esméralda, *Un été en enfer* (Paris: Exils, 2004), 31–32.

21. SHAT, 1H2524, "La guerre psychologique. Conférence no. 3," Centre d'Instruction Pacification et Contre-Guérilla, 8.

22. SHAT, 1H2425, "Psycho-sociology musulmane." Fiche no. 9-Annexe I. Centre d'Instruction Pacification et Contre- Guérilla, 2.

23. CAOM, SAS/Doc/5 A.B.C, 15.

24. *Mémento de l'officier d'action psychologique en Algérie*, 6.

25. Claude Cabanne, "Formes et problèmes de la décolonization," *Revue Militaire d'Information*, no. 328 (June 1961), 25. See also General M. Boucherie, "Les bureaux Arabes: Leur role dans la conquête de l'Algérie, *Revue de Défense Nationale* (July 1957): 1062–64. Boucherie asserted, "A Muslim even when he does not practice, always remains a Muslim." He reached this conclusion upon observing that an Algerian officer in the French army, Colonel Ben Daoud, a graduate of Saint-Cyr Academy "who even commanded a French regiment [but] resumed wearing the burnous when he retired, and with it the Muslim life." See p. 1063.

26. SHAT, 1H2524, 2.

27. Ibid., 5.

28. Nevertheless, the handbook indirectly points to the problematic colonial status of Algerians in outlining the sociopolitical and economic dimensions of psychological action. For example, both Algerians and Frenchmen were to be told of "the good that France has done for Algeria, including training of an intellectual elite." Ibid., 15, 6–7.

29. SHAT, 1H2524, "La guerre psychologique. Conférence no. 2," Centre d'Instruction Pacification et Contre-Guérilla, 8–9.

30. Ibid., 5. The text ambiguously toys with the idea of the "sacred" and the sanctification of war, which purportedly provides the same emotional release as celebrations of holy festivals did in the old days.

31. SHAT 1H3196D1, *Rapport sur la campagne d'Algérie*, No. 1952/DO/3/OPE.S, November 19, 1956, 7.

32. SHAT, 1H3196D1, *Rapport sur la campagne d'Algérie*, No. 175/S/110o RIM/CDT/SEM, November 8, 1956, 7.

33. SHAT, 1H3196D1, *Rapport sur la Campagne d'Algérie*, No. 174/COL/S, November 15, 1956, 5.

34. SHAT, 1H2403D1, *Fiche. Organisation de la section "Relations Nationales,"* March 26, 1959; April 15, 1959.

35. *Rapport* No. 175, 7.

36. SHAT, 1H3196D1, *Rapport particulier du Chef d'Escadron Jouanno, commandant le groupe de transports 385 sur la campagne d'Algérie*, No. 755/EM/S, November 6, 1956. 2. Referring to colonists, Jouanno noted that "sheltering animals and farm equipment seems in their eyes to be more important than the military men who came to defend their interests."

37. SHAT, 1H3196D1, *Rapport sur la campagne d'Algérie*, No. 252/44, 4ème Division d'Infanterie Motorisée, 12ème Régiment de Dragons, November 1956, 2.

38. The quality of interpreters was frequently evaluated by the army. For example, Report No. 154/3/2RSA/DV issued by the 2nd Régiment des Spahis Algériens notes the "absence of good interpreters at the 3rd and 4th Squadrons—Very average at the 1st; Good at the 2nd—; Very good at the Joint Chiefs of Staff." See p. 2.

39. 1H3196D1, Rapport No. 188/III/24o. R.A., November 17, 1956, 5.

40. Abdelhamid Benzine, *Journal de marche* (Alger: Editions ANEP, 2002), 54.

41. SHAT, 1H2461D2.

42. SHAT, 1H3196D1, *Rapport sur la campagne d'Algérie*, No. 931/EM/3, November 8, 1956, 2. This report was written by Lieutenant-Colonel Carribou, commanding the operational zone of Tlemcen.

43. SHAT,1H3196D1, *Rapport sur la campagne d'Algérie*, no. 174/COLS/S, November 15, 1956, 7–8, 4.

44. SHAT, 1H1100D1, *Note annexe no. II* to Letter N. 125/IGCI of March 8, 1960, 5.

45. SHAT, 1H1493, *Utilisation des CTT à des fins non-conformes à leur vocation*, N.40 I.G.C.I., March 24, 1960.

46. SHAT, 1H1261D4, *Directive générale no. 6, au sujet de l'activité du maintien de l'ordre en Algérie, "* March 7, 1957, 1, 2.

47. Ibid., 3.

48. See several discussions under the rubric of "Action politique et militaire" of a "pacification" proposal, SHAT, 1H2537D2.

49. SHAT, 1H2537D1, *Note de service*, No. 153/OR, May 30, 1957, 2.

50. SHAT, 1H2537/D1, *Réflexions sur l'action militaire et politique à mener dans le quartier de Warnier*, No.1549/2/9oRC, signed by Chief Battalion Domens.

51. SHAT, 1H1493, *Inspection du CMI et de quatre CTT de la zone ouest Constantine*, June 13, 1961, No. 222/I.C.I. See *Fiche concernant le camp militaire d'internés de Ksar Thir*, 1.

52. 1H1493, *Inspection Du CMI*, 3

53. Paret, *French Revolutionary Warfare*, 64. Fanon also described some of the brainwashing techniques used by psychological action experts. However, he appears to have been unaware of Salan's secret strategy. He also underestimated the effects of brainwashing on combatants other than those labeled "intellectuals": He surprisingly argued that because torture was used on ordinary combatants as a means of brainwashing, their symptoms were more physical than mental, and thus not "serious." See *The Wretched of the Earth*, 285–89.

54. See SHAT, 1H2537D3, *Note de service opération "Jumelles,"* No. 23/Artois/5/OPS/S, September 8, 1959.

55. 1H1493, *Inspection du CMI*, 2.

56. See Saïd Ferdi, *Un enfant dans la guerre* (Paris: Editions Du Seuil, 1981). See also Brahim Sadouni, *Destin de Harki 1954. Le témoignage d'un jeune Berbère enrôlé dans l'armée française à 17 ans* (Paris: Cosmopole, 2001).

57. SHAT,1H1100D1, *Fiche sur l' action psychologique dans les centres d'internement*, September 30, 1959, 2.

58. SHAT, 1H1493, *Note*, No. 23/I.C.I, January 23, 1962.

59. *Fiche sur l'action psychologique*, 4.

60. Général Robert Gaget, *Commando Georges* (Paris: Grancher, 2000), 65, 70. See also SHAT, 1H2486D1, articles on Bigeard in Paris-Presse l'Intransigeant, March 1959; Mai 1959; and September 10, 1959.

61. Commandant Si Azzedine, *On nous appelait fellaghas* (Paris: Stock, 1976), 55, 57, 58.

62. Ibid., 59.

63. Gilles Manceron and Hasan Remaoun, *D'une rive à l'autre* (Paris: Syros, 1993), 141.

64. Benzine, *Journal de marche.*

65. Azzedine, *On nous appelait fellaghas*, 66–67.

66. Ibid., 65, 52.

67. Ibid., 67–69.

68. See Saïd Benabdellah, *La justice du FLN pendant la guerre de libération* (Alger: Société Nationale d' Edition et de Diffusion, 1982), 101.

69. Bellahcène Bali, *Mémoires d'un jeune combattant de l'ALN à Tlemcen et sa région: 1956–1958* (Beyrouth: Al-Achraf, 1999), 164, 165. Bali cried after executing his friend, and told his chief, Si Salah, that the next time he ordered him to carry out an execution, he would commit suicide (164). But, he was ordered to

execute a number of informants after this episode, some of whom were women. See pp. 167–84.

70. Azzedine, *On nous appelait fellaghas*, 69.
71. Benzine, *Journal de marche*, 24, 35, 17, 24–25.
72. Azzedine, *On nous appelait fellaghas*, 77
73. Benabdellah, *La justice du FLN*, 65–72.
74. Azzedine, *On nous appelait fellaghas*, 70.
75. Ibid., 59.

CHAPTER 4
MODELS OF PACIFICATION

1. See *Bataille d'Alger, bataille de l'homme* (Desclée de Brouver, 1972), 66.
2. See SHAT, 1H3196D1, *Rapport du chef d'Escadron Scheibling commandant PRVT le quartier de Mondovi*," 2o D.I.M and Z.E.C, Secteur de Bône, No. 390/Q.5/5/S, September 18, 1957, 1.
3. See Lacheroy, *De Saint-Cyr à l'action psychologique*, 119. See also John Stewart Ambler, *The French Army in Politics 1945–1962* (Ohio State University Press) 1996, ch. 12.
4. SHAT, 1H2403D1, *Note au sujet des officiers itinérants*," December 4, 1958, 2.
5. See SHAT, 1H2537D1, *Analyse: NDS, No.2 530/CAC/FY* dated August 28, 1957, of *Réflexions du Capitaine Desgranges*, Corps d'Armée de Constantine, No. 247/BI/5/SC. See also 1H2537D1, *Commentaires du Commandant du Secteur de Bordj Menaiel*.
6. Lacheroy, *De Saint-Cyr à l'action psychologique*, 9.
7. John Stewart Ambler, *The French Army in Politics*, 319. Ambler uses Jean Planchais's inadequate categorization: "national-communism."
8. John Stewart Ambler cites Jean Planchais's typology of military ideology: nationalism, "national-Catholicism" and "national-communism." Ibid.
9. Antoine Argoud, *La décadence, l'imposture et la tragédie*, 143–45.
10. Serge Chakotin, *The Rape of the Masses*, xvii.
11. Argoud, *La décadence, l'imposture*, 100, 149, 114–16, 155.
12. Ibid., 156.
13. Ibid., 147
14. Ibid.
15. Ibid., 128, 129.
16. Ibid., 157.
17. Racinet, *Les capitaines d'Avril* (Paris: Editions France-Empire), 5–47, 72, 234, 235.
18. Ibid., 93, 47, 89, 92.
19. Ibid., 94, 95, 97, 82.
20. Ibid., 253, 70, 232, 99–100.
21. Ibid., 230, 70.
22. Ibid., 108.
23. Ibid., 109, 110, 277.

24. Jean Pouget, *Bataillon R.A.S. Algérie* (Paris: Presses de la Cité, 1981), 142, 141.

25. Ibid., 132.

26. Ibid., 143, 144, 150.

27. Ibid., 147, 149, 349–63.

28. Quoted by Argoud, *La décadence, l'imposture*, 152.

29. Pouget, *Bataillon R.A.S.*, 156, 161, 309.

30. Ibid., 306, 308, 310.

31. Ibid., 318, 319, 329, 309.

32. Ibid., 334, 338.

33. Henry Descombin, *Guerre d'Algérie 1959–1960. Le cinquième bureau* (Paris: L'Harmattan, 1994), 32, 63.

34. Ibid., 141–42, 39.

35. Ibid., 76, 77.

36. Ibid., 33, 107, 58.

CHAPTER 5
DOING TORTURE

1. A book written by John E. Talbott bore the apt title *A War without a Name* (New York: Knopf, 1980).

2. Quoted in Vaujour, *De la révolte à la révolution*, 129–30.

3. Vidal-Naquet, *Les crimes de l'armée*, 167.

4. Vaujour, *De la révolte à la révolution*, 356, 373, 358, 360. Vaujour nevertheless admitted that "information, intelligence, is obviously a means of governing, and thus crucial," pp. 34–35.

5. Branche, *La torture et l'armée*, 236.

6. Denis Lefebvre, *Guy Mollet face à la torture* (Paris: Editions Bruno Leprince, 2001), 84.

7. Ibid., 245, 260–61, 250.

8. SHAT, 1H1369D4, no. 1675 EM/ORG/1, April 7, 1958 and no. 2293EMA/1.0, May 19, 1958.

9. SHAT, 1H1156. See also Vidal-Naquet, *Les crimes de l'armée*, 115.

10. SHAT, 1H1369D4, Ministère des Armées "Terre," No. 1763-EMA/1.0, April 23, 1959.

11. Cornélius, "Morale, droit et guerre révolutionnaire," *Verbe*, no. 92 (April 1958): 69. Cornélius was a pseudonym under which one or several counterrevolution advocates wrote in this Cité Catholique journal.

12. Delarue was a priest working under the authority of the titular chaplain for the 10th DP (Division Parachutiste), Father Chevalier. See Xavier Boniface, *L'aumônerie militaire française, 1914–1962* (Paris: Les Editions du Cerf, 2001), 505.

13. Pierre Vidal-Naquet, *Torture: Cancer of Democracy: France and Algeria 1954–62* (Harmondsworth: Penguin Books, 1963), 42.

14. Branche, *La torture et l'armée*, 60–61.

15. Vidal-Naquet, *Les crimes de l'armée*, 158. Estoup asserted that General Massu gave the order to torture. See p. 157.

16. This villa is also at times erroneously referred to as Susini.

17. Florence Beaugé, *Algérie, une guerre sans gloire* (Alger: Editions Chihab, 2006), chapter 8.

18. H. G. Esméralda, *Un été en enfer* (Paris: Exils, 2004), 71.

19. Henri Alleg, *La question* (Paris: Editions de Minuit, 1961), 15–16, 55.

20. Béchir Boumaza et al. *La gangrène* (Ryad El Feth, Alger: Editions Rahma, 1992), 42. Originally published by Les Editions de Minuit, 1959.

21. Alleg, *La question*, 55.

22. Vittori, *On a torturé en Algérie*, 43.

23. Alleg, *La question*, 47.

24. Vittori, *On a torturé en Algérie*, 43, 45.

25. Vittori's narrator includes an office where intelligence files were kept in his description of the premises of the DOP and where he tortured prisoners. See p. 42.

26. Vidal-Naquet, *Les crimes de l'armée*, 101, 102, 105.

27. Aussaresses, *Services spéciaux*, 158.

28. Vittori, *On a torturé en Algérie*, 40

29. Ibid., 42, 53, 27.

30. Ibid., 46.

31. See, among others, Henri Alleg's description of his torturers Charbonnier and Erulin, in *La question*. See also *Dossier sur la torture et la répression en Algérie. Nous accusons*. Memorandum addressed to René Coty, president of France, and General de Gaulle in 1958 by the Ligue des Droits de l'Homme and four committees (Maurice Audin; Résistance Spirituelle; Vigilance Universitaire; and Centre d'Information et de Coordination pour la Défense des Libertés et de la Paix).

32. Ibid., 165.

33. Ibid., 28, 49.

34. Ibid., 45.

35. Esméralda, *Un été en enfer*, 30–31.

36. Ibid., 54.

37. Ibid., 81, 72–73.

38. Boumaza, *La gangrène*, 49.

39. This explanation of torture by bottle "sitting" was also given by the president of the Commission for the Safeguard of Individual Rights and Liberties, M. Patin. See Simone de Beauvoir and Gisèle Halimi, *Djamila Boupacha* (Paris: Gallimard, 1962), 1, fn. 1, 69, 73–74, 90.

40. Abdelhamid Benzine, *Lambèse* (Alger: Editions ANEP, 2001), 26, 83, 50, 59.

41. I have always been struck by the similarities in sexual imagery used by working-class Pieds-Noirs and urban disaffected Algerian men. The expression "I'll lower his pants," to refer to a man one wants to harm, was commonly used by both.

42. Vittori, *On a torturé en Algérie*, 101.

43. See *Dossier sur la torture*.

44. Vittori, *On a torturé en Algérie*, 138–39, 57. A torturer explained that electricity was meant to make the victim "feel pleasure." See Vidal-Naquet, *Les crimes de l'armée*, 75.

45. Mark Simpson, *Male Impersonators* (New York: Cassell, 1994), especially chapter 2.

46. Boumaza, *La gangrène*, 17. As he was about to undergo torture by electricity, Boumaza resignedly thought of becoming impotent and felt relieved that he already had one child.

47. Klaus Theweleit, *Male Fantasies,* trans. Stephan Conway in collaboration with Erica Carter and Chris Turner (Minneapolis: University of Minnesota Press, 1987), 302.

48. Ibid., 19.

49. Patrick Rotman, *L'ennemi intime* (Paris: Editions du Seuil, 2002), 62.

50. The movie *The Battle of Algiers* depicts instances where the blowtorch was used. For witness accounts of the use of this tool, see Benyoucef Ben Khedda, *Alger, capitale de la résistance, 1956–1957* (Alger: Editions Houma, 2002), 149.

51. Alain Maillard de La Morandais, *L'honneur est sauf* (Paris: Editions du Seuil, 1990), 207.

52. Conversation with Louisette Ighilahriz, Staouéli (Algeria), June 16, 2006.

53. *Dossier sur la torture*, 28.

54. Ibid., 37.

55. Vidal-Naquet, *Les crimes de l'armée française*, 70.

56. General Yusuf paid ten francs for a pair of ears in the nineteenth century; see Olivier Le Cour Grandmaison, *Coloniser, exterminer*, 138–39.

57. Vittori, *On a torturé en Algérie*, 79, 71.

58. Ibid., 11.

59. Ibid., 54.

60. Ibid., 11.

61. See Karl Warnke, ed., *Lais de Marie de France* (Paris: Librairie Générale Française, 1990), 116–33.

62. Mattei, "Jours Kabyles," 15.

63. Branche, *La torture et l'armée*, 68, fn. 3.

64. Vittori, *On a torturé en Algérie*, 12–15.

65. Ibid., 12.

66. Ibid., 53.

67. Ibid., 96.

68. Ibid., 118–19.

69. Boumaza, *La gangrène*, 81.

70. Vittori, *On a tortur en Algérie*, 108.

71. General Aussaresses claims that Ben M'hidi was not tortured, but that he drove him to a suburb of Algiers after his "interrogation" and hanged him, on General Massu's order, after considering poisoning him with cyanide. See his *Services spéciaux, Algérie 1955–1957* (Perrin, 2001), 161–71. See also Ben Khedda, *Alger, capitale de la résistance*, 113–21.

72. Vittori, *On a torturé en Algérie*, 129.

73. Ibid., 107.

74. Aussaresses, *Services Spéciaux*, 70.

75. Vittori, *On a torturé en Algérie*, 120.

76. See Aussaresses, *Services spéciaux*, 197.

77. Vidal-Naquet, *Les crimes de l'armée*, 118.
78. Vittori, *On a torturé en Algérie*, 126.

CHAPTER 6
WOMEN

1. See SHAT, 1H2461D1, *Organisation féminine de la zone autonome d'Alger*, 10e Région Militaire, Corps d'Armée d'Alger, Etat Major, 2e Bureau, No. 4026/C.A.A.A./2.S. October 8, 1957.

2. This focus on women in times of crisis also harks back to the Vichy France campaign aimed at redefining women as mothers and homemakers. See Francine Muel-Dreyfus, *Vichy and the Eternal Feminine*, trans. by Kathleen A. Johnson (Durham and London: Duke University Press, 2001).

3. SHAT, 1H2461D1, *Fiche sur l' émancipation de la femme*, 10e Région Militaire, Corps d'Armée de Constantine. No number. See also 1H2461D1, *La femme musulmane*, May 1958, 50.

4. Lieutenant-Colonel Marey, a deputy of Colonel Godard, forwarded a report to the general command detailing an FLN plan elaborated by Zohra Drif to enlist women in an underground network of propaganda and social action to counteract the work of the SAS. The plan was apparently foiled by the arrest of Yacef Saadi, chief of the Zone Autonome d'Alger, during the "battle" of Algiers. SHAT, 1H2461D1, "Organisation féminine de la Z.A.A," Zone Nord-Algérois. Secteur Alger Sahel, 2ème section, no. 1722/2/C.S., October 2, 1957. The plan called for one women's section to document cases of torture.

5. This strategy of stealing the "revolution" initiated by the FLN was clearly articulated by Racinet, as discussed in chapter 4.

6. SHAT, 1H2461D1, "Organization féminine de la Z.A.A.

7. SHAT, 1H2461D1, *Action sur les milieux féminins*, 7.

8. SHAT, 1H2524, "Sociologie musulmane. Causerie no. 9. Les caractères essentiels de la mentalité des F.M.," 1. "F.M." means "Français-Musulmans."

9. Some reforms of family law did take place. See Marnia Lazreg, *The Eloquence of Silence: Algerian Women in Question* (New York: Routledge, 1994), 90–92.

10. SHAT, 1H2461D1, *Fiches*, 10e Région Militaire/Commandement des Forces Terrestres en Algérie, Etat Major-5e Bureau, ACT/EMSI, March 4, 1959.

11. SHAT, 1H2461D1, *Action sur les milieux féminins en Algérie*, Etat Major Interarmées, 3ème Bureau, No. 888/2.500, October 12, 1959, 15.

12. Ibid., 1.

13. SHAT, 1H2524, "La guerre psychologique. Conférence no. 3," Centre d'Instruction Pacification Contre-Guerilla," 3.

14. SHAT, 1H2461D1. *Document capturé sur Si Boumédiène, Nahia 4 Nord, Mintaqa 8*. This combatant had been killed on November 26, 1958. Copies of this document were disseminated among all EMSI.

15. See Djamila Amrane Minne, *La guerre d'Algérie (1954–1962). Femmes au Combat* (Alger: Editions Rahma, 1993).

16. SHAT, 1H2461D1, "La femme algérienne dans la révolution," an article initially published in the FLN paper *Renaissance algérienne*, no. 1, *wilaya* 3, De-

cember 1957. The text lists rural women's functions in the war and reports that one woman took an ax to a French soldier.

17. SHAT, 1H2461D1, "La femme algérienne," excerpt from the FLN, *Renaissance algérienne*, no. 2, *wilaya* 3, 1957.

18. SHAT, 1H2461D1, *Fiche no. 1*. Body hygiene was the unstated precondition for indoctrination seen as a sort of psychological hygiene. This method was similar to those used by the Centre d'Etudes des Problèmes Humains (CEPH). See Jackie Clarke, "Engineering a New Order," especially 76, 82.

19. SHAT, 1H2461D1, *Fiche no. 5*.

20. SHAT, 1H2461D1, *Action sur les milieux féminins*, 5.

21. SHAT 1H2461D1, *Fiches no. 2 and 3*.

22. SHAT, 1H2461D1, *Etude des "Directives FLN,"* Etat Major, 5ème Bureau, February 12, 1959.

23. SHAT, 1H246D1, *Action, sur les milieux féminins*, 5.

24. SHAT, 1H2461D1, *Fiche concernant une action psychologique à mener sur les rebelles Kabyle*s, January 23, 1959.

25. SHAT,1H2461D1, *Action sur les milieux féminins*, 15.

26. Aspirant Olivier Hamon, "*Objectif population: Action et guerre psychologiques en* Algérie," in *Service historique de l'armée de Terre* 1992 (Château de Vincennes, 1995), 203. In 1960 there were about 315 sociomedical workers, divided up into 171 teams numbering 141 Algerian women, 80 Frenchwomen from France, and 94 Pieds-Noirs. See also SHAT, 1H2461, *Annexe. Action sur les milieux féminins*, August 19, 1960.

27. See SHAT, 1H2461D1, *Fiche de renseignement*, P.R.G., Blida, May 29, 1957. This was a copy of a talk that the Imam of Bou Arfa mosque was supposed to give at the Friday prayer of May 17, 1957.

28. Quoted in Hamon, *Objectif population*, 219.

29. SHAT, 1H2641D1, *Action sur les milieux féminins*, 9.

30. SHAT, 1H2461D1, *Fiche* No. 1019/CAB/Mil./10, September 20, 1958. See also 1H2461D1 *Fiche* dated September 5, 1958, from the military cabinet in Algiers. No number.

31. See also Jacque Massu, *Le torrent et la digue. Alger du 13 Mai aux barricades* (Paris: Plon, Editions du Rocher, 1972), 329. The Massus also adopted a young Algerian girl, Malika, whom they converted to Catholicism. A picture of the girl sporting a chain with a cross pendant appears in the book. The emphasis placed on music was part of the propaganda technique of combining sound with image in order to influence the psyche.

32. SHAT, 1H2461D1, *Renseignment ambiance. Vu côté femmes (dans le quartier du sous-secteur d'Hussein Dey)*, August 22, 1960.

33. SHAT, 1H2461D1, *Fiche de renseignements*, 10e Région Militaire, 5e Bureau, August 23, 1958.

34. SHAT, 1H2461D1, *Message*, No. 1118/RM.10/5/EMS from 10e R.M. Command, 5e. Bureau.

35. Jean-Luc Einaudi, *La ferme Améziane. Enquête sur un centre de torture pendant la guerre d'Algérie* (Paris: L'Harmattan, 1991), 105–7. Monique Améziane was Mouloud Améziane's half-sister. Their father (whose real last name was Ben Hamadi) had been bachagha of the city of Constantine. Mouloud had given his

father's farm to the FLN before it was turned into a torture center by French troops. See p. 104.

36. Ibid., 106.

37. Frantz Fanon, *A Dying Colonialism* (New York: Grove Press, 1967), esp. chapter, "Algeria Unveiled."

38. See SHAT, 1H2461D1, *La femme musulmane*, 54–55.

39. SHAT, 1H3434D1, *Note de Service: Compte rendu de la fouille du village de Sidi Youcef*, No. 658/9oRIMA/2/3/S, February 28, 1959, 5.

40. 1H3434D1. *Note sur l'attitude et le comportement des unités*, No. 241/Z.E.A./S, March 3, 1959, 2. The advocate of this attitude, General Faure, had in January 1959 warned against acts that caused damage to the reputation of the army. He berated the fearful [*timorées*] units in ZEA [Zone Est Algérois] and argued that the adversary avoided units he deemed tough and attacked the softer ones.

41. Pierre Leulliette, *St. Michael and the Dragon: Memoirs of a Paratrooper* (Boston: Houghton Mifflin Co., 1964), 314–16.

42. Like this anonymous woman, in February 1960, Djamila Boupacha, accused of having placed a bomb in a café, noticed some "turned" Algerian men among her torturers. Beauvoir, *Djamila Boupacha*, 33–34.

43. Leulliette, *St. Michael and the Dragon*, 316.

44. Vidal-Naquet, *Les crimes de l'armée française*, 112.

45. SHAT, IH1100D1, Centre d'Instruction Pacification et Contre-Guérilla, X° Région Militaire, Principes généraux d'action sychologique, 2. The text describes the FLN psychological action.

46. SHAT, 1H2537D3, *L'opération "Jumelles,"* Note liminaire, 8.

47. See a virulent racist article by A. Fourier, P. Michaux, and J. Thiodet, "Aspects pariculiers à la criminalité algérienne," *Alger Université* (June 1957): 5.

48. Rotman, *L'ennemi intime*, 108, 78.

49. Ibid., 77.

50. Esméralda, *Un été en enfer*, 69.

59. Mouloud Feraoun, *Journal* (Alger: ENAG Editions, 1998), 232. The event was confirmed by the mother superior of the White Sisters Order on January 14, 1957. See p. 235.

52. Ibid., 232, 233.

53. Ibid., 366.

54. Ahmed Bencherif, *L'aurore des mechtas* (Alger: Société Nationale d'Edition et de Diffusion, 1969), 18.

55. Leulliette, *St. Michael and the Dragon*, 178–79.

56. Jauffret, *Soldats en Algérie*, 299.

57. Leulliette, *St. Michael and the Dragon*, 14.

58. Feraoun, *Journal*, 367, 410, 178–79.

59. Ibid., 366.

60. Ibid.

61. Bencherif, *L'aurore des mechtas*, 61–62.

62. Vidal-Naquet, *Les crimes de l'armée française*, 112.

63. I was denied access to a file on military bordellos during the Algerian war

by the Service Historique de l'Armée de Terre, and thus could not ascertain the fact.

64. See Marnia Lazreg, *The Eloquence of Silence: Algerian Women in Question* (New York: Routledge, 1994), 54.

65. Interviews quoted in Florence Beaugé, *Algérie: Une guerre sans gloire*, 160–61, 156.

66. Ibid., 162.

67. Branche, *La torture et l'armée*, 309. see also Djamila Amrane Minne, *La guerre d'Algérie (1954–1962)*, 310.

68. This was a ritual question that Djamila Boupacha was also asked by the president of the Commission for the Safeguard of Individual Rights and Liberties when he interviewed her pursuant to her complaint about having been tortured. Beauvoir, Djamila Boupacha, 109 (handwritten letter), 120–21.

69. Ighilahriz, *Algérienne*, 98–104, 111.

70. Ibid., 112.

71. Ibid., 116–17.

72. Ibid., 257–58.

73. Beaugé, *Une guerre sans gloire*, 242.

74. Beauvoir, *Djamila Boupacha*, 51, 24.

75. After her torture, Boupacha was also subjected to psychological action. The captain who directed her torture took her for a walk during which a prearranged meeting with an agent took place. Subsequently, the agent exhorted Boupacha to keep out of trouble, and offered his friendship to her. Ibid., 37.

76. Ibid., 140. The doctors feared for their own safety should they attribute faded scars (their examination of the victim took place five months after she had been tortured) to torture.

77. Ibid., 142, 49. The doctor used the French expression "troubles des règles qui sont de nature constitutionnelle," which could mean "disturbances due to menses," or inherent to the victim's constitution.

78. Ibid.

79. Boupacha's cellmate, Zineb Laroussi, a common prisoner was promised (and given) release from jail in exchange for testifying that she had not seen Boupacha coming from the torture chamber unconscious and bleeding. She had also testified that Boupacha had not talked to her about her torture, and had been cheerful as well as engaged in banter with soldiers. Laroussi recanted several months later before a judge in the city of Caen to which Boupacha's trial had been transferred, and later in Algiers, before a military tribunal. Ibid., 184–85, 106.

80. *Dossier sur la torture et la Répression en Algérie*, 15, 28.

81. Esméralda, *Un été en enfer*, 28, 64.

82. Andrée Dore-Audibert, *Des françaises d'Algérie dans la guerre de libération: des oubliées de l'histoire* (Paris: Karthala, 1995), 89.

83. See ibid., 33, 36–40, 144–56, 38.

84. Ighilahriz, *Algérienne*, 73–74.

85. Esméralda, *Un été en enfer*, 26, 73.

86. Vittori, *On a torturé en Algérie*, 125.

87. Outside the torture chamber, raping women became routine. A longtime

lawyer of Algerian women arrested by the police or the military, Gisèle Halimi, noted: "I cannot imagine a woman being arrested and interrogated who was not also raped. . . . all those I defended had been. Branche, *La torture et l'armée*, 304.

88. Rotman, *L'Ennemi Intime*, 217, 309.

89. Jauffret, *Soldats en Algérie 1954–1962*, 299.

90. Andrew Orr, *Ceux d'Algérie* (Paris: Payot, 1990), 67; Branche, *La torture et l'armée*, 309.

91. Mauss-Copeaux, *Les appelés d'Algérie*, 156.

92. Dore-Audibert, *Des françaises d'Algérie*, 48–51. Some of the social workers refused to cooperate in a police operation that would have jeopardized their standing in the Algerian community. Others wrote a petition of support to the government, See pp. 53–54.

93. The Arabic plural of Hammam is Hammamat.

94. Leulliette, *St. Michael and the Dragon*, 282.

95. Vidal-Naquet, *Les crimes de l'armée française*, 36.

96. Ibid., 112.

97. Vittori, *On a torturé en Algérie*, 169.

98. Bellahcène Bali, *Mémoires d'un jeune combattant de l'A.L.N. à Tlemcen et sa région: 1956–1958* (Beyrouth: Al Achraf, 1999), 176–77, 184, 173.

99. Figures used in SHAT, 1H2461D1, *La femme musulmane*, 45.

100. SHAT, 1H2461D1, *Action sur les milieux féminins*, 13.

CHAPTER 7
CONSCIENCE, IMPERIAL IDENTITY, AND TORTURE

1. It goes without saying that the troops had different attitudes towards the war. There were also soldiers who refused to fight, or disobeyed orders to execute prisoners. Nevertheless, the bulk of the troops did fight, making Jean-Charles Jauffret's judgment that the war "was more tolerated than accepted" problematic in its implications. It sanitizes the war and fits in with the view that abuses committed during the war were isolated incidents attributed to a few soldiers. See Jauffret, *Soldats en Algérie*, especially, 45.

2. Mauss-Copeaux, *Appelés en Algérie*, 20, 21.

3. Orr, *Ceux d'Algérie*, 127, 183.

4. Mauss-Copeaux, *Appelés en Algérie*, 233.

5. Morandais, *L'honneur est sauf*, 221–96.

6. R. P. Louis Delarue, *Avec les Paras* (Paris: Nouvelles Editions Latines, 1960), 192.

7. Mauss-Copeaux, *Appelés en Algérie*, 247.

8. Ibid., 244.

9. Robin, *Escadrons de la mort*, 61.

10. Ibid., 10.

11. Ibid.

12. Salan, *Mémoires*, 441.

13. Robin, *Escadrons de la mort*, 11.

14. Vittori, *On a torturé en Algérie*, 213, 217, 209.

15. See Mauss-Copeaux, *Appelés en Algérie*, 195. One man is reported to have

said: "Those who sent me over there made me an accomplice to the deaths of numerous Algerians. I will never forgive them."

16. Orr, *Ceux d'Algérie*, 196, 203, 198, 204, 205.

17. Mauss-Copeaux, *Appelés en Algérie*, 74, 164, 165.

18. Ibid., 66.

19. Rotman, *L'ennemi intime*, 12.

20. Mauss-Copeaux, *Appelés en Algérie*, 256, 251.

21. Ibid.

22. Ibid., 272, 261, 259.

23. *Le Procès des Généraux Challe et Zeller. Texte intégral des débats* (Paris: Nouvelles Editions Latines, 1961), 23, 45, 49.

24. Rotman, *L'ennemi intime*, 153.

25. Ibid., 88–93, 252.

26. Ibid., 158.

27. François Mauriac, *Bloc notes* (Paris: Editions du Seuil, 1993), vol. 1, 1952–1957, 536.

28. SHAT, 1H2486/1, "Le cas de conscience du Soldat Liechti," *Libération*, March 9, 1959; see also "Alban Liechti emprisonné en Algérie," *L'Humanité*, March 13, 1959.

29. Comité pour la paix en Algérie, *Et ils pacifièrent Alger* . . . (Chênée, 1959), 22–38, 30.

30. The "battle of Algiers" was not a "battle" but a military operation mounted against the population of the Casbah. See Henri Alleg, *Retour sur la question* (Bruxelles, Belgique: Editions Aden 2006), 19.

31. Saadi Yacef, *Souvenirs de la bataille d'Alger* (Paris: René Julliard, 1962), 17–19.

CHAPTER 8
THE CHRISTIAN CHURCH AND ANTISUBVERSIVE WAR

1. All Souls' Day is followed by the Day of the Dead (*La Fête des Morts*) on November 2. A notable historian of the Algerian War titled the first of his four volumes, *Les fils de la toussaint* (The Sons of All Souls' Day). See Yves Courrière, *La guerre d'Algérie—I Les fils de la toussaint* (Paris: Fayard, 1969).

2. Hacène Ouandjeli, *Flash sur la révolution* (Alger: ENAL, 1984), 38.

3. André Nozière, *Algérie: Les Chrétiens dans la guerre* (Paris: Editions Cana, 1979), 23. See also *Le chanoine Jules Tournier. La conquête religieuse de l'Algérie 1830–1845. La nouvelle église d'Afrique* (Paris: Plon, 1930), 50. Tournier writes that on July 6, 1830, Count de Bourmont, head of the invading expedition, "planted the cross on the highest elevation of the city [wall]. And thus ended the great drama that for several centuries pitted Christian Europe against the Africa of Muslim pirates," 49, 23.

4. During the war, Abbot Victor Vaugarni, chief chaplain in Algiers, is said "to have thrown more blessed water on General Massu, ardent advocate of torture, than on the walls of the chapel" he dedicated to paratroopers on May 13, 1958. Given their historical context, these were not isolated cases of religious conscience gone awry. See Nozière, p. 129.

5. Jewish communities had been assimilated into the European population with which they identified politically after citizenship was extended to them by the Crémieux Decree of 1871.

6. See chapters 3 and 6.

7. In the 1800s missionary activity was frowned upon by the military, fearing it might cause further unrest. Monsignor Charles Lavigerie, fought his way into missionary work, founding the order of the White Fathers. However, conversions, except of orphans of the famines of 1865–66 and scattered villagers in mountain villages in *Grande Kabylie* met a strong resistance from the native population.

8. Nozière, *Algérie*, 29, and fn. 17; 28, 35.

9. Christiane Alix, "Le Vatican et la Décolonisation," in Marcel Merle, ed. *Les églises chrétiennes et la décolonisation*. Cahiers De La Fondation Nationale Des Sciences Politiques (Paris: Librairie Armand Colin, 1967 (Paris: Armand Colin, 1967), 17, fn. 3.

10. The law did not apply to the colonies.

11. On the extreme right was Cité Catholique, and on the left, Témoignage Chrétien.

12. Nozière, *Algérie*, 56, 76, 236. The FLN critique sought to reveal that Monsignor Duval was still playing colonial politics, although changing times required him to transcend local constraints and embrace a future without colonial rule.

13. Ibid., 239.

14. François Méjean, *Le Vatican contre la France d'Outre Mer* (Paris: Librairie Fischbacher, 1957), 87.

15. Nozière, *Algérie*, 100.

16. Méjean, *Le Vatican*, 167.

17. Nozière, *Algérie*, 111, 109, 100.

18. Ibid., 123. Xavier Boniface points out that the chaplaincy was the first to have been organized on both ends of conscripts' itinerary, in France and in Algeria.

19. Nozière, *Algérie*, 123.

20. Ibid., 124. Nozière charges that it had engaged in suppressing the voices of the troops.

21. Ibid., 125, 126.

22. Le Cardinal Feltin: "Hommage à l'armée française," *Itinéraires*, no. 15 (July–August 1957): 122–23. Text of a speech made by the cardinal.

23. Morandais, *L'honneur est sauf*, 93.

24. Ibid., 93.

25. The essay was published by *Alger-Université*, the Pied-Noir paper of the General Association of Algiers Students in June 1957, pp. 4, 6. Most of the essay was also reprinted in the powerful *Témoignage Chrétien* on June 21, 13. Excerpts with a commentary also appeared in Morandais, *L'honneur est sauf*, 342–46.

26. Delarue pointed out that the document was meant for internal use, although his subsequent agreement to have it circulated with minor revisions casts doubt on his intentions.

27. See Morandais, *L'honneur est sauf*, 93.

28. Ibid. See also *Témoignage Chrétien*, 13.

29. Alger-Université, "Réflexions d'un prêtre sur le terrorisme urbain," June 1957, p. 4.

30. For Pius XII's problematic pronouncements about decolonization, see Allix, "Le Vatican et la decolonization," 83.

31. Delarue argued that Pius XII's Christmas message liberated him from the "the lies inherent in the pseudo-Christian language of capitulation, and of this false religion of emasculated men." *Alger-Université*, 4.

32. Morandais, *L'honneur est sauf*, 343. Delarue uses the euphemism "information" for interrogation under torture that must be "conducted."

33. *Témoignage Chrétien*, June 21, 1957, 13; Morandais, *L'honneur est sauf*, 345.

34. Delarue did not contemplate the possibility of torture resulting in the death of the innocent, except in alluding by way of comparison to the death penalty sometimes being mistakenly ordered against the wrong person.

35. Morandais, *L'honneur est sauf*, 345.

36. Nozière, *Algérie*, 132–33. Monsignor Badré wrote that Delarue had shown his "notes" to Massu. According to Xavier Boniface, the text was disseminated outside the army in April 1957 in Algiers, Lyon, Grenoble, and Paris. See *L'aumônerie militaire française de 1945 à 1962*, 504.

37. Quoted in Nozière, *Algérie*, 133, 134.

38. Boniface, *L'aumônerie militaire*, 506, 507.

39. Ibid., 508, 509.

40. See "Le Dossier Jean Muller," *Les Cahiers du Témoignage Chrétien*, no. 38 (September 1957): 1–29.

41. Nozière, *Algérie*, 135.

42. Morandais, *L'honneur est sauf*, 202, 221, 280.

43. Henri Peninou, *Réflexions sur les devoirs du soldat. Notre vie chrétienne en Algérie*, May 1959, Présenté par Jean-Charles Jauffret (Montpellier: UMR 5609 du CNRS-ESID, 1998): 47–48. Jauffret did not display sensitivity to the racial implications of his own statement about racism among the troops. He wrote: "these men of color" had been mistreated by "paratroopers with a very high IQ." See fn. 2, p. 47, 26.

44. Ibid., 28, 54, 58, 48–49. See fn 1, p. 48, 51. Again, in a footnote, Jauffret evinces a strong desire to interpret the text as meaning that the FLN had never controlled the entire country, and thus pacification signified the "conquest" of the population. These were the precepts of the theorists of revolutionary war, which Jauffret made his. See fn. 1.

45. Ibid., 55, 62, 63.

46. Nozière, *Algérie*, 146.

47. SHAT, 1H2486/1, "La lettre aux Evêques," *France Observateur*, April 12, 1959; "Monsignor Badré's Letter to Military Chaplains," *La France Catholique*, May 10, 1959; see also clippings from other newspapers in the same folder.

48. Nozière, *Algérie*, 14; Boniface, *L'aumônerie militaire*, 510–11. The designation "Green Document" comes from the color of the folder containing the text entitled "A Study of Moral Behavior in Revolutionary War." Ibid., 510.

49. Morandais, *L'honneur est sauf*, Annex 4, 351, 352.

50. Ibid., 353.

51. SHAT, 1H2486/1, "Monsignor Badré's Letter to Military Chaplains," *La France Catholique*, May 10, 1959. See also clippings from other newspapers in the same folder.

52. Morandais, *L'honneur est sauf*, 353–54.

53. Nozière, *Algérie*, 141. It must be noted that Morandais did not reproduce this passage in his excerpt of the Green Document. Because the provision denied all the principles that the document harnessed against torture, it was dropped from official documents and statements emanating from the chaplaincy made later on.

54. Ibid.

55. Ibid., 166–70. As the war continued, Protestant missions were sent from France to provide a range of social services to the poor in shantytowns. A schism took place at Boufarik, near Algiers, as a result of a clash between Pastor Tartar, committed to keeping Algeria French through religious understanding, and the rest of the Protestant community leery of his method. Tartar, an orientalist, founded in July 1959 the Union of Believers, open to Muslims, Christians, and Jews, in the hope that true "brotherhood" might be achieved under the political aegis of France (p. 180). He consequently decided to start a new church, the Eglise Protestante d'Algérie (p. 181).

56. Ibid., 207–13.

57. Garrigou-Lagrange, "Intégrisme et national-catholicisme," 521. The double-entendre of the concept "cité (city) helped to conflate the city of God with the secular city.

58. La Cité Catholique, *Pour qu'il règne* (Paris: Cité Catholique, 1959), 697.

59. Quoted in Garrigou-Lagrange, "Intégrisme et national-catholicisme," 536.

60. La Cité Catholique, 700. On Catholic action see Général de Cathelineau, "L'Action Catholique," *Itinéraires*, no. 15 (July–August 1957): 2–16.

61. Boniface, *L' aumônerie militaire*, 480. See also Robin, *Escadrons de la mort*, 160–61.

62. Boniface, *L'aumônerie militaire*, 480. Robin estimates that out of four hundred cells, two hundred were in the military.

63. Paret, *French Revolutionary Warfare*, 109.

64. Robin, *Escadrons de la mort*, 158–64.

65. Etienne Fouilloux, "Ordre social chrétien et Algérie française," in François Bédarida and Etienne Fouilloux, eds., *La guerre d'Algérie et les Chrétiens*, Cahiers de l'Institut d'Histoire du Temps Présent, no. 9 (October 1988): 68, 74.

66. La Cité Catholique, *Pour qu'il règne*, 700. See also Ousset's letter to *Itinéraires*, no. 17 (November 1957): 116–18.

67. Quoted in Garrigou-Lagrange, "Intégrisme et national-catholicisme," 522.

68. See Monsignor Bressolles, "Guerre juste et croisade," *Verbe*, no. 86 (October 1957): 72–79. See also no. 81 (January–March 1957).

69. Garrigou-Lagrange, "Intégrisme et national-catholocisme,"25, 519, 537.

70. Robin, *Escadrons de la mort*, 160–61, 515.

71. Quoted in Ibid., 515.

72. *Itinéraires*, no. 18 (December 1957): 103.

73. *Itinéraires*, no. 15 (July–August 1957): 140.

74. *Itinéraires*, no. 11, (March 1957): 101–2.

75. Quoted in Fouilloux, "Ordre social chrétien," 72.

76. *Itinéraires*, no. 11 (March 1957): 102; and Fouilloux, "Ordre social chrétien," 76–77.

77. With the exception of the group of Catholics who directed the review *Economie et Humanisme*, and those at *Témoignage Chrétien*, little understanding of the colonial causes of the war was evinced.

78. Garrigou-Lagrange's notion that Catholic fundamentalist nationalism was adept at using Catholicism not as religious faith but as a (political) ideology is correct.

79. The fact that Muslims have tortured other Muslims does not detract from the added religious dimension that torture acquires when a Christian priest condones its use against people of a different faith perceived as former competitors, and present enemies.

80. Nozière, *Algérie*, 216–22, 226.

81 The Chaulets trained Algerian students headed for the *maquis* in first aid.

82. Interview in Bédarida and Fouilloux, eds., *La guerre d'Algérie et les chrétiens*, 149. Christian members of the *Association de la Jeunesse Algérienne pour l'Action Sociale* or AJAAS also shared Berenguer's and Mandouze's sense of outrage at the inequities of the colonial system.

83. Charles-Robert Ageron raises the question and, after a hurried discussion, concludes that the religious factor cannot be ignored. See "Une guerre religieuse?" in Bédarida and Fouilloux, eds. *La guerre d'Algérie et les chrériens*, 27–29.

84. Cornélius, "Morale et guerre révolutionnaire," *Verbe*, no. 90 (February 1958): 87–88.

85. Nozière, *Algérie*, 154, 161.

86. Merle, *Les églises chrétiennes et la décolonisation*. Merle notes that this is a tradition of the Catholic Church.

87. Audiotape of an interview carried out on December 8, 1997. SHAT, 3K28.

CHAPTER 9
FANON, SARTRE, AND CAMUS

1. See, among others, Jean-Pierre Rioux and Jean-François Sirinelli. *La guerre d'Algérie et les intellectuels français* (Paris: Editions Complexe, 1991); James D. Lesueur, *Uncivil War: Intellectuals and Identity Politics during the Decolonization of Algeria*, 2nd ed. (London, Lincoln: University of Nebraska, 2005).

2. Henry Alleg, *La question*, 107.

3. Ibid., 86.

4. Ibid., 84, 79.

5. Ibid., 84, 177–78.

6. Ibid., 44, 43.

7. Ibid., 83, 80.

8. Ibid., 83. Fanon's conception of decolonization inspired a vast literature. For an analysis of various trends among his followers and critics, see Benita Parry, "Problems in Current Theories of Colonial Discourse," *Oxford Literary Review*, vol. 9, 1–2 (1987): 27–58; Henry Louis Gates, Jr., "Critical Fanonism," *Critical Inquiry* 17 (Spring 1991), 457–70. See also Hussein Abdilahi Bulhan, *Frantz Fanon and the Psychology of Oppression* (New York: Plenum Press, 1985); and Lewis R. Gordon, *Fanon and the Crisis of European Man: An Essay on Philosophy and the Human Sciences* (New York: Routledge, 1995).

9. Frantz Fanon, *The Wretched of the Earth*, 35–58.

10. Ibid., 94, 54.

11. Jean-Paul Sartre, *Situations V. Colonialism and Neo-Colonialism*, "Les damnés de la terre" (Paris: Gallimard, 1964), 181. This essay was originally published as the preface to F. Fanon, *The Wretched of the Earth*, 7–31.

12. Sartre, *Situations V*, 181, 180, 179, 27.

13. Ibid., 58.

14. For a discussion of the religious reformist movement, see Ali Merad, *Le réformisme musulman en Algérie de 1925 à 1940* (Paris: Mouton, 1967).

15. Sartre, *Situations V*, "Les damnés de la terre," 170.

16. Ibid., 175, 174.

17. Ibid., 187, 189, 190.

18. Ibid., 186, 192.

19. Ibid., 191, 161.

20. See Martha Crenshaw Hutchinson, *Revolutionary Terrorism* (Stanford: Stanford University Press, 1978).

21. Albert Camus, *Réflexions sur le terrorisme*. Texts chosen and introduced by Jacqueline Levi-Valensi, commentaries by Antoine Garapon and Denis Salas (France: Nicolas Philippe, 2002), 47, 48.

22. Albert Camus, *L' homme révolté* (Paris: Gallimard, 1951), 15, especially 35, 48; 358, 292. Camus felt that revolt acquires its full "meaning" only in the West. A thorough analysis of the book is beyond the scope of this book. I am focusing on its implications for the Algerian War.

23. Camus, *Réflexions sur le terrorisme*, 152, 153, 157. Camus was unwilling to accept the Tunisian struggle for independence as anything but "fellaghisme" a neologism that dismissed the struggle as simple banditry. Similarly, although he made a speech on March 15, 1957, in Paris commemorating the first anniversary of the Hungarian uprising against Soviet rule that was published as an introduction to a book by Tibor Meray, he failed to see the similarities between the Hungarians' struggle for freedom and the Algerians'. See "Kadar Has Had His Day of Dread!" in Tibor Meray, *That Day in Budapest, October 23, 1956*, trans. Charles Lam Markmann (New York: Funk and Wagnalls, 1969), 3–11.

24. Camus, *L'homme révolté*, 32, 33.

25. Albert Camus, *Actuelles III: Chroniques algériennes 1939–1958* (Paris: Gallimard, 1958), 19–20.

26. Albert Camus, *Le mythe de Sisyphe. Essai sur l'absurde* (Paris: Gallimard, 1942), 87.

27. *Le Monde*, December 14, 1957, quoted in Wolf Albes, *Jean Brune et Albert*

Camus (Friedburg: Editions Atlantis, 1999), 55. Before the row provoked by this sentence, Camus wrote *Le Monde* a letter in which he pointed out that he felt closer to the Algerian student than to many Frenchmen "who speak about Algeria but do not know her. *He* knew what he was talking about. His face revealed no hatred, but despair and misfortune. I share his misfortune; his face is that of my country." Perhaps, but the Stockholm speech clearly indicated that they did not share the same mother. See p. 56.

28. See Albert Camus, *Neither Victim nor Executioner* (Chicago: World Without Wall Publications, 1972).

CHAPTER 10
MORALIZING TORTURE

1. Michael Walzer, "Political Action: The Problem of Dirty Hands," in Sanford Levinson, ed., *Torture* (New York: Oxford University Press, 2005), 63.

2. Walzer, "Political Action," 64–65.

3. See Lefebvre, *Guy Mollet face à la torture.*

4. See Manceron and Remaoun, *D'une rive à l'autre*, 145. The authors argue that the most lethal bomb before the Battle of Algiers began was detonated by French policemen on November 8, 1956.

5. George Wilhelm Fiedrich Hegel, 1770–1831, *Hegel's Philosophy of Right*, trans. T. M. Knox (Oxford: Clarendon Press, 1945), 86–104.

6. Hegel, *Philososphy of Right*, 79, 82, 84.

7. Ibid., especially 92–98.

8. Ibid.

9. Ibid., 98.

10. See, among others, William Outwaite, *New Philosophies of Social Science: Realism, Hermeneutics and Critical Theory* (New York: St. Martin's Press, 1987).

11. Hegel, *The Philosophy of Right*, 98.

12. Walzer, "Political Action," 72.

13. Positive references to Camus's work should take into account the philosophy of the absurd that informs it. Without it, the political views he expresses in a theatrical form appear normative when they could just as well be taken as embodiments of a philosophy that is "morally" dubious.

14. Henry Schue, "Torture," in Sanford Levinson, ed., *Torture*, 57.

15. Søren Kierkegaard, *Fear and Trembling, Repetition* (Princeton: Princeton University Press, 1983), 54 (para. 105), 60.

16. http://www.theatlantic.com/doc/200310/bowden, 2006. *Atlantic Monthly* (October 2003). Retrieved October 17, 2006.

17. Elshtain, "Reflection on the Problem of 'Dirty Hands,'" 85.

18. See John Conroy, *Unspeakable Acts, Ordinary People* (New York: Alfred A. Knopf, 2000), 6.

19. Aussaresses, *Services spéciaux*, 156.

20. Discussion with the author, June 16, 2006. Staouéli (Algeria).

21. Esméralda, *Un été en enfer*, 10.

22. Title of Esméralda's book, *Un été en enfer.*

23. Jean Bethke Elshtain, *Just War against Terror: The Burden of American Power in a Violent World* (New York: Basic Books, 2004), 27, 162, 26, 44.

24. Elshtain, "Reflections on the Problem of 'Dirty Hands,'" 83.

25. J. Vialatoux, *La répression et la torture* (Paris: Les Editions Ouvrières, 1957), 129.

26. Ibid., 85, 79.

27. See Alan Dershowitz, "Tortured Reasoning," in Sanford Levinson, ed., 263.

28. Michael Ignatieff, *The Lesser Evil: Political Ethics in an Age of Terror* (Princeton: Princeton University Press, 2004), 140.

29. Carl Schmitt, *Political Theology: Four Chapters on the Concept of Sovereignty*, trans. George Schwab (Chicago: University of Chicago Press, 2005), 14.

30. Giorgio Agamben, *State of Exception* (Chicago: University of Chicago Press, 2005), especially chapter 1.

31. Ibid., 20, 141, 21, 10, 32.

32. Ibid., 8, ix, 12.

33. Vialatoux, *La répression*, 20–21.

34. Ibid., 21.

35. Elshtain passes judgment on Islam and Muslim women but hardly reflects on the significance of invoking Catholic casuistry in justifying the torture of Muslims. See *Just War*, chapters 9, 10. Ignatieff is guilty of a similar bias.

36. See Elaine Scarry's critique of Alan Dershowitz's advocacy of torture warrants: "Five Errors in the Reasoning of Alan Dershowitz," in Sanford Levinson, ed., *Torture*, 281–90.

37. See Edward Peters, *Torture*. Exp. Ed. (Philadelphia: University of Pennsylvania Press, 1996), especially chapter 2.

38. Elshtain, *Just War*, 166.

CHAPTER 11
REPETITIONS: FROM ALGIERS TO BAGHDAD

1. Ahmed Taleb-Ibrahimi, *Mémoires d'un Algérien*, Tome 1: Rêves et épreuves (1932–1965) (Alger: Casbah Editions, 2006), 191–205. For charges of torture, see also Séverine Labat, *Les islamistes algériens* (Paris: Editions du Seuil, 1995), 257.

2. Jacques Vergès, *Lettre ouverte à des amis algériens devenus tortionnaires* (Paris: Albin Michel, 1993), 21, 38, 31.

3. Ahmed Merah, *Le terrorisme judiciaire d'une mafia au pouvoir* (Alger: Editions Merah, 2001), 27–45.

4. It must be noted that violence in Algeria was also committed by groups and individuals that remained anonymous, for reasons such as settling scores, greed, or simply spite.

5. The French generals were tried for the putsch they staged in April 1961. Charges of torture were also made, but ultimately the generals were pardoned.

6. Lahouari Bouhassoune, *Nezzar-Souaïdia. Procès d'une décennie* (Oran: Editions Dar El Gharb, 2002), 37, 45, 48, 57–60.

7. Alberto R. Gonzales, "Memorandum for the President," in Mark Danner,

Torture and Truth: America, Abu Ghraib, and the War on Terror (New York: New York Review of Books, 2004), 83, 84.

8. The Geneva Convention on the Treatment of Prisoners of War, article 38.

9. Gonzales, "Memorandum," 84, 92.

10. Ibid., 85–87. GPW is a shorthand for Geneva Convention III on the Treatment of Prisoners of War. III refers to part III of the text of the Convention.

11. Danner, *Torture and Truth*, 108–10, 112, 155. See also Yoo's defense of torture in his *War by Other Means: An Insider's Account of the War on Terror* (New York: Atlantic Monthly Press, 2006).

12. Esméralda, *Un été en enfer*, 34–40.

13. Danner, *Torture and Truth*, 155.

14. Department of the Army, Field Manual 2.22.3 (FM34–52) (Washington, D.C., September 6, 2006), vi.

34. http://www.fcnl.org/issues/item_print.php?item_id=1860&issue_id=119. Retrieved September 3, 2006, 1–2.

16. Kate Zernike, "Top Republicans Reach an Accord on Detainees," *New York Times*, September 22, 2006.

17. Kate Zernike and Sheryl Gay Stolberg, "Differences Settled in Deal over Detainees," *New York Times*, September 23, 2006.

18. A list of the torture methods used at Abu Ghraib can be found in Mark Danner, *Torture and Truth*, 292.

19. Mark Danner uses the felicitous phrase "shame multiplier." *Torture and Truth*, 19, 23.

GLOSSARY

Centres d'Hébergement — Internment (concentration) camps where prisoners (mostly political prisoners) were sent for the duration of the war. Although their official name was Centres d'Hébergement (lit. Hospitality Centers) they were referred to in common parlance as internment camps.

Dechra — Small village.

Djema'a — Assembly of village notables or elders.

Djounoud — (sing. *Djoundi*) Soldiers.

Douar — Small rural community, word used synonymously with hamlet. Etymologically, it refers to a group of rural houses/families.

Fellaga — Also spelled *Fellagha*. Arabic for "(head) splitter," or bandit. Term borrowed from the Tunisian struggle for independence from France to signify FLN combatant qua bandit.

Gourbi — (plur. *graba*) Poor rural dwelling built with a combination of reeds, mud, wooden beams, and at times corrugated iron sheets.

Harka — (sing. *Harki*) Auxiliary corps of men serving with the French colonial army; they were recruited among rural villagers, and captured FLN combatants after they were subjected to psychological action.

Katiba — Company in the FLN military organization.

Makhzen — (sing. *Makhazni*) Armed guards supplementing soldiers at the SAS.

Maquis — Literally, shrub. Refers to the Resistance movement in France during World War II. Similarly, in Algeria it meant combatants hiding in the mountains. A combatant was also called a *maquisard*.

Mechta — Used during the war interchangeably with *douar*, or hamlet. Original meaning varied with regions. It could mean a rural house surrounded by a garden, or a group of such houses. Original meaning: house where one spent the winter.

Mintaqa — Zone in the FLN military organization.

Moudjahed — Also spelled *Moudjahid*; pl. *moudjahidine*. FLN combatant.

Nahia — Subdivision of *mintaqa* in the FLN military organization.

Pieds-Noirs — Self-attributed nickname referring to French settlers born in Algeria. They included French, Spanish, Italian, and Maltese immigrants to the colony.

Spahis — Originally Turco-Algerian cavalry. Incorporated in colonial military cavalry.

Wilaya — FLN military region. Also means administrative division. Sometimes erroneously spelled *willaya*.

Qism — Sector in FLN military organization.

REFERENCES AND SELECTED BIBLIOGRAPHY

Agamben, Giorgio. *State of Exception*. Translated by Kevin Attell. Chicago and London: Chicago University Press, 2005.
———. *Means Without End. Notes on Politics*. Translated by Vincenzo Binetti and Cesare Casarino. Minneapolis and London: University of Minnesota Press, 2000.
Ageron, Charles-Robert, ed. *L'Algérie des Français*. Paris: Editions du Seuil, 1993.
———. "Complots et purges dans l'armée de libération algérienne." *Vingtième Siècle. Revue d'Histoire*, no. 59–60 (1968): 15–27.
———, ed. *La guerre d'Algérie et les Algériens*. Paris: Armand Colin, 1997.
Ainad Tabet, Radouane. *Le 8 Mai 1945 en Algérie*. Alger: Office des Publications Universitaires, 1985.
Albes, Wolf. *Jean Brune et Albert Camus*. Friedberg: Editions Atlantis, 1999.
Alexander, Martin, Martin Evans and J.F.V. Keiger, eds. *The Algerian War and the French Army, 1954–1962. Experiences, Images, Testimonies*. Houndmills: Palgrave Macmillan, 2002.
Alford, Fred C. *Narcissisms: Socrates, the Frankfurt School, and Psychoanalytic Theory*. New Haven: Yale University Press, 1988.
Alleg, Henri. *La question*. Paris: Les Editions de Minuit, 1961.
———. *Prisonniers de guerre*. Paris: Les Editions de Minuit, 1962.
———. *Mémoire algérienne*. Paris: Stock, 2005.
———. *Retour sur "La question."* Bruxelles: Editions Aden, 2006.
Ambler, John Stewart. *The French Army in Politics 1945–1962*. Columbus: Ohio State University Press, 1996.
Anderson, Benedict. *Imagined Communities: Reflections on the Origins and Spread of Nationalism*. London, New York: Verso, 1991.
Appiah, Kwame Anthony. *The Ethics of Identity*. Princeton: Princeton University Press. 2005.
Argoud, Antoine. *La décadence, l' imposture et la tragédie*. Paris: Arthème Fayard, 1974.
Aron, Raymond. *L'Algérie et la république*. Paris: Plon, 1958.
———. *La tragédie algérienne*. Paris: Plon, 1957.
Asad, Talal. *Formations of the Secular: Christianity, Islam, Modernity*. Stanford: Stanford University Press, 2003.
Aussaresses, Paul Général. *Services spéciaux. Algérie 1955–1957*. Paris: Perrin, 2001. Translated by Robert L. Miller as *The Battle of the Casbah: Counter-Terrorism and Torture*. New York: Enigma Books, 2002–2006.
Azan, Paul Général. *Conquête et Pacification de l'Algérie*. Paris: Librairie de France, 1931.
Bali, Bellahcène. *Mémoires d'un jeune combattant de l'A.L.N à Tlemcen et sa région: 1956–1958*. Beyrouth: Al-Achraf, 1999.

Barkat, Sidi Mohammed. *Des Français contre la terreur d' état (Algérie 1954–1962)*. Paris: Editions Reflex, 2002.

Baudrillard, Jean. *The Transparency of Evil: Essays on Extreme Phenomena*. New York: Verso, 1993.

Beaugé, Florence. *Algérie, une guerre sans gloire*. Alger: Editions Shihab, 2006.

Beauvoir, Simone de, and Gisèle Halimi. *Djamila Boupacha*. Paris: Gallimard, 1962.

Bédarida, François and Etienne Fouilloux, eds. *La guerre d'Algerie et les chrétiens*. Cahiers de l'Institut d'Histoire du Temps Présent, no. 9 (October 1988).

Benabdellah, Saïd. *La justice du F.L.N. pendant la lutte de libération*. Alger: Société Nationale d' Edition et de Diffusion, 1982.

Benchérif, Ahmed. *L'aurore des mechtas*. Alger: SNED, 1969.

Benkhedda, Benyoucef. *Alger, capitale de la résistance 1956–1957*. Alger: Editions Horma, 2002.

Benzine, Abdelhamid. *Journal de marche*. Alger: Editions ANEP, 2002.

———. *Lambèse*. Alger: Editions ANEP, 2001.

Berque, Jacques. *L'Islam au défi*. Paris: Gallimard, 1980.

Blatt, Deborah. "Recognizing Rape as a Method of Torture," *NYU Review of Law and Social Change*, no. 19 (1991–1992): 821–865.

Bois, Jean-Pierre. *Bugeaud*. Paris: Arthème Fayard, 1997.

Boisson-Pradier, Jean. *L'église et l'Algérie*. Paris: Etudes et Recherches Historiques, n.d.

Bollardière, Général Jacques Pâris de. *Bataille d'Alger. Bataille de l'homme*. Paris: Desclée de Brouver, 1972.

Bonnet Gabriel. *Les guerres insurrectionnelles et révolutionnaires de l'Antiquité à nos jours*. Paris: Payot, 1958.

Bosworth, William. *Catholicism and Crisis in Modern France: French Catholic Groups at the Threshold of the Fifth Republic*. Princeton: Princeton University Press, 1962.

Boumalit Djemil. *Du mystère de la tragédie de Melouza à l'abomination de Sakiet Sidi Youssef*. Tunis: Editions Bouslama, n.d.

Boumaza, Béchir, et al. *La gangrène*. Alger: Rahma, 1992.

Bourdel, Philippe. *Le livre noir de la guerre d'Algérie. Français et Algériens 1945–1962*. Paris: Plon, 2003.

Branche, Raphaëlle. *La torture et l'armée pendant la guerre d'Algérie 1954–1962*. Paris: Gallimard, 2001.

———. "Des viols pendant la guerre d'Algérie." *Vingtième Siècle. Revue d'Histoire*, no. 75 (Juillet–Septembre 2002): 123–132.

———. "Entre droit humanitaire et intérêts politiques: Les missions Algériennes du CICR." *Revue Historique*, no. 609 (January–March 1999): 101–125.

Brison, Susan J. *Aftermath: Violence and the Remaking of the Self*. Princeton: Princeton University Press, 2002.

Bruge, Colonel André. *Guerre psychologique. Le poison rouge. Guerre sans frontières*. Nice, 1969.

Bulhan, Hussein Abdilahi, *Frantz Fanon and the Psychology of Oppression*. New York: Plenum Press, 1985.

Camus, Albert. *Neither victims nor Executioners*. Chicago: World Without War Publications, 1972.

———. *Actuelles III: Chroniques Algériennes 1939–1958*. Paris: Gallimard, 1958.

———. *Lettres à un ami allemand*. Paris: Gallimard, 1945.

———. *Réflexions sur le terrorisme*. Text selected and introduced by Jacqueline Levi-Valensi, commentary by Antoine Garapon et Denis Salas. France: Nicolas Philippe, 2002.

———. *L'homme révolté*. Paris: Gallimard, 1951. Translated by Anthony Bower under the title *Rebel*. Harmondsworth: Penguin Books, 1971.

Card, Claudia. *The Atrocity Paradigm: A Theory of Evil*. Oxford: Oxford University Press, 2002.

Carlier, Omar. *Entre nation et jihad. Histoire sociale des radicalismes algériens*. Paris: Presses de La Fondation Nationale des Sciences Politiques, 1995.

Cassirer, Ernst. *The Myth of the State*. New Haven: Yale University Press, 1961.

Chakotin, Serge. *The Rape of the Masses*. London: George Routledge and Sons, 1940.

Charles, Pierre, Joseph Folliet, Pierre Lorson, and Ernest Van Campenhout. *Racisme et catholicisme*. Paris: Casterman, 1939.

Clarke, Jackie "Engineering a New Order in the 1930s: The Case of Jean Coutrot," *French Historical Studies* 24, no. 1 (winter 2001): 63–86.

Clausewitz, Carl Von. *On War*. Edited and translated by Michael Howard and Peter Paret. Princeton: Princeton University Press, 1984

Colley, Linda. *Captives: Britain, Empire and the World, 1600–1850*. New York: Anchor Books, 2004.

Collot, Claude. *Les institutions de l'Algérie durant la période coloniale (1830–1962)*. Paris: Editions du CNRS, 1987; Alger: Office des Publications Universitaires, 1987.

Comité Pour la Paix en Algérie. . . . *Et ils pacifièrent Alger . . . Chênée, 1959*.

Commandant Azzedine. *Et Alger ne brûla pas*. Paris: Editions Stock, 1980.

———. *On nous appelait fellaghas*. Paris: Stock, 1976.

Conger, Y. "Mentalité de droite et intégrisme." *La Vie Intellectuelle* (June 1950): 644–666.

Connelly, Matthew. *A Diplomatic Revolution: Algeria's Fight for Independence and the Origins of the Post–Cold War Era*. New York: Oxford University Press, 2002.

Conroy, John. *Unspeakble Acts, Ordinary People: The Dynamics of Torture*. New York: Alfred A. Knopf, 2000.

Contat, Michel, and Michel Rybalka, eds. *The Writings of Jean-Paul Sartre*. Vol. 2. Evanston, IL: Northwestern University, 1974.

Cooper, Frederick. *Colonialism in Question: Theory, Knowledge, History*. Berkeley and Los Angeles: University of California Press, 2005.

Cornaton, Michel. *Les camps de regroupement et la guerre d'Algérie* (Paris: L'Harmattan, 1967.

Courrière, Yves. *La guerre d'Algérie-II. Le temps des léopards*. Paris: Arthème Fayard, 1969.

———. *La guerre d'Algérie- IV. Les feux du désespoir*. Paris: Arthème Fayard, 1971.

Danner, Mark. *Torture and Truth: America, Abu Ghraib, and the War on Terror*. New York: New York Review of Books, 2004.

Das, Veena, Arthur Kleinman, Mamphele Ramphele, and Pamela Reynolds. *Violence and Subjectivity*. Berkeley: University of California Press, 2000.

Davies, Nicholas. *Ten-Thirty-Three: The Inside Story of Britain's Secret Killing Machine*. Edinburgh: Mainstream Publishing, 1999.

De Gaulle, Charles. *Mémoires*. Paris: Gallimard, 2000.

Derrida, Jacques. *Donner la mort*. Paris: Galilée, 1999.

Descombin, Henry. *Guerre d'Algérie 1959–1960. Le cinquième bureau*. Paris: L'Harmattan, 1994.

Dore-Audibert, Andrée. *Des Françaises d'Algérie dans la guerre de libération: des oubliées de l'histoire*. Paris: Karthala, 1995

Dossier sur la Torture et la Répression en Algérie. "*Nous Accusons.*" Memorandum sent to Mr. René Coty, President of the Republic, and to General de Gaulle, Council President, 1958.

Duverger, Maurice. *Demain, la république*. Paris: René Julliard, 1958.

Einaudi, Jean-Luc. *La bataille de Paris*. Paris: Seuil, 1991.

———. *La ferme Améziane. Enquête sur un centre de torture pendant la guerre d'Algérie*. Paris: L'Harmattan, 1991.

———. *Octobre 1961*. Paris: Fayard, 2001.

El Madani, Tewfik. *Mémoires de combat*. Translated from Arabic by Malika Merabet. Alger: Entreprise Algérienne de Presse, 1989.

Elshtain, Jean Bethke. *Just War against Terror: The Burden of American Power in a Violent World*. New York: Basic Books, 2003.

Evans, Martin. *The Memory of Resistance: French Opposition to the Algerian War (1954–1962)*. Oxford: Berg, 1997.

Faivre, Maurice. *Les archives inédites de la politique algérienne 1958–1962*. Paris: L'Harmattan, 2000.

Fanon, Frantz. *The Wretched of the Earth*. Translated by Constance Farrington. New York: Grove Press, 1963.

———. *A Dying Colonialism*. Translated from the French by Haakon Chevalier. New York: Grove Press, 1967.

Favrelière, Noël. *Le déserteur. Récit*. Paris: J. C. Lattès/Edition Spéciale, 1973.

Favrot, Charles-Henri. *La révolution algérienne*. Paris: Plon, 1959.

Feraoun, Mouloud. *Journal 1955–1962*. Alger: ENAG, 1998.

Ferguson, Niall. *Empire: The Rise and Demise of the British World Order and the Lessons for Global Power*. New York: Basic Books, 2002.

Ferdi, Saïd. *Un enfant dans la guerre*. Paris: Editions du Seuil, 1981.

Ferro, Marc, ed. *Le livre noir du colonialisme*. Paris: Robert Laffont, 2003.

Folliet, Joseph. *Guerre et paix en Algérie. Réflexions d'un homme libre*. Paris: Chronique Sociale, 1958.

Forestier, Patrick. *Confession d'un émir du G.I.A.* In collaboration with Ahmed Salam. Paris: Bernard Grasset, 1999.

Foucault, Michel. *Discipline and Punish: The Birth of the Prison*. Translated from the French by Alan Sheridan. New York: Vintage, 1979.

France, Marie de. *Les lais de Marie de France*. Edited by Karl Warnke. Paris: Librairie Générale Française, 1990.

Freud, Sigmund. *Character and Culture*. Edited by Philip Rieff. New York: Collier Books, 1963.

Gaget, Général Robert. *Commando Georges. Renseignements et combats*. Paris: Grancher, 2000.

Gates, Henry Louis, Jr. "Critical Fanonism" *Critical Inquiry* 17 (Spring 1991), 457–470.

Garrigou-Lagrange, Madeleine. "Intégrisme et national-catholicisme." *Esprit* (November 1959): 515–542.

Gérard, Jean-Louis. *Dictionnaire historique et biographique de la guerre d'Algérie*. Hélette: Editions Jean Curutchet, 2000.

Gérin-Ricard, Lazare de, and Louis Truc. *Histoire de l'Action Française*. Paris: Fournier Valdes, 1949.

Girardet, Raoul. *La société militaire de 1815 à nos Jours*. Paris: Perrin, 1998.

———. *Le nationalisme français 1871–1914*. Paris: Armand Colin, 1966.

———. *Mythes et mythologies politiques*. Paris: Editions du Seuil, 1986.

Gordon, Lewis R. *Fanon and the Crisis of European Man: An Essay on Philosophy and the Human Sciences*. New York: Routledge, 1995.

Gosnell, Jonathan K. *The Politics of Frenchness in Colonial Algeria, 1930–1954*. Rochester, NY: University of Rochester Press, 2002.

Grandmaison, Olivier Le Cour. *Coloniser, exterminer. Sur la guerre et l'état colonial*. Paris: Arthème Fayard, 2005.

Greer, Donald. *The Incidence of Terror during the French Revolution: A Statistical Interpretation*. Cambridge: Harvard University Press, 1935.

Greig, Ian. *Subversion: Propaganda, Agitation and the Spread of the People's War*. London: Tom Stacey, 1973.

Grigore-Muresan, Madalina. *La terreur de l'histoire dans l'imaginaire littéraire du XXe siècle*. Thèse, Université d'Angers, 1998.

Guenaneche, Mohammed. *Le mouvement d'indépendance en Algérie entre les deux guerres (1919–1939)*. Translated from the Arabic by Sid Ahmed Bouali. Alger: Office des Publications Universitaires, 1990.

Guentari, Dr. Mohammed. *Organisation politico-administrative et militaire de la révolution algérienne de 1954 à 1962*. 2 vols. Alger: Office des Publications Universitaires, 2000.

Guilhaume, Jean-François. *Les mythes fondateurs de l'Algérie française*. Paris: l'Harmattan, 1992.

Guillon, Jean-Marie. *Paul-Albert Février. Un historien dans l'Algérie en guerre. Un engagement chrétien 1959–1962*. Preface by Pierre Vidal-Naquet. Postscript by André Mandouze. Paris: Cerf, 2006.

Harbi, Mohammed, and Benjamin Stora. *La guerre d'Algérie 1954–2004. La fin de l'amnésie*. Paris: Robert Laffont, 2004.

Harbi, Mohammed, and Gilbert Meynier. *Le FLN. Documents et histoire 1954–1962*. Paris: Arthème Fayard, 2004.

Hardeman, Hilde. *Coming to Terms with the Soviet Regime*. Dekalb: Northern Illinois University Press, 1994.

Hardt, Michael, and Antonio Negri. *Empire*. Cambridge: Harvard University Press, 2000.

Hardy, Michel, Hervé Lemoine, and Thierry Sarmant. *Pouvoir politique et autorité militaire en Algérie française. Hommes, textes, institutions 1945–1962*. Paris: L'Harmattan/Service Historique de l'armée de Terre, 2002.

Haroun, Ali. *La 7ème Wilaya. La guerre du FLN en France 1954–1962*. Paris: Editions du Seuil, 1986.

Harries, Jill. *Land and Empire in Late Antiquity*. Cambridge: Cambridge University Press, 1999.

Hegel, Georg Wilhelm Friedrich, *Hegel's Philosophy of Right*. Translated by T. M. Knox. Oxford: Oxford University Press, 1945.

Heggoy, Alf Andrew. *Insurgency and Counterinsurgency in Algeria*. Bloomington: Indiana University Press, 1972.

Hillyard, Paddy. *Suspect Community: People's Experiences of the Prevention of Terrorism Acts in Britain*. London, Boulder: Pluto Press, 1993.

Hillyard, Paddy, and Janie Percy-Smith. *The Coercive State*. London: Pinter Publishers, 1988.

Horne, Alistair. *A Savage War of Peace. Algeria 1954–1962*. New York: The Viking Press, 1977.

Ighilahriz, Louisette. *Algérienne. Récit recueilli par Anne Nivat*. Paris: Fayard/Calmann-Lévy, 2001.

Jauffret, Jean-Charles. *Soldats en Algérie. Expériences contrastées des hommes du contingent*. Paris: Editions Autrement, 2000.

Jeanson, Francis. *L'Algérie hors-la-Loi*. Paris: Editions du Seuil, 1955.

Jenkins, Brian. *Nationalism in France: Class and Nation since 1789*. Savage: Barnes and Noble Books, 1990.

Journal of Strategic Studies. "France and the Algerian War 1954–62. Strategy, Operations and Diplomacy." Special Issue. Vol. 25, no. 2 (June 2002).

Jünger, Ernst. *Storm of Steel*. London: Penguin, 1961.

Kaddache, Mahfoud. *Et l'Algérie se libéra 1954–1962*. Paris: EDIF, 2000, 2003.

Kelly, Gail Paradise. *French Colonial Education: Essays on Vietnam and West Africa*. New York: AMS Press, 2000.

Kelly, George Armstrong. *Lost Soldiers: The French Army and the Empire in Crisis, 1947–1962*. Cambridge: MIT Press, 1965.

Khelifa, Laroussi. *Manuel du Militant Algérien*. Vol. 1. Lausanne: La Cité, 1962.

Kierkegaard, Søren. *Fear and Trembling. Repetition*. Edited and translated by Howard V. Hong and Edna H. Hong. Princeton: Princeton University Press, 1983.

Kleinman, Arthur, Veena Das, and Margaret Lock. *Social Suffering*. Berkeley: University of California Press, 1997.

Kristeva, Julia. *Powers of Horror: An Essay on Abjection*. New York: Columbia University Press, 1982.

Labat, Séverine. *Les islamistes algériens*. Paris: Editions du Seuil, 1995.

La Cité Catholique. *Pour qu'il régne*. Paris: Cité Catholique, 1959.

La guerre d'Algérie. Dossier et témoignages réunis et présentés par Patrick Eveno et Jean Planchais. Paris: La Découverte/Le Monde, 1989.

La guerre d'Algérie au miroir des décolonisations françaises. Actes du colloque en l'honneur de Charles-Robert Ageron. Sorbonne, November 2000. Paris: Société Française d'Histoire d'Outre-Mer, 2000.

La répression en Algérie. Document edited by the Mouvement National Judiciaire and the Comité d'Information et d'Action pour la Solution Pacifique des Problèmes d'Afrique du Nord. Paris, 1956.

Lacan, Jacques. *The Four Fundamental Concepts of Psychoanalysis*. Edited by Jacques-Alain Miller. Translated by Alan Sheridan. New York: Norton, 1978.

Lacheroy, Colonel Charles. *De Saint-Cyr à l'action psychologique. Mémoires d'un siècle*. Charles Lavauzelle, 2003.

Lacouture, Jean. *Algérie, la guerre est finie*. Pari: Editions Complexe, 1985.

Lacouture, Jean, and Dominique Chagnolland. *Le désempire. Figures et thèmes de l'anticolonialisme*. Paris: Editions Denoël, 1993.

Lancaster, Donald. *The Emancipation of French Indochina*. London, New York: Oxford University Press, 1961.

Larbi, Lyès. *Dans les geôles de Nezzar*. Paris: Paris-Méditerranée, 2002.

Lasch. Christopher. *The Minimal Self: Psychic Survival in Troubled Times*. New York: W. W. Norton, 1984.

Lauret, Jean-Claude, and Raymond Lasierra. *La torture et les pouvoirs*. Paris: Balland, 1973.

Lazreg, Marnia. *The Eloquence of Silence: Algerian Women in Question*. New York: Routledge, 1994.

Le Bon, Gustave. *La civilisation des Arabes*. Alger: SNED, 1969.

———. *La psychologie des foules*. Paris: Félix Alcan, 1895.

———. *Lois psychologiques de l'évolution des peuples*. Paris: Félix Alcan, 1916.

Le dossier Jean Muller. Les Cahiers du Témoignage Chrétien, no. 38, 1957:1–29.

Le droit à l'insoumission. "Le dossier des 121." Paris: François Maspéro, 1961.

Le Genre Humain. Juger en Algérie 1944–1962. Paris: Seuil, September 1997.

Le Goff, Jacques. *Histoire et mémoire*. Paris: Gallimard, 1988.

Le Procès du Général Raoul Salan. Paris: Nouvelles Editions Latines, 1962.

Le Procès des Généraux Challe et Zeller. Texte Intégral des Débats. Paris: Nouvelles Editions Latines, 1961.

Lea, Henry Charles. *Superstition and Force: Essays on the Wager of Law, the Wager of Battle, the Ordeal, Torture*. Amsterdam: Fredonia Books, 2003. First published in 1892.

Lebjaoui, Mohammed. *Bataille d'Alger ou bataille d'Algérie?* Paris: Gallimard, 1972.

Leclair, Capitaine, M. L. *Disparus en Algérie*. Paris: Jacques Grancher. 1986.

Lefebvre, Denis. *Guy Mollet face à la torture*. Paris: Bruno Leprince, 2001.

Lehureaux, Léon. *Islam et chrétienté en Algérie*. Alger: Imprimerie Baconnier, n.d.

Leonard, Roger Ashley Leonard. *A Short Guide to Clausewitz On War*. New York: G. P. Putnam's Sons, 1967.

Lesueur, James. *Uncivil War: Intellectuals and Identity Politics during the Decolonization of Algeria*. 2nd ed. London, Lincoln: University of Nebraska, 2005.

Leulliette, Pierre. *St. Michael and the Dragon: Memoirs of a Paratrooper*. Boston: Houghton Mifflin, 1964.

Levinson, Sanford. *Torture: A Collection*. Oxford: Oxford University Press, 2004.

Liauzu, Claude, and Gilles Manceron, eds. *La colonisation, la loi et l'histoire*. Paris: Editions Syllepse, 2006.

Lichtheim, George. *Imperialism*. New York: Praeger. 1972.

Lorcin, Patricia M. E. *Imperial Identities: Stereotyping, Prejudice and Race in Colonial Algeria*. London: I. B. Tauris, 1999.

Lyautey, Pierre. *L'Empire Colonial Français*. Paris: Les Editions de France, 1931.

Mahfoufi, Mehenna. *Chants Kabyles de la guerre d'indépendance. Algérie 1954–1962.* Paris: Editions Séguier, 2002.

Maitre, Jacques. "Le catholicisme de droite et la croisade anti-subversive." *Revue Française de Sociologie* II, no. 2 (1961): 106–117.

Major Addresses of Pope Pius XII. Edited by Vincent A. Yzermans. Volume I: *Selected Addresses.* St. Paul: North Central Publishing Company, 1961.

Mamdani, Mahmood. *Imperalism and Fascism in Uganda.* London: Heinemann Educational Books, 1983.

Manceron, Gilles. *Marianne et les colonies. Une introduction à l'histoire coloniale.* Paris: Editions la Découverte, 2003.

Manceron, Gilles, and Hassan Remaoun. *D'une rive à l'autre. La guerre d'Algérie de la mémoire à l'histoire.* Paris: Syros, 1993.

Mann, Michael, *Incoherent Empire.* New York: Verso, 2003.

Massu, Jacques. *Le Torrent et la Digue. Alger du 13 Mai aux Barricades* (Paris: Plon, Editions du Rocher, 1972.

———. *La vraie bataille d'Alger.* Paris: Plon, 1971.

Mattéi, G. M. "Jours Kabyles (Notes d'un rappelé)," *Les Temps Modernes* (July–August 1957), 137–138.

Mauriac, François. *Bloc-Notes.* Vol. I. 1952–1957. Vol. II. 1958–1960. Paris: Editions du Seuil, 1993.

Maurras, Charles. *La contre-révolution spontanée. La recherche, la discussion, l'émeute 1899–1939.* Paris: H. Lardanchet, 1943.

———. *Réflexions sur la révolution de 1789.* Paris: Plon, 1948.

Mauss, Marcel. *The Gift.* New York: Norton, 1967.

Mayer, Arno J. *The Furies: Violence and Terror in the French and Russian Revolutions.* Princeton: Princeton University Press, 2000.

———. *Dynamics of Counter-Revolution in Europe, 1870–1956: An Analytic Framework.* New York: Harper Torchbooks, 1971.

McClintock, Michael. *Instruments of Statecraft: U.S. Guerilla Warfare, Counter-Insurgency, and Counter-Terrorism, 1940–1990.* New York: Pantheon books, 1992.

Mégret, Maurice. *L'action psychologique.* Paris: Arthème Fayard, 1959.

———. *La guerre psychologique.* Paris: Presses Universitaires de France, 1956.

Méjean, Jean. *Le Vatican contre la France d'outre-mer.* Paris: Fischbacher, 1957.

Meray, Tibor. *That Day in Budapest, October 23, 1956.* Translated by Charles Lam Markmann. New York: Funk and Wagnalls, 1969.

Merleau-Ponty, Maurice. *Humanism and Terror.* Boston: Beacon Press, 1969.

Messikh, Mohammed-Sadek. *Les trois dames de la Kasbah de Pierre Loti.* Alger: Editions Raïs, 2006.

Meunier, Gilbert. *Histoire intérieure du FLN 1954–1962.* Paris: Arthème Fayard, 2002.

Meynaud, Jean. "Les militaires au pouvoir." *Revue Française de Sociologie* II, no. 2 (1961): 75–87.

Milgram, Stanley. *Obedience to Authority: An Experimental View.* New York: Harper and Row, 1974.

Miller, John. *Egotopia: Narcissim and the New American Landscape.* Tuscaloosa: University of Alabama Press, 1997.

Minne, Danièle Djamila Amrane. *La guerre d'Algérie (1954–1962). Femmes au combat.* Alger: Editions Rahma, 1993.

Montagon, Colonel André. *Une guerre subversive. La guerre de Vendée.* Paris: La Colombe, 1959.

Moran, Daniel, and Arthur Waldron, eds. *The People in Arms: Military Myth and National Mobilization since the French Revolution.* Cambridge: Cambridge University Press, 2003.

Morandais, Alain Maillard de. *L' honneur est sauf.* Paris: Editions du Seuil, 1990.

Muel-Dreyfus, Francine. *Vichy and the Eternal Feminine.* Translated by Kathleen A. Johnson. London, Durham: Duke University Press, 2001.

Naville, Pierre. "Les arguments sociaux de la stratégie." *Revue Française de Sociologie* II, no. 2 (1961): 4:14.

Nedjadi, Boualem. *Les tortionnaires de 1830 à 1962.* Alger: Editions ANEP, 2001.

Nietzsche, Friedrich. *The Use and Abuse of History.* Indianapolis: Bobbs-Merrill, 1978.

Nora, Pierre. *Lieux de mémoire.* Vol. 2, *La Nation.* Paris: Gallimard, 1984.

Nord, Pierre. *L'intoxication. Arme absolue de la guerre subversive.* Paris: Fayard, 1971.

Nord, Pierre, and Jaques Bergier. *L'actuelle guerre secrète.* Paris: Encyclopédie Planète, 1969.

Nozière, André. *Algérie: Les chrétiens dans la guerre.* Paris: Editions Cana, 1973.

Odell, Jack S. *On Consequentalist Ethics.* Toronto: Wadsworth, 2004.

Onwuanibe, Richard C. *A Critique of Revolutionary Humanism.* St. Louis: Warren H. Green, 1983.

Orr, Andrew. *Ceux d'Algérie. Le silence et la honte.* Paris: Editions Payot, 1990.

Ouandjeli, Hacène. *Flash sur la révolution algérienne.* Alger: ENAL, 1984.

Paret, Peter. *French Revolutionary Warfare from Indochina to Algeria.* New York: Frederick A. Praeger, 1964.

Paret, Peter, ed. with Gordon A. Craig and Felix Gilbert. *Makers of Modern Strategy: From Machiavelli to the Nuclear Age.* Princeton: Princeton University Press, 1986.

Parry, Benita. "Problems in Current Theories of Colonial Discourse," *Oxford Literary Review*, vol. 9, 1–2 (1987): 27–58.

Peninou, Henri, "Réflexions sur les devoirs du soldat. Notre vie chrétienne en Algérie," May 1959. Présenté par Jean-Charles Jauffret. Montpellier: UMR 5609, CNRS-ESID, 1998.

Pervillé, Guy. "La guerre subversive en Algérie: La théorie et les faits." *Relations Internationales*, no. 3 (1975): 171–194.

Peters, Edward. Inquisition. Berkeley: University of California Press, 1989.

———. *Torture.* Philadelphia: University of Pennyslvania Press, 1996.

Planchais, Jean. *L'empire embrasé 1946–1962.* Paris: Denoël, 1990.

———. *Le malaise de l'armée.* Paris: Plon, 1958.

———. "Crise de modernisme dans l'armée." *Revue Française de Sociologie* II, no. 2 (1961): 118–123.

Pouget, Jean. *Bataillon R.A.S. Algérie.* Paris: Presses de la Cité, 1981.

Puy-Montbrun, Déodat. *L'honneur de la guerre.* Paris: Albin Michel, 2002.

Racinet, Jean-Claude. *Les capitaines d'Avril*. Paris: Editions France-Empire, 1976.

Rejali, Darius M. *Torture and Modernity: Self, Society and State in Modern Iran*. Boulder: Westview Press, 1994.

Rioux, Jean-Pierre and Jean-François Sirinelli. *La guerre d'Algérie et les intellectuels français*. Paris: Editions Complexe, 1991.

Robin, Marie-Monique. *Les escadrons de la mort: L'école française*. Paris: La Découverte, 2004.

Rocard, Michel. *Rapport sur les camps de regroupements et autres textes sur la guerre d'Algérie*. Paris: Mille et Une Nuits, 2003.

Rotman, Patrick. *L'ennemi intime*. Paris: Editions du Seuil, 2002.

———, and Bernard Tavernier. *La guerre sans nom: les appelés d'Algérie 1954–1962*. Paris: Editions du Seuil, 1992.

Roy, Jules. *J'accuse le Général Massu*. Paris: Editions du Seuil, 1972.

Sadouni, Brahim. *Destin de Harki 1954. Le témoignage d'un jeune berbère enrôlé dans l'armée française à l'age de 17 ans*. Paris: Cosmopole, 2001.

Sahlins, Peter. *Unnaturally French: Foreign Citizens in the Old Regime and After*. Ithaca, NY: Cornell University Press, 2004.

Salan, Raoul. *Mémoires. Fin d'un empire*. Paris: Presses de la Cité, 1971.

Sari, Djilali. *A la recherche de notre histoire*. Alger: Casbah Editions, 2003.

Sartre Jean-Paul. *Situations, V. Colonialisme et néo-colonialisme*. Paris: Gallimard, 1964. Translated by Azeddine Haddour, Steve Brewer, and Terry McWilliams under the title *Colonialism and Neocolonialism*. New York, London: Routledge, 2001.

———. *Essays in Existentialism*. Secaucus, NY: The Citadel Press, 1974.

———. *La nausée*. Paris: Gallimard, 1938.

———. *L'engrenage*. Paris: Editions Nagel, 1948.

———. *Huis Clos*. Paris: Gallimard, 1962.

———. *Morts sans sépulture. Pièce en trois actes*. Lausanne: Marguerat, 1946.

Savarèse, Eric. *Histoire coloniale et immigration*. Paris: Séguier, 2000.

Scarry, Elaine. *The Body in Pain: The Making and Unmaking of the World*. New York: Oxford University Press, 1985.

Schacter, Daniel, Elaine Scarry. *Memory, Brain, and Belief*. Cambridge: Harvard University Press, 2001.

Schmitt, Carl. *Political Theology: Four Chapters on the Concept of Sovereignty*. Translated by George Schwab. Chicago: University of Chicago Press, 2005.

Schopenhauer, Arthur. *The World as Will and Idea*. London: Routledge and Kegan Paul, 1957.

Sederberg, Peter C. *Terrorist Myths: Illusion, Rhetoric and Reality*. Englewood Cliffs, NJ: Prentice Hall, 1989.

Servan-Schreiber, Jean-Jacques. *Lieutenant en Algérie*. Paris: Presses Universitaires de France, 1971.

Shennan, Andrew. *Rethinking France: Plans for Renewal 1940–1946*. Oxford: Clarendon Press, 1989.

Sigg, Bernard W. *Le silence et la honte: Névroses de la guerre d'Algérie*. Paris: Messidor/Editions Sociales, 1989.

Simon, Pierre-Henri. *Actes du colloque de Rome suivis de Contre la Torture*. Paris: Les Editions du Cerf, 1999.

Sinnott-Armstrong, Walter. *Moral Dilemmas*. Oxford: Basil Blackwell, 1988.

Sivan, Emmanuel. *Communisme et nationalisme en Algérie 1920–1962*. Paris: Presses de la Fondation Nationale des Sciences Politiques, 1976.

Sontag. Susan. *Regarding the Pain of Others*. London: Hamish Hamilton, 2003.

Soustelle, Jacques. *Le drame et la décadence française. Réponse à Raymond Aron*. Paris: Plon, 1957.

Sudry, Yves. *Guerre d'Algérie: Les prisonniers des djounoud*. Paris: L'Harmattan, 2005.

Sun Tzu. *The Art of War*. Translated and with an introduction by Samuel B. Griffith. New York: Oxford University Press, 1971.

Taussig, Michael. *Shamaanism, Colonialism and the Wild Man: A Study in Terror and Healing*. Chicago: University of Chicago Press, 1987.

Thénault, Sylvie. *Une drôle de justice. Les magistrats dans la guerre d'Algérie*. Paris: Editions de la Découverte, 2001.

Theweleit, Klaus. *Male fantasies*. 2 vols. Translated by Stephan Conway with Erica Carter and Chris Turner. Minneapolis: University of Minnesota Press, 1987.

Tillion, Germaine. *Algeria, the Realities*. New York: Knopf, 1958.

———. *Les ennemis complémentaires*. Paris: Editions de Minuit, 1960.

Tocqueville, Alexis de. *De la colonie en Algérie*. Paris: Editions Complexe, 1988.

Tournier, Jules le Chanoine. "La nouvelle église d'Afrique." *La conquête religieuse de l'Algérie 1830–1845*. Paris: Plon, 1930.

Trinquier, Colonel Roger. *Guerre, Subversion, Révolution*. Paris: Robert Laffont, 1968.

Truc, Gustave. *Paysages d'Algérie. Economie et traditions, 1900–1930*. Alan Sutton, 2000.

Tse-tung, Mao. *On War*. Dehra Dun: Current Events Press, 1966.

Vaujour, Jean. *De la révolte à la révolution. Aux premiers jours de la guerre d'Algérie*. Paris: Albin Michel, 1985.

Vergès, Jacques. *Lettre ouverte à des amis algériens devenus tortionnaires*. Paris: Albin Michel, 1993.

Vergès, Jacques, Michel Zavrian, and Maurice Courrège. *Les disparus. Le cahier vert*. Lausanne: La Cité Editeur, 1959.

Vialatoux, J. *La répression et la torture. Essai de philosophie morale et politique*. Paris: Les Editions Ouvrières, 1957.

Victor, Pierre. *La terreur sous le directoire: Histoire de la persécution politique et religieuse après le coup d'état du 18 Fructidor (4 Septembre 1797) d'après des documents inédits*. Paris: Retaux-Bray, 1887.

Vidal-Naquet, Pierre. *L'affaire Audin (1957–1978)*. Paris: Les Editions de Minuit, 1989.

———. *La torture dans la république*. Paris: Les Editions de Minuit, 1972.

———. *Les assassins de la mémoire*. Paris: Editions de la Découverte, 1987.

———. *Les crimes de l'armée française. Algérie 1954–1962*. Paris: La Découverte, 2001. Originally published by Maspéro in 1975.

———. *Torture: Cancer of Democracy. France and Algeria 1954–1962*. Baltimore: Penguin Books, 1963.

Vittori, Jean-Piere. *On a torturé en Algérie. Témoignages recueillis par Jean-Pierre Vittori*. Paris: Editions Ramsay, 2000.

Wallon, Henri Alexandre. *La terreur: Études critiques sur l'histoire de la révolution française*. Paris: Hachette, 1881.

Walzer, Michael. *Just and Unjust Wars: A Moral Argument with Historical Illustrations*. New York: Basic Books, 1977.

Weber, Eugen. *Action Française: Royalism and Reaction in Twentieth-Century France*. Stanford: Stanford University Press, 1962.

Werner, Eric. *De la violence au totalitarisme. Essai sur la pensée de Camus et de Sartre*. Paris: Calmann-Lévy, 1972.

Wilder, Gary. *The French Imperial Nation-State: Negritude and Colonial Humanism between the Two World Wars*. Chicago: The University of Chicago Press, 2005.

Yacef, Saadi. *Souvenirs de la bataille d'Alger. Décembre 1956–Septembre 1957*. Paris: René Julliard, 1962.

Yoo, John. *War by Other Means: An Insider's Account of the War on Terror*. New York: Atlantic Monthly Press, 2006.

Archives

Archives Nationales, Algiers
#F/17.15.4; 6F/17.15.8; 7F/17.15.5; 12P/31.3.2; 262.I.13

Service Historique de l'Armée de Terre (recently renamed Service Historique de la de Défense)
1H series
1097D1; 1100D1; 1152D6; 1158D1; 1158D2; 1158D3; 1158D5; 1158D6; 1158D7; 1237D2; 1261D4; 1263D4; 1369D4; 1493; 1494D1; 2403D1; 2461D1; 2461D2; 2485D2; 2486D1; 2524; 2537D1; 2537D2; 2537D3; 2556D1; 2556D2; 2581D1; 2591D1; 3196D1; 3434D1; 4608D1; 4712D3.
Audio tape: 3K28.

Centre des Archives d'Outre Mer, Aix-en-Provence
2H73; 1H17; 1H4; 1H131; 16H2; 2H32; 2SAS/56; 2SAS/76; 2SAS/140; 8SAS /50; SAS/5;10K; 14CAB171; 14CAB62; Bib12.982.

Bibliothèque Nationale de France (site Richelieu)
F19/2487; F19/6123; F19/6314.

Journals

Esprit
Itinéraires
Nation Française
Revue de Défense Nationale
Revue Française de Sociologie
Revue Militaire d'Information
Témoignage Chrétien
Verbe

INDEX

HUMAN RIGHTS AND CRIMES AGAINST HUMANITY

Edited by Eric D. Weitz

This series provides a forum for publication and debate on the most pressing issues of modern times: the establishment of human-rights standards and, at the same time, their persistent violation. It features a broad understanding of human rights, one that encompasses democratic citizenship as well as concerns for social, economic, and environmental justice. Its understanding of crimes against humanity is similarly broad, ranging from large-scale atrocities like ethnic cleansings, genocides, war crimes, and various forms of human trafficking to lynchings, mass rapes, and torture. Some books in the series are more historically oriented and explore particular events and their legacies. Others focus on contemporary concerns, like instances of forced population displacements or indiscriminate bombings. Still others provide serious reflection on the meaning and history of human rights or on the reconciliation efforts that follow major human-rights abuses. Chronologically, the series runs from around 1500, the onset of the modern era marked by European colonialism abroad and the Atlantic slave trade, to the present. Geographically, it takes in every area of the globe. It publishes significant works of original scholarship and major interpretations by historians, human-rights practitioners, legal scholars, social scientists, philosophers, and journalists. An important goal is to bring issues of human rights and their violations to the attention of a wide audience and to stimulate discussion and debate in the public sphere as well as among scholars and in the classroom. The knowledge that develops from the series will also, we hope, help promote the development of human-rights standards and prevent future crimes against humanity.